Intellectual Origins of Islamic Resurgence in the Modern Arab World

SUNY Series in Near Eastern Studies
Said Amir Arjomand, Editor

Intellectual Origins of Islamic Resurgence in the Modern Arab World

Ibrahim M. Abu-Rabiʿ

State University of New York Press

Published by
State University of New York Press, Albany

Printed in the United States of America

For information, address State University of New York
Press, State University Plaza, Albany, N.Y., 12246

Production by E. Moore
Marketing by Theresa Abad Swierzowski

Library of Congress Cataloging-in-Publication Data

Abu-Rabi', Ibrahim M.
Intellectual origins of Islamic resurgence in the modern Arab world / Ibrahim M. Abu-Rabi'.
p. cm.—(SUNY series in Near Eastern studies)
Includes bibliographical references (p.) and index.
ISBN 0-7914-2663-7 (alk. paper).—ISBN 0-7914-2664-5 (pbk.: alk. paper)
1. Islam—20th century. 2. Religious awakening—Islam. 3. Quṭb, Sayyid, 1903–1966. I. Title. II. Series.
BP60.A26 1995
297'.2'0904—dc20 94-44054
CIP

10 9 8 7 6 5 4 3 2 1

To the Memory of my Mother

Contents

Foreword

Modern Islamic intellectual history continues to be the subject of much debate in both Western and Muslim academic circles. This strange and fascinating phenomenon which swept the Middle East for the last century and a half has puzzled, frightened and often angered the Western media and political establishment. The date of its actual beginning, its course and purpose and its future direction have occupied Western scholars for nearly the same period of time.

Conversely, the West has throughout this long period attracted and repelled the makers of modern Islamic thought and history. It was likewise during this period that Islam began to find a new home in the West. Thanks to the rapid growth of the Muslim community in Europe and the Americas, Islam is no longer the Oriental stranger which evoked so much fear and fascination in the Western psyche since the days of the Crusades.

Until recently, the Islamic and Western academic circles had little contact beyond the fact that Western scholars studied Muslim intellectuals as living representatives of a confused and romantic phenomenon which refuses to go away. There was little intellectual or academic dialogue between Muslim and Western scholars of Islam. This situation, however, began to change with the increasing number of Muslim students who came to study Islam in the West and to occupy important positions in institutions of higher learning alongside their Western colleagues.

Another factor which brought living Islam to Europe and North America has been the increasing numbers of Muslim emigres and converts who work and live in practically all Western urban centers. Thus modern Muslim intellectual history has since World War II become part of Western history as well. Muslim emigres now include well-known activists who carry on their intellectual work in major European and American cultural centers. Therefore, Muslim scholars are increasingly having to use Western methodologies in their research and analysis of Islamic thought and history and present their findings in an idiom which is familiar to both their Western and Muslim readers.

It may be argued, for the purpose of this study, that the roots of the Arabo-Islamic renaissance of the nineteenth century lay in the pre-modernist Wahhābī movement of the eighteenth century. Wahhābism shocked the Arab and Muslim world with its violent call for the reform of Islam as a pre-condition for the reform of Muslim society. The Wahhābī shock was matched by another and no less significant jolt, namely the Arab discovery of Europe.

The Wahhābīs awakened Arab Muslim intellectuals to the possibilities of religious reform which, they held, is a necessary condition for a true revival of Muslim unity and power. The discovery of Europe brought home the possibilities that science and technology could have in transforming a religiously self-confident Muslim *ummah* into a world power. It may be further argued that Arab-Islamic modernism has been a long and persistent attempt toward the marriage of reason and religion in a determined effort to recover Islam's past glory. The story of this quest is a painful tale, but also a fascinating one.

The present study by a young Arab intellectual may itself be regarded as yet another chapter in this story. Ibrahim Abu-Rabiʿ provides a comprehensive analysis of modern Arab Islamic intellectual history based on its primary sources as well as the most current social scientific theories and methodologies. He is academically rigorous in his approach, but above all, he is an honest scholar with genuine academic and intellectual integrity.

Abu-Rabiʿ's sound research and personal involvement, the wise choices of subjects and personalities for closer examination, and his comprehensive and clear presentation of a vast and complex subject, makes his work a notable contribution to the entire field of Arab studies.

The Shiʿite dimension, while being an integral part of modern Arab Islamic history, its roots lay elsewhere. Shiʿite intellectual history is rooted in the worldview of suffering, martyrdom and messianic eschatology. The intellectual history of the Arab people is not yet a finished story. It is therefore hoped that in future editions of this important work the Shiʿite dimension will be better historically and theologically contextualized and more fully treated.

Mahmoud M. Ayoub

Acknowledgments

This work was conceived inititially as a comprehensive study of Sayyid Quṭb, the theoretician par excellence of Islamic resurgence in the modern Arab world. After further reflection, I decided to write additional chapters that provide a historical and philosophical background to the ideas of Sayyid Quṭb and contemporary Muslim revivalists in the Arab world.

A great variety of studies on Islamic resurgence have appeared in the past two decades. Most treat the subject of "political Islam" and the ramifications of the relationship between religion and the nation/state in the postindependence era. This study does not follow the same lines of analysis of the well-known studies in the field of Islam and politics. The objective is to attempt to lay down the epistemological, philosophical, and theoretical foundations, principles, and orientations of modern and contemporary Islamic resurgence in the Arab world. Further, it seeks to fill a lacuna in the intellectual history of the modern Arab world—a need that has always been felt since the publication of Albert Hourani's pioneering work, *Arabic Thought in the Liberal Age*.

It took me almost five years to complete this work. In this regard, I wish to register my great appreciation to the generous financial help which I received from the Rockefeller Foundation during the academic year 1990–1991 when I had the benefit of staying one full year at the Middle East Center at the University of Texas in Austin to further my research. The Virginia Foundation for the Humanities in Charlottesville also gave me support and space in the Summer of 1990, and the American Council of Learned Societies enabled me to travel to different Arab countries in 1992 to collect further data and conduct personal interviews. Of the numerous colleagues who read either my entire manuscript or chapters thereof, I would like to thank the following: Cliff Edwards and Johnnie Scofield of Virginia Commonwealth University; Sulayman Nyang of Howard University; Ralph Coury of Fairfield University; Kevin Lacey of Binghamton University; John Voll of the University of New Hampshire; John Esposito of Georgetown University; Antony Sullivan of the University of Michigan; Basheer Nafi and Yusuf Talal DeLorenzo of the International Institute of Islamic Thought in Herndon, Virginia; Mahmoud Ayoub of Temple University; Ramadan ʿAbdallah and Mazen Najjar of the World and Islam Study Enterprise in Tampa, Florida; Yushau Sodiq of Christian Texas University; Rula Jurdi AbiSaab of Yale University; Julia Clancy-Smith of the University of Arizona, Sadiq Jalal al-ʿAzm of the University of Damascus; and Wadiʿ Haddad, David Kerr, Miriam Theresa Winter, Steve Blackburn, and William McKinney of Hartford Seminary. I also wish to thank the following students of mine for their enormous help: Cindy Mosher; Irfan Omar; Joseph Wei; Ealy Bennett; Fawaz Damra; Tarik Hamdi; and Basit Koshul. In addition, I wish to thank the staff of Hartford Seminary Library for their indispensable help. My thanks go in particular to Carolyn Sperl and Marie Rovero.

Over the years, Meltem, my wife, and I shared the pain and excitement of scholarship and intellectual life. She is partly responsible for some of the ideas that I express in this book. I am truly grateful to her.

Chapter 1

The Context: Modern Arab Intellectual History, Themes, and Questions

Few subjects can be as subtle and elusive as intellectual history. In studying the main features of modern Arab and Muslim thought, one stands before a colossal tradition of methodology that needs to be sifted and incorporated in a meaningful study. On the one hand, one must be adequately acquainted with the different theories of Islamic knowledge and their historical and social background. On the other, one must be abreast of recent developments in Western critical theory, sociology, philosophy, history, and the humanities in general. In other words, a scholar must be versed in several languages and disciplines in order to fulfill the task of a comprehensive and serious study of this important topic. It is, no doubt, pivotal to present critically and afresh the major themes and suppositions—not only of modern Arab thought, but also of the Islamist discourse—as a distinct historical, philosophical, ideological, and, sometimes, dominant mode of thought in the modern Arab world.

We should be careful lest we reduce the multivariant domain of modern Arab intellectual history to one religious essence or secular tendency. Instead, one could easily argue that it is more comprehensive than that. As shall be amply illustrated in the following chapters, the Islamist discourse, in its different manifestations, histories, conditions, and ideological pronouncements, is a distinctive intellectual formation that must be located within the larger context of Arab intellectual history that has been weltering with all sorts of discourses, both secular and religious. In one important sense, we must be far from assuming, as many commentators on "political Islam" often do, that the Islamist discourse is essentialist, purist, homogeneous, one-dimensional, antimodernist, and irrationally anti-Western.[1] Although some Islamist activists, out of ignorance, speak of the Islamist discourse in essentialist terms (that is, Islam is the solution), this does not reflect in any real measure the religious, intellectual, social, and political burdens under which serious Islamist thinkers have labored.[2]

One may argue, in retrospect, that it is somewhat simple to discern the underlying epistemological principles of Islamic intellectual history during its formative phase (eighth to thirteenth century), when Islam was distinguished by a high level of urbanism and intellectual maturity, as represented by its literati class (*'ulamā'*) and hetrogeneous nature of its religious, intellectual, and cultural production.[3] The picture of the intellectual domain in the modern Arab world, however, might not be as easy to discern or comprehend. This is due to several factors, which may be summarized as follows: (1) the breakdown of the totalistic vision of Islam which considered Islam and the state to be one; (2) the rise of different intellectual currents, especially in the nineteenth century, that challenged the long-established authority of the *'ulamā'*; and (3) the political division and subdivision of the Arab world in the wake of colonialism.

These developments came about as a result of the confluence of internal and external factors that helped to diminish the role of Islam as the main political, social, and even cultural system of the modern Arabs. Although some leading historians and political economists prefer to speak in terms of one Arab nation, it is doubtful that one can speak of a homogeneous Arab culture, let alone a unified Islamic culture.[4] What that means in terms of Arab intellectual history is that it is hazardous to assume that there is some objective intellectual reality that might be brought to the fore merely by discussing it. In fact, the issue is far more complicated. Hence, one of the major goals of this chapter is to lay out the central issues of modern Arab thought as seen by a variety of Arab thinkers and scholars who belong to different intellectual traditions and who seem to propose a number of different solutions to the issues facing them. My discussion, especially in this chapter, focuses on the intellectual (and religious or antireligious) outlook of a selected number of Arab thinkers, some of whom (such as Muhammad Aziz Lahbabi and Malek Bennabi) were steeped in the colonial moment. Others (such as Hichem Djait, Muḥammad al-Bahiy, and Muḥammad ʿĀbid al-Jābirī) were products of a different era that can roughly be termed the *nationalist* one (from 1952 to the present).

Besides dealing with the common concerns of modern Arab thought, my purpose in this work is to discuss, in a systematic manner, the intellectual history of Islamic resurgence, as a specific but multifarious trend in the modern Arab world, and I shall do so by examining in depth the major issues, questions, and problems tackled by the leaders of that movement. Such an approach will undoubtedly shed light on the influence which organized religious thought might have had on social, political, and cultural life in Arab societies. To contextualize Islamic resurgence in modern Arab thought, I will highlight a number of key terms, concepts, and issues which have been pivotal to the intellectual development of the Arab world in the last one hundred years or so. Such concepts as Islamic tradition (*turāth*), decline, renaissance (*nahḍah*), Westernization/modernity/modernization, authority, knowledge, reconstruction, and critique have definitely gone through important metamorphoses in the minds of modern Arab thinkers. In that sense, one must bear in mind that these conceptual formations do not exist in a historical or social vacuum. They influence—and are influenced by—all sorts of subjective and objective factors. In other words,

> Intellectual history cannot claim to be the true or only history. . . . It exists only in connection with, and in relation to, the surrounding political, economic, and social forces. The investigation of subjects of intellectual history leads beyond the purely intellectual world, and intellectual history per se does not exist.[5]

Intellectual history does not follow a specific method of analysis. That is to say, "Intellectual history is not a whole. It has no governing problématique."[6] In the same vein, modern Arab intellectual history, far from being reduced to one problematic, is distinguished at the core by a variety of conceptual issues with varying degrees of intensity and interrelationship. To be more precise, the bare outlines of modern Arab thought, just as with any other collective human thought, may consist of the following:

> the history of ideas (the study of systematic thought, usually in philosophical treatises), intellectual history proper (the study of informal thought, climates of opinion, and literary movements), the social history of ideas (the study of ideologies and idea diffusion), and cultural history (the study of culture in the anthropological sense, including world views and collective *mentalités*).[7]

Tackling the central issues and questions that have preoccupied thinkers in the modern Arab world, whether religious or secular, is a formidable task. A cursory reading of this chapter and other studies in the field presents us with a major problem. Specifically, the problem is the dearth of committed and articulate interpretations of modern Arab thought as compared, let us say, to modern British to French thought. The issue becomes even more confounding in relation to the intellectual foundation of Arab Islamic resurgence. Most existing studies in Arabic and European languages are primarily confined to the analysis of a single salient feature, falling under the general rubric of "political Islam." As a consequence, there is an appalling failure to treat systematically the main issues at hand, both conceptually and theoretically.

The accepted method for comprehending the nature and flow of modern Arab intellectual history has been to speak in terms of certain binary opposites, such as tradition/modernity, renaissance/decline, decadence/renewal, stagnation/revival, and elite/popular cultures.[8] We must not take these distinctions at face value, nor as rigid and mutually exclusive classifications of thought. One example could serve to illustrate the dilemma. Many scholars have viewed the intellectual leaders of Islamic resurgence (such as Ḥasan al-Bannā and Sayyid Quṭb) as popular leaders, on the supposition that, to a certain extent, their ideas reflect the conditions and needs of the masses. But what prevents us from considering them as "elite intellectuals"? Although it is correct to assume that these figures expressed popular ideas, they also had access to—and were in dialogue/confrontation with—the elite culture of their age, be it the religious culture of the *'ulamā'*, or the secular culture of Egypt at the time.

Undoubtedly, it is an academic imperative to identify the main features of modern Arab thought, and the role that Islamist discourse might play in this thought. On the whole, Hamilton Gibb's observation of 1947—especially when applied to a systematic treatment of the intellectual history of Islamic resurgence—remains, more or less, true in the 1990s. "One looks in vain for any systematic analysis of new currents of thought in the Muslim world."[9] To grasp the intellectual formation of Islamic resurgence as a relatively new current of thought is to shed new light on the interaction between society and religion, elite and popular cultures, and the role of religious intelligentsia in the modern or secular nation/state. Also, one must raise a number of questions concerning the historical nature and specificity of the Islamist discourse. It is taken for granted that thought—including the most speculative, abstract, and metaphysical ones—never arises in a vacuum, but is organically connected to and conditioned by a set of conceptual, social, and historical precedents and processes.

What type of intellectual history is to be written? I do not purport to write an elite intellectual history in the traditional Islamic sense. That is, I am not interested in writing about the theological formulations and philosophical theses of the *'ulamā'* in the modern Arab world.[10] Neither does space allow me to tackle popular culture in depth. In this context, my aim is to write an explicit intellectual history of what has proven, to a certain extent, to be a popular religious movement, a movement that was founded by lay Muslim intellectuals who, very often, did not belong to the traditional religious elite in their countries.[11] One may describe these leaders as religiously-oriented intelligentsia who, sprouting from various intellectual and social backgrounds, aimed at tackling some of the most perplexing religious, social, and intellectual issues in the modern Arab world. Although, on the whole, the various attempts by Islamists to seize power and establish an Islamic political system have ended in failure,[12] they have exerted, nonetheless, a strong and enduring religious, social, and intellectual influence on a significant portion of Arab society.

Finally, what about the question of continuity and discontinuity in modern Arab thought? Michel Foucault raises this question in a theoretical way in several of his works, and especially in *The Archeology of Knowledge*,[13] in which he speaks of epistemological acts and thresholds, of the displacements and transformations of concepts, and of the problem being "no longer one of tradition, of tracing a line, but one of division, of limits; it is no longer one of lasting foundations, but one of transformations that serve as new foundations, the rebuilding of foundations."[14] In other words, Foucault argues—and dangerously so—that the historian of thought is in no position to write a total and general history of ideas, let alone be comfortable to trace the same concept to the past. Discontinuity, epistemic ruptures, and continuous shifts in conceptual boundaries are what define the space of ideas, be they modern or classical.[15]

While it is feasible to speak of conceptual ruptures in the modern Arab world—for example, liberalism is not as dominant a discourse in contemporary Arab thought as it was in the 1930s—one is justified, nevertheless, in speaking of continuities. These continuities, however, should be understood against the background of historical change. One still hears in contemporary Arab society similar cries to those of the nineteenth century on the necessity of reforming education, of facing up to the challenges of Westernization, of adaptation to modern realities and norms. One might interpret the contemporary calls all over the Arab world for the return to Islam as a reflection of a crisis, a rupture, and as a response to social and cultural displacements and transformations. However, these calls could also be interpreted as an affirmation of the inner continuity of the Islamic discourse—or discourses—and as rebuilding on old foundations. In sum, the notion of continuity and discontinuity is very useful in describing the recurring themes and discourses of modern Arab thought. An epistemic rupture might well be the other side of the conceptual formation.

Nahḍah as a Problem in Modern Arab Thought

The gestation of modern Arab intellectual history must be understood against the backdrop of the Arab *nahḍah* (rebirth or renaissance)[16] of the nineteenth century. *Nahḍah* is

> a vast political and cultural movement that dominate[d] the period of 1850 to 1914. Originating in Syria and flowering in Egypt, the *nahḍah* sought through translation and vulgarization to assimilate the great achievements of modern European civilization, while reviving the classical Arab culture that antedates the centuries of decadence and foreign domination.[17]

Besides favoring Western achievements, the *nahḍah* movement, especially in its Muslim part, stood against the degeneration of Islamic thought which, according to Gibb, "stayed put—that is it remained fixed in the molds created for it by the scholars, jurists, doctors, and mystics of the formative centuries and, if anything, decayed rather than progressed."[18] Muslim *nahḍah* thinkers—most notably Rifāʿah R. al-Ṭahṭāwī,[19] Jamāl al-Dīn al-Afghānī,[20] and Muḥammad ʿAbduh[21]—basically postulated that a regeneration of Islam and an acceptance of the "positive" features of the West were not at all incompatible. This is perhaps what justifies a scholar such as Hisham Sharabi to postulate that the *nahḍah* "did not constitute a general cultural break in the sense the European Renaissance did; for on the one hand, it did not achieve a genuine transcendence of inherited structures of thought . . . , and on the other, if failed to grasp the true nature of modernity."[22] The feelings of the Muslim *nahḍah* thinkers and their ambivalence toward European challenges and scientific progress are best illustrated by the nineteenth-century Moroccan *'ālim* and traveller Muḥammad al-Saffār, who was baffled by the cleanliness of the French, their industrious nature, the advance of their technology, and the strength of their army.

> So it went until all had passed, leaving our hearts consumed with fire from what we had seen of their overwhelming power and mastery, their preparations and good training, their putting everything in its proper place. In comparison with the weakness of Islam, the dissipation of its strength, and the disrupted condition of its people, how confident they are, how impressive their state of readiness, how competent they are in matters of state, how firm their laws, how capable in wars and successful in vanquishing their enemies—not because of their courage, bravery, or religious zeal, but because of their marvelous organization, their uncanny mastery over affairs, and their strict adherence to the law.[23]

It is true, one can argue, that a man like al-Saffār, who was firmly rooted in the Islamic culture of his urban literati class, would be concerned with power and how to restore the dignity of Islam that was being severely challenged by a new mode of European hegemony. However, it is equally true that his reflections on the West were a sign of religious and intellectual crisis, an indication that a mutation in lives and goals was about to take place, and a telling manifestation of a deep ambivalence about an inherited mental space that does not seem to match the space of modern life. In the words of Albert Hourani, the generation of the *'ulamā'*, to which al-Saffār belonged, was in no position to be complacent about the past any longer. It was a generation of religious, social, and cultural crisis.

> At another level, we can notice in this period a deep disturbance in the lives of educated men, not only those trained in the new schools but those formed in the traditional ways of thought; not only do their careers take different paths, but the ways in which they see their own lives begin to change.[24]

With the onslaught of colonialism and the gradual dissemination of Westernization as a cultural phenomenon in the traditional milieu of

Islam, Muslim thinkers were alerted to a multitude of ruptures in their societies that were political, social, economic, and even linguistic. This is what justifies a scholar such as W. C. Smith theorizing that the modern period of Islamic history "begins with decadence within, intrusion and menace from without; and the worldly glory that reputedly went with obedience to God's law [was] only a distant memory of a happier past."[25] At about this time, "Western civilization was launching forth on the greatest upsurge of expansive energy and power vastly accumulated. With them, the West was presently reshaping its own life and soon the life of all the world."[26] The *nahḍah* intelligentsia, therefore, reacted to decline in the Muslim world as they understood it and theorized on the options for renaissance, while not neglecting Western possibilities for such a renaissance.

One can easily argue that the *nahḍah* phenomenon is based on a complex epistemological structure which has both Islamic and Western components. As such, the *nahḍah* was translated by the Arab intellectual pioneers of the nineteenth century into a historical and social movement, and has, consequently, revived a significant number of issues and debates revolving around the Islamic heritage and the challenges of the present—namely, Islam and the question of Arab cultural identity, Islam and the West, the question of women, and the issue of freedom of expression.

According to Mohammed Arkoun, the encounter between the Arab world and the West created new conditions to which Arab and Muslim thought responded by creating new expressions.[27] These expressions represented the new philosophical, sociocultural, psychological, and linguistic orientations of the modern Arab world. In order to understand the background of these new expressions, one must take into account the concomitant cultural side of colonialism, which is Western modernity, its nature and contents, and the impact it could have had on modern Arabic and Muslim thought.[28] "The historian of thought," in Arkoun's words, "is bound to go deeper and analyze the relations between material and intellectual modernity."[29]

Arkoun sets forth to explore the impact of modernity on Arab thought and philosophy. He maintains that the Arab world accepted Western modernity and its educational and cultural underpinnings only "slowly and reluctantly." One of the main consequences of the interaction between Arab and Western thought is a new philosophical thinking characterized by criticism, innovation, and a futuristic orientation. Arkoun does not reflect much on the present condition of Muslim critical thinking in the Arab world, although he calls, nonetheless, for a critique of Islamic reasoning as a means of reviving contemporary Arab thought.[30]

The *nahḍah* thinkers—as the product of the new age of crisis and mutation—were confronted with the problem of how to interpret the vast Islamic tradition of the Qur'ān, *Ḥadīth*, law, and philosophy in a sociopolitical and scientific environment which was foreign to them because it was dominated by the West. It is somewhat true that these thinkers "lived and acted in an Islamic community that was intellectually still relatively coherent and united,"[31] but it might be equally true that the preindustrial and precapitalist notions and concepts of Muslim thought were inadequate to meet the challenges perpetuated by an aggressive Western world-view. The essential question posed by the *nahḍah* thinkers was how Muslims can be authentic and modern at the same time. They saw the need for a total revitalization of Islam in the face of an encroaching Western culture because "the attack of the West on the Arab world, aside from its political effects, was also a direct attack against Islam as a religion."[32]

The *nahḍah* intellectuals attempted to salvage "Islamic Reason" from many centuries of slumber and decadence.[33] They argued for the viability of Islamic reasoning in the modern age because they believed that Islam was inherently rational.[34] Arming themselves with what they considered to be authentic Islamic criteria for thinking and discourse, they sought to improve both the internal Muslim situation and fight external Western cultural and political encroachment.[35] Thus, historical continuity with the Islamic tradition—what Arkoun calls epistemic continuity—was hailed as an answer to historical, cultural, and religious rigidity and stagnation. This continuity, furthermore, paved the way toward forging a new and important synthesis that reflected, on the one hand, the maturity of Muslim thinkers, and, on the other, the deep sense of crisis facing Muslim society.

Generally speaking, three main concepts can sum up the progression of Arab thought from the early nineteenth century until the present: (1) *nahḍah* (renaissance), (2) *thawrah* (revolution), and (3) *'awdah* (return to the foundations). These three concepts imply the following: (1) reviving Muslim thought from within by affirming continuity with the past, and from without by borrowing from western sources; (2) emergence of the nation state in the wake of resisting the political and economic domination of the west, and (3) translating Islam as an ideology of combat which indicates, besides the nonfeasibility of nationalism as an alternative to the current state of affairs, a deep confrontation between the status quo upheld by a basically secular and military state and all sorts of Islamist movements carrying the banner of *'awdah* (return) to what they hold to be the "true religion."

At a more conceptual level, modern Arab thought has positioned itself to deal with the *nahḍah* problematic through three different modes of discourse: (1) doctrinal, (2) philosophical, and (3) historical/political discourse. To begin with, doctrinal discourse concerns the purification of the fundamentals of religion. As Laoust aptly puts it, "No doctrinal reform is possible without return to an original source."[36] Reform or *iṣlāḥ* can be defined as the return to the just form of religion, and the affirmation of transcendent truth in a modern setting. The reformist program has dominated Arab intellectual activity up to the present time, and it revolves around the affirmation of "a traditionalist method and language" in a modern setting. Therefore, contemporary Muslim philosophers and intellectuals find themselves face-to-face with a set of social and historical questions that await theological answers. It is clear that many a Muslim intellectual remains faithful to his or her vision of past Muslim history, a vision based on the significant role which revelation plays in the process of history. However, as a result of the rise of political secularization in the Arab world in the wake of Western colonization, "the reign of the *faqīh*s (jurists and theologians) was substituted, for better or worse, by that of the [technical] experts and the leaders of the masses. This new situation necessitated a new mental attitude and new criteria."[37]

The objective of philosophical discourse, as it appears in the early writings of the noted Egyptian philosopher, Shaykh Muṣṭafā ʿAbd al-Rāziq[38] (d. 1947), is to prove the authenticity of traditional Islamic philosophical discourse, and its relevance to the needs of modern Muslim societies. ʿAbd al-Rāziq played a major role in focusing the attention of Arab thinkers on the importance of philosophy as a medium of intellectual discourse. In his major work, *Tamhīd li tārīkh al-falsafah al-Islāmiyah (Prolegomena to the History of Islamic Philosophy*), ʿAbd al-Rāziq proposes the following: (1) the Qur'ān, as the sacred book for Muslims, encourages free rational speculation (*naẓar ʿaqlī ḥurr*); (2) a literalist interpretation of the Qur'ān is inadequate to portray its rationalistic depth and attitude; (3) Islamic rationalism, which is intrinsic to the Islamic revelation, should not be confused with the Greek logic and philosophy that Muslim thinkers adopted and modified; and (4) the Arab race is as capable of philosophy and comprehensive thought as any other people.[39] In this, ʿAbd al-Rāziq goes against the grain of nineteenth-century orientalist thought, whose best representative, Ernest Renan, argued that

> We can not demand philosophical insights from the Semitic race. It is only by a strange coincidence of fate that this race instilled a fine character of power in its religious creations, [for] it never produced any philosophical treatise of its own. Semitic philosophy

> is a cheap borrowing and imitation of Greek philosophy. This should be, in fact, said about Medieval philosophy in general.[40]

Reacting to the preceding thesis, ʿAbd al-Rāziq attempts to prove the originality and authenticity of Islamic philosophy by elaborating on the inner theoretical dynamics of Islamic culture and by stressing the strong bond between philosophy, on the one hand, and sufism, *kalām*, jurisprudence, and the *Sharīʿāh*, on the other.[41] His final aim, however, is to prove the compatibility of traditional Islamic philosophy with the rationalism of modern thought.

The historical/political discourse of the *nahḍah* describes the religion/state relationship. This relationship has undergone many transformations since the nineteenth century. In the first phase of the *nahḍah*, Islam assumed a nationalistic meaning, the purpose of which was to build a strong state that would be able to compete with the West. In the second phase, Islam was expressed by Jamāl al-Dīn al-Afghāni, Muḥammad ʿAbduh, and Rashīd Riḍā in pan-Islamic terms. The goal was to reinstitute the Muslim *ummah* (community of believers) in the image of the Ottoman Empire. Furthermore, Islamic resurgence rose in the form of the Muslim Brotherhood movement. Ḥasan al-Bannā, the founder, opted to create an Islamic state. His program attempted to assert the sacred law in all walks of life. Politics, as a result, dominated philosophy and theology. A rupture between the *ʿulamāʾ* (the custodians and defenders of the classical Sunni tradition) and the Ikhwan (as a mass-based movement) was inevitable. The Ikhwan viewed the *ʿulamāʾ* with great distrust. In the Ikhwan's view, the *ʿulamāʾ* were upholders of the same status quo that the Ikhwan were attempting to abolish. As the following chapters show, one must not presuppose that the Ikhwan—or Islamic resurgence in general—is a mere political phenomenon. Resurgence must be treated in philosophical terms as well, and it should be placed in the larger category of modern Arab intellectual history. The Ikhwan discourse was born in reaction to relatively modern historical and political crises affecting the modern Arab world, and, as a result, it has always attempted to provide solutions on the basis of a new—and sometimes aggressive—understanding of the colossal Islamic tradition.

To conclude, *nahḍah* provides an essential conceptual tool for the analysis of the evolution of modern Arab thought, and it describes the way in which Arab thinkers—both secular and religious—have wrestled with issues of heritage and present demands. Far from being monolithic, the concept of *nahḍah* has been interpreted variously in the intellectual domain of the Arab world. Two essential components of the *nahḍah* remain the same, however. They are Westernization and the Islamic tradition.

Orientalist Reconstruction of Modern Arab Intellectual History: Decline and Westernization

It is known that, aside from its political and sometimes religious motivation, orientalism has contributed widely to the revival of many Islamic fields of study that are now considered to be classical. What is less known, perhaps, is the orientalist position on modern Arab thought and philosophy. Serious orientalists—people such as Hamilton Gibb, von Grunebaum, Louis Gardet, and Robert Brunschvig—discussed thematically what they considered as the decline of the Arab world, and came up with a unanimous method and alternative to this supposed problematic, namely "Westernization" as a response to the intellectual, religious, and cultural decline of the world of Arabs and Islam. To paraphrase many an orientalist attitude, "Westernization should be the intellectual problem of modern Islam."

One can distill a general orientalist position on decline and renaissance which is distinguishable, in some ways, from the "Arab position" on the same issue. In this section, I discuss the formulations of Gibb, Smith, and von Grunebaum on modern Arab thought, and the position which the theme of renaissance/decline occupies in them. This discussion will be more revealing when compared to that of the next section that sums up the attitudes of a representative number of contemporary Arab thinkers on the same phenomenon.

Gibb claims that, around the turn of this century, and under the powerful impact of technical Westernization—that is, modernization, Islam started to disintegrate as an organic theological and social system. Although "the vital forces of Islam, as a creed, as a rule of life, and as an ethical system remain unimpaired"[42] in the modern Arab world, argues Hamilton Gibb, "Islam as the arbiter of social life is being dethroned."[43] This is a remarkable development in view of the fact that, for centuries, Islam had not lost its grip on either the Muslim elite or the masses. Gibb, as well as many modern orientalists, understands Westernization in three interdependent ways: (1) it is the adoption of Western military apparatus and technique—that is to say, it is an external and concrete scientific tool of progress; (2) Westernization is a worldview—or it is a process of rationalization; and (3) Westernization is a philosophical and educational outlook. A mere cumulative technological dimension of life can not be judged to be advanced if it is unaccompanied by a rational mentality, which can be cultivated only through education.[44] To Gibb's mind, "The main—indeed, if the word is taken in a wide enough sense, the only—sound agent of Westernization is education, and it is by the criterion of its education in Western thought, principles, and methods that the extent of Westernization in the Muslim world is to be judged."[45] Put differently, in order to guarantee the success of Westernization in the Arab world, its elite culture has to change enormously, from that of the traditional Islamic understanding of life to a Western outlook. A necessary component of this shift in intellect and spirit is a new type of intelligentsia.[46] Gibb, of course, does not think of the leftist intelligentsia as an option because he prefers a secular, procapitalist one.

To Gibb, the proliferation of a new Westernized mind-set in the Arab world has not been completely successful. In a later study, Gibb turns his attention to the reasons that inhibit the "Arab mind" from achieving full progress. These reasons, he feels, are quite obvious. The "Arab mind,"[47] shaped by the long Islamic centuries, is resistant to accepting Western notions of progress. Put differently, Arabs and Muslims display internal or essentialistic obstacles to progress along Western lines. The structure of the "Arab mind" is not solid enough to affect and grasp recent Western scientific achievements and discoveries. The Arab mind lacks comprehensive vision and outlook.

> The student of Arabic civilization is constantly brought up against the striking contrast between the imaginative power displayed . . . in certain branches of Arabic literature and the literalism, the pedantry, displayed in reasoning and exposition, even when it is devoted to these same productions. It is true that there have been great philosophers among the Muslim peoples and that some of them were Arabs, but they were rare exceptions. The Arab mind, whether in relation to the outer world or in relation to the processes of thought, cannot throw off its intense feeling for the separateness and individuality of the concrete events.[48]

This, according to Gibb, explains the aversion of Muslims to the thought-processes of rationalism. The real cause of decline, according to Gibb, is the inability of the "atomistic" Muslim mind to catch up with the rationalist modes of Western thought. "The rejection of rationalistic modes of thought and of the utilitarian ethic which is inseparable from them has its roots, therefore, not in the so-called 'obscurantism' of the Muslim theologians but in the atomism and discreetness of the Arab imagination."[49] According to Pruett, the assumption that Islam is an unchanging "religion" and a fixed abstraction against which all modern developments—such as liberalism, nationalism, and modernism—are to be judged, permeates Gibb's *Modern Trends in Islam*. Gibb sees his task as that of "explaining what he sees as the clearly anomalous and disintegrated character of the religion of Islam."[50]

Gibb contends that Islam faces the same fundamental problems as in the past because it is still

> confronted with searching questions as to the validity of its metaphysics, its ideal constructions abstracted from the material world, and of the resulting frames of reference within which its doctrines are formulated and expounded. The problem which Islam must face is that its traditional formulations necessarily include certain elements of reasoning which are based on intellectual concepts no longer accepted, and that it must be continually adapting its apologetic to more acceptable concepts.[51]

To achieve progress, the "Arab and Muslim mind" should emancipate itself from the categories of the Qur'anic revelation—those same categories that have made Islam "a classical example of an entirely self-sufficient, self-enclosed, and inbred culture."[52] As a supposedly rigid and closed epistemological system which shuns outside influences, Islam does not meet modernity, not even half way. The problem becomes even more grave if viewed from a historical perspective.

> After the thirteenth century or so, it is assumed that, from a religious angle, Islam stayed put—that it remained fixed in the molds created for it by the scholars, jurists, doctors, and mystics of the formative centuries and, if anything, decayed rather than progressed. In some respects, this view is apparently justified, and it is, indeed, held by a number of modern Muslim scholars themselves.[53]

Although Edward Said suggests that Gibb prefers the *'ulamā'* to the modernists,[54] it is clear from the above discussion that Gibb sees hope for Muslims only if they transcend—and not modify or synthesize—their "ancient categories of thinking" and follow, more or less, a reformist program that subcribes to the relativist demands of modern life and that is not afraid to make concessions to science.

Von Grunebaum shares Gibb's basic contention that the foundations of the "Arab mind" need to be radically reoriented toward Western rationalism. He also argues that cultural Westernization is the only viable cultural system in modern times that is capable of giving a sense of direction and meaning to the Third World, including the Muslim world. Westernization seeped into the upper stratum of Muslim societies because of power differentials and Muslim dependency on the West. However, to ensure a complete transformation of the Arab world, it is insufficient to allow "Western technology or natural science or military art to be grafted onto the traditional intellectual structure. New content would not be enough, nor would new methods. The change ha[s] to be admitted down to the very roots, that is, the vantage point of the civilization and its objective."[55] As Western culture is the most productive of all world cultures, it is but natural that there should be a cultural flow between the center (Europe) and the periphery (the world of Islam).

Von Grunebaum discusses the necessity of transforming the "antiquated culture" of Islam, and of cultural borrowing from the West under the auspices of colonialism. He does not discuss the impact of European colonialism on all aspects of modern Arab society and life. He limits his disucssion to the "religious and epistemological contents" of the "Arab mind." His major concern is to clear any impediment or obstacle between the source—namely, Westernization—and the receiving culture so as to ensure an uninterrupted flow of Western cultural influence and directives. As a psychological goal, Westernization can be achieved only if one knows who the enemy is, or the real causes of decline. Von Grunebaum sums up the basic characteristics of progress and those of decline in the following terms:

> When contacts were first made, the basic concepts of both worlds were absolutely incompatible. Whereas, in the East, the individual was incorporated into and subordinated to family, clan, tribe, and ethnic-religious unity, with the state providing, as it were, only a modicum of outside coordination, the West represented the primacy of the human being and his integration at the same time into the "organic" state. The formal restraint of thought, in which the preservation of the known was at stake, collided with the West's passionate devotion to scientific progress, to domination of nature, to knowledge as an unending process. To the cult of the inherited, the West opposed active interference in social conditions and problems. Loyalty to persons was opposed by loyalty to an impersonal whole, to institutions. Whereas the Arab was prepared to satisfy himself with a suprara-

> tional interpretation of the real, the European insisted upon rationalistic criticism. As a corollary, the Arab was (and still is) inclined toward "personalization of problems"; he feels enemies, humiliations, and triumphs where the Occidental makes allowances for material, objective, and, in any event, impersonal difficulties.[56]

Von Grunebaum goes a step beyond Gibb by advocating the creation of an Arab or Muslim occidentalist, as a counterpart to the Western orientalist. To him, Arab occidentalism must carry the double task of liberating the modern "Arab mind" from past influences and spreading the seeds of Westernization so that the masses may master basic Western notions and principles.

Westernization is the worldview par excellence that the modern-day occidentalist must adopt and nurture as part of his cultural space. Colonialism has acted as a catalyst in freeing the "Muslim mind" from supposedly moral and intellectual paralysis and stagnation. Did not the great Ibn Khaldūn postulate that the conquered always adopt the mannerism and culture of the conquerors? To von Grunebaum, the answer is very clear—Muslims felt the urge to be colonized.

> Colonialism is not a political whim but a historical necessity. One succumbs to colonization only when one is colonizable. And one does not cease to be colonized before one ceases to colonizable. Does not the Qur'ān (*sūrah* 13:12) state that God changes the status of a nation only when it has changed its spiritual bearing?[57]

It is interesting that von Grunebaum, in his analysis of colonialism, borrows in toto the main ideas of the Algerian thinker Malek Bennabi as outlined in his painstaking study, *Vocation de l'Islam*.[58] Bennabi, writing under the influence of French culture and colonialism, is deeply perturbed by what he perceives as the moral and social chaos of modern Islam. Colonialism has not been that menacing. "The man of Europe unknowingly played the role of the dynamite that explodes in a camp of silence and contemplation."[59] But colonialism, one must remember, led to the creation of a novel type of sophisticated hegemony which has not escaped the attention of every serious secular and religious intellectual in the Arab world. On the Islamist side, colonialism has been used as a reason to free Arab and Muslim lands from Western hegemony.

Louis Gardet, unlike both Gibb and von Grunebaum, explains Muslim decline in purely religious terms. He traces decline to premodern Europe, to the thirteenth century that saw the destruction of the ʿAbbasid caliphate. Political disintegration was preceded by "fixation in the religious sciences."[60] Fixation, stagnation, rigidity, and obscurantism were central features of the traditional Islamic sciences, such as theology, exegesis, mysticism, and *Ḥadīth* studies. In Gardet's view, the "ossification" of Muslim religious sciences was a necessary outcome of "the absence of a living and a doctrinal authority,"[61] similar to that of Catholicism. The real cause of decline is not military nor political. It lies in the inner structure of the Islamic religion and its inability to adapt to external changes and exigencies. Gardet agrees with another French scholar, R. Brunschwig, that the real problem facing modern Islamic thought is that modern-day Muslims still situate their historical ideal in the past, and that is why "a resolute rejection of innovation marks modern Islamic thought."[62] As a result, *taqlīd* (blind imitation) has replaced *ijtihād* (rational exertion) as the basis of thought.

In making a clear distinction between Islam, as both method and praxis, and Westernization, as technique and process, modern orientalists state, with sufficient clarity, their preference for Westernization as the only viable intellectual option to modern Arabs and Muslims. Orientalists in general—and this is shared by some Islamist thinkers—downplay the rich dynamics of Arab and Muslim history in the Ottoman period. They prefer to speak in the general terms of stagnation and decline. They all seem to share the conclusion that a real *nahḍah* cannot take a proper course unless it renounces "Islamic dogmatism," obscurantism, atomism, mythology, and ancient beliefs.

The Problem of Westernization and Tradition as Viewed by the Modern Arab Intelligentsia

Strangely enough, a good number of Muslim (even Islamist) authors agree with the basic orientalist premise that decline had been pervasive in the house of Islam up until the European intervention in the nineteenth century. A large number of Muslim-oriented thinkers assume that true Islam developed against the tumultuous background of the first few centuries, and that a general theological and subsequent social and political decline set in from the thirteenth century.[63] In spite of agreeing with orientalism on this particular thesis of decline, the solutions the majority of the Arab and Islamist intelligentsia offer are at variance with those of orientalism. To preserve the religious integrity of Islam, and to promote Muslim consciousness in all fields of life, these thinkers propose that it is the urgent task of modern Muslims to revive and practice the old solid foundations of Islam. This basic concern—the revival of Islam—is commonly shared by conservative and modernist Muslims alike. This is the bridge connecting people such as Abū al-Ḥasan al Nadwī and Ḥasan al-Bannā with Malek Bennabi and Muḥammad al-Bahiy.

Arab Religious Response to Decline and Westernization

Abū al-Ḥasan al-Nadwī, an Indian by birth, occupies a unique position in contemporary Arab Muslim thought, especially in the current history of revivalism. His, *What Has the World Lost as a Result of the Decline of Muslims?*,[64] translated into Arabic from the Urdu and introduced by Sayyid Quṭb just a few months before the latter joined the Ikhwan in 1951, sheds some light on the historical consciousness of many an Islamist thinker. Further, Nadwī's response to Muslim decline is the more interesting because of his own affiliation by birth and training to the *'ulamā'* class in India, and because the solutions he offers are based on radical changes in every department of Muslim life at present.

Nadwī follows the orientalist method in tracing Muslim decline to the premodern era. In fact, he tells us, decline started in the wake of the reign of the four Rightly Guided caliphs, and its first symptoms were seen in the de facto separation between religion and state as practiced by the Umayyads and 'Abbasids. The religious establishment was unable to prevent this cleavage between state and religion, and some *'ulamā'* were actually guilty of justifying and propagating secular activities and tendencies. Nadwī elaborates on the theme of *'ulamā'* and power in modern Muslim societies, and accuses a great number of *'ulamā'* of "intellectual prostitution." He argues that the intellectual core of Islam, as represented by its theological class, has disintegrated because of the willingness of that class to play into the hands of politicians. The *'ulamā'*, who are supposed to take the general welfare (*maṣlaḥah*) of the community into account, have neglected their traditional duties, and "are even open to purchase by the highest bidder. They have put themselves up for auction."[65]

The religion-state dichotomy has had far-reaching consequences on the morality, mental aptitude, and religious thinking of Muslims. Nadwī argues that, far from allowing moral degeneration to direct their lives, Muslims adopted Greek and foreign dectrines, methods, and ways of thought that were incompatible with the intellectual and theological orientation of the Qur'ān and, as a result, revealed and man-made law became confused. "If the Divine Law becomes tainted by human intervention," Nadwī maintains, "it will cease to be what it should—a guarantee for success in this world and the next. Neither will the human intellect submit to it, nor will the mind of man be won over."[66]

In spite of certain attempts at renaissance and the rise of the Ottomans as a major world power in the fourteenth and fifteenth centuries, the grandeur of Islam as practiced by the Rightly Guided caliphs was never recaptured. The Turks became guilty of the same malpractices of their predecessors and, worse yet, they allowed their minds to be static, and intellectual sterility became the accepted norm.[67] Nadwī bewails this lamentable state of affairs and says that

> the fifteenth century was definitely the last to reveal any real intellectual life among the followers of Islam. It was during this century that Ibn Khaldūn wrote his *Prolegomena*. In the sixteenth century, the indolence of mind, slavish pedantry and blind imitation became complete. One does not find even one in a hundred among the ulama of the last four centuries who may, with justice, be called a genius, or who may have produced anything to set beside the bold and noble intellectual activities of the earlier centuries.[68]

In a sense, Nadwī maintains that Muslims would not have been colonized in the modern era had they not had the dispensation to be colonizable. He shares this sentiment, as has already been pointed out, with both von Grunebaum and Malek Bennabi.

Against this gloomy picture, it was but natural for the European powers, emerging fresh in the wake of the Reformation and Industrial Revolution, to compete successfully with Muslim power and affect the whole texture of Muslim life and thought. Moral, social, and mental degeneration leads naturally to borrowing from and imitation of the superior culture. Here Nadwī follows a Khaldūnian analysis and critique of Muslims in decline. "Dazzled by the power and progress of the western nations, Muslims began to imitate Western social and economic institutions regardless of the consequences. . . . The prestige of religion was diminished. The teachings of the Prophet were forgotten."[69] It is hard to believe that modern-day Muslims profess the same ideology as did their noble ancestors.

Nadwī seems to be uncertain about how to approach the whole question of technological modernity and Westernization. On the one hand, he levels a critique at industrial society because, in his view, technological society has reduced man to a shallow being and robbed him of his pristine nature and moral loftiness. On the other, he compliments the West for its organizational and educational skills and the consciousness of its citizenry. He also considers the West to be further advanced in terms of its technology than any other nation or region in the world. Therefore, he advocates that Muslims learn from the technological superiority of the West, but only as long as they remain steeped in their own intellectual and moral traditions.[70]

Nadwī is, however, troubled by the philosophical spirit underlying the Western world. This world in his view is characterized by imperialism, capitalism, and communism—all of which are exported to the Third World. Looking deeper at the West, he postulates, one may notice the following: (1) religion has been pushed to the periphery. As a result, moral degeneration and spiritual malaise have been rampant; (2) aggressive nationalism is the norm, and has proven to be destructive to the Muslim *ummah*; and (3) religious ethics and secular power have been separated. Atheistic materialism, according to Nadwī, is the logical consequence of the conditions prevalent in Europe.

Exported to the Third World, materialism has had the pernicious effect of swaying Muslims from their faith, even to the point where one notices in modern Muslim societies a perplexing alliance between Muslims and Paganism. Nadwī asserts that, "The modern Muslim has totally given up the idea of leadership; he has lost faith in himself. His whole mental attitude is being molded by the undercurrents of Paganism. Muslim states exhibit the same materialistic tendencies which are the hallmark of the Western social system."[71] Nadwī does not, at this stage, make any distinction between the ruling and intellectual elite and the masses in the Muslim world. He seems to suggest that the spirit of Westernization, in terms of materialism and paganism, has invaded every domain of Muslim life.

The solution to this state of degeneration requires radical intellectual revolution. "The Qur'ān and the *Sunnah*," argues Nadwī, "can still revitalize the withered arteries of the Islamic world."[72] It is necessary, therefore, to establish a highly conscious and pragmatic Muslim leadership that is aware of the menaces surrounding the Muslim *ummah* and which exhibits a strong sense of integrity in order to combat the multitude of evils that has crept into the inner Muslim reality. One of the first tasks of this leadership is to analyze the power structure in Muslim societies, and critique the power elite that does not hesitate for a minute "to mortgage the destiny of [its] people and walk away with it."[73]

What Nadwī cannot admit, along with his contemporary disciples, is that the Islamic discourse, however it is defined, does not—and, indeed, cannot—constitute an autonomous discourse in modern Arab intellectual history. It is, indeed, true that the Islamic discourse, in its various contents and forms, is an impressive and diverse arena of thought, which must be understood against the multitude of, especially, secular currents of thought, some of which display open hostility to any religious interpretation or worldview.

Although agreeing with some of Nadwī's basic theses about Islamic history, the Azharite thinker and former rector of the Azhar university, Muḥammad al-Bahiy, tackles the whole issue of decline and Westernization from a totally different angle than does Nadwī and, indeed, from the majority of Muslim Arab writers in the twentieth century. In his ground-breaking, *Modern Islamic Thought and its Relation to Western Colonialism*,[74] al-Bahiy places the "Muslim problematic" squarely within the context of modern colonialism and its cultural tool, simply understood as orientalism. His method brings home a host of contemporary issues without going back to the distant past, as do Nadwī and others.[75]

Colonialism is an integral part of the modern Muslim consciousness, in spite of the fact that it is not of the making of Muslims. In other words, al-Bahiy begins with the thesis that the "colonial fact" must be the basis of any discussion about modern Islamic thought. The primary goal of colonialism, he argues, is the weakening of Muslim doctrine, and consequently the weakening of Muslims themselves. Colonialism uses different tools to achieve its goals, but the most efficient is the way in which it spreads its intellectual hegemony in the Muslim world. To ensure its "control over and direction of Islamic thought in realizing this goal [that of intellectual hegemony],"[76] colonialism has launched a two-pronged attack:—first, encouraging indigenous Muslim thinkers, such as Sayyid Aḥmad Khān and Mirza Ghulām Aḥmad of India, to establish movements in the name of reforming Islam; and second, establishing educational training centers with the sole purpose of educating a sufficient number of missionaries and orientalists whose primary task has been, in recent history, to highlight the doctrinal differences and schisms among Muslims, assert political, economic, and geographical differences between the peoples that make up the Muslim *ummah*, and elevate the status of Christianity, Western civilization, and its political regimes at the expense of the principles of Islam.[77] In complete agreement with a number of Arab thinkers in the 1950s and 1960s, al-Bahiy links missionary—educational and religious—activities to colonialism.[78] He also considers orientalists to be the modern heirs to the crusaders. He argues that, a priori, they distort the meaning and message of Islam. In this, he agrees with one of the main theses of Muḥammad Asad that, "As those orientalists are not a special race by themselves, but only exponents of their civilization and their social surroundings, we must necessarily come to the conclusion that the occidental mind, on the whole, is for some reason or another prejudiced against Islam as a religion and as a culture."[79]

Al-Bahiy concludes by saying that orientalism is the cultural side of colonialism, and it, indeed, becomes a dangerous phenomenon when a number of prominent Muslim thinkers adhere to its basic premises and postulates. In short, it is a "cultural venom."[80] Therefore, it comes as no surprise that pro-colonialist and pro-orientalist trends exist in modern Islamic thought, and that this matter must not be taken lightly.

On the other hand, anti-colonialist and anti-orientalist trends have been in the making since the nineteenth century through the efforts of Jamāl al-Dīn al-Afghānī, Muḥammad ʿAbduh, and Muḥammad Iqbāl. These eminent thinkers and their numerous disciples share their fight against the intellectual hegemony of the West by asserting the principles of Islam and their applicability in the modern world. However, after their deaths, another indigenous reform movement—represented in the main by Ṭāha Ḥusayn—"followed in the footsteps of European thought—in its direction, rules, and method of solving life's problems. And the chosen place of this reform movement is the national Egyptian university, headed by free and independent scholars."[81]

What solution does al-Bahiy then give to this state of affairs? Al-Bahiy stands for the reformation and reconstruction of modern Islamic thought, and advocates that it rids itself of the pro-colonialist current by bridging the gap between the way Islam is practiced as culture and the way that its ideal is perceived. He maintains that, as a result of colonialism, there has been an intense polarization in the modern Muslim identity. This polarization can be overcome only if the national liberation movements—such as Nasserism—that were suffering from the vacuum created by colonialism, were to practice Islam as a system of life. Instead, "the indigenous liberation movements, after becoming movements for political independence, have become movements of isolation (*ʿazl*), cutting off the Muslim masses from real life, and permitting the materialist, atheist, and orientalist Western thought to infiltrate and consolidate both polarization and vacuum."[82]

Al-Bahiy does not go too far in criticizing the Egyptian nation/state. After all, as a rector of the Azhar, he is a state functionary.

However, the final solution, as he sees it, is the reform of the Azhar. (His book was written several years before the actual reform of the Azhar in the late 1950s under Imām Maḥmūd Shaltūt.[83]) What is surprising is that he does not refer explicitly nor implicitly to the Muslim Brotherhood Movement and its intellectual leaders at the time, mainly Ḥasan al-Bannā and Sayyid Quṭb.

Secular Arab Analysis of Decline and Westernization: Traditionalism or Historicism or Marxism?

The religious problematic has proven to be at the center of modern Arab intellectual debate. Although, on the whole, secular Arab thinkers pursue different premises and methodologies than those of religious-oriented thinkers, they nevertheless cannot escape dealing with the religious issue. Laroui's thinking on the matter represents the radical—or Marxist—critique of Arab society, culture, and its religious underpinnings.[84] "Criticism of religion is the premise of all criticism."[85] Thus declares Marx in his writing. Abdallah Laroui follows this maxim rather passionately and applies it to the intellectual history of the modern Arab world which, in his estimation, has not as yet transcended the "problem of religion." In order to place religion in its proper place and dilute its popular effectiveness, Laroui proposes a critical method based on philosophy. "Philosophy," he tells us, "is born, develops, and lives again in polemic. It is not by re-examining old problems with the old terminology that it can save itself from ever-threatening anachronism; it renews itself only by occupying itself with the questions that are the stuff of everyday social practice, and these first appear in the form of critical polemic."[86] Laroui deals with the religious question rather reluctantly. His own philosophy is guided by a secular, democratic, progressive, and even atheist vision that aims to transform Arab society from a state of "backward tradition and religion" to one that seeks a radical transformation and liberation of the Arab individual and the creation of a socialist society. To achieve this end, religion must be done away with. However, the obsession with the problem of religion, which permeates the entire work of Laroui, acts as a reminder of the centrality of religion in the modern Arab discourse, as pointed out earlier.

Laroui's *oeuvre* is illuminating, perhaps not for the answers it gives, but for the questions and issues which it raises. Throughout his work, he raises the following fundamental questions: (1) What is colonialism? Is it economic and political hegemony or the consciousness of Western modernity? (2) What is revolution, and what role does the nation state play in it? (3) What are the reasons standing behind decline and stagnation in Arab society? and (4) What position does the religious question with its ever-present weapon, *turāth*, occupy in the modern context?[87]

These questions, in Laroui's view, summarize what he terms "*la problématique arabe*,"[88] as opposed to the Islamic problematic in al-Bahiy's view. Laroui's version of the problematic reflects the way in which modern Arabs deal with their transitional epochs and the challenges that they produce. It also contains four basic conceptual elements: authenticity, continuity, universality, and artistic expression. One must, however, investigate these elements historically in relation to three state-formations in the modern Arab world: the colonial state, the liberal state, and the national state.[89]

There are, Laroui proposes, three principal ideological currents that deal with the questions perturbing Arab society: (1) the religious current, best represented by the cleric or the shaykh; (2) the political, best represented by the liberal politician who, to varying degrees, sees in the West his only chance for intellectual and material survival; and (3) the technical, represented by scientists and technocrats who are concerned with the efficient introduction of science and technology into society.

In Laroui's view, the cleric, as the guardian of tradition, cannot rid himself of the ancient polarization and conflict between Islam and Christianity. He still thinks according to these defunct categories, Laroui claims. Thus, his religious consciousness does not allow him to grasp the fundamental changes taking place in the West since the Renaissance and their distinctive secular traits. Nonetheless, the religious consciousness of the cleric is marred by a duality. "The conscience of our cleric is religious when he analyzes society, but he becomes liberal when he critiques the West."[90]

The liberal politician, although not dismissing Islam in public, has borrowed all of his basic concepts about consultation and democracy from the West. However, he sometimes gives them an Islamic umbrella, as in his use of the terms *shūra* and *ijmāʿ*. He still appeals to the Islamic tradition as both a symbol of legitimation and an indicator of cultural authenticity.

The technocrat, on the other hand, pays lip service to both religion and politics. He sees the difference between the Arab world and the West, not in terms of religion or political organization, but in the way in which each has acquired applied science.[91] The technocrat reminds others of the following maxim: "Today's civilization is entirely based on industry, and its culture is science and nothing but science, whereas the culture of agrarian societies is that of literature, religion, and philosophy." In addition, the technocrat—in the words of Laroui—has totally neglected the religious question and tradition. "The technocrat does not feel any need of interpreting the dogma or even changing its traditional meaning; he simply ignores doctrine totally."[92] Laroui is perhaps justified in drawing our attention to this latter idea mainly because the modern Arab technocrat grew up in the shadow of either colonialism or secular nationalism, both of which attempted to relegate religion to a peripheral status.

After outlining the main currents of "contemporary collective Arab ideology," Laroui discovers that the tenacious presence of tradition and the traditional mentality, far from being anachronistic and obsolete, still dominate contemporary Arab thinking. Laroui's relevance to our present endeavor is derived from his scathing critique of what he terms "Islamic traditionalism," and its pervasive presence in contemporary Islamic societies. Laroui struggles specifically with the notion of the Islamic tradition per se. Although he ends up dismissing the entire theological and philosophical heritage of Islam as obsolete, he maintains that traditional categories of thought still dominate the mental product of a large number of the Arab intelligentsia. "Arab intellectuals think according to two rationales. Most of them profess the traditionalist rationale [*salafī*]; the rest profess an eclecticism. Together, these tendencies succeed in abolishing the historical dimension."[93] According to Laroui, the real crisis of the traditionalist Arab intelligentsia is to be sought in the foundations that give birth to their thought. This mental dependency on and refuge in the past makes the chances of historical consciousness and progress quite remote. What is, therefore, the alternative? Laroui argues that the only means to do away with the traditionalist mode of thinking, "consists in strict submission to the discipline of historical thought and acceptance of all its assumptions."[94] Laroui is not quite clear about the real nature of this historical school. Yet, his challenge to the functioning categories of the modern Arab mind still awaits an answer. In the words of Hourani, Laroui calls for the adoption of historicism, "that is to say, a willingness to transcend the past, to take what was needed from it by a 'radical criticism of culture, language, and tradition,' and use it to create a new future."[95]

It is true that Laroui brings out a number of important terms that summarize his position on a number of crucial issues. Such terms as hegemony, tradition, historicism, and revolution cannot be valued in a historical sense unless they are understood in the context of the power dynamics in modern Arab society, as well as the way in which this society produces knowledge and culture. One could argue, therefore, on the basis of Laroui's thinking that the real problem facing the modern Arab world is not Westernization, cultural alienation, nor historical alienation, but the preservation of rigid and traditional categories of thought which do not show inner readiness to combat and solve current problems.

Laroui's point of departure is similar to that of al-Bahiy's. Both share the same sentiment about colonialism and even orientalism, and they both display a common goal, which is to overcome cultural and intellectual backwardness in the Arab world. However, they display different approaches in treating the issue at hand. Laroui proposes to overcome the past by suggesting its total abolition from the existing memory or Arab society, whereas al-Bahiy does not see revival except within the context of the traditional Islamic formulations. In other words, al-Bahiy and many Islamist thinkers admit of the disintegration of Islam as doctrine, ethics, and community in the modern world, and argue for its restoration as religion, way of life, and state. Laroui takes the disintegration of Islam as an indicator of the incompatibility of its basic formulations with modernity. Here he shares, more or less, the orientalist thesis that "the traditional Islamic mentality includes elements of reasoning which are based on intellectual concepts no longer accepted." Laroui, however, goes further than the orientalists in suggesting Marxism, as a world-view, method, and ideology, is the only viable alternative to the crisis of traditionalism.[96]

Deconstruction of "Arab and Muslim Reason": An Alternative to Decline?

In an illuminating piece on the difference between theology and philosphy, Paul Tillich argues that "epistemology, the knowledge of knowing, is a part of ontology, the knowledge of being, for knowing is an event within the totality of events. Every epistemological assertion is implicitly ontological. Therefore, it is more adequate to begin an analysis of existence with the question of being rather than with the problem of knowledge."[97] Muḥammad ʿĀbid al-Jābirī does not take Tillich's advice, and prefers, instead, to interpret the present problems of Arab and Muslim existence by analyzing the cognitive components that have gone into making the Muslim mind since the inception of

Islam.[98] What are the benefits of an epistemological critique of the "Arab mind"—both classical and modern?

Al-Jābirī argues that a thorough deconstruction and critique of the structure of the Arab mind is a necessary step toward building a viable Arab future. In *al-Khiṭāb al-ʿarabī al-muʿāṣir (Contemporary Arab Discourse*), he maintains that the Arab *nahḍah* of the nineteenth century did not result in a major epistemological and philosophical breakthrough because of the failure of its representatives to critique the Arab mind itself. Al-Jābirī upholds the orientalist position that there was a deep decline in the Arab world on the eve of the European intervention.[99]

Al-Jābirī considers the question of decline (*inḥiṭāṭ*) to be one of the main problematics of modern Arab thought and philosophy. He declares that no intellectual trend has been immune from discussing the reasons and nature of this situation. He argues that Muslim thinkers, especially revivalist Muslim thinkers, have failed to present a viable alternative to the problem of decline.[100] He further argues that both "the Islamic tendency" and "the liberal Westernized tendency" have not succeeded in diagnosing the intellectual malaise of the Arab world. The former tendency locates the solution in the Islamic past, in the Golden Age, whereas the latter locates it in the European Renaissance, which was the antecedent of European colonialism. In other words, the liberal tendency, according to al-Jābirī, cannot seek Western philosophical answers to questions and issues arising in the context of the modern Arab world. Finally, al-Jābirī concludes that the *nahḍah* discourse in modern Arab thought—be it Islamic, liberal, nationalist, or Marxist—is a compromising and self-contradictory one, mainly because it offers ready-made solutions and theses.

Al-Jābirī, as with any modern Arab philosopher, is preoccupied with the correct method of investigating and interpreting the intellectual achievements of the Arab world in the last century or so. He contends that the various components that make up the *nahḍah* discourse—especially the political, Arab nationalist, liberal, and Islamic philosophical ones—have paid lip service to the real and fundamental issues and questions facing the Arab world. As a result, the "Arab mind has failed to build up a coherent discourse which could deal with any of the numerous issues and questions debated in the past one hundred years."[101] Al-Jābirī reaches the grim conclusion that the conceptualizations of the *nahḍah* discourse were based on prefabricated models that do not necessarily reflect the current social and cultural conditions.

Al-Jābirī inquires, along Foucauldian lines,[102] about the possible relationship between knowledge and power in modern Arab societies. Knowledge is cognition and power is ideology. To understand the deep and complex relationship between cognition and ideology in the modern Arab world, al-Jābirī begins by analyzing the constitutive epistemological principles of what he calls the "Arab mind."[103]

What is the relationship between the cognitive and the ideological? In *Takwīn al-ʿaql al-ʿarabī* (*Formation of the Arab Mind*), al-Jābirī attempts to show that the structure of the Arab mind is different, for instance, from that of the French or Chinese mind. Following in the footsteps of the French epistemologist Lalande, al-Jābirī draws a distinction between "La raison constituante" and "La raison constituée."[104] The former is a mental activity that differentiates between principles and consequences, and the latter is defined as the epistemological principles of mind that resist major change.

Al-Jābirī claims that the Arab mind is "*une raison constituée*." That is to say, it "is a constituted reason: it is the summation of all those principles and rules offered by Arab culture to its adherents as a means of gaining knowledge. In other words, a culture imposes these rules and principles as an epistemological system."[105] Elaborating on the preceding thesis, al-Jabiri argues that the Arab mind, which has been formed since the *jāhiliyah*, has taken its epistemological shape and depth in the formative phase of Islam, and has thus resisted any later historical and political transformations, especially in the modern period.

Al-Jābirī goes on to add that the history of Arab thought is based on three broad epistemological structures: (1) *Jāhiliyah* epistemology; (2) Islamic epistemology; and (3) *nahḍah* epistemology. In this classification, al-Jābirī goes against the grain of many Muslim thinkers who hold firmly to the idea that the Islamic system of knowledge abolished the *jāhilī* one,[106] and that both Islam and *jāhiliyah* are mutually exclusive. Al-Jabiri is closer to the ideas of Goldziher and Izutsu, who maintain that Islam, far from abolishing *jāhiliyah* thinking, modified its epistemology and directed its worldview in an Islamic way. It is interesting to note that in his analysis of the history of Arab thought, al-Jabiri subscribes to the notions that explain the evolution of Arab thought linearly and monolithically. In that sense, he views the *nahḍah* problematic as a historical event that can only be understood against the backdrop of pre-Islamic, Islamic, and Western epistemologies and world-views.

Although there have been some epistemic ruptures in the long history of Arab thought, this thought must be understood as an archeology of knowledge rather than an epistemic mutation. Therefore, there has always been, al-Jābirī concludes, strong connections between epistemology and ideology, or tradition and ideology. The Islamic heritage serves several social and political purposes in the modern Arab world. Its utility has been the main source of its strength and longevity.[107]

Al-Jābirī's analysis neglects to mention or give value to the nonliterate Arab mind, to folk culture, and to practices in the Arab world that form a major portion of social and cultural tradition. Whereas the literate Arab mind was formed in the era of *tadwīn* (recording), the same does not apply to folk culture, which is still a dominant factor in the Arab world today. Therefore, it seems to me that, when we document the *nahḍah* epoch, we should not neglect the conditions of folk cultures and their eminent contributions to revival.

Al-Jābirī explains that one of the most important steps taken by the literate Arab mind was to build foundations for the Arabic language. Consequently, "after mummifcation, the Arabic language was frozen . . . But social life can neither be mummified nor frozen."[108] This is the main crisis facing the Arab intelligentsia today, because they write in a language that contains elaborate mechanics and linguistic distinctions, thus forcing them to use concepts and terminologies created by the forefathers. He claims that today's Arabic is not equipped with the proper linguistic tools to reflect the colossal historical changes affecting the modern Arab world. Here al-Jābirī reiterates Abdallah Laroui's thesis on the anachronism of the Arabic language. "The *salafī* (traditionalist) imagines that his thoughts are free. He is mistaken: in reality, he is not using language to think within the framework of tradition; rather, it is tradition that lives again through language and is 'reflected' in him."[109] Both preach the liberation from language because Arabic, as a medium of communication, is both ahistorical and unimaginative. Therefore, the first step toward true emancipation comes in the form of freeing the Arabic language from the "epistemological constraints and shackles" of the Grand Ancestors. This, in turn, would liberate the Arab intelligentsia from the burden of double thinking at the expense of driving them away from rich intellectual and literary tradition creation by the Arabic language and civilization in the medieval period.

Al-Jābirī, following in the footsteps of Joseph Schacht[110] and George Makdisi,[111] maintains that Islamic civilization is that of *fiqh* (jurisprudence). *Fiqh* was established during the *tadwīn* movement and doubly supported by the *'ulamā'* and the state. The state and its supporters prevented the recording of what they perceived as intransigent material and, therefore, according to al-Jābirī, the thinkable and unthinkable were forced to coexist in the Muslim world. Al-Jābirī argues that liberating modern Arab thought from both the language and *fiqh* of the past would restore intellectual rigor and freedom.

Personalism or Cultural Westernization?

One must understand the neo-structuralist attempts at deconstructing Arab reason as a means of transcending decline in the larger context of modern Arab intellectual history. It is clear that al-Jābirī is indebted mainly to the French deconstructionist school as well as to the leading attempts of both Laroui and Arkoun in applying Western notions of critique to the thought structure of the modern Arab world. The effect of French philosophy in its Begsonian and Sartrian senses is visible in the work of Muhammad Aziz Lahbabi (d. 1992), unquestionably one of the most important intellectual figures in contemporary North Africa. Born in French Morocco and alerted to the enormous cultural and political gaps between his native country and the more advanced West, Lahbabi has been in a unique position to comment on the viable issues and concerns of the modern Arabs.

Lahbabi's thought, far from being static, has been subject to a series of epistemological transitions from personalism to realism and to Third-World futurism.[112] Further, his thought is a catalyst of two historical moments, phases, exigencies, and conditions. On the one hand, he responds to the challenges of colonialism and Westernization, especially in North Africa, and he utilizes in his early philosophical work a Western philosphical trend, known as *personalism*.[113] On the other, he is overwhelmed by the concerns of the postindependence Muslim world—that is, the nation state's phase, as part of the Third World, and takes an aggressive stand against the West.[114]

Just like P. Tillich,[115] who also was influenced by European existential philosophy in the interwar period, Lahbabi sees the problem of modern Arab society to be that of searching after the true meaning of its own existence, that of *aṣālah* or authenticity. Lahbabi's ontology, especially in his early philosophical work, is defined as a "web of interaction between man, self, and world." Man's awareness of this interaction is what gives him a sense of freedom and destiny. In his view—as well as in the view of others who have written on the subject—"a person . . . is a complex unity of consciousness, which identifies itself with its past self in memory, determines itself by its freedom, is purposive and value-seeking, private yet communicating, and potentially rational."[116] To Lahbabi, freedom presupposes responsibility, and responsibility presupposes destiny.[117] Freedom is the freedom of the function or will of man, and man's principal trait is autonomy. Here, he agrees with Hegel's understanding of the history of the world as "the progress of the consciousness of freedom."[118] Lahbabi's Hegelianism, which is similar to that of the early Marx, stresses the idea that living human beings make their history, and that man per se is free to function because he possesses a complete rational self. Freedom is experienced as deliberation, decision, and responsibility. These three elements of freedom constitute man's destiny. He is aware however that freedom and destiny, besides encouraging individual participation, assume a healthy integration between the person and his or her social milieu.[119] He further maintains that man is distinguished by *telos* (the inner aim) which is the basis of his process of actualization. Participation is essential for the individual, and not accidental. This participation guarantees the relational aspect of human life. Man is related to God and to other beings.

Lahbabi's arguments center around propositions and concepts that make up the mental space of the Western world. He seems to be more concerned, at an early stage in his philosophical career, with the crisis of orientation and spiritual malaise in Western societies than he is with the problems of colonization and decolonization in Arab and Muslim societies. Therefore, in his discussion of being (*être*),[120] Lahbabi is concerned with Western ontology and its constituent elements. The term *being* means the whole of human reality—the structure, the meaning, and the aim of existence. Lahbabi says that Hegel was the first Western philosopher to give the term *being* a whole philosophical meaning. "Finally, with Hegel, the concept of being is understood for the first time as a dynamic and logical movement of concepts. The human being is thought, and thought cannot be reduced to 'I think.'"[121] Lahbabi is, therefore, immersed in the Hegelian principle of dialectics and vitality, in which vitality reflects the inseparable relationship between being and thought, and being and existential freedom. Therefore, man's dynamic interaction with reality is a complex process that leads to continuous self-growth and self-consciousness. Man is distinguished from animals by consciousness. In addition to dynamics and form, man is distinguished by vitality and intentionality. Intentionality presupposes an inner aim (*telos*), and *telos* is the source of social dynamics and growth. Intentionality is defined as a human capacity to relate to meaningful structures, to live in universals, to grasp and shape reality. In other words, man is distinguished by his ability to create technical as well as conceptual tools that relate him to reality in its inclusive sense.

Lahbabi took major strides to apply his personalistic ideas to cultures and civilizations in general. In 1961, he wrote a book on how a national culture, especially that of North Africa, can attain universal principles of action, humanism, and dynamism.[122] He contends that a national culture is defined as "a totality of spiritual, intellectual, and material values and forms that are conceived by a nation in the process of its evolution."[123] A national culture can achieve total integration with the world civilization only if its creative energies are translated experientially and existentially. In sum, political independence should lead to the solidification of the national culture, and the vitality of national culture is sought in its contributions to world civilization.

Only in 1964, after Moroccan independence, does Lahbabi concern himself with Islamic personalism (*al-shakhṣāniyah al-Islāmiyah*) in the publication of *Le Personnalisme Musulman* (Paris 1964). Lahbabi is concerned with the universal traits of the Islamic message and with the normative universal issues that should distinguish the Muslim person from others. "To live as a Muslim," Lahbabi maintains, "is to grasp oneself as a consciousness embodied and committed in this world to seek personal authenticity."[124] For the whole *ummah* to achieve autonomy—and, henceforth, collective commitment—a great emphasis on the creative energies of the *ummah* must be stressed:

> It is unfortunate for the Islamic culture that *ijtihād* has never been respected especially by the *fuqahā'*, who have installed themselves as the protectors of *tashrī'* [legislation], and struggled in favor of *taqlīd* [blind obedience to the text]. In other words, they have refused any effort toward personal interpretation or any adaptation of the text to reality. *Taqlīd* is the triumph of the sheep-like spirit. The formalistic and literal spirit has triumphed by neutralizing any spirit of initiative or criticism.[125]

Lahbabi equates Sufism with the absence of autonomy and individual will. He argues that, with Sufism, Muslims began to succumb to the various aspects of fatalism (*tawakkul*), dependence, the belief in the precariousness of time, the nonreality of the world, and, consequently, the renunciation of this world.[126] Lahbabi considers that the Sufi's retreat from the world has gone in an opposite direction to all cultural and social progress, as well as to the directions of the Qur'ān and the Sunnah. Sufism, according to him, occupies only a marginal position in respect to the official religious sciences in Islam. "Because the origin of mysticism is not Islamic, almost all the practices of the

Sufis are not Islamic. That is why in the eighth Islamic century, the great Muslim thinker Ibn Taymiyah defined the mysticism of Sufism as an "ensemble of *wasāwis* (hallucinations)."[127] Lahbabi's critique of Sufism as an irrational—and, implicitly, an irrelevant—religious movement appears very clearly in his early writings as a young man enchanted with the scientific and rational contributions of Western civilization. Therefore, in his analysis of Sufism, he argues that it has been unable to produce an adequate and precise language of discourse because its fountainhead is the irrational and unknown.

In addition to the previously mentioned postulates, Lahbabi proposes that even the modern *salafiyah* of Jamāl al-Dīn Afghānī and Muḥammad ʿAbduh, which sought to transcend backwardness by renovating religion, failed to meet the demands of the modern age.

> The *salafiyah* can be viewed from two different perspectives. In the first place, it is a movement of purification, of the return to the origins as a means of rejecting all the superstition and myths that have accumulated over the centuries in Islam. In the second place, it is a struggle for the opening of the door of *ijtihād*. Considering this situation—opening the door of *ijtihād*—the *salafiyah* has begun to make new interpretations in order to actualize Islam and create an atmosphere of adaptation in the wake of the encounter with the West.[128]

Nevertheless, he goes on to argue that, "we should not blind ourselves to the difficulties and inadequacies facing the *salafiyah*. Its promoters, it seems, in the late nineteenth century and the beginning of the twentieth, did not possess, as was necessary, any consciousness of the dynamism of industrial societies, nor did they understand the leading role played by bankers and technicians in contemporary society."[129] The modern *salafiyah* has thought of religious problems as being independent of the new context of industrialization—a context of development that created new psychological and social problems, especially among the working classes.

In conclusion, Lahbabi applies what he has learned from the philosophies of personalism and existentialism to the modern Muslim world. A transition is made in his thought from speculative thinking to experiential reality. The connection between thought and being must be translated as dynamism, vitality, responsibility, and destiny. Lahbabi was concerned, until his death in 1992, with the destiny of Arabs and Muslims. His appraisal of contemporary Muslim culture is based on premises of rationalization, industrialization, and the creation of a new and efficient intelligentsia. Modern Muslims, in order to survive, have to reappropriate modern culture and its achievements.

Islamic Hegelianism?

In his two perceptive studies, *La Personnalité et le Devenir Arabo-Islamique* and *Europe and Islam: Cultures and Modernity*, the Tunisian philosopher Hichem Djait probes into the concerns of what he calls the Arabo-Islamic personality—its present, its future, and its relationship with the West. Djait represents a new brand of Francophone authors and philosophers who are totally immersed in the issues and questions that underlie the Muslim world, and he brings a novel brand of European philosophical insights, especially Hegelian and Existentialist, into his analysis.[130]

As a serious student of cultures, Djait delves into the Islamic heritage as a means of finding answers to his present concerns. Nevertheless, he turns Islamic religious belief and the inherited Arabo-Islamic culture into "a subject of critical assessment."[131] He argues that Islam, in its classical age and vigor, was characterized by a high sense of religious and cultural homogeneity and historical consciousness. This was obvious in the writings of the *'ulamā'* and thinkers who ventured to discover the realm of the unknown in the human and social sciences. The elite culture of Islam, Djait tells us, "pursued all the forms of learning with fierce vigor: history, geography, law, scholastic theology, philosophy, medicine, and mathematics. But, in the meantime, it was seized and shaken by an underlying force: a fascination with God."[132] However, the obsession with the divine did not limit itself to the realm of history nor to that of the secular, in general. It took on a strong scriptural fascination as well. The Sacred Text (such as the Qur'ān) created a long interpretive tradition, which forms the second major tradition in Islam today, after the Qur'ān itself.[133] Furthermore, the Sacred Text became the embodiment of the Islamic search for the ideal. Thus, a total picture of the majesty that was Islam emerges before our eyes. We are talking about an undeniably theological unity that elevated human culture to the level of the sacred. However, the historical continuity of this culture was broken well before the Western intrusion into Muslim lands.

Therefore, Djait enquires about the theological and cultural homogeneity of the modern Muslim world, and reaches the conclusion that a new terminology, in the form of dialectical epistemology, must be used in order to shed light on the modern situation. Djait sees a historical breakup in modern Islam, and argues for the use of the bipolar concept of historical continuity and discontinuity as a yardstick against which the nature and achievement of the Arab *nahḍah* are judged. This is a better measure than "the rather hollow dyads of apogee/decline, decadence/renaissance, Arab/non-Arab, orthodoxy/heterodoxy, not to menition the recent dialectic between tradition and modernity."[134] The multipolar cultural character of modern Islam emerging in the wake of its political and historical breakup destroyed its "living network of human and cultural exchanges, [thus] condemning each region to a solitary existence or to an exclusive dialogue with the past."[135]

To Djait's mind, Islam started to decline when its cultural and political homogeneity broke down, and that is when Muslims were awakened to a violent encounter with Europe. In a sense, decline means the breakup of the homogeneity that classical Islam attained. It further means the accentuation of tension between the specific or particular and the universal, as well as between the real and the ideal in Islam.

Decline also means the inability of the *'ulamā'*, as the leading intellectual class in Islamic societies, to produce relevant theological knowledge that could be used to offset the rising tide of secular knowledge. Thus, we are talking about a fundamental inner mutation in the modern setting of Islam—its cultural and social milieu. This mutation is further accentuated by the political disintegration of modern Islam and by industrial and military weakness. Thus, a question arises: can an Islamic intellectual movement in the Arab world today salvage the classical homogeneity of Islam after its historical breakup?

Djait alludes to the lack of philosophical knowledge in modern Islamic resurgence as a popular religious movement, and says that the Islamic movements of today are in an undeniably pitiful and unenviable position. On the one hand, the Islamic resurgence benefitted greatly at the mass level from the failure of liberalism, Arab nationalism, Arab socialism, and state-capitalism. On the other, it has not been able to forge a coherent alliance between knowledge and action, or philosophy and movement. On the contrary, Islamic resurgence has had to face an unholy alliance between secular knowledge and power.

The colonial shock has produced, in the modern Arab society, a dialectical situation. The contradiction between the colonizer and the colonized produced the bourgeoisie, the petty bourgeoisie, and an oppositional intelligentsia. In other words, this encounter has produced a new constellation of power relations that did not exist in the precolonial epoch. One of these changes is that "the power holder (politician) and the intellectual have become unified in their thinking, especially in the priority they accord praxis over theory, and in the distance they have instituted between reality and truth, or between the true and the said. But, because of his function, the politician, nevertheless, stays as the man of reality, and the intellectual, because of his vocation, stays as the man of truth."[136] Djait goes on to argue that

> The major drama of the Arab intellectual rests not only in his witnessing the devaluation that is behind his reason for existence and pride—knowledge and culture—but in being prevented from accomplishing his civilized mission, which is criticism and free speculative thinking. It is even strange to note that the active segment of the Arab intelligentsia has invested its debating power in the notion of social justice, thus neglecting a concept similar in beauty and truth, which is liberty.[137]

According to Djait, then, contemporary Arab society must unleash the power of reason as a means of attaining freedom in a true sense. This is more possible in the case of those Arab intellectuals who have come in touch with the Western philosophy and critical theory, such as in North Africa.[138]

Conclusions

In spite of his double-criticism approach, the Moroccan philosopher Abdelkebir Khatibi states that "Contemporary Arab knowledge cannot, without experiencing a radical rupture, escape its own theological and theocratic foundations which characterize the ideology of Islam and of all monotheism."[139] Clearly, the treatment of Islam and the Islamic tradition by modern Arab intellectuals is unavoidable in liberal, Marxist, nationalist, and religious works. The preceding notion is in agreement with the thesis that the modern and contemporary intellectual history of the Arab world has not yet been able to establish an independent personality of its own outside the periphery of religion. Therefore, a major component of modern Arab thought—especially in its Islamic dimension, and in spite of modern encounters with the West as the "other"—has preserved a fundamental historical connection to the Medieval Islamic heritage of thought. Consequently, a scholar is compelled to deal with modern Arab intellectual history in the context of its historical and cultural specificity. Modern European thought, which broke away from medieval Christian thought, cannot act as the criteria against which one must measure the intellectual contributions of modern Arab society.

Putting the question of continuity aside, this chapter revolves around the richness and diversity of contemporary Arab intellectual history. Arab thinkers have been alerted to the need to produce ideas and philosophies that have a bearing on present intellectual, social, and cultural issues.[140] Because no intelligentsia of any society can be monolithic and dull in terms of its theoretical reflections and ideas, it is taken for granted that the concerns of the Arab intelligentsia are diverse. It could be said that Arab intellectual life of the twentieth century is more rich and profuse than that of the previous century. This is due to several causes. First, whereas pre-nineteenth-century Islamic thought is characterized by the absence of the West as a political, religious, and intellectual problematic and threat,[141] post-nineteenth-century Islamic thought is bewildered by the questions and issues which the West and colonialism have engended in the modern Muslim world. With the end of colonialism and the rise of the independent nation/state, new issues came to the fore. Life became more complex, and a noticeable shift of emphasis is seen from struggles against colonialism to building a national culture. Second, postcolonial Arab societies have struggled with issues of identity—especially religious identity—and the task of defining the relationship between the nation/state and religion—namly, Islam—became the more urgent. Third, the end of official colonialism did not mean the end of Western cultural and scientific influence on the Arab and Muslim world. In certain ways, the Western influence upon some Arab countries increased by leaps and bounds. Today, instead of direct Western military, economic, and political hegemony, Arab societies cannot afford to ignore the tremendous Western influence in terms of ideas, commerce, and modernization plans which have ushered the West into a new form of hegemony. An appreciation of this new situation—emerging especially in the wake of the defeat of Iraq in the Gulf war of 1991 and the ensuing New World Order in the Arab world—and a better grasp of the shifting role of religion are necessary.

The colonial and postcolonial moment in the Arab world has led to a noticeable erosion in the religious and social position of the *'ulamā'* as the traditional intelligentsia class in the world of Islam. The function of the traditional *'ālim* is to preserve and transmit religious knowledge.[142] A new type of Muslim intellectual (the Islamist) is being born—one who is critical of the *'ulamā'*, yet who, nevertheless, shares nearly the same world-view of Islam. The new Muslim intellectual takes a more activist role, and is forced, therefore, to interpret the contents of Islam in a new way.

It is somewhat ironic that most of the thinkers whose work has been analyzed in this chapter share a common thesis: the European thrust on the Arab world (and the land of Islam in general) and its concomitant political and ideological hegemony mark the birth of modern Arab and Islamic thought. In other words, modern Arab and Islamic thought is greatly steeped in the colonialist moment, and, in retrospect, it is even difficult to speak of the inner movements and transformations in modern Islam without considering a phenomenon of great importance that once seemed to be external—that is, colonialism and Westernization.

Second, the reaction to the European onslaught has taken the form of two movements, each of which has its staunch supporters in Arab and Muslim lands. One is reformist and seeks to reconstitute modern Muslim thought on the basis of rebuilding Muslim culture and education. The second is modernist, is more Western in essence and orientation than the first, and does not see any contradiction between learning from both the great Islamic tradition and appropriating the best features of the Western world.

Third, in spite of their numerous disciples and the intellectual subcurrents they have generated since the late nineteenth century, both Muslim reformism and modernism have failed to transform their ideas into mass movements. Although one must examine the Muslim Brotherhood movement as the social movement par excellence in the modern Arab world against the backdrop of both reformism and modernism, it is a continuation of neither, and, in fact, the literature of Islamic resurgence is highly critical of both.

Fourth, in speaking of the role of Islam in the modern world, a variety of opinions and interpretations have arisen. The reactions to the onslaught of colonialism have never been monolithic nor uniform, and this state of affairs testifies to two fundamental facts: (1) the dynamism of thought in modern Islam, and (2) the variety of political, ideological, and social positions held by the leaders of both secular and religious thought.

Fifth, a number of basic terms and phrases might summarize the issues around which modern Arab thought revolves—colonialism, secularization, *nahḍah*, revolution, return to the origins, rejection of medieval shackles, culture, inferiority complex, dynamism, and the premise that Islam is fit for all times and places. Therefore, it was necessary in this chapter to review and analyze the work of leading secular, religious, and Western thinkers who have tackled these issues from different angles.

Sixth, Western orientalists and their intellectual allies in the Arab and Muslim world—that is, modernists—subscribe to the thesis that Islam is a dogmatically rigid religion, and that its basic assumptions, concepts, and formulations that had been formed in the ancient past are no longer capable of interpreting a progressively dynamic modern situation resulting from the thrust of Western modernity. The radical Arab secularist goes even a step further by preaching the abolition of religion and even expunging the Arabic language from the present intellectual domain of the Arab world.

Finally, many an orientalist believes that modern Arab thought must keep itself distant from the religious underpinnings of Islam if it is to avoid dogmatism, atomism, literalism, mental lethargy, and apologetic tendencies. In this, one may argue that the orientalist might agree with some of the positions of the radical secularist.

Chapter 2

Turāth Resurgent? Arab Islamism and the Problematic of Tradition

The preceding chapter has drawn our attention to the notion of "Islamic tradition" *(al-turāth al-islāmī)* as a major historical and philosophical problematic in modern Arab intellectual history.[1] The present chapter addresses itself to the following three main questions: First, what is tradition in general, and Islamic tradition in particular? Second, what does the revival of Islamic tradition in the twentieth century mean? And, third, what is Islamic resurgence, and what are the reasons behind its emergence?

Generally speaking, it is possible to distinguish three main positions on Islamic tradition as discussed in the first chapter of this book: first, orientalist thought—along with secular thought, and especially Arab Marxist thinking—which disputes the efficacy of tradition in the context of intellectual Westernization and industrial advancement; second, Muslim thought—especially the conservative/traditionalist type—which calls for the revival of the past in a modern setting; and third, a middle-of-the-road position which advocates a rapprochement between the Islamic tradition and Westernization. This latter aspect is best represented by the works of Hichem Djait and Muhammad A. Lahbabi.

As noted in the preceding chapter, the question of tradition occupies a central place in modern Arab thought. How can one, then, define the epistemological parameters of religious tradition and its impact on the present?

To start with, rational and empirical criteria of judgement might be insufficient to define and analyze the different components of tradition, especially if it is characterized by a strong metaphysical edge, such as Islam is a monotheistic religion that strongly believes in a transcendent God. In addition to its metaphysical and intangible part, tradition can also be tangible, especially if we refer to the concrete cultural, social, and literary practices and habits of a people. Both tangible and intangible dimensions of tradition often belong to the past, and they both invoke a sense of authority, or an implicit one at least. In addition, in the minds of some, tradition is synonomous with order, meaning, sacredness, and equilibrium. In the minds of others, tradition is anachronistic religiosity, mental backwardness, lack of creativity, and fear of innovation.

It is a known fact that religious traditions are often transmitted from one generation to another, either orally or in a written form. Both "high culture" and "folk culture" play a significant part in this transmission. The object of transmission, besides dissemination and conservation of tradition, is also to foster ways of managing the religious tradition by believers. In that sense, it is also understandable how believers often impose a sense of homogeneity on their tradition of the distant past. Tradition gets reified, abstracted, and, sometimes, atomized and sliced into a fine and thin piece. When a generation is beset by problems or imbued with a sense of insecurity vis-à-vis an aggressive culture, such as Western culture in the Third World, there is always a longing for, and aspiring to, a pure and managable past. A classical phase is appealed to as a form of alleviating present difficulties, and classicism as a movement of thought emerges. Aside from its psychological appeal, therefore, classicism, to paraphrase von Grunebaum, is seen as authoritative in the case of questionable and disputed matters. Classicism also is double-sided. On the one hand, it is a dynamic and dynamizing concept. On the other, it is a static notion of perfection. The latter sense always leads to imitation, and satisfation with past criteria of thought and action.[2]

In delineating the core structure and comprehending the nature of the Islamic tradition, one must define its central intellectual pieces—which are mainly the Qur'ān and the Sunnah—and how they have interacted throughout Islamic history with all sorts of persons, forces, and situations to create the Islamic canon of doctrine, philosophy, ethics, and social and political attitudes and notions. This is what Wilfred Cantwell Smith appropriately terms "the cumulative tradition," by which he means a religio-historical construct. "It is diverse, it is fluid, it grows, it changes, it accumulates."[3] As a social and historical construct—and in large measure—the cumulative tradition can be "something intelligible, and empirically knowable."[4] That is to say that one can determine the "movers and shakers" of tradition, with a certain historical precision—depending, of course, on the available data and documentation.

As a universal and monotheistic phenomenon, the Islamic cumulative tradition has been distinguished by a sacred text, which naturally lies at its very heart. This sacred text forms its central tradition, and is complemented by the *Ḥadīth* as a subtradition. Both the Qur'ān and the *Ḥadīth*, however, have accumulated a substantive body of interpretation. This body, in turn, has formed its own distinctive traditions. Both the primary tradition of the Qur'ān, and the body of interpretation created around it, have been in constant interaction. It is also usually difficult to understand one without the other. The American sociologist Edward Shils comments with great insight on the process of tradition-formation in the high cultures of the world, including that of Islam.

> The intellectual tradition of religious belief is two-sided. There is, on the one side, the tradition of the sacred text itself. The formation of that tradition, the amalgamation of sacred texts into a canon is a process of great complexity. It is not merely a matter of the transmission of manuscripts. It is a matter of determining which variants are best and which belong in the canon. Not wholly separate from this is the tradition of interpretation of the text. The meaning of the text is a creation of the interpretation tradition.[5]

It was, therefore, natural for the Islamic tradition, produced against a complex background and over a long historical period, to establish certain basic mechanisms of both conservation and expansion. Tradition is also not immune to cultural and intellectual borrowing and adaptation. In its formative phase, Islam was not hesitant to incorporate Hellenistic elements—especially in the domain of philosophy and logic—into its mental fabric.[6] Consequently, "Every major tradition is a product of the confluence of contributory traditions, not only at its origin but in the course of its history."[7]

In addition to the Qur'ān and the *Ḥadīth*—the two major components of Islamic tradition—Islam, as a great sacral culture, has been distinguished by a sacred language through which it was possible to imagine the Islamic *ummah* as a universal community of believers. In the words of Benedict Anderson, "All the great classical communities conceived of themselves as cosmically central, through the medium of a sacred language linked to a superterrestrial order of power."[8] He also correctly notes that, "In fact, the deader the written language—the farther it was from speech—the better; in principle everyone has access to a pure world of signs."[9] Although Qur'anic Arabic is not a dead language, it has been challenged by the rise of the vernaculars that was made possible as a result of the introduction of print media in the nineteenth century. Nevertheless, Arabic has served as a binding sacred force since the birth of Islam, and it continues to play a similar role in spite of the emergence of nationalisms in different Muslim lands. In the Middle East, the collapse of the Ottoman caliphate and the rise of Turkish and Arab nationalisms dealt a heavy blow to the political vision of Islam, but it is doubtful that its religious integrity—that is, the ability of Islam to still imagine itself as a universal *ummah* that is bound by a sacred language—suffered the same damaging blows.

In fact, the rise of Islamic resurgence in the wake of the abolition of the Ottoman caliphate could be explained in part as a continuation of Islam to imagine itself as a universal *ummah*, as opposed, let us say, to a particular community or nation. Perhaps the central reason for the ambivalence of Arab nationalism toward Islamic resurgence, as a religious and political movement, lies in the fact that Arab nationalism, from the very moment of its emergence, has been unable to abolish or transcend one of the central components of Islam—the Arabic language. In the words of Halim Barakat, "There is, in fact, unanimous agreement among theoreticians of Arab nationalism on the great significance of [Arabic] language."[10] Language is the pulse of both Arabism and Islam.[11] Then too, Islamic resurgence—in spite of its confrontation with the Egyptian nation/state in the 1950s and 1960s, the Syrian nation/state in the 1980s, and the Algerian in the 1990s—did understand the special role of Arabism and the Arabic language.[12]

Although Islam as an "imagined religious community" has not disintegrated totally in the wake of the collapse of the Ottoman state, Muslim culture and institutions have been challenged to the core, especially under the impact of hegemonic and aggressive Westernization. As has already been noted in the preceding chapter, Muslim *nahḍah* thinkers perceived the Western encroachment in the guise of colonialism to be, first and foremost, a substantive threat to the "Islamic tradition"—to the central sources of the Islamic way of life, the Qur'ān and the Sunnah. They conceived of *nahḍah* as an intellectual movement capable of imagining Islam afresh and in light of outside challenges. However, some of the Muslim intelligentsia who opted for a secular path—especially in the first part of this century—lost confidence in the truth of their religious tradition, and assimilated the central tenets of Western culture.[13]

It is undoubtedly clear that one consequence of the modern confrontation between the Islamic religious tradition and mentality on the one hand, and the Western world-view on the other, has been a renewed interest in the problematic of Islamic tradition. It is common knowledge that the authority of tradition is invoked, albeit in various degrees, when there is a major trauma in society. Islamic tradition has been invoked by all sorts of forces in modern Islam, ranging from the Wahabbis in Arabia to the Ikhwan in Egypt and the rest of the Arab world. It is perhaps true that the Islamic tradition has been invoked and manipulated differently by various people for the sake of safeguarding their own interests and objectives in times of crisis and predicament.[14] Traditional symbols come to the fore, and neo-traditionalism as sociopolitical and religious force begins to emerge, "when the traditionalist begins to come more deeply to grips with the Western challenge, he may become a 'neo-traditionalist.' Here, too, we may discern 'rejectionist' and 'adaptionist' extremes. Neo-traditionalism may be viewed as a transitional phase on the way to secularism, modernism, and radical Islamism."[15] One can see Islamic resurgence, therefore, as a neo-traditional Islamism, which, in many ways, has felt the impact of the West and has been compelled to forge a kind of an intellectual and political synthesis in order to respond to the formidable challenge of the West. This is perhaps what differentiates it from other traditionalist and conservative tendencies in the modern Arab world that did not take the Western threat seriously. In other words, Islamic resurgence is not a strident assertion of old values in a condensed and purified form, but is a reaction to an aggressive Western and capitalist modernity.

Historically speaking, the Muslim Brotherhood Movement has carried the task of resurgence since 1928. Emerging in Egypt as a direct response to British hegemony, the Ikhwan has generated and revived a host of religious, social, political, and civilizational debates. In one sense, at least, modern Muslims must be indebted to Islamic resurgence for promoting intellectual and religious revival that has proved to be very urgent and necessary in view of the sterility of the intellectual formulations of the traditional *'ulamā'* class, and, perhaps, the unfortunate debacle of Islamic modernism.[16]

The view, promoted by some scholars, that a total vacuum of Islamic intellectualism exists in the modern Arab world neglects to consider the phenomenal emergence, growth, and resilience, in spite of political repression, of Islamic resurgence throughout the Arab world. What is significant about Islamism, especially when seen in the context of Arab intellectual history, is that, aside from being a political and sociological fact, it has emerged as a viable intellectual movement invoking the authority and seeking the legitimacy of the central Islamic tradition. It has undoubtedly shown a great ability to utilize and depend on a complex Islamic tradition, and it has thus competed successfully with secular and Westernized trends, especially in translating its notion of the Islamic tradition in a popularly managable way, thus securing the support of the masses. What that means is that the Islamic religious tradition and its relevant symbols, which had been pushed to the side before the resurgence of religious neo-traditionalism, are occupying a center stage again, to the extent that even the most secular politician and thinker of all in the contemporary Arab world cannot neglect this significant development. In the words of Issa Boullata, contemporary Arab thinkers have only recently begun to realize "that Arab culture and the Islamic heritage will inevitably have to be taken into serious consideration in any modernization process."[17] The point that must be made here is that neither the orientalist solution *à la mode* of H. Gibb, nor the Arab Marxist solution *à la mode* of A. Laroui of transcending the Islamic tradition reflects adequately the process of the reconstruction and resurgence of neo-traditionalism in the contemporary Arab world. Although it is true that the process of modernizing Arab society had been under way since the latter part of the nineteenth century, that did not preclude, but perhaps facilitated, the emergence of Islamism. Consequently, the Islamic tradition, besides occupying center stage, has been transformed into a radical ideology, a program of action, and a competing paradigm in the ideological and intellectual landscape of the contemporary Arab world. This is a far cry from the position that Islam held in the 1920s and the 1930s when its very symbols, articulations, and even cognitive (revelational) core had been under severe attack by secular ideologies. Instead of facing erosion and attrition, the Islamic tradition has become the center of debate.[18]

One can use Eric Hobsbawm's recently coined phrase "the invention of tradition" to refer to the process initiated by neo-traditional Islamism.[19] What is very significant about today's Islamic resurgence is perhaps, not its political slogans nor various attempts to seize political authority, but its invention of the Islamic tradition in such a way that *turāth* is not understood as a belonging to the past, but as forming the center of the contemporary Arab intellectual discourse.[20] Inventing the *turāth*, and not merely preserving it, also means ascribing an ideological value to tradition, such as the use of Islam as an ideological weapon against all sorts of enemies. It is not my intent here to argue that the ideological side of Islam is a novel phenomenon. One might argue—and indeed many have—that Islam has been an ideological religion since its inception.[21] However, what is distinctive about Islamic resurgence is the particular milieu in which it was born. This milieu is significantly different from that which gave birth to Islam. Although it is a universal religious phenomenon, Islam does not form a center as it did in its formative phase. In this sense, what Edward Shils has to say about the past expansion of the Islamic center is very instructive.

> One of the most successful expansions of a center is the expansion of Islam from Mecca into the realms of other societies and cultures of Asia and Africa. . . . The expansion of Islam, militant, and intellectual and organizationally superior to the rest of the sparsely settled, intellectually and organizationally weak, Arabian peninsula, was a simple matter. The expansion into the realm of Hellenistic and Graeco-Roman traditions was more complex. The intellectual tradition of this area, pagan and Christian, was still very strong, while militarily the eastern Roman Empire and what remained of the western Empire were weak. The consequence was military triumph, and the diminution of adherence to the hitherto dominant traditions of the area to very small enclaves. The expansion of the Islamic center replaced those previously dominant traditions. The changes did not only take place at the periphery; Islamic traditions also changed in the course of their expansion. Greek philosophy and science entered into Islamic thought. Islamic theology had to adapt itself to these, undergoing the changes necessary to incorporate them.[22]

One cannot but contrast this marvelous historical expansion of Islam to the modern state of affairs in which the Islamic center, both geographically and intellectually, had been under incessant external attack and internal contraction and loss of vitality. This historical reversal of fortune forms the backbone of the argument of Islamism that there needs to be a new form of Islamic expansion, especially in the wake of the failure of nationalism in delivering Arab society from its woes and problems.

One may look at the novel thrust of neo-traditionalism as sending shock waves into the secular domain of thought in Arab society. In the words of the Syrian thinker Kamal Abu-Deeb, the phenomenon of the resurgence of Islam—best understood as "the shock of tradition"—has dealt a heavy blow to the secular center of thought. "The center, with its relatively long history of liberalism, secularism, nationalism (both regional and Pan-Arab), socialism, and closeness to the West and Western culture in particular, was dealt a heavy blow and began to crack."[23] The traditional base of Arab society has proven to be stronger than that of many other contemporary societies.[24]

This newly invented traditionalism, in the form of Islamic resurgence, juxtaposes the present state of decline of the Muslim world and its increasing peripherality to the Islamic center of the past, when Islam was confident of itself, expanding beyond its original territory and winning new converts. Islam and Muslims are no more the center of the world, and shrinkage was experienced over the centuries, not only in terms of territory but, worse yet, in terms of beliefs, ideas, and concepts.

To elaborate on these notions, it is possible to argue that one cannot understand the historical dynamics of the modern Muslim world except in relation to Western modernity. One can generally define *modernity* as an objective historical, social, and cultural movement and phenomenon, emerging mainly in Europe in the post-Industrial Revolution era and seeking to stamp the modern age with a new, rational, vital, and dynamic outlook and ideology.[25]

From its inception, modernity espoused a highly visible rationalist attitude. Whether it was Hegel who first developed "a clear concept of modernity,"[26] or Rousseau being the "archetypal modern voice in the early phase of modernity,"[27] or Luther being its greatest modern anxiety-ridden religious personality,[28] there is almost a universal agreement shared by the intellectual historians of modernity that early modernists were troubled, lonely, and anxious human beings. Just like the early nationalists in the colonized Third World in the nineteenth century, who "were lonely, bilingual intelligentsias,"[29] early modernists sought a total break with their inherited intellectual and social tradition, especially religion.[30] Further, early modernists suffered a great deal from theoretical and conceptual solitude. In many ways, they produced their own concepts without reference to religious foundations or epistemologies.[31]

One of the main premises of modernism is the belief in the infinite capacity of the human mind to transform and control social and natural phenomenon. This presupposition challenges the theistic or Islamic mind at its foundation. Reason, in the crude words of Hegel, is what "distinguishes us from the brutes."[32] Therefore, modernist thinkers view man as being endowed with reason, self-consciousness, a sense of individualism, progress, *esprit systematique*, freedom, and as a maker of history. In the words of Kojeve, "there is something in Man, in every man, that makes him suited to participate—passively or actively—in the realization of universal history."[33] Modern man, and not God, is the maker of history,[34] which contrasts sharply with the Islamic view of history.

One of the main features of modernity in the nineteenth century was the pursuit of progress. For instance, Reinhold Niebuhr contends, along the same lines of the main eighteenth and nineteenth century thinkers, that the concept of progress reflected a highly volatile rational movement, which is best understood as "a tremendous affirmation of the limitless possibilities of human existence, and as a rediscovery of the sense of a meaningful history." To Niebuhr's mind, the movement of rationalism took many forms of expression and gave rise to diverse philosophical, religious, and social movements, such as Cartesian rationalism, the French enlightenment, liberalism, Marxism, secular utopianism and Nietsczhean nihilism.[35] However, "In all of these multifarious expressions, there is a unifying principle. It is the impulse toward the fulfillment of life in history."[36]

In addition to progress, Europe was bent on the universalization of its human reason. Therefore, eighteenth and nineteenth century philosophers and thinkers were in search of universal epistemological criteria in order to subdue the mysteries of nature and man. Looking in retrospect at the unfolding of Western civilization since the Renaissance, one can discern essential and substantial qualities and consequences produced against the tumultuous background of this complex history. One of these consequences is secularization which has persisted ever since. This, it seems to me, has never been a minor factor in the history of the West for the mere reason that theology has ceased to capture the imagination of the Western mind. By ceasing to perceive God as an epistemological problematic, Western man has endeavored to find other avenues of expressing his potential.

A nagging philosophical issue faced by European modernists was "the theory of knowledge." There was an urgency to establish new foundational knowledge, not legitimized by Metaphysics or monotheism. One sees the transition from a Metaphysics-bound knowledge to a rational one in the works of Locke, Descartes, and Kant, and their various disciples and admirers. This led definitely to the secularization of knowledge. In addition, European modernists had to find an answer to the question pertaining to the possible relationship between philosophy, as epistemology or foundation of knowledge, and other arenas of life, such as society, ethics, and history. Rorty maintains that there was a real secularization of many areas of thought, including the moral aspect of life.

> The secularization of moral thought, which was the dominating concern of European intellectuals in the seventeenth and eighteenth centuries, was not then viewed as a search for a new metaphysical foundation to take the place of theistic metaphysics. Kant, however, managed to transform the old notion of philosophy—metaphysics as "queen of sciences" because of its concern with what was most universal and least material—into the notion of "most basic" discipline—a foundational discipline. Philosophy became "primary" no longer in the sense of "highest" but in the sense of "underlying."[37]

Therefore, knowledge is not to be searched for in the realm of metaphysics, but in the domain of fluctuating human history. Exported to the Muslim world under the auspices of colonialism, this idea had a major impact on producing a new type of indigeneous intelligentsia that no longer saw its role as that of preserving but critiquing tradition and even Islam as a monotheistic phenomenon.

To look at it from a different angle, capitalist nihilism—as in the negation of divine Metaphysics and the role of God as stipulated by monotheism—promoted a double-edged approach in the wake of the Western expansion overseas. On the one hand, it offered the indigenous people, especially the educated, an abundance of social, educational, and economical opportunities. On the other, it stripped the "natives" of their traditional values and standards. This approach had a major bearing as well on sacred space in traditional Muslim society. The ancient Muslim city, with the mosque, the *madrasah*, and the bazaar at its center, no longer performs a useful function in the eyes of modernist capitalism. Far from being sacred and stable, space is subject to continuous change. This view has led to a more pronounced segregation of people in terms of poverty and wealth, and a gradual alienation of the sacred city from the affairs of secular urbanism. Woven into this complex process is that traditional values—which, more or less, had given a sense of security to the people—came under rampant assault. In a sense, when talking about the progression of nihilism in Muslim lands, it is important to note that, far from being limited to an assault on the Qur'anic foundations of revelation and knowledge, it also led to the depreciation of a traditional mode of life that had been entrenched for many centuries.[38] Both knowledge and modern values, as propagated by secular capitalism, are no longer in need of foundational structures and contents. They do not need to arrive at ultimate causes, or bring to life a historically-based norm and behavior. Thus, nihilism, simply defined as supremacy of the human mind over divine matters, becomes reified, not only in the modernist consciousness of a few selected natives who go to the schools of Europe, but is appropriated by the process of modernization as well. This process of modernization, simply defined as a systematic commitment to rationality, tends to push forward what it perceives as new universal principles, derived mainly from European conception of progress and evolution. It is understandable why, in its process of expanding overseas, capitalist modernity sought to bypass the traditional mentality and implant a new one. That is why a clash between the traditional and the modern in a colonized context was unavoidable. Added to the agony resulting from this direct collision between two fundamentally different world-views is another deriving from the lack of a self-critical attitude of both modernity and traditionalism.

Modernity is intrinsically unsettling and disturbing. Its strong commitment to rationalization underscores its enigma and gradual progression toward more commitment to reason. In its universal march aimed at modernizing the world, modernity has swept away, in quite unprecendented fashion, many a traditional mode of behavior. The new institutions in modern society, such as those crafted by the majestic touch of modernity, supercede the somewhat limited scope of traditionalism. In the words of Anthony Giddens, four major institutions define modern society: (1) industrialism or transformation of nature; (2) capitalism or capital accumulation in the context of competetive labor; (3) military power or the control of the means of violence in the context of industrialization of war; and (4) surveillance or the control of information and social supervision, distinguish modern society from traditional insitutitions.[39] Perhaps the most unsettling aspect of these modern institutions is the assault on traditional bases of knowledge or, in Giddens' words, "modernity effectively involves the institutionalization of doubt."[40]

Western modernity has, thus, translated itself in the modern Muslim world into a complex political, economic, and cultural phenomenon known as "colonialism," which possesses a radically different outlook than that of Islam. That is what makes Islamism, as a modern religious movement, a reaction to the onslaught of modernity and its philosophical outlook.

As a result of the enduring impact of modernity, one cannot but view the thought of Islamic resurgence in the context of the social and historical transformations of colonial and post-colonial Arab society. Undoubtedly, colonialism as a major political, social, cultural, and psychological phenomenon has deeply affected the workings of the modern Arab/Islamic mind, and it is naive to assume that the inner developments in contemporary Islamic thought are immune to the impact of colonialism and its aftermath. It is as strong a component—sometimes negative, sometimes positive—in modern Arab societies as the Qur'anic impact on the Arab mind.

As a result of the engrossing impact of colonization—understood later on as modernity and modernization—there ought to have been a response at all levels of thought. The Islamic thought was no exception to that. Therefore, when studying the main manifestations of the Ikhwan thought, especially before the *thawra* phase of 1952, one cannot fail to notice the great strides of critical thinking in this discourse. This critical orientation produced a multifarious and complex process at the metaphysical, theological, religious, cultural, literary, and political levels. I believe that the task of the historian of ideas is to develop a reflective philosophical approach in order to study this complex Islamist discourse. Because of the immense theological and historical significance of the Qur'ān in the world of Islam, a serious scholar must study the way the Qur'ān has been understood and interpreted by the Islamist discourse. Quṭb's grandiose exegesis, as analyzed in chapter 6 of this book, is just one example of how serious and critical the Islamist tendency was in orientation and method.

Reacting to Westernization and its various cultural and political forms and expressions, Islamic resurgence, in the form of the Muslim Brotherhood Movement, aimed, from its very beginning at finding the *al-ḥall al-islāmī* (Islamic solution)—a famous slogan of all Islamist organizations—to the problem of alienation, education, economic organization, and social justice in society. As shall be seen in our discussion of al-Bannā, Quṭb, and Faḍlallah, Islamism is a total revolutionary ideology that advocated an Islamic nation without separation of religion and state. Next, it proposed an Islamic educational system with the goal of creating the "Muslim individual, the Muslim house, the Muslim nation, and the Muslim government." Third, it attempted to create an economic infrastructure based on Islamic principles to solve social injustice. This is, in a nutshell, what defines the normative as well as the social nature of Islamic resurgence in the Arab world.

Salient Features of Islamic Resurgence in the Arab World: Toward a Multidimensional Approach

So far, I have tried in this chapter to address the first two questions posed at the beginning. It is worthwhile at this stage to discuss briefly the salient features of Islamic resurgence in the Arab world and the reasons for its emergence on the basis of some of the most advanced literature in the field. To be sure, it is difficult to discuss all that has been written on Islamic resurgence, simply because of its immense volume. However, it is important to discuss a number of select positions on Islamic resurgence in relation to the full range of issues and questions that underlie modern Arab intellectual history in general.

To Hisham Sharabi and his "radical school of critics" of Arab society, Islamic resurgence is one of the fundamental manifestations of neopatriachal structure and discourse in modern Arab society. Sharabi defines neopatriarchy as a mode of being that is neither modern nor traditional, and that is born out of deformed modernization.[41] Sharabi argues that, as a result of the failure of critical modernity (such as Marxism) to gain a strong foothold in Arab society, "[t]he relations and values of neopatriarchy have gained the ascendancy (1970s and 1980s), and Islamic fundamentalism has moved to the center of the political stage."[42] In Sharabi's view, the main distinguishing fact about Islamism is its modern character and the fact that it was born in dialectical reaction to imperialism.

> The movement of Islamic radicalization accompanied the process, of "modernization" and was dialectically linked to it. Islamic fundamentalism, like Westernization and "modernization," was a psychosocial phenomenon taking form under European domination and in direct reaction to it. But militant Islam (fundamentalism) ought to be interpreted not simply as a rejection of foreign values and ideas but rather as an attempt to give a new Islamic content to the meaning of self and society by refomulating a redemptive Islamic dogma.[43]

It is plausible to argue, as does Sharabi, that Islamism's identity, especially in its first stage, is highly embedded in imperialism. It has criticized colonialism on the grounds of religious alienation and cultural dependency. Its deep commitment to retrieve authenticity (*aṣālah*) is a reflection of the deep anxiety and crisis of identity permeating modern Arab society. To the majority of Islamists—especially those who follow in the footsteps of Sayyid Quṭb and Yūsuf al-Qaraḍāwī—the modern nation/state, emerging in the wake of colonialism's eclipse, did not stem the tide leading to foreign intellectual hegemony. Instead, it propagated cultural dualism and further dependency on the West.[44] The modern nation/state also has espoused a national policy of education in the fields of history and philosophy in which only dead issues are raised—hollow issues that have no relevance whatsoever to the great social, political, and cultural problems besetting modern Muslim societies. This is best expressed by Rashid al-Ghanoushi of Tunisia.

> What difference does it make for us when we, defeated Muslims . . . , know the Mu'tazilite position on God's attributes . . . or Ibn Rushd's understanding of the universe . . . or Ibn Sina's opinion of the self . . . ?[45]

The bone of contention of many Islamist movements is their critique of oppressive social and political reality as well as passive and subdued intellectual environment. In short, Islamism has emerged as a viable protest movement in the Arab world. In the words of Halim Barakat, himself a radical critic of Islamic fundamentalism, "religion has been used by the colonized and the oppressed as a mechanism of instigation against their colonizers and oppressors . . . In fact, one of the most significant reasons for what is called the Islamic resurgence is the active involvement of religious movements in opposition to colonization and dependent, repressive regimes."[46] This observation gains further significance if it is extended to cover the conflict between different Arab regimes, espousing Arab nationalism (as in Egypt and Syria), and Islamic resurgence. From the point of view of resurgence, nationalism is an alien and repressive ideology.

Therefore, Islamic resurgence is undoubtedly a modern phenomenon—the product, to a large extent, of modern conditions which ironically enable it to use Islamic symbols to face the new situation. Some Muslim scholars, best represented by Khurshid Ahmad, argue that modern Islamism is part of an overall Islamic historical pattern, known as *tajdīd*, and is, consequently, "a perennial phenomenon in Islamic history and therefore not particularly new or modern."[47] It seems to me that the resurgence is Islamic only to the extent that it has utilized and re-invented the main Islamic symbols of *tajdīd* (renewal), *iṣlāḥ* (reform), *ijtihād* (reasoning), and *ḥarakiyya* (dynamism) in a modern setting.[48] However, one must perceive Islamic resurgence as a socioreligious phenomenon evolving mainly in reaction to the Western thrust into the Muslim world. Further, the nature of the West itself as a capitalist system, with its complex culture of advanced industrial societies, has a direct bearing on the emergence of resurgence initially, at least, as the movement of the oppressed.

In its foundational phase, Islamism focused on the issue of social justice as its leading social concern. This is true in the case of both Sunni and Shi'ī resurgence in the Arab world as will be shown in our analysis of the work of both Quṭb and Faḍlallah. One may agree with Samir Amin's observation that, "It seems realistic to start from the bold observation that capitalist development and imperialist conquests have created the situation [of Islamic resurgence] we are experiencing. Like it or not, the problems facing us are those engendered by this development."[49]

John Voll, on the other hand, provides a more general thesis on the origins of modern resurgence, "Islamic fundamentalism is . . . a distinctive mode of response to major social and cultural change introduced either by exogenous or indigenous forces and perceived as threatening to dilute or dissolve the clear lines of Islamic identity, or to overwhelm that identity in a synthesis of many different elements."[50] The point to be made here is that both the external factors—the West, capitalism, and social and economic forces—and the internal factors—Islamic *tajdīd*, and the like—have produced this phenomenon, and that both sets of factors are modern themselves. Islamic resurgence in the modern Arab world is a socioreligious and political movement that represents social interests, perhaps those of the "alienated petty bourgeois mass and its proletarian extension."[51] It has nevertheless given rise to a variety of voices and expressions, and has been unrelenting in pursuing its major goal, which is to alter or supplant some portion of the existing culture and society, either through legal peaceful means or revolutionary methods. As a social movement, Islamic resurgence is revolutionary because it seeks to introduce radical changes and transformations in the philosophical bases as well as the social, economic, and political structures of the status quo. The Iranian revolution, carried out in the name of Islam, has been a real indicator that Islam can be a vehicle of revolutionary change in twentieth-century Muslim societies.

Moreover, Islamic resurgence, besides being a social and political movement, is part of an intellectual and religious formation which must be adequately accounted for within the social formation sphere.

One could agree to a certain extent with Eric Davis's assessment that many a study of Islamic resurgence lacks theoretical and intellectual rigor and orientation, and that a great majority of "Western and non-Western scholars . . . have presented a reified, reductionist, and ultimately ideological understanding of the relationship between Islam and politics. An escape from this theoretical *cul-de-sac* requires a historical examination of the articulation of Islamic political movements with the surrounding social structure, state formation, competing ideologies, and exogeneous forces such as colonialism and the world market."[52] While all of these criteria are necessary to examine Islamic resurgence, none sheds enough light on its theological and intellectual formation. In a sense, as a radical political ideology, Islamic resurgence appeals to a revolutionary tradition in normative Islam.

One major religious premise of Islamism is that "correct Islam" cannot be practiced in the twentieth century except in the context of an Islamic political system. Therefore, one conspicuous goal of Islamic resurgence, especially its radical wing, is the establishment of an Islamic political regime. Seen against the context of the current regimes in the Arab world, Islamic resurgence has adopted an ideological position that seeks to transcend the status quo, and is, thus, seen as a counterstate ideology. It is somewhat ironic, notes Nazih Ayubi, that the postcolonial state in the Arab world which has, in the most part, neglected to define itself in religious or theocratic terms, has paved the way for Islamism to use one of its strongest weapons—that is, religion:

> [T]he fact that the contemporary State lays claim to secularism has enabled some forces of political protest to appropriate Islam as their own weapon. Because the State does not embrace Islam (except in a "defensive" reactive way), it cannot describe its opponents as easily as the traditional State could as being simply heretic cults. Political Islam [Islamism] now reverses the historical process—it claims "generic" Islam for the protest movements, leaving to the State the more difficult task of qualifying and justifying its own "version" of Islam.[53]

From this viewpoint, one can come to one possible conclusion that Islamism did not participate in any substantial sense in erecting the foundations of the modern or secular state, and, therefore, it finds itself compelled to condemn a system that it considers to have failed on all counts. Condemnation of the political system complements a rejection of all forms of secular ideologies that make up the intellectual landscape of the modern state. In this particular sense, one might well define Islamism as "the recourse to the vocabulary of Islam, used in the postcolonial period to express within the state, or more often against it, an alternative political program."[54] This program, to be sure, is based on a certain reading of Islamic history and culture.

It is also possible to argue that Islamism is a reaction to the crisis of the secular nation/state, especially in the wake of the 1967 Arab defeat with Israel.[55] Philip Khoury elaborates this thesis in an important article and concludes that "Islamic revivalism can best be understood as a reaction to a crisis in the modern secular state. This crisis can be defined as "state-exhaustion." The reaction is to the state's inability to bring the whole society into modernity."[56] While this might be true, one can not forget that a large segment of the leadership of Islamism is Western-trained, and that some use their Westernized education as a means of asserting their tradition in a highly volatile and changing world. In this particular sense, Islamic resurgence does assimilate one major component of modernity—namely, technology and science.[57]

As shown in this discussion, Islamic resurgence's relation to the Islamic tradition has been a complex one. Although it is true that "The 'resurgence of Islam' is, at least in some of its aspects, a utilization of tones and symbols that have deep roots within the Islamic tradition,"[58] it has nevertheless offered a unique interpretation of a major part of the corpus of the Islamic tradition that is consonant with the conditions of the modern world. As a religio-social movement, it attempted to explain and transcend the challenges posed by the modern world to Islam. Its understanding of tradition is, thus, innovative and not anachronistic, elastic and not rigid.

In its attempt to overcome the modern challenge, Islamic resurgence has emphasized, theoretically at least, the reconstruction of an Islamically based authority; of the Islamic nation, which is a gradual reconstitution of the Muslim *ummah*; and the building of a comprehensive system of Islamic law, government, education, and ethics in the modern world. The reconstitution of the *ummah* in the modern world is considered possible if there is a return to the original sources of Islam. This cry has been a response to the forces of secularization and modernization in Arab societies. The preceding thesis raises the important question of the relationship between Islamism and nationalism.

To come to grips with the relation of nationalism to religion, let us look briefly at Benedict Anderson's *Imagined Communities*, one of the few works that treat the relationship between religion and nationalism as a theoretical problem.[59] In the words of Partha Chatterjee, Anderson's book is a highly unorthodox intervention in the literature of nationalism, because Anderson "refuses to 'define' a nation by a set of external and abstract criteria. On the contrary, he fundamentally subverts the determinist scheme by asserting that the nation is 'an imagined political community.' It is not uniquely produced by the constellation of certain objective social factors; rather, the nation is 'thought out,' 'created'."[60]

The following treatment of Anderson's work is quite necessary at this stage because it is impossible to have a proper understanding of, for example, Sayyid Quṭb's religious thought of the 1950s and 1960s without shedding enough theoretical light on the problematic of religion and nationalism in general. As will be seen later, few of the intellectual leaders of Islamic resurgence have provided any systematic treatment of the subject of nationalism, but one must concede that the second important variable in the making of Islamic resurgence in the Arab world after colonialism has been nationalism. The intellectual history of Arab Islamic resurgence gains a new epistemic force during the time in which Arab nationalism is gaining political power. Sayyid Quṭb's thought is a clear representative of that.[61]

What does Benedict Anderson say? Anderson skillfully treats what he calls "the anomaly of nationalism" in the context of modern European history without underestimating the unique nature of non-European nationalisms. "[I]n Western Europe," he arguess, "the eighteenth century marks not only the dawn of the age of nationalism but the dusk of religious modes of thought."[62] That this argument is not new is unimportant. What is important however is that nationalism "is an imagined political community—and imagined as both inherently limited and sovereign."[63] The crux of the argument is that nationalism is able to invent a new community, as opposed to the ancient religious constellation of community, and give it new parameters and meanings.

Although it would be simpleminded to assume a historical congruence between Western nationalisms and Muslim nationalisms—or nationalisms in the Muslim world—they nevertheless share similar ideological and philosophical bases. Although one could argue that the early leaders of the Ikhwan did not object to Arab nationalism as long as an Islamic state could be established, one must note that religion, and all it stands for, occupies a peripheral status in nationalist thought. Nationalism reached this conclusion through a complex process of interaction between different historical and social variables and factors that are not the same in each country. However, one thing is clear. "The great sacral cultures . . . incorporated conceptions of immense communities . . . Christendom, [and] the Islamic *Ummah* . . . imagined itself . . . as central . . . [religious communities] were imaginable largely through the medium of a sacred language and written script."[64] One can possibly argue therefore that Arab nationalism, as both an intellectual and political force, was able to imagine a limited and sovereign political community that is not congruent with the universal ideals of Islam. As a result, it produced a new type of intelligetsia—an intelligentsia that does not subscribe to the traditional modes of religious thinking, as it had been enunciated by the *'ulamā'*, and that does not see itself as part of "a cosmological hierarchy of which the apex [is] divine."[65] It is understandable, therefore, that Arab nationalist intelligentsia would not agree with the basic aims of Islamic resurgence which revolve around "(1) intellectual and religious reconstruction of Islamic thought; (2) reconstruction of Muslim society and polity; and (3) approximation of some of Islamic cooperation, Islamic unity, Islamic solidarity, i.e. closeness between the different peoples who make up the Muslim *ummah*."[66]

Anderson argues that nationalism in the Third World was a response to the colonialist/capitalist intervention in its gestation period. With the expansion of capitalism to the Third World in the context of colonialism, a number of fundamental changes take place: (1) the book industry and journalism in the colonies encourages local or vernacular dialects at the expense of the language of the elite culture; (2) missionaries establish Western-oriented educational institutions to train the indigenous intelligentsia to think in Western terms; and (3) some of the Western-trained intelligentsia carry the banner of nationalism. Anderson's assessment of the subject is all the more useful.

> It is generally recognized that the intelligentsia were central to the rise of nationalism in the colonial territories. . . . [Their] vanguard role derived from their bilingual literacy, or rather literacy and bilingualism. . . . Bilingualism meant access, through the European language-of-state, to modern Western culture in the broadest sense, and, in particular, to the models of nationalism, nation-ness, and nation/state produced elsewhere in the course of the nineteenth century.[67]

However, Anderson comments with brutal sarcasm on the cultural state of this bilingual intelligentsia produced in the schools of the West. "The expansion of the colonial state which, so to speak, invited 'natives' into schools and offices, and of colonial capitalism which, as it were, excluded them from boardrooms *meant that to an unprecendental extent the key early spokesmen for colonial nationalism were lonely, bilingual intelligentsia unattached to sturdy local bourgeoisie* [Emphasis added]."[68] Colonial nationalism showed little interest in indigenous religions, whereas the second generation of nationalists, who were still influenced by the West, showed a certain interest in their religion and even tried to incorporate a religious language into their nationalist thought.[69] However, in the mind of the Islamist intelligentsia, the nationalist intelligentsia, while being able to fight colonialism politically, was unable to shake off the spiritual and intellectual influence of Westernization.

To a large extent, one could argue that the emergence of Islamic resurgence in the Arab world, specifically in Egypt, coincided with the "crisis of orientation" in the life of the nationalist intelligentsia.[70] Both were, more or less, reacting to similar forces—foreign presence, and lack of internal political and social cohesiveness. However, Islamic resurgence envisioned the Muslim *ummah* as the answer to this state of affairs, whereas Arab nationalism was more limited in its imagining. There is no doubt that Islamic resurgence has been been politically romantic in its imagining of the *ummah* as a gradually reconstituted religious and social community. Perhaps this romanticism is the dynamo that propels the movement into action, and that has littered its lenghty way with tragic pitfalls and hazards.

Anderson's theoretical formulation has drawn our attention once again to the crisis theory discussed earlier in this chapter. To some, the crisis did not result from any historical conflict between nationalism and religion in the Arab world, but from the historical rupture between the Islamic ideal and real. This rupture, they claim, resulted in an endemic spiritual and social crisis. They also claim that the real thrust of Islamic resurgence has been to "correct the spiritual crisis" in modern Islam by endevouring "to strike a balance between the divine promise of earthly success to the Muslims and their contemporary situation."[71] In short—and according to this view—Islamism is a reflection of a pathological crisis that is deeply rooted in Muslim society. Crisis theory is also articulated in political terms.

> An outstanding characteristic of religious fundamentalist movements is their cyclical propensity, consisting of successive periods of dormancy and resurgence. A casual pattern can be discerned whereby manifestations of religious resurgence correspond to periods of intense spiritual, social, and political crisis. Islamic fundamentalism is no exception to this historical pattern. Indeed, throughout Islamic history, the incidence of fundamentalist resurgence has been closely associated with periods of great

turmoil when the very existence of the Islamic polity and/or its moral integrity were under threat.[72]

Once again, the great historical transformations that led to the rise of nationalism in the modern Arab world are seen as enough reason for this crisis, but the argument quoted here stipulates that crisis has been the most distinguishing characteristic of both classical and modern Islamic history. If this theory is to be taken at face value, what prevents us from considering total human history to be crisis prone? Other crisis theorists are somewhat sensible in that they do not trace the origins of the modern crisis to the distant past. Instrad, they see Islamism as a reflection as well as a major reason for the crisis of contemporary Arab society. The Sudanese scholar Ḥaydar Ibrāhim ʿAlī writes that "Islamic resurgence is principally a movement of crisis,"[73] and that it is "the result of a deep psychological, social, economic, political, and civilizational crisis, and in turn, it [Islamism] gets transformed to become itself a reason for a far more complicated and deeper crisis as has been the case lately in a number of Arab societies, such as Tunisia, Algeria, and the Sudan."[74] Some Islamist writers propose a similar line of argument, but reach different conclusions, arguing that Islamism is a self-conscious effort to deal with crisis. In their view, Islamism is the last defense mechanism that contemporary Muslim societies resort to in order to transcend internal fragmentation, loss of autonomy and inner unity, and is a means of bridging social, political, cultural, sectarian gaps and problems caused by the modern secular state. "In most cases, Islamism is a conscious attempt to contain all these contradictions by bypassing them, and is a response to foreign hegemony as well as the failure of the regional state internally."[75] Halim Barakat more or less reiterates the preceding position by concluding that religion—as an expression of the frustration, exploitation, and sense of illusion of the masses—cannot be a truly revolutionary force. What Barakat has to say summarizes in a nutshell the attitude of the contemporary Arab left toward the problem of resurgence.[76]

It is clear that the crisis of the independent nation/state in many Arab countries has indeed led to a political and even intellectual vacuum that Islamic resurgence has not been oblivious to. What facilitated the efforts of Islamic resurgence in confronting the nation/state and taking advantage of this vacuum is perhaps the modernized element of resurgence. Although, "at the beginning of the twentieth century Islamic revivalism did not appeal to the majority of the educated Arabic-speaking people in urban centers such as Cairo and

Damascus,"[77] a large number of its intellectual leaders, including both Ḥassan al-Bannā and Sayyid Quṭb, were products of secular and educated background. There is reason to believe that the theoretical formulations of contemporary Islamic resurgence are not confined to traditional-minded intelligentsia, but that a large number of professionals, including many who received Western education, espouse the ideas of the Ikhwan in a variety of forms.[78] This gives resurgence an aggressive intellectual edge, to say the least. John L. Esposito corroborates this view by saying that, "In the nineties, Islamic revivalism has ceased to be restricted to small, marginal organizations on the periphery of society and instead has become part of mainstream Muslim society, producing a new class of modern-educated but Islamically oriented elites who work alongside, and at times in coalition with, their secular counterparts."[79] Therefore, the nation/state of the contemporary Arab world finds itself at loggerheads with an aggressive religious movement that is, to a large extent, the product of the modern conditions.

Conclusions

One can discern the following identifiable qualities of Islamic resurgence: (1) it represents a modern Islamic discourse that has been produced against the dynamics of modern Arab history; (2) it is an anti-establishment movement, both politically and religiously; (3) it does not agree with the basic premises of Arab nationalism; and (4) it has re-interpreted Islamic tradition in a way that lends itself to a revolutionary meaning. The failure of Islamic resurgence so far to accomplish its grandiose scheme of the political reconstruction of the *ummah* has placed it in a head-on conflict with the current secular regimes in the Arab world.

Chapter 3

Ḥasan al-Bannā and the Foundation of the Ikhwan: Intellectual Underpinnings

Man can be satisfied only by action. Now, to act is to transform what is real. And to transform what is real is to negate the given.

—Alexander Kòjeve, Introduction to the Reading of Hegel: Lectures on The Phenomenology of Spirit (Ithaca, N.Y. 1980) 54

One of the most potent attractions of a mass movement is its offering of a substitute for individual hope. This attraction is particularly effective in a society imbued with the idea of progress. For in the inception of progress, "tomorrow" looms large, and the frustration resulting from having nothing to look forward to is the more poignant.

—Eric Hoffer, The True Believer: Thoughts on the Nature of Mass Movements (New York 1951) 23–24

In speaking of the formative phase of Islamic resurgence in the modern Arab world, only a few thinkers can be said to have played a pivotal role in the formation and later dissemination of the Ikhwan's ideas. Four people stand out for having exerted lasting influence on the theoretical foundations of the thought of the Ikhwan and its current proliferation throughout the Arab and Muslim world. They are Ḥasan al-Bannā, the founder; ʿAbd al-Qādir ʿAwdah, a lawyer by profession and one of the early followers of al-Bannā;[1] Sayyid Quṭb, who became a member of the Ikhwan movement in the early 1950s, and Muḥammad al-Ghazālī, a prolific author and teacher who is esteemed by many for having kept alive the thought of the Ikhwan even after the deaths of the first three thinkers.[2] Especially since the expansion of the Ikhwan beyond its physical and intellectual center in Egypt, other figures of importance have also emerged. In this context it is worthwhile to mention Yūsuf al-Qaraḍāwī of Egypt;[3] Musṭafa al-Sibāʿī of Syria;[4] Saʿīd Ḥawwā of Syria;[5] Ḥasan Turābī of Sudan,[6] and Rāshid al-Ghanoushī of Tunisia.[7]

In this work, the thought of Ḥasan al-Bannā and Sayyid Quṭb will be highlighted. The ideas of Muḥammad Ḥusayn Faḍlallah, A shiʿī *ʿālim* activist in Lebanon, will also be analyzed. The intellectual contributions of Quṭb—who was, as will be seen later, the intellectual and ideologue par excellence of the Ikhwan—will receive special attention, while the work of other relevant figures in Arab Islamism will also be considered.

This chapter is confined to discussing the intellectual career of Ḥasan al-Bannā, but with a dual objective: (1) to trace the growth and evolution of Ḥasan al-Bannā's ideas which paved the way toward creating an intact ideological movement, or rather a counterstate ideological movement, and (2) to examine the impact of this counter-ideology on the Ikhwan after the assassination of al-Bannā in 1949. Under the latter objective, I will also discuss the way the counter-ideology was interpreted and developed by subsequent intellectual leaders of the Ikhwan, and by Sayyid Quṭb and Yūsuf al-Qaraḍāwī in particular.

Ḥasan al-Bannā and his followers were convinced that their interpretation of Islam as both faith and ideology was the correct one. The other side of this belief was that the prevalent interpretations of Islam as a complex tradition—whether of the Sufis, the *ʿulamā'*, or the modernists such as Muḥammad ʿAbduh and Rashīd Riḍā—were inadequate to meet the tasks that Ḥasan al-Bannā and the early Ikhwan leaders had in mind. Therefore, if we are ever to have an idea of how al-Bannā's ideas developed, the reasons and conditions that led to these convictions must be analyzed. An elaborate discussion of Ḥasan al-Bannā's ideas is in order because, as a charismatic leader, he

> was the Brotherhood in the early stages of its development. He gave his Brethren (Ikhwan) their group characteristics as well as their program; he inspired them with his ardor and sincerity; and his magnetic personality attracted an ever-swelling stream of adherents to the movement. Until within a few months of the end of his life, Ḥasan al-Bannā kept the power in his own hands and personally directed the program and the policies of his organization.[8]

Although it is plausible to argue that al-Bannā was not a profound thinker in the same way that Muḥammad ʿAbduh was, his ideas and career paved the way toward the construction of a viable modern Islamist discourse which proved to be a competitor, not only to all sorts of secular discourses in the modern Arab world, but to traditional religious discourse as well.

In laying out and analyzing the major intellectual, religious, philosophical, and political themes of Ḥasan al-Bannā's world-view, special attention will be given to the metamorphosis it underwent in the wake of al-Bannā's assassination in 1949. Al-Bannā planted the intellectual seeds of a socio-religious and mass-oriented movement that has played a significant role in the politics and society of the Arab Middle East and North Africa. According to Muḥammad A. Khalafallah, the charisma of Ḥasan al-Bannā stems from his being the sole founder of the largest religious movement in the modern Middle East, his execution of his work with utmost care, and his having "defined the parameters of its mission, purposes, and methods."[9] One must note that, in spite of the controversial political stands of the Muslim Brotherhood in various Arab nations today, the Brotherhood has undoubtedly made a strong ideological impact on a significant section of the Arab and Muslim intelligentsia.[10] Generally speaking, Ḥasan al-Bannā's contribution to the debate on the revival of Islam in the twentieth century must be understood as that of a religious-minded and rising middle-class intellectual of the Third World laboring under the impact of cultural Westernization and political weakness at home. Those who continued the legacy of al-Banna came from more or less similar social and educational backgrounds.

Some have discussed, albeit briefly, Ḥasan al-Bannā's political philosophy for the purpose of investigating the political power and influence of the Ikhwan during the interwar period.[11] In fact, the political power of the Ikhwan has always been in doubt. Their ambivalence toward the pragmatic world of politics—as Richard Mitchell shows clearly throughout his well-researched *The Society of the Muslim Brothers*—does little to portray their ideological convictions with any degree of precision. Therefore, my purpose here will not be to investigate the Ikhwan's dabbling in politics, but rather to examine the system of ideas which al-Bannā laid out, because that is what is truly at the center of Islamist thought. In other words, if one is to write the intellectual history of the Ikhwan, one must start with the types of problems and issues with which al-Bannā dealt.

As already mentioned, al-Bannā must be perceived as a Third-World intellectual who "was born into a feudal society . . . [which was] undermined by [both] British imperialism,"[12] and the secular and rational outlook of Western modernity. Consequently, throughout his entire career as an ideologue/activist, al-Bannā viewed the West as a great political and intellectual challenge. He grew up against an established peasant background, and he had no exceptional religious training except that he was a member of a Sufi order. While a teenaged student at Dār al-ʿUlūm in Cairo, he opted for a secular path in education.[13] In the first part of his life, he represented the Islam of the effendis with his "effendi's coat, tie, and tarbush."[14] Alienation in the big city—a major theme discussed by many Egyptian intellectuals with rural backgrounds at the turn of the century[15]—opened new vistas of hope for the young al-Bannā who began viewing himself as duty-bound to tackle the malaise of Islam and Muslims. He explains this situation in the following manner:

> After the last war [World War I] and during the period I spent in Cairo, there was an increase in spiritual and ideological disintegration, in the name of intellectual freedom. There was also a deterioration of behavior, morals, and deeds in the name of individual freedom . . . I saw that the social life of the beloved Egyptian nation was oscillating between her dear and precious Islamism which she had inherited, defended, lived with, and become accustomed to, . . . and this severe Western invasion which is armed and equipped with all the destructive and degenerative influence of money, wealth, prestige, ostentation, material enjoyment, power, and means of propaganda.[16]

In treating the ideas of Ḥasan al-Bannā, one must assume that his thoughts, far from arising in a vacuum, crystallized in the context of the debates arising in Egypt in the interwar period over religious, economic, political, social, and intellectual conditions and matters. The thought structure of the Ikhwan, as molded by al-Bannā, is based on a world-view of Islam understood as a religion, a civilization, a way of life, an ideology, and a state. Some tend to believe that this world-view, espoused in totality by al-Bannā, is essentialist, unchanging, and beyond the rules of history. Al-Bannā's Islamist discourse, however, was born against the tumultuous events of the interwar period and, to a certain extent, al-Bannā had to compromise his ideological Islamist stands in order to deal with the dominant system. While it is correct to argue that the Ikhwan, theoretically speaking, can not be "regarded as a more-or-less deviant type of offshoot from Islam,"[17] it is nonetheless a new phenomenon which emerged in response to certain conditions on the ground. Al-Bannā's philosophy, therefore, is that of an intellectual-leader and organizer who had a large stake in the world of events in Egyptian society at the time. For a clear elucidation of his basic ideas, I propose to examine the following themes and questions distilled from his basic writings, speeches, memoirs, and the growing corpus of secondary material on his life and thought.

1. Islamic decline and renaissance;
2. Westernization, colonialism, and the encounter with the West;
3. Social, economic, and political conditions;
4. The role and function of the *'ulamā'* as the literati class in Islam; and
5. Islam as a system of life and ideas.

These themes, as already shown in the first chapter of this work, constitute the backbone of modern Arab intellectual history.

Ḥasan al-Bannā's *Memoirs* As a Source of the Ikhwan's Early Intellectual History

Hasan al-Bannā's *Mudhakarāt* (*Memoirs*), written a few years before his assassination in 1949, reveal the intimate side of his life and shed considerable light on his intellectual and religious development. Al-Bannā's *Mudhakarāt* is written in the first person, and this is perhaps what distinguishes it from traditional Islamic *tarjama*. A *tarjama* in the words of Dale F. Eickelman, "is generally written in the third person, even if autobiographical, suggesting a distancing from self, an appeal to set standards and understandings. The components include a genealogy, an account of formal education and Qur'anic memorization, a list of teachers (often including close relatives, which indicates family support for religious learning), the books and subjects studied, and selections from the subject's poetry, aphorisms, or other contributions to learning."[18] In a reflective, but straightforward style, al-Bannā offers a clear portrait of a troubled self—a self that is torn between its passion for things Islamic and irritation at things un-Islamic.

Four distinguishing characteristics of his *Mudhakarāt*[19] emerge. First, there is the solemn atmosphere of his birth place in Maḥmūdiyya in Upper Egypt, an inspiring milieu that fills the heart with feelings of nostalgia, relatedness, and meaning in life. Perhaps this environment, more than anything else in al-Bannā's life, always weighed heavily on his mind, and it symbolized the perfection of tradition and authority. Al-Bannā often refers to his father and his influence on him, but he rarely mentions his mother, and it is difficult to judge whether al-Bannā was concerned about the plight of women in Egyptian society at the time. Second, al-Bannā portrays the religious environment of Maḥmūdiyya, and discusses in detail the impact of sufism on his personal growth and development. Third, al-Bannā devotes a section to the teachers who influenced him and the books that he read. In this, he follows the model of the classical Islamic *tarjama*. Fourth, he documents in minute detail his journey to Cairo in 1922 as a young student, and the shock that resulted from his first encounter with a big and secular city.

In this autobiography, al-Bannā is clearly aware of the different forces that exerted influence on him in his youth, and he is clear about the steps to be taken for the achievement of his goals. In short, his *Mudhakarāt* plays a multiple function of explicating, justifying, and shedding light on the formation of the young mind of Ḥasan al-Bannā.[20]

How great was the influence of Sufism on al-Bannā's life? It is evident that al-Bannā's mystical training and allegiance to the Ḥaṣafī mystical school,[21] as a young man, molded his entire personality. In my view, that was the single most important factor in al-Bannā's establishing and sustaining an active religious and social organization with a clear social and political mission. That sufism suited the mental and spiritual inclinations of the young al-Bannā was but a natural result of the idealist training which he received from his father at home. The spiritual side of Sufism did not prevent the young adept from perceiving the great practical benefits of the *ṭarīqah* and the effects of its socialization process. What impressed him the most, he tells us, was the practical side of preaching of the Ḥaṣafī school and its unique power to preserve and propagate the noble ideals of the Islamic religion. Taking the oath of allegiance to the *ṭarīqah* while still eighteen years old automatically placed him in the ranks of the most esteemed and educated disciples.[22] This had the double effect of (1) enabling al-Bannā to distance himself from his family and childhood friends, and (2) forming a new mentality that was based on the distinction drawn by Sufism between the *khāṣṣah* and *'āmmah* (the elite and the commoners).[23] Al-Bannā thought of himself as belonging to a special class of people, as a person responding to a special call, and as a true believer with a mission. However, precisely because of his social background and his Sufi training, he felt it was his duty to alleviate the suffering of the common people. Because of his position, he was able, as Afaf Marsot puts it, to talk "to common folk in an idiom they understood, one that came from their traditions and was related to their needs. He did not talk of democracy or constitutional rights, or use the elaborate terminology of the lawyers trained in Paris."[24] He was always mass-oriented.

Al-Bannā records that one of the principles emphasized by the shaykh of the Ḥaṣafī *ṭarīqah* at the time was not to discuss controversial theological and philosophical matters before commoners who were not in a position to appreciate the theological and intellectual articulation of Islam. Theological and mystical discussions were the subject of the "special sessions"[25] which al-Bannā attended regularly. Al-Bannā became the secretary and an active member of the Hasafi Welfare Society, which had the double mission of (1) propagating the ethical and social ideals of Islam as understood by that *ṭarīqah*, and (2) fighting the Christian missionary activities that had become widespread throughout the Egyptian countryside and small cities.[26] Al-Bannā understood the mission of the Welfare Society as a form of struggle to spread the social and egalitarian ideals of Islam, and he tried to mold the early beginnings of the Ikhwan in this fashion, that of a social organization concerned about the social welfare of society.[27] Nevertheless, al-Bannā never restricted his mission to that of a social reformer, or even to that of a revolutionary and radical critic. He, therefore, referred to the Ikhwan in his later writings not as a benevolent organization, nor as a political party, but as "a new spirit making its way into the heart of this nation."[28]

Besides considering Sufism as a method of spiritual training, a way of life, and a world-view, al-Bannā maintained that it was a historical necessity. When Islam expanded from its center in Arabia, and then engulfed the world with its religious zeal and passion, it was natural that some Muslims would amass great wealth and prefer this world to the Hereafter. Al-Bannā goes on to argue that, as a result of the rapid social transformations in early Islam, and the renunciation of the simple pattern of the Prophet's life and that of his companions, "it was but natural that a group of righteous and pious people would emerge to preach against the pleasures of this mortal life. Early mystics emphasized the building of moral character and obedience to God. In fact, mysticism, which I call the science of education and behavior, is the kernel of Islam. Mystics, undoubtedly, have achieved a very distinguished place in this science."[29]

Ḥasan al-Bannā basically remained a committed Sufi even after he founded the Ikhwan. This contrasts sharply with the negative views which a good number of contemporary Ikhwan leaders hold about Sufism. For instance, Samīḥ A. al-Zayn, an influential contemporary pro-Ikhwan thinker, wrote a book for the purpose of unraveling what he called "the evils of Sufism."[30] In that work, al-Zayn contends that

Islam and Sufism are two poles apart, and that, whereas the earlier is the primordial religion (*dīn al-fiṭrah*), the latter is a vehicle of both moral and physical decay.[31]

As a political movement, the Ikhwan discarded al-Bannā's early Sufi ideas and, as a result, they were able to present a tremendous challenge to popular Sufism in modern Egyptian society. Michael Gilsenan, for example, argues that the dynamic asceticism that characterized the Ikhwan found no place in popular Sufism. Al-Bannā's aims, according to Gilsenan, were comprehensive and inner-worldly. His success occurred because his call presented a positive response of a militant traditionalist nature to social and political conditions. Gilsenan is of the opinion that the Sufi orders offered nothing to the modern Muslim save an image of intellectual irrelevance, and superstitious beliefs and practices that degraded Islam.[32]

To conclude, Sufism exerted an undeniable influence on the emotional maturity and mental outlook of al-Bannā, and there is no evidence in his writings or in his life that it ever ceased to influence him. According to the Egyptian scholar Muḥammad Bayyūmī, al-Bannā, who was a pragmatic man, "at an early age, revolted against the Sufi way . . . He refused to organize his movement as a Sufi order; instead, he wanted it to be 'a general movement based on knowledge, education and *jihād*.'"[33] This thesis, however, is untenable in view of the fact that al-Bannā applied all that he acquired from his early Sufi training—in terms of self-discipline, obedience to the leader or shaykh, and fulfillment of the ethical rules and standards of Islam—to the Ikhwan movement. It is indeed difficult to believe that al-Bannā's charisma lost its mystical substance once the Ikhwan was founded. In a sense, I. M. Husaini, a leading Palestinian scholar and sympathizer of Islamic resurgence,[34] is correct to state that "it is apparent that al-Bannā was a Sufi and remained a Sufi. But this was a particular kind of Sufism which aimed at reform through religion, or rather just one of the aspects of Sufism to which he clung, while abandoning all others."[35] In other words, Sufism was the spiritual engine that propelled him to action and, in the final analysis, he saw no contradiction between its ethical and spiritual goals and his own social praxis.

Toward a New Synthesis

The Islamic discourse at the turn of the century was far from monolithic, and it comprised at least four different tendencies as Egypt moved into the 1930's. Those tendencies were (1) the *'ulamā'*, (2) the modernist, (3) the secularized Muslim, and (4) the Muslim Brotherhood. Christina Harris calls the latter a "militant reactionary reform group."[36] She gives the following reasons for such a description:

> Their founders believed that "modernism" had already gone too far in Islamic society; they were convinced that the fundamental beliefs and institutions of Islam were thereby threatened. And because they blamed Western politico-economic intrusion in their world for the Westernization of their society, they became xenophobic and anti-Western. Chief among these associations was the Ikhwān al-Muslimūn, the Muslim Brotherhood, founded in Egypt in 1928. This was a militant reactionary reform group which began life as a religious revivalist movement.[37]

This characterization of the Ikhwan as a militant and xenophobic religious organization fails to come to grips with the reasons behind the emergence of such a movement and the early mystical life of its founder. Al-Bannā, according to a contemporary Ikhwan theorist, was aware of the total dependency of the Muslim world on the West. He understood that "Islam, far from being a philosophical doctrine or cultural trend, was a social movement aiming at social improvement in all aspects of life. In other words, it was necessary [in al-Bannā's view] to formulate an Islamic ideology, i.e. a holistic Islamic theory capable of putting forth a cure for prevailing social conditions."[38]

The nascent Ikhwan movement under the leadership of al-Bannā spoke in its early phase (1928–1939) in terms of the necessity of the propagation and preservation of Islam, and also in anti-imperialist terms. This was perhaps necessary for three reasons. First, al-Bannā needed a sort of popular terminology in order to spread his movement to the masses whom he claimed to represent. Second, he essentially saw his movement as replacing the centers of Islamic power in an Egyptian society that he considered to be incompetent and waning,—namely, Azhar; Sufis, and the lay Muslim groups. Organizationally speaking, al-Bannā thought of transcending these units because he did not consider them to be effective enough in fulfilling their mission. Intellectually speaking, however, he was more indebted to Sufism than to any other current of thought prevalent in Egypt at the time. Finally, al-Bannā was decidedly anti-imperialist, and he considered secularism as being anathema to the true spirit of Islam. It was obvious to him, not only that the Islamic forces had failed to treat the modern malaise of Islam, but that the secular/liberal and Islamic modernist forces had fallen short as well.

Let us now consider the following formulation. While the society treated is not modern Egypt, but modern India, the sort of conclusions derived might shed light on the subject at hand:

> The 19th century [Indian] intelligentsia may have genuinely welcomed the new ideas of reason and rationality, and some may even have shown considerable courage and enterprise in seeking to "modernize" social customs and attitudes. *But the fundamental forces of transformation were absent in colonial society. . . . Liberalism stood on highly fragile foundations. . . . In India, bourgeois opposition to imperialism was always ambiguous* (Emphasis added).[39]

Although one might argue that it is difficult to draw comparisons between the Indian and Egyptian exeriences, certain similarities do come to mind—particularly their shared colonialist backgrounds and the responses of indigenous forces. Ḥasan al-Bannā must have understood that the predicament of Islamic modernism resulted from the inflexible structure of a colonial society which gave modernism no chance to articulate itself fully. Further, the indigenous secularists were too far removed from the religious and cultural concerns of Egyptian society to envision Islamic discourse as a way out of the predicament of colonialism. Amid this failure and fragility of opinion, al-Bannā emerged as a stern and resilient critic of prevailing conditions.

In addition to the propagation and preservation of Islam and the choice of Sufism as a religious way of life, two major factors influenced the life of al-Bannā in the interwar period: (1) abolition of the Ottoman caliphate by Atatürk in 1924, and (2) the progressive secularization of Egyptian education as witnessed in the increased influence of foreigners over Egyptian education in general and Cairo university in particular.[40] This state of affairs alerted the young al-Bannā to the discrepancy in Egyptian life between the vast Islamic tradition that Egypt had inherited over fourteen hundred years and "the fierce attack of Western thought and culture" on the indigenous cultural milieu.[41] Gradually, al-Bannā reached the conclusion that, in fact, an all-encompassing malaise of spiritual, social, and intellectual nature had struck at the roots of modern Muslim culture, and that a thorough complacency had infected the so-called protectors of Islam and its core intelligentsia, the *'ulamā'*.

One particular anecdote, narrated in his *Mudhakarāt*, illustrates the depth of al-Bannā's anxiety, his perception of impending crisis, and the acute sense of mission compelling him to reform the conditions of the *ummah*. One day, he visited a prominent Azharite shaykh to whom he felt close, owing to the shaykh's Sufi inclinations. When al-Bannā complained to Shaykh Dajawī about the deterioration of religion in Egyptian society, the shaykh advised the young al-Bannā to do his best to steer clear of trouble and to take care of himself. The sensitive al-Bannā did not accept the shaykh's advice, and his bitter and intense response to the shaykh illustrates al-Bannā's inner crisis and sense of alienation.

> I disagree with you totally, sir. I think that it [your advice] is a reflection of weakness and laziness [on your part] and an escape from responsibility. What are you afraid of? The government or the Azhar? Your pension has you confined to your [comfortable] home . . . Must you be no different from the rest of this nation, the naive Muslim nation that wastes its precious time in the coffee houses? This nation, which in fact radiates with belief, is a discarded power, a fact that enables the atheists and the immoral to propagate their ideas and publications ceaselessly. This is taking place while you [the *'ulamā'* of the Azhar] show negligence and carelessness. My reverend shaykh, if you fail to act on behalf of God, then at least act for the sake of the salary you receive in the name of Islam. Since, if Islam were to vanish, you, as the *'ulamā'*, would find neither food to eat nor money to spend. Hence, at least do something to protect your own interests, even if you fail to protect the interests of Islam. Act on your own behalf in this world, even if you show no consideration whatsoever toward the Hereafter, or else you will lose both this life and the next.[42]

This anecdote illustrates a theme that has preoccupied the intellectual leadership of the Ikhwan since the founding of the movement—namely, the relationship between the *'ulamā'* establishment and the Ikhwan. Rifa't al-Sa'īd argues that, although Ḥasan al-Bannā was antagonistic to the *'ulamā'* and the interests they represented, he never severed his relationship with them. Moreover, he was careful about developing a relationship, albeit a cautious one, with the official religious establishment, and he never went all the way to condemn the *ūlamā'*.[43] To my mind, this assessment is inaccurate because it obscures the bitter debate which arose shortly after Ḥasan al-Bannā's death among several of his supporters, most notably Shaykh Muḥammad al-Ghazālī and the secular intelligentsia represented by the famous Khālid M. Khālid, about the nature and function of the *'ulamā'*class in Egyptian society.

The debate that sparked the controversy revolved around two issues: (1) the Ikhwan's call for "a return to religion," and (2) the *'ulamā'*"s seizure of the new opportunity created by the Ikhwan's radicalism to promote a state-oriented religion. The liberal attack on the *'ulamā'* as a priestly and parasitical class was spearheaded by the ex-Azharite *'ālim* Khālid M. Khālid. This debate, to be sure, was reminiscent of two previous cases in Egyptian intellectual life represented also by Azharites-turned-liberals, Ṭāha Ḥussain and 'Alī 'Abd al-Rāziq.[44] In his still-relevant, but controversial work, *From Here We start*,[45] Khālid argues bitterly that there is a Muslim priesthood in contemporary Muslim societies which is "pregnant with pernicious doctrines and deadly principles."[46] The sole aim of this class has been to exploit people's spirituality and devotion to religion. It also "commingled its interests with religious doctrine itself, thereby completing the desecration of religion . . . Later on, the priesthood, with consistency and with perseverance, went about envenoming everything with its deadly poison, consecrating economic and social reactionism and preaching eloquently the virtues and excellence of poverty, ignorance, and disease."[47] In Khālid's view, then, the type of truth represented by the priestly class is "a form of mental and religious terrorism."[48]

Khālid continues by criticizing, implicitly at least, the Ikhwan's doctrine of religion/society and religion/state compatibility by advocating the notion of liberating society from the bondage of religion. This is necessary in his view, because any "priestly class"—ancient or modern, *'ulamā'*-oriented or Ikhwan-oriented—serves as the embodiment of social injustice and exploitation of the poor. This class—"the fastest runner after booty, wealth, and pride," promotes superstitions instead of rationalism and poverty instead of wealth.[49] Khālid draws the conclusion that any meddling of religion in the affairs of society is apt to "annihilate the personality of the nation, to drag the whole people down into an abyss of servility and subjection, and to breed an instinct of following."[50] Religion, therefore, is far from being a liberating force in society. Instead, it subjugates humankind to the whims and desires of an egotistical, stagnant, and wealth-driven mentality.

Muḥammad al-Ghazālī also held the view that some of the *'ulamā'* he knew acted just like parasites sucking the blood of the poor.[51] In a scathing critique of Khālid M. Khālid's book, *From Here we Start*, al-

Ghazālī wrote, just a year after the assassination of al-Bannā, that there had, indeed, been a number of influential *ʿulamāʾ* who cared more about their personal welfare than the general happiness of Muslims.

> The men who now lead the defense of Islam are, without exception, bringing shame to themselves and their cause . . . The service of God and Mammon cannot be combined; nor can the duty of jihad be compatible with the pursuit of pleasure and comfort. It requires a really deranged mind to bring these opposites together in any system of human life. Such must be the minds of those Azharites who grow fat while Islam grows thin, and repose in comfort while [Muslims] suffer in anguish. These deceivers have devised devilish means for escaping the genuine duties of Islam. They are more crafty and sly than those *ḥashīsh* smugglers who escape justice and the police. On one hand, we have a group of men satisfied merely with the performance of personal worship. When they are asked to take care of the public, or observe the social duties of Islam, they answer despondently, "politics is not our business." . . . On the other hand, we have a group that fights sectarianism and worship of the dead, yet its members profess to belong to Muḥammad bin ʿAbd al-Wahāb. They silently worship the living and sheepishly submit to the tyrants and despots of their "Wahabi" [Saudia Arabia] land . . . We have seen many leaders of al-Azhar who did not leave their office chairs until their pockets bulged with riches, though they claimed to be the "spiritual continuation" of the legacy of Muḥammad ʿAbduh and Jamāl al-Dīn.[52]

One must keep in mind that these internal Islamic debates contain a large dose of self-criticism that might have affected the intellectual environment in which the early Ikhwan leadership grew. In one sense, what one witnesses here is a severe critique directed by one Muslim group or camp against another. The view held by some that the Ikhwan avoided intellectual and theological disputations with other Muslim groups for the sake of unifying the diverse views in Islam does not hold water. The Ikhwan launched their movement in protest to what they perceived as "the declining state of Islam," and in response to the ineffectiveness of the guardians of Islam in defending and promoting it. The thesis that "the Brethren belong to no one special sect but are devoted to the bare essence of religion" cannot be tested against the historical background of the Ikhwan.[53] Second, Ikhwan thought on many matters, although shaped by the intellectual veracity of al-Bannā, did not end with his death. New developments were a necessary element in the post-al-Bannā stage.

Al-Bannā makes certain that a distinction is drawn between religion per se and the religious establishment. He develops this theme in some of his later lectures. The conclusion he reached was that some Muslim religious authorities of high rank had allied themselves with the colonialists, and that this situation wreaked havoc in the world of Islam. He argued that this alliance with "the exploiters" is just a reflection of "their choice of selfish interests and worldly ambitions over the welfare of the country and the nation."[54]

This is a flaw within the worldly establishment of the *'ulamā'* and not within the faith of Islam. Al-Bannā's severe criticism of the Azhar establishment and the mentality it bred has, from the beginning, been a major feature of the Ikhwan's thought and ideology. This situation created doubts and suspicion in the mind of al-Bannā about the efficacy of the Azhar to offer even the most necessary remedies to the inflicted state of Muslims. This mistrust led to a wide gulf between al-Bannā and the Azhar, and one of its logical consequences was his desire to establish an independent movement capable of meeting the demands of contemporary life. Therefore, from the start, al-Bannā shunned the support of the Azhar and its intelligentsia, and his was a movement that grew parallel to the Azhar in attempting to win the allegiance and support of the masses.[55]

In 1927, al-Bannā moved to the city of Ismā'iliyah on the Suez Canal. The noticeable presence of foreigners there, especially the British, and the ineffectiveness of the different indigenous religious groups, Sufis and non-Sufis, in practicing "genuine Islam" compelled him to first withdraw from the scene altogether, and then practice his religion in seclusion and silence.[56] This attitude of withdrawal from others and shying away from the multiplicity of religious organizations is reminiscent of the earlier Imām Abū Ḥāmid al-Ghazālī's (d. 1111) attitude as described in his autobiography.[57] Just as al-Ghazālī before him, al-Bannā experienced anxiety, confusion, and uncertainty, as well as mental irritation and disease. Under the circumstances, seclusion became a necessity. However, this was no ordinary seclusion. Rather, it was on the order of getting out of the whale in order to maneuver later on. Blind imitation, useless knowledge, and unsound argumentation were the landmark of the religious milieu in Ismā'iliyah. Once more, the anxious al-Bannā asked himself, "What is to be done? Is it time to draw away from the long-desired goal of promoting Islam?" The answer that al-Bannā put forward was to establish the Ikhwan as a movement with radical aims in mind—as a movement of instilling the truth, propagating Islam, establishing a just Islamic society, and disseminating Islamic knowledge throughout society. Al-Bannā describes with considerable emotion the day when six prominent people from Ismaiʿliyya, all of whom were his disciples, pleaded with him to establish that organization.

> Influenced by my speeches and lectures, the six of them sat at my feet, talking with clear determined voices, radiant eyes, and faithful faces saying, "After listening to you, we pondered deeply what you had to say and felt extraordinarily impressed. We know not the road to the salvation of Islam and glory of Muslims. We, however, have grown impatient with the life of degradation and captivity. The indigenous Arabs and Muslims of this country have been deprived of their status and prestige. These foreigners consider them to be their obedient servants. All we possess is the blood that runs in our veins, our spirits that radiate with belief . . . and this little money of which our children have been deprived. We cannot comprehend as much as you do what afflicts this country and the best way to serve the *ummah*. We are ready to offer you whatever we possess so that we feel relieved of our duties toward God. We ask you to guide us in the field of action. We are sure that any group of people that is determined to serve God and sacrifice itself toward reaching that goal, certainly deserves success, however limited it may be.[58]

Al-Bannā's mind, so far, responded to three needs: (1) spiritual and religious conditions, (2) political and economic deprivation, and (3) organizational necessities. Launching the Ikhwan movement in those early years in Ismāʿiliyah proved to be very difficult indeed. The internal malaise of which al-Bannā had spoken all his life did not wane with the foundation of his movement. On thc contrary, he tells us in his autobiography that many rumors surfaced accusing him of being dictatorial in nature, of spending the Ikhwan money freely, and of forming a close clique around him. Some went so far as accusing him of asking his followers to worship him in place of God. These accusations were levelled against al-Bannā by some of his chief disciples, some of whom were prominent *ʿulamā*ʾ and teachers. Al-Bannā was discouraged by what he perceived as the inclination of some to sow dissension (*fitnah*) that nearly wreaked havoc in the ranks of the early Ikhwan. Nevertheless, al-Bannā went about organizing his movement with ceaseless zeal, bringing about radical changes in certain key concepts and practices.

One of the changes al-Bannā hoped to introduce was the status of the mosque, bringing it from a static place of worship to a center of the Islamic revolution, as a place of radical transformation and renewal.[59] The mosque in al-Bannā's mind offers a multiplicity of functions. First, it is a place of worship. "It links the people of this earth with the affairs of heaven."[60] In addition to reflecting human spirituality, worship, in al-Bannā's view, reflects the social, political, and ethical values of the three major systems of government known to man—communism, dictatorship, and democracy. Al-Bannā captures the connection between Islamic prayer and the three systems in the following:

> Islamic prayer . . . is nothing but a daily training in practical and social organization, uniting the features of the Communist regime with those of the dictatorial and democratic regimes. . . . the moment [the believer] enters [the mosque], he realizes that the mosque belongs to God and not to any one of His creatures; he knows himself to be the equal of all those who are there, whoever they may be; here there are no great, no small, no high, no low, no more groups or classes. . . . And when the muezzin calls, "now is the hour of prayer," they form an equal mass, a compact block, behind the imam. . . . That is the principal merit of the dictatorial regime: unity and order in the will under the appearance of equality. The *imām* himself is in any case limited by the teachings and rules of the prayer, and if he stumbles or makes a mistake in his reading or in his actions, all those behind him have the duty to tell him of his error in order to put him back on the right road during the prayer, and the imam himself is bound to accept the advice and, forsaking his error, return to reason and truth. That is what is most appealing in democracy.[61]

In other words, the mosque, far from being an abstract metaphysical locus, is placed by al-Banna squarely within this world and its secular systems.

The second function of the mosque is that it is the abode of the newly found religiosity. Here, the secular domain and space cease to exist. The space of the mosque is protected by the divine and not by the political elite of the country. Al-Bannā attempts to instill in the minds of his followers the notion that sovereignty belongs, finally, to none other than God, and that secular rulers are temporal and helpless in the final analysis.

Third, the mosque is the criterion against which the religiosity of society is judged. It is the symbol of Islamic rule.

Fourth, mosques, in al-Bannā's words, "are the schools of the commoners, the popular universities, and the colleges that lend educational services to the young and old alike."[62] A mosque should have the triple function of (1) being a place of worship for people, (2) a place of education, and (3) and a hospital for the spiritually, mentally, and physically sick. In this, al-Bannā invokes the early experience of the Prophet in Medina when the latter saw the mosque as the concrete embodiment of Islamic belief and as a culmination of many of the ideals that he had preached in Mecca. The mosque as a pedagogical school for the oppressed gains a new significance with the emphasis al-Bannā places on the negative impact which secularization and missionary activities had had on young Egyptian minds. Unlike the Prophet who was laying down the blueprint for a new Islamic society and state, al-Bannā's vision by this stage did not transcend the purely religious and cultural realm. The mosque is a place of cultural buildup and dissemination.

It is easy to notice a qualitative change in the use of language in al-Bannā's *Mudhakarāt*. At the surface, he uses more or less conventional Islamic terminology common to all who share the Muslim cultural space. His use of the mosque as a key term is significant for the meaning which it denotes and for the social and political functions that it can serve. That is to say, the physical space—the mosque itself—is interpolated with the cultural and religious space—namely, the mosque's functions. Thus, al-Bannā emphasizes the mosque as a key term in order to demonstrate its usefulness, and in order to cleanse it of the meanings attached to it by other religious groups, especially the *'ulamā'*. In the words of Terry Eagelton, "The word is the 'ideological phenomenon par excellence,' and consciousness itself is just the internalization of words, a kind of 'inner speech.' To put the point differently, consciousness is less something 'within' us than something around and between us, a network of signifiers which constitute us through and through."[63] The mosque in al-Bannā's understanding denotes a network of signifiers, a whole system of inner-oriented meanings and outer-oriented practices and mores.

In addition, al-Bannā's perception of the mosque as a dynamic domain for the propagation of Islam and the preparation of an active Muslim group must be understood against the social context of the early days of the Ikhwan. At the time—and this is perhaps different today—the Brotherhood attracted the poor and the uneducated, "The first Muslim Brethren were humble Egyptians: the lowliest workers, the poor peasants, impoverished students—the undernourished and the underprivileged of all classes."[64] Therefore, the mosque, as a sacred place, and as a place that gives emotional comfort and security to the poor, was the ideal medium for the preaching and transmission of the Ikhwan's ideas.

By the time al-Bannā moved to Cairo, he had succeeded in establishing the Ikhwan as a legitimate Islamic movement based on a flexible and broad understanding of Islam which promotes social and political causes. His Sufi inclinations never wavered even at this stage, although he was enveloped by the secular environment of Cairo. Al-Bannā urged his followers to practice the method of correct dissemination of ideas. Therefore, in his days in Ismā'iliyah, just before he moved his organization to Cairo in 1932, he stressed certain duties that every member of the Ikhwan should shoulder, such as brotherhood, cordiality, responsibility, sacrifice, attendance, and persistence. On the other hand, al-Bannā defines what he terms the ten evils (*al-mūbiqāt al-'ashr*). They are colonialism; political, personal, and sectarian differences and divisions; interest taking; foreign corporations; emulation of the West; secular laws; atheism and intellectual chaos; desires and lewdness; immorality and weak leadership; and the lack of scientific method in discourse and analysis.[65]

Al-Bannā's understanding of the Qur'ān as an ideological text is far more radical than that of the reform movements of the nineteenth and early twentieth century. It is true that, in both cases, the Qur'ān was understood as an all-encompassing document. However, in al-Bannā's case, the Qur'ān provides the criteria for social reform and political unity. Al-Bannā postulated that the Medina experience would have been impossible had the Qur'ān not provided the basis for political and moral regeneration. In his view, the disintegration of the Islamic state has set in because of five problems which he listed as political and religious differences; self-indulgence and luxury; the transfer of authority to non-Arabs; indifference to applied sciences; and Muslim infatuation with authority.[66]

Al-Bannā's Third-Worldism and the West

To elaborate on al-Bannā's views of the West, let us state at the outset that he draws distinctions among Western colonialism, Western civilization, and Christianity. Although he appears to reject the West totally in his *Mudhakarāt*, one must not suppose that this had been his position throughout his life. For instance, in a pamphlet he co-wrote with two early leaders of the Ikhwan in 1929, al-Bannā, in the words of one commentator, "admonishes the reader to follow the Western examples as far as religious primary education is concerned. According to the authors of the pamphlet, in the West it is nowadays generally recognized that religious education is of the utmost importance for the well-being of a child and for the welfare of society. This Western insight should be a lesson for the Muslims."[67] In terms of the latter aspect, al-Bannā points out that there is a substantial Christian community in Egypt, indigenous to Egyptian soil and not part of the Western conquest. European Christianity, in his view, was used by the secular West to colonize the rest of the world. "Europe retained its Christianity only as an historical heirloom, as one factor among others for educating the simple-minded and naive among the masses, and as a means for conquest, colonization, and the suppression of political aspirations."[68]

In terms of the distinction that he makes between Western civilization and colonialism, al-Bannā rejects the latter, once and for all. In terms of civilization, he is ready to accept the material benefits that the West has brought about, and, in this, he is in line with Nadvi's position previously referred to. According to Husaini, the Ikhwan's rejection of imperialism is based on religious principles.

> Their political program, with its cornerstone of liberation from foreign authority, is in reality a reaction to imperialist rule. If there had been no such rule as this it would be safe to assume that the movement would be devoid of such a political tendency . . . [The Ikhwan] opposed imperialism on a religious basis and not only on a civil one. They hold that Islam cannot tolerate foreign rule or foreign domination, and they saw all of the countries of Islam without exception under this rule.[69]

Al-Bannā contends that the most harmful consequences of exporting Western ideas to the Muslim people, under the guise of missionary activities and colonialism, lie in the field of education. In the realm of education, he argues, Western powers were able to found educational and scientific schools in the heart of Islam

> . . . which cast doubt and heresy into the souls of its sons [Muslims] and taught them how to demean themselves, disparage their religion and their fatherland, divest themselves of their traditions and beliefs, and to regard as sacred anything Western, in the belief that only that which had a European source could serve as a model to be emulated in this life.[70]

What is even more harmful is that education was a tool used by the colonial powers to create an indigenous mercenary intellectual class made up of "the sons of the upper class alone."[71] Consequently, the masses were deprived of basic education in religious and secular sciences. Al-Bannā further argues that *mental colonization*, a theme later picked by the intellectual leaders of the Ikhwan, especially Sayyid Quṭb, was a major consequence,

> This drastic, well-organized campaign had a tremendous success, since it was rendered most attractive to the mind, and would continue to exert a strong intellectual influence on individuals over a long period of time. For this reason, it was more dangerous than the political and military campaigns so far.[72]

Al-Bannā's thought on this matter can be adequately judged against the background of Egypt's cultural life in the 1920s and 1930s while he was reaching adulthood and intellectual maturity.

Al-Bannā realizes that an influential part of the indigenous intelligentsia—a good part of whom was educated at the Azhar—had gone secular and, in the process, tried to undermine both the textual and political bases of Islam. In 1926, Ṭāha Ḥussain published *Fī al-shi'r al-jāhilī* in which he applies critical nontraditional methods to the explication of the Qur'anic text. This was followed by another intellectual blow from the pen of a long-established Azharite *'ālim* 'Alī 'Abd al-Rāziq who, in *al-Islām wa uṣūl al-ḥukm*, argues that the Qur'ān does not stipulate the establishment of a religious government.[73]

Al-Bannā maintains that materialism has been the most pervasive influence on modern Western civilization, and has consequently rendered Western spirituality sterile.[74] Thus, he associates Western civilization with apostasy, licentiousness and adultery, egoism, usury, and moral and political bankruptcy. In terms of the latter, he argues that Western civilization is now bankrupt and is in decline.

> Its foundations are crumbling, and its institutions and guiding principles are falling apart. Its political foundations are being destroyed by dictatorships, and its economic foundations are being swept away by crises. The millions of its wretched unemployed and hungry offer their testimony against it, while its social foundations are being undermined by deviant ideologies and revolutions which are breaking out everywhere. Its people are at a loss as to the proper measures to be taken and are wandering far astray. Their congresses are failures, their treatises are

> broken, and their covenants torn to pieces: their League of Nations is a phantasm, possessing neither spirit nor influence, while their strong men, along with other things, are overthrowing its covenant of peace and security.[75]

What al-Bannā has in mind is the rise of totalitarian movements in the interwar period and the political disunity of Europe at the time. It is the opinion of Husaini that al-Bannā and the early Brethren distinguished between the indigenous Western culture with its scientific, moral, and religious side, and aggressive colonialism abroad.[76]

Al-Bannā seems to understand the rise of Third-World nationalism as a genuine response to colonial penetration. He maintains that "Near Easterners realize the necessity of freeing themselves from the yoke of Western occupation which has curtailed their honor and independence and has imposed upon them heavy sacrifices in money and in blood."[77] *Waṭaniyyah* (patriotism) and *qawmiyyah* (nationalism), in their essence, do not contradict the precepts of Islam. Both require Muslims to spread Islam beyond a particular region.

Al-Bannā's understanding of Islam is innovative. He does not present Islam as a parochial religion or system, but as a universal faith with a strong sense of ideological mission. To his mind, Islam is not just a reform movement but a radical movement of change. The following illustrates his position:

> Our aims include anything that the word Islam stands for. The term *islām* has a very wide meaning and is not adequately defined by that narrow interpretation which is given to it by many people. We believe that Islam comprises and regulates all human affairs and does not shrink from new problems and necessary reforms. It is not restricted to religious and spiritual matters. . . . We understand, however, the word *islām* in a different sense. We understand it in a very wide sense, as regulating all the affairs of this life and the next. This interpretation of Islam is not of our making. This is derived from the study of the Qur'ān and the manner of life (*sīrah*) led by the first Muslims. If the reader desires to understand how it is possible for the Ikhwan to claim that they promote an idea which, it would seem, has a wider meaning than that implied in the term *islām*, let him take his Qur'ān and strip his soul from desire (*hawa*) and purposefulness (*ghāyah*). Then he will understand the actual meaning of the Qur'ān, and he will recognize its identity with the propaganda aims of the Ikhwan.[78]

The flexibility that al-Bannā gave himself and the organization of the Ikhwan in interpreting Islam was justified by direct reference to the Qur'ān, as the foundation of Islam. Al-Bannā was clearly dissatisfied with the current interpretations, and he felt his search for new ones was warranted by the miserable plight of Muslims.

Al-Bannā also opted to transcend what he considered the ethical and reformist attempts of al-Afghānī, ʿAbduh, and Riḍā. The Ikhwan's ideology revolved around three basic interdependent pillars: (1) a determined leadership, (2) believing workers, and (3) a proper program of action as contained in the Qur'ān and the Sunnah.[79] This understanding was basically a response to the mental and cultural fragmentation experienced by Egyptian society at the time, and which al-Bannā witnessed himself. Muslim nations had been assailed by imperialist aggression, internal factionalism, economic and social injustice perpetrated mainly by foreign financial interests, intellectual anarchy, and spiritual poverty.[80] In the words of Husaini, the Ikhwan movement "is distinguished from preceding Islamic movements by four points: (1) all-inclusiveness; (2) a tightly knit organization; (3) popular orientation and appeal; and (4) interaction with local events in Egypt."[81] The Ikhwan's ideology is distinguished by the following characteristics: (1) Islam is an all-encompassing and comprehensive system that treats the affairs of this and the next world; (2) the foundations of Islam are both the Qur'ān and the tradition of the Prophet; and (3) Islam is applicable to every time and place.[82] The Ikhwan movement, therefore, is in continuation with all aspects of Islam, both metaphysical and historical. To al-Bannā, the Ikhwan is (1) a *salafī* movement, because its fountainhead is the Qur'ān and the Sunnah; (2) a Sunni path because it is inclined toward applying the Prophet's way of life; (3) a Sufi truth (*ḥaqīqah ṣūfiyyah*) for its emphasis upon virtue and purity; (4) a political organization for the views it carries; (5) an athletic group; (6) a cultural and scientific body; (7) an economic enterprise, and (8) a social idea.[83]

A contemporary leftist Egyptian historian, Rifaʿat al-Saʿīd, maintains that al-Bannā's attack on and critique of the West are not based on "a clear understanding of the concept of colonialism, and he [al-Bannā] does not offer a specific solution to the problem of colonialism. In al-Bannā's views, colonialism is just a 'European crusade' or Christian colonialism."[84] Al-Bannā's understanding of imperialism might not be as well-developed or sophisticated as that of Lenin or Mao, but he is, nevertheless, obsessed with colonialism as a multidimensional Western ideological and hegemonic presence that has affected all dimensions of Muslim life and thought. In a historical sense, at least, al-Bannā fell under the influence of Afghānī, 'Abduh, and Riḍā, all of whom had something to say about imperialism and its dangers on Muslim societies.

The Muslim Brotherhood: From Discourse to Ideology

The American and European proponents of "the end of ideology" thesis[85] in the 1950s and 1960s were oblivious to the pervasive influence of all sorts of ideologies on the Muslim world, and were, thus, unable to acknowledge the roles of nationalism, Marxism, and religious resurgence. Today, almost every Western thinker with an international reputation prefers to speak of the menace that the ideology of Islamic fundamentalism supposedly poses to Western interests in the Middle East, North Africa, and the rest of the Muslim world. That the "end of ideology" thesis is untenable in our context is clear from the various ideological pronouncements and practical stands of the Ikhwan.

Ḥasan al-Bannā, the ideologue par excellence of the emerging Ikhwan in the 1930s and 1940s, was a charismatic although tragic figure possessed with grandiose notions of reconstruction, revival, dynamism, and change.[86] That he did not conjure his movement out of the void, and that he responded to what he and many other Muslims perceived as an entrenched social and moral malaise in society, are notions taken for granted by almost every one who studies the early history of the movement. Conditions were ripe for such a movement to arise.[87] What Ḥasan al-Bannā did, with his outstandingly tragic personality, was to amass what seemed to be enough power, organization, and following to change conditions for the better. What he did not realize, however, was that conditions had been stagnant for a few hundred years, and one person, however creative and resilient he might be, cannot possibly muster enough energy to change them. Al-Bannā's answer, however, was his profound conviction and deep commitment to the cause.

He felt he was in the presence of some irresistible power, or that he had deep faith in a great nebulous entity, however undefined. He attempted, although unsuccessfully, to translate the deep anxiety underlying the bases of his devout life, and the poignant anxiety of the masses whom he claimed to represent, into certitude, devotion, and meaning. The three dimensions of time—past, present and future—played a significant role in giving direction to the aspired meaning. The present was always shunned for the sake of a glorious past and a hopeful future. Clinging to an ideal past—and using it as a means of reassurance—was his answer to the cruelty and meaninglessness of the present, for the present is the abode of half-hearted existence, and the realm of the annihilated and nonexistent selves. The Ikhwan, as a mass movement, appealed in its early phase to the downtrodden. In every place and time, the downtrodden are "those who crave to be rid of an unwanted self. A mass movement attracts and holds a following, not because it can satisfy the desire for self-advancement, but because it can satisfy the passion for self-renunciation."[88] A charismatic leader always tries to bolster hope in the future by having recourse to a meaningfully glorious past. Al-Bannā was just such a charismatic leader. His stated objectives were indeed bold. He opted to transcend the whole fabric of the status quo by simply eliminating it. The more he realized the impossibility of fulfilling such a task, the more fanatic in his endeavors and the more uncompromising he became. In one sense, at least, he became the victim of his own ambitions—a scapegoat of objective conditions, and a martyr of his movement.

What type of an intellectual was Ḥasan al-Bannā? How did he consider the problem of knowledge, and was his vision utopian? Finally, what social and political interests did he represent? These questions must be answered in the context of his early intellectual formation, and the key concepts that make up his entire thought system.

As a young intellectual, al-Bannā stands before three intellectual giants—Jamāl al-Dīn al-Afghānī, Muḥammad ʿAbduh, and Rashīd Riḍā. He is similar in many ways to Riḍā because he chose a secular path at the beginning of his career. Riḍā chose journalism and al-Bannā education. However, the major difference between al-Bannā and Riḍā is that, whereas the former came from a humble religious and social beckground, the latter came from an established religious class, which is described by Albert Hourani as follows:

> By the eighteenth century, there seems to have been achieved a certain stability in the ideal human type here described: that of the man learned in tradition and law, initiated into a Sufi order within the bounds of the Shariʿā[h], respectful of authority, willing to serve it but keeping his distance from it, giving leadership to the urban population, linked by interest with the preservation of a fabric of ordered and prosperous city life, and having a certain fear and disdain of the forces of the countryside.[89]

This image of an ideal *ʿālim* started to change with the advent of European colonialism to Muslim lands. The pace of the deep political, social, and cultural changes which Muslim societies underwent in this period reflected itself on educated men and women. Again, in the words of Hourani, "We can notice in this period a deep disturbance in the lives of educated men, not only those trained in the new schools but those formed in the traditional ways of thought; not only do their careers take different paths, but the ways in which they see their own lives begin to change."[90] The new forces at play exerted a major influence on the traditional milieu, and in many ways the *'ulamā'* were the first to pave the way for a more progressive way of seeing things. Hourani comments on this situation by saying that, in this case, "there takes place a kind of mutation in the ideal type of the *'ālim*."[91] The deliberate choice of a new path and vocation is, "a sign of a disturbance in himself as well as in his world."[92] It is clear that, especially after the European penetration into Muslim lands, a good number of the high official *'ulamā'* could not afford to close themselves off to the changes taking place around them, and that a certain measure of openness was needed to ameliorate the conditions of Muslim societies. Although Ḥasan al-Bannā was exposed to a perturbing situation, both within himself and around him, he chose, unlike a good number of nineteenth century *'ulamā'*, to close himself off to Western ideas and belief systems. The fact that al-Bannā is not an ecclesiastic intellectual in the Gramscian sense, in that he does not belong to a class of people known for its monopoly over religious knowledge—such as the *'ulamā'*,[93]—does not exclude him from being an organic intellectual, one who performs social functions on behalf of a certain class in society—namely, the emerging religious lower and middle class. As already shown, al-Bannā's background is markedly religious, but this was the religion of the petite bourgeoisie and not that of the landed aristocracy, to which the *'ulamā'* were attached in Egypt in the 1930s and 1940s.

What is an organic intellectual? Gramsci, for instance, maintains that every social class creates within itself, organically, one or more groups of intellectuals who give it homogeneity and consciousness of its function in the economic, social, and political fields.[94] Therefore, every class in society has its own organic intellectuals. The following question is in order: Does the Muslim Brotherhood form a class at this stage? Undoubtedly, besides preaching the Qur'ān and the treasures of paradise, the Ikhwan was fighting for certain social and political interests. Its claim for representing the disadvantaged defines its social interest. In that sense, al-Bannā was both an "organic" and an "innovative traditionalist." In other words, al-Bannā's social position as an ideologue and an intellectual was defined by the social interests which he articulated—those of the poor and emerging middle class. His thoughts did not arise in a vacuum. In the words of Gramsci, "there is no such thing . . . as an autonomous intellectual stratum. All intellectuals are attached to a social class and perform the function of articulating the view of the social world appropriate to their social class."[95]

In its early phase—and as an emerging and aggressive socio-religious movement—the Muslim Brotherhood was in the process of exercising moral, social, and political hegemony over a significant number of the Egyptian masses. However, this was all done under the most adverse of political circumstances. Because hegemony "critically involves ideological domination,"[96] the Ikhwan's engineering of consent was based on a number of factors, including the charisma of the founding leader, an established Islamic world-view, and appropriate social and political conditions. In its drive toward rooting its ideology in the Egyptian soil, the Ikhwan failed to assimilate or "conquer ideologically"[97] two broad social strata: (1) the secularized indigenous classes, and (2) the institutionalized *'ulamā'* class. This failure resulted from the Ikhwan's emerging badly bruised from its political confrontation with the regime. In short, although the Ikhwan succeeded in articulating the social interests and political aspirations of a sizable number of the Egyptian masses, it failed, for all sorts of internal and external reasons, to embody these in a viable political system.

Is the Ikhwan's ideology utopian? Karl Mannheim, for instance, defines utopia as a "state of mind [which] . . . is incongruous with the state of reality within which it occurs. This incongruence is always evident in the fact that such a state of mind in experience, in thought, and in practice is oriented toward objects which do not exist in the actual situation."[98] Every ideology, whether dominant or subdued, has a strong utopian edge. The Ikhwan's ideology, as a reflection in large measure of an embattled state of mind, especially in its early phase, is inevitably utopian. The utopia of the ascendant Ikhwan was the idea of establishing an Islamic state along the classical lines of the *ummah* which was dealt a heavy, if not shattering, blow by imperialism, secularism, and nationalism. The idea was—and still is, at least in part—a real utopia. Hidden in this utopian conception, however, is an ideological position which is critical of the status quo, be it nationalist, secularist, or even semireligious. Underlying this ideological position is also a theoretical method aiming at transcending the present order and establishing a new one. However, as long as the dominant group which controls and manages the existing order is able to protect its interests, the opposing group—such as the Ikhwan—will not be able to transcend its utopian state, because it is dissatisfied with the current state of affairs.

To be sure, there is, in this argument, an implicit assumption pertaining to the notion of freedom as understood by an emerging mass movement. Except in perhaps rudimentary and primitive fashion, al-Bannā does not offer an explicit notion of freedom in his speeches and writings. However, implicit in his critique of the status quo is the notion of freedom—collective freedom that must be derived at the expense of dismantling the existing order. It is a type of freedom that is hampered by the power of the dominant group to keep its hegemony and by the failure of the Ikhwan to affect the texture of this hegemony.

Let us recap our argument in the following manner. So far, we have stressed the discourse of Islamic resurgence as it develops in the life of the leader-founder who, in spite of the availability of various interpretations of Islam throughout history and at present, takes a novel approach. We have also seen how al-Bannā's discourse was shaped, to a large extent, against the Egyptian background of the interwar phase, and how crucial was the phenomenon of the West in creating his thinking. Further, al-Bannā's thinking goes beyond the framework of discourse to encompass the notion of ideology. In other words, it is necessary to elaborate on the possible connection between ideology and discourse in al-Bannā's world-view.[99]

As an ideological formation, this discourse necessarily serves an important social function. It represents the religious, social, and economic interests of one class or social group. Therefore, as a means of comprehending its social function, we can distinguish three major characteristics of al-Bannā's ideological discourse: (1) religion, (2) history, and (3) political organization. Three interrelated orientations control and define the ideological expression in the Third World. They are the relationships with tradition, the Western world, and the masses. At the heart of al-Bannā's worldview is the notion that tradition (*turāth*) must be superior to modern culture, especially because of the impact of the West. Because of such incompatibility, al-Bannā eliminates any form of rapprochement between Islamism and the West.

Conclusions

The intellectual history of a major socio-religious organization, especially when it is bogged down by political and organizational problems and misfortunes, develops against the complex interplay between the ideas of the leadership or leader—in this case, Ḥasan al-Bannā—and the material circumstances surrounding the movement.

That this is clear enough could help to elucidate two principal processes that have shaped the Ikhwan since its development.

First, Ḥasan al-Bannā was busy laying down the intellectual and practical foundations of a socio-religious organization that was struggling to leave an imprint on Egyptian society and politics. This was a lengthy and complex process, and it took place in an atmosphere of rapid change, political disunity, and mental confusion.

Second, because al-Bannā's career ended abruptly as a result of assassination, his ideas were left to others to develop. There is no doubt, however, that al-Bannā left an indelible mark on the Ikhwan as a new movement, but it is doubtful that he solidified its intellectual structure. The Ikhwan takes on a new intellectual shape with the contributions of Sayyid Quṭb, one of the most perceptive, and perhaps tragic personalities of the post-al-Bannā Ikhwan.

Ḥasan al-Bannā, as Richard Mitchell ably shows in his well-researched study, *The Society of the Muslim Brothers*, entered the political fray immediately after moving the headquarters of his movement to Cairo in 1932. From that time until his assassination in 1949, al-Bannā attempted to be a key player in Egyptian political life. His heavy involvement in politics defined, to a large extent, the intellectual and ideological agenda of the Ikhwan. However, it is a mistake to consider his nonpolitical or religious ideas to be peripheral to his whole conceptual scheme. It is true, however, that he was bereft of time to pay sufficient attention to cultural and religious issues.

Ḥasan al-Bannā and the intellectual leadership of the Ikhwan in general did not forsake Islam or Islamic ideas in the reconstruction of their system.[100] That is to say, the Ikhwan tradition is based on a novel understanding and presentation of the wider tradition of Islam. The entrenched concepts, presuppositions, and intellectual standards of al-Bannā's discourse, although derived from Islam in general, carry new meaning that had hitherto been unknown to many Muslims.[101] In his own way, al-Bannā realized the complex situation brought about by the eruption of Western modernity in the Arab and Muslim world, and he showed a novel reaction. He did not express naive curiosity and admiration of Europe, nor did he even try to learn from it. A century earlier—and as seen in the first chapter of this book—the pioneers of the Egyptian *nahḍah*, such as Jabartī and Ṭahṭāwī,[102] admired the progress that Europe had attained and did all they could to transplant progressive European ideas in Egyptian soil. For instance, the nineteenth-century thinker Ṭahṭāwī often comments on the apparent physical and cultural advances of the French over the Egyptians. This observation was the cornerstone of the *nahḍah* problematic: Why are we as Arabs and Muslims not as advanced and as strong as the West? Ṭahṭāwī identified with Western progress and hoped that Egypt would follow the same road. Ṭahṭāwī's fascination with the West brought about a critical re-evaluation of tradition. Nevertheless, he did not abandon Islam entirely. In short, the thinkers of this period, "were not able to overcome the contradiction between their desire to preserve their own individual characteristics and their will to catch up with Europe."[103] The main reform desired was moral and cultural rather than economic and military. European technology was acceptable provided it was stripped of all cultural implications. This compromising attitude, in both theory and practice, is also a characteristic of contemporary Arabic thought. This attempt was totally rejected by al-Bannā. He considered the West to be a physical and intellectual threat to the welfare of Islam and Muslims, and his response centered around two axes: (1) reinterpretation of the complex Islamic culture and tradition in a fresh manner, and (2) resistance to the military, economic, and political encroachment of the West in Muslim lands.

There is no indication whatsoever in the writings or life of al-Bannā that he or the Ikhwan ever deviated from what might be termed "mainstream Islam."[104] However, does that mean that the Ikhwan simply replicated other current ideas on—or interpretations of—Islam? As it has been suggested, the answer is "No." However, the Ikhwan were not simple pundits or imitators. In this, the conclusion that Husaini reaches after he performs an in-depth study of the Ikhwan's principles is simply inadequate. "The [Islamic] tenets are numerous in the writings of al-Bannā and all of the Brethren without exception. Inevitably, this leads to the conclusion that the Brethren are imitators and not innovators; that they add nothing new but revive the old and resurrect the dead, since all of these teachings were taken originally from religion itself."[105]

Al-Bannā and the early Ikhwan never attempted to revive the philosophical tradition of classical Islam, nor did they concern themselves with the scholastic theology of the reform school of Muḥammad ʿAbduh or his disciples. This can be explained by the humble social origins of the early Ikhwan leadership, and by their emphasis upon social and political matters which, in their view, were intractably linked to the essence of the religious quest in Islam. Their movement was primarily religious and social in nature and orientation.

There is an implicit admission on the side of al-Bannā that secularization had been a de facto state of affairs in the Muslim world for many years. Also, there is a strong association among colonialism, cultural Westernization, and missionary activities.

It has taken centuries for the complex Islamic tradition—with its two substrata, the Qur'ān and the Sunnah—to emerge. The heart of this tradition has been defined and redefined by a multitude of Muslim scholars belonging to different social strata and carrying various political convictions. In Islam, a body of religious experts called the "*'ulamā'*" has traditionally played a key role in interpreting, preserving, and transmitting what was seen as the sacred tradition. These above functions had to coalesce with authority. The Sacred Text is the residue of authority, and political authority very often had to depend on this textual authority as a means of legitimation. However, the world of the *'ulamā'* was privy to two incompatible realms of discourse: the elite and the popular. The endless theological debates, commentaries and subcommentaries did not appeal to the masses because the masses simply did not understand them. On the other hand, in order to legitimize their existence, the *'ulamā'* had to channel their ideas to the masses or to popular culture. To a certain extent, only a thin line existed between the popular culture of the people and the elite of the *'ulamā'*.

Part of the *'ulamā'*'s elite culture, especially the Qur'anic one, had to be digested by the masses. Ḥasan al-Bannā went through almost similar channels in order to rally support and legitimation. He realized that the *'ulamā'* had lost their efficacy and mass appeal and that a new popular Islamic movement was needed. He gave the Qur'ān and the Sunnah an enhanced position, he abhorred abstract theological debates and disagreements, and he derived a novel notion of authority and power that was based on the Qur'ān. Al-Bannā realized that "the authority of [his] entire Islamic tradition had been challenged by the triumph of colonial, non-Muslim forces,"[106] and that the *'ulamā'* were not up to the task of meeting this tremendous challenge.

Al-Bannā's formidable challenge to the authority of the *'ulamā'* in society would have been impossible without his appeal to the same popular forces that the *'ulamā'* had, themselves, appealed to for support. Al-Bannā realized that the bulk of the indigenous intelligentsia had become completely secularized, and that to start working on this group to win back their support to Islam would have proved difficult if not impossible at that stage. It was easier to win the support of the masses for the obvious reason that, socially, they were disenchanted with the system and, culturally, they had not been overcome by secularization and other Western ideas. What al-Bannā hoped to achieve at the religious and cultural levels was to create an independent, socially based, and strong religious movement that would wield authority and consequently substitute all forms of decadent Islam and culture for newer, more vigorous, and aggressive interpretations.

Chapter 4

Sayyid Quṭb: The Pre-Ikhwan Phase

I have always sensed that the writings of the freedom-loving fighters do not go in vain, mainly because they [writings] awaken the sleepy, inflame the senses of the half-hearted, and lay the ground for a mass-oriented trend following a specific goal . . . Something must be happening under the influence of writing.
—Sayyid Quṭb, Dirāsāt Islāmiyah *(Cairo 1967) 135*

What is the response of the indigenous Third-World intelligentsia to colonialism and its corollary, cultural alienation? What role does religion—such as—Islam—occupy in this response? How is tradition being reinterpreted and manipulated? Can one draw the line between the Islam of the *'ulamā'* and the Islam of the Ikhwan? Can the *'ulamā'* be a tool in the hands of colonialism? Is there an inherent conflict between Islam and capitalism? What is the meaning of Islam in an age of political and social change and turbulence?

Sayyid Quṭb's ideas between 1933 and 1952 shed enough light on these questions to warrant our treating them as representative of an important and unique phenomenon in modern Arab intellectual history. This phenomenon is not solely preoccupied with politics per se, but with all the manifestations of education and culture under imperialism, and with the pivotal role of religion, interpreted in a certain fashion, in lending credence to the whole process.

For the sake of simplicity, I distinguish between two broad phases of Sayyid Quṭb's intellectual life: the pre-Ikhwan and the post-Ikhwan phases. At the beginning of the first phase—and far from committing himself to the intellectual problems of Islam and Muslims—Quṭb considered Islam and the Arabic language as foreign to the Egyptian mentality. His interest in Islamic matters became more pronounced in the 1940s and brought about a major shift in his thought and commitments. In my view, his Islamic commitment crystallized with his 1949 publication of *Social Justice in Islam*. The shift to the Ikhwan's point of view took place clearly in the late 1940s and early 1950s, especially with the publication of his critical study of Muslim religious hierarchy and capitalism in *The Battle Between Islam and Capitalism*. The purpose of this chapter will be to analyze systematically the pre-Ikhwan thought of Quṭb by highlighting some of its major themes in relation to the larger Egyptian culture and society.

Sayyid Quṭb's Oeuvre

Sayyid Quṭb's intellectual life spanned a period of almost 34 years during which he distinguished himself as a literary, social, and religious critic and writer.[1] It is reasonable to argue that he is one of the few Arab authors who, after his death, still influenced several generations of Islamically committed intellectuals. Quṭb's work can be classified under the following categories: (1) poetry and literature;[2] (2) Qur'anic aesthetics;[3] (3) philosophy of social justice;[4] (4) sociology of religion;[5] (4) Qur'anic exegesis;[6] and (5) Islam and the West.[7]

It is the view of many a scholar that Sayyid Quṭb is the most significant thinker of Islamic resurgence in the modern Arab world.[8] His importance stems from a number of factors. First, after a long involvement with the intellectual environment in Egypt—especially the secular side of that environment during the interwar period—he was able to construct a sophisticated and comprehensive system of thought that presented the Islamic view on a number of substantive issues and problems besetting Arab and Muslim societies. Second, it is possible to discern in his complicated system of thought a significant number of themes and motifs that are still shared by a major portion of the contemporary Muslim intelligentsia. As Emmanuel Sivan points out, Quṭb's influence, although starting in Egypt, went beyond Egypt and the Arab world to the Muslim world. "Quṭb's thought of the 1950s and 1960s left a clear mark on Turkey, a country that is not Arabic-speaking but which has a Sunni majority. In Pakistan his important works have been translated into Urdu, and in Malaysia, a series of classical writings of the Sunni revival (including Quṭb's) has been published recently."[9] Third, in addition to defining certain issues for the Muslim intelligentsia, Sayyid Quṭb's thought constituted the premises of many a radical Muslim group, especially in Egypt in the 1970s. In short, Sayyid Quṭb's theoretical formulations of the philosophical, social, economic, and religious issues and questions besetting Egyptian and Muslim societies lie at the core of much contemporary Islamist thinking and organization. His thought remains unparalleled.

It is true that there is a prodigious amount of information, explanation, and interpretation about the phenomenon of Islamism. Yet, Quṭb occupies a central place in the scholarly output on Islamic fundamentalism. His thought, his activism, and finally his execution by the Nasser regime in 1966 exemplify the life of a Muslim ideologue/activist that many in the Muslim world aspire to imitate. Furthermore, Quṭb's example highlights the cultural, intellectual, social, and economic polarities obtaining in the modern Muslim world.

At least three historical moments intersected to shape the theoretical output of Sayyid Quṭb and to define what I would call the "Quṭbian discourse," which is his intellectual formation spanning a period of at least three decades—namely, (1) the pre- and postrevolution political situation of Egypt, (2) the intellectual environment of Egypt, and (3) the personal experience of Quṭb that ended with his political ordeal and subsequent execution in 1966.[10]

Quṭb's various works—especially his magnificent exegesis of the Qur'ān, *Fī Ẓilāl al-Qur'ān*—are distinguished by the central position that methodology occupies within them. As I will show later, Quṭb's point of departure in his Islamically committed oeuvre is to develop a reflexive theological, historical, and sociological method with which to investigate the main themes and arguments of the Islamic religious phenomenon and its relevance to modern times. In one sense, Quṭb performs what Christian thinking terms *Systematic Theology*.[11] In another, however, he goes beyond systematic theology to ideology, and to change at all levels of thought and culture. Broadly speaking, the underlying presuppositions of Quṭb's Islamic discourse include the following:

First, since the emergence of Islam, the interpretations of religious phenomenon provided by scholars have given rise to different views and premises. This diversity in views has shown the vitality of Islam as a universal religion.

Second, these hermeneutical approaches or discourses have been conditioned by the concepts, mental formations, economic conditions, and political attitudes of their particular historical situation. Therefore, in rendering a judgement on somebody's behavior, one has to pose questions about the historical conditions in which that discourse was produced. In this case, for example, Quṭb tackles the controversial role of the Jews in his Qur'anic exegesis. He comes to the conclusion that they opposed the Islamic message because of two factors: (1) their privileged social and economic position in Arabian society, and (2) their literate culture that put them in a place far above that of the nomadic Arabs.

Third, Quṭb's methods of exegesis, *da'wah*, and thinking allow us to elaborate on the possible connection between ideology and discourse. This relationship, being central in Quṭb's thought and practice, has brought to the fore the problem of authority and legitimacy in the modern Islamic discourse. In short, the Quṭbian methodology is concerned about the real meaning of discourse and utterances. "Words change their meaning from one discourse to another, and conflicting discourses develop even where there is a supposedly common language. Among this . . . it is not the language which determines the meanings of words and phrases in discourse. The real 'exterior' of those meanings has nothing at all to do with linguistic properties. Indeed, meanings are part of the 'ideological sphere' and discourse is one of ideology's specific forms."[12] Quṭb's ideological practice of the 1950s and 1960s ran counter to that of the nascent Egyptian state of Nasser and the Free Officers. The two imaginations—that of the state and that of the Ikhwan as represented by Sayyid Quṭb—did not coalesce. In fact, they were incapable of coexisting under the same ideological sphere.

It should be noted that one must examine the Quṭbian problematic—that is, Quṭb's ideological formulation of Islam and its viability in the modern world—against the background of competing discourses in modern Arab intellectual history, including (1) renaissance or *nahḍah* discourse; (2) political discourse; (3) national discourse; (4) philosophical discourse; and (5) Islamic doctrinal discourse. These discourses, discussed at length in the first chapter, provide the conceptual background to many of Quṭb's Islamic ideas. Here, I will seek to establish two premises: (1) that Quṭb's ideas did not develop in a social or intellectual vacuum, but that they responded to actual situations; and (2) that Quṭb's reliance on the Qur'ān or the Islamic tradition in its totality was not an escape from the present, but an attempt to come to terms with it.

Social life in Egypt in the phase under consideration was the scene of collision and struggle between opinions and parties. Generally speaking, intellectual life at the time was tumultuous and agitated. Quṭb did not belong to the theological environment of the Azhar, nor did he develop, at this early stage in his life, a systematic philosophical doctrine. Far removed from theological and philosophical disputes, he was drawn to the world of literature and literary criticism. Quṭb's inward intellectual maturing culminated with his transition from the world of literature to that of religion. Undoubtedly, Quṭb experienced the sort of bitter inward struggles that are characteristic of those who have a high measure of intellectual and social consciousness.

Sayyid Quṭb's Formative Phase: Emergence of a Literary, Cultural, and Religious Critic

In order to appreciate the early intellectual orientation of Sayyid Quṭb and the reasons that led him to take an active Islamic role in Egyptian intellectual life, it is necessary to consider his early literary preoccupations. Nothing better elucidates Quṭb's anti-Islamic and antitraditionalist attitude as a young critic and man of letters than two articles that he published in 1938 on the psychological underpinnings of the Arabic language. There, Quṭb shows his preference for Egyptianism at the expense of both Islam and the Arabic language.

Influenced by nineteeth-century concepts of progress and evolution—and by the new school of literature represented by ʿAbbās al-ʿAqqād, Ibrāhim al-Māzinī, and Ṭāhā Ḥussain—Quṭb picked up the theme of the quarrel between traditionalists and modernists in modern Arab language and literature.[13] The conclusion he reached was that the traditionalist school of Arabic, with its numerous adherents, had failed to cope with the changes and demands of the modern age, mainly because of its rigid view of language and literary expression. Quṭb argues that "language is a living organism adaptable to the environment of its speakers, and it parallels the progress of ideas and science, and is influenced by politics, economics and society. [Language], just like the characteristics of other living organisms, evolves and grows."[14] At its core, this quarrel was just another reflection of fundamental differences between two temperaments, mentalities, and ways of expression.

Quṭb speaks more like an Egyptian than he does an Arab or a Muslim. He argues that the Arabic language should not only adapt itself to historical changes, but also to the unique temperament, and social and historical needs of the Egyptian nation. "We should not be hesitant to proclaim that this language (Arabic) is not our native tongue, but that of another nation (the Arab nation) that differed from our own in its mores, traditions, thoughts, environment, political, and economic conditions—in the same way that any two nations differ from each other."[15] It is possible to argue on the basis of this premise that, to be true to their Egyptian image, the Egyptian people must rediscover their social roots and identity through a new medium of expression that would supersede the principle of the Arabic language. Egyptianism must find a new expression through flexibility and openness to outside influences.

He continuce to argue that

> Far from being a quarrel over language and literature, as perceived by some, the quarrel (between traditionalists and modernists) is in essence a difference between two mentalities that barely agree in their respective views on language and expression, let alone in their outlook upon life in its totality and particularity. The ancient school is shallow in feeling, primitive in consciousness, and ill-equipped psychologically and experientially, as compared to the expansive world of feeling of the modernist school and its rich psychological ammunition and existential experience.[16]

Although at this stage, Quṭb does not tackle the question of Westernization in Egyptian culture as a whole, he nevertheless opts for a modernist approach in language, mental outlook, and cultural orientation. This modernist approach stands in contradiction to the regressive orientation of Arabic language and literature and, consequently, to the whole of the Arab and Islamic tradition.

Quṭb clearly did not believe in the sacredness of the golden age of Arabic language and literature. Rather, he was more influenced by the Darwinian school of evolution, and viewed language as a continuously evolving organism. Quṭb shunned the idea that classical poetry was the best Arabic poetry. He wrote that, in the view of the traditionalists, "Jāhilī poetry is the best, followed by early Islamic poetry, then the Ummayad's, then the ʿAbassid's. And when we consider today's poetry, it is in their opinion that it is backward and stagnant (*muta'khir wa munḥaṭ*) . . . Therefore, we are forced in their view to pay homage to the past until we lose ourselves."[17] What is interesting in this context is perhaps not Quṭb's views on poetry, nor even literature in general, but the way in which he considers the question of the past and its relevance to any creative young person. Far from seeing the past as an intellectual burden and an unacceptable religious legacy, he dismisses it totally for the sake of the present and contends that the present and the future are pregnant with possibilities that were outside the pale of the past. To be modernist in outlook is to negate the given past. The past does not even exist as a historical objectivity.

Aesthetically speaking, Quṭb—who perceived himself as a poet, critic, and man of letters—conceived of poetry as the highest expression of man's inner feeling and his outside world. Here, he developed the concept of harmony or integration in poetry which, later on, became one of the major concepts applied to his study of the Qur'ān.[18] He prefers the poet to the philosopher mainly because "the poet is [totally] engaged in life; he feels its feeling, is conscious of its consciousness, and he interacts with it. Then he discusses what he feels, or what life wants to discuss about itself."[19] The philosopher, on the other hand, cannot but afford to present elitist feelings and thoughts, because he is an ivory-tower intellectual. The juxtaposition between the poet and the philosopher in Quṭb's early thought reflects two themes that preoccupied Quṭb: intimacy and alienation. The poet is a symbol of intimacy, subjective consciousness, and linguistic permutations, whereas the philosopher is a symbol of alienation, objective and rigid utterings, and linguistic stagnation. In other words, Quṭb considers the poet to be the intellectual par excellence, a person who has a real mission, a social *engagé*, and a man of profuse ideas.[20]

Far from remembering his childhood or reflecting romantically on nature, the poet should be the one to delve deep into his feelings and externally reflect on them as a means of conveying the rich panorama of life. In his expression, "the poet is influenced by time and place and all that surrounds him . . . since his feeling is, to a large extent, born out of these factors."[21] Quṭb argues that young Egyptian poets have expressed in their poetry the gloomy and, according to some, pessimistic conditions of life in Egypt in the interwar period. These poets expressed their authentic selves because "they are an example of Egyptian temperament in recent years—a phase distinguished by transition, uncertainty, and conflict in the political, economic, and social fields."[22] This pessimism, contradiction, and alienation is but a reflection of a living *ummah*. Once again, Quṭb uses the expression "living organism," and here he sees the organic connection between growth in language and life in people.[23] The poet is that superior and distinguished being who can convey the burning feeling of a whole nation. Quṭb does not claim at this stage that the poet is the savior—the poet is the socially engaged.

One can trace Quṭb's formative phase as a poet and thinker, in a general sense, to the immense influence that his traditional peasant milieu had on him, especially when he was a teenager. This influence is best described in detail in his autobiographical sketch, *Ṭifl min al-Qaryah* (*A Child from the Village*), in which he tries to imitate the most famous autobiography of the blind Egyptian man of letters, Ṭāhā

Ḥussain.[24] Here, the literary influence of Ḥussain is most visible as Quṭb mentions that explicitly in his critical essay, *Naqd Mustaqbal.* In *Ṭifl min al-Qaryah*, one can see the influence, not only of literature and poetry on Quṭb's style and method, but also of criticism as a tool of dissecting the present social, religious, and economic conditions, and as a means of offering an alternative of hope to the masses. Quṭb is aware of the significance of criticism in a culture that does not appreciate it. He follows the maxim that he lays down in *Kutub wa Shakhṣiyāt* that the main function of criticism [*wadhīfat al-naqd*] is to destroy before it builds. Destruction [*al-hadm*] leads to necessary explosions, ruptures, and fundamental changes. *Al-hadm* is the only useful means of waking up those fools who are surrounded by ancient stagnation.[25]

In *Ṭifl min al-Qaryah*, Quṭb weaves a comprehensive and illustrative picture of how life in the Egyptian village was in the first twenty years of this century. It is a traditional peasant life distinguished by the dominance of popular culture in which the Sufis play a predominant role. Quṭb discusses the educational differences between the traditional Islamic *madrasah*, prevalent in the village then, and the modern-type school that he enrolled in. He talks about his early formation as a young man lucky enough to have meaningful cultural exchanges, especially with the Cairene students who often visited the village. He discusses his deep passion for the village and his special love for girls. As a young man, he favored the teaching of girls and boys in the same classroom.

Quṭb is especially critical of the practitioners of folk religion in the village. His criticism withstanding, the practices of the shaykh (or the holy man) do not seem to disrupt the harmonious relationship the village has established with its surroundings. Quṭb describes mockingly the practices of the shaykh who "rarely takes a shower"[26] and yet who, after bathing, would have his family distribute the water in which he bathed to the people of the village as a sign of blessing (*barakah*). The spiritual *barakah* of the shaykh also had its material rewards. Many visitors went to the house of the shaykh in search of *barakah* and bearing lavish gifts. Quṭb notes, however, that the shaykh's house was a hospital for the physically sick, and that the shaykh was distinguished by his charisma, popularity, uniqueness and blessing. The interplay between religion and society in such a peasant environment was kept harmonious by the special spiritual gifts of the shaykh.[27]

Quṭb's rejection of the mediating role of the shaykh was transformed later on in his life to a severe critique of the role of the religious establishment in society. I will demonstrate this clearly in my analysis, later in this chapter, of Quṭb's most important work, *Ma'arakat al-Islām wa'l Ra'smāliyah* (*The Battle Between Islam and Capitalism*). Quṭb's rejection of folk religion was, in essence, a triumph for rationality in a culture of superstition, myths, mysterious links with the divine, and uncertainty about the future. He does not leave his description of the atmosphere of exploitation in the village without mentioning the role of the village leader or the *'umdah*, a figure who had knowledge beforehand of 90 percent of the thefts that took place in the village.[28]

Quṭb's condemnation of the village shaykh and the village leader illustrates the wider social concern that Quṭb became committed to as a young man. Later, this concern is translated into a deep sympathy with and commitment to uncover the plight of the poor in Egyptian society. As a result, Quṭb seeks solutions to this overwhelming social problem and finds them in Islam. Emerging from a traditional peasant background, where the social gradations are more or less unpronounced, the social and economic misery of the countryside weighs heavily on him. There is no real indication in *Ṭifl min al-Qaryah* that Quṭb distinguishes himself from the people of the village. He is one of them and their plight is his. Musallam's description of Quṭb's postvillage experience sheds light only on his feelings toward the poor, "The memory of these and other childhood experiences with the underprivileged was to haunt Sayyid Quṭb later in life and make him feel that he was an exploiter of these workers and the millions like them who planted the Nile Valley with gold in return for starvation."[29]

As a young critic, Quṭb moves into another field of criticism that seems at the outset, at least, to be more complicated than that of literary criticism—namely, the criticism of culture and education. Quṭb is challenged at heart by the conclusions of Ṭāhā Ḥussain in *Mustaqbal al-Thaqāfah fi Miṣr*, one of the few landmarks in liberal and Westernized Arab thought.

Mustaqbal al-Thaqāfah fi Miṣr, written in the interwar period, is a theoretical liberal justification for a better and more democratic system of education in Egypt.[30] In it, Ṭāhā Ḥussain argues passionately for complete immersion of the Egyptian mind in Western civilization and its scientific and cultural contributions. "It is our opinion that the criterion for material progress either individually or collectively is based on our borrowing from the material life of Europe."[31] On the whole, Quṭb is impressed with Ḥussain's literary qualities and persuasive arguments concerning the state of education and culture in Egyptian society. At this stage, Quṭb defines himself as an independent intellectual with a distinct method that does not subscribe to parties and denominations. Yet, Quṭb is troubled with Ḥussain's central thesis that the Egyptian mind has always been Westernized because of the geographical proximity of Egypt to Europe. To Ḥussain's mind, the affinity with Europe was always mental—that is, the mental make up of Egyptians is the same as that of Europeans.

Ḥussain further argues that this affinity goes back to the early interaction between the ancient Egyptian and Greek civilizations. Quṭb finds this argument difficult to accept for two main reasons: First, the ancient Greek presence in Egypt took the form of cultural colonialism that was promoted by the rulers, "the pharaohs who were hated by the [common] people."[32] Here, Quṭb alludes to the political situation in Egypt under British influence, stating that "Egypt cannot tolerate an unrestricted colonialism that robs it of its sovereignty and general polity."[33] Therefore, the common denominator presented by Ḥussain—mental affinity—does not hold water for Quṭb. Second, consider the belittling of the role of the Arabic language and Islam as a source of unity. Quṭb argues that Ḥussain does not accept religion as a source of unity, and that, according to Ḥussain, Muslims were more influenced by Greek philosophy than by religion. Quṭb counters by arguing that Greek philosophy influenced only the educated elite in Islam, and that Islam had "influenced the Egyptian nation and given it a unique stamp, and spread over it its pure Arab spirit which is the strongest in the world."[34] Furthermore, Islam, as religion, law and civilization, has restructured the cultural and social bases of Egyptian society. "The Qur'ān has placed the Egyptian mind, like all the other minds that fell under its sway, in a certain context—that of Qur'anic legislation and the Qur'anic worldly system."[35] In sharp contrast to his two essays on the Arabic language, already discussed, Quṭb is alerted to the cultural and intellectual consequences of the liberal project in Egyptian society. He begins to see this project as a challenge to the future of Egyptians as part of Arabism and Islam. Quṭb's thought becomes polarized. On the one hand, he dismisses both Arabic and Islam. On the other, he refuses to accept Ṭāhā Ḥussain's liberal orientation.

Quṭb's claim to objectivity and a free critical investigation of such ideas as Ḥussain's is a sign of confusion in his intellectual life at this stage. Contrary to the attempt of Ḥussain to assert the Westernization of the Egyptian mentality, Quṭb attempts to prove that "the Egyptian mind" is distinctly different and autonomous from the Western one. He also decides that there is a deep polarization in Egyptian society between the European mind adopted by the educated Egyptians and "our doctrines, traditions, and conscience."[36]

Quṭb perceives the conflict to be a civilizational one because of two major facts: (1) the Islamic influence on the Egyptian mind, and (2) Western, especially British, colonialism under whose shadows Western ideas and mores spread into Egyptian society. Ṭāhā Ḥussain does not shy away from calling on Egyptians to adopt European methods of education and even worldview from the advanced European West.

> Our educational system is . . . based on exclusively European methods, which are applied throughout our primary, secondary, and higher schools. If, for the sake of argument we suppose that the mentality of our fathers and grandfathers may have been Eastern and essentially antithetic to the Europeans, we must see that our children are quite different. We have been putting into their heads modes of thought and ideas that are almost completely European. I cannot conceive of anyone seriously advocating abandonment of the European system in our schools in favor of reviving techniques used by our ancestors. As a matter of fact, the Europeans borrowed the methods that prevailed in the Islamic world during the Middle Ages. They did then just what we are doing now. It is essentially a matter of time.[37]

Sayyid Quṭb rejects the call for a total integration with the European educational system and, 13 years later, he links Ḥussain's liberal project to modernize Egyptian education and society with British colonialism and its overt means to subjugate Egypt. Quṭb then levels a major critique to Ḥussain's intellectual and liberal project. In Quṭb's view, Ḥussain had become a pawn in the hands of the colonialists. "They [the British] know the Francophile tendencies of this man [Ḥussain]. They realized when he became the Minister of Education that British culture would be in jeopardy. That is when they remembered that Ṭāhā Ḥussain was a significant man of letters deserving to be invited to Britain. . . . [British] colonialism is wary that its conspiracies in the Ministry of Education would be uncovered and shaken."[38]

In sum, Ḥussain offers a solution to the crisis of education in Egyptian society based entirely on Western methods and concepts and arguing for free elementary education for all classes of society while having in mind a far-reaching goal which is the promotion of democracy and sovereignty of the Egyptian state. These liberal ideas were not shared by Quṭb to the same degree. Quṭb agrees with Ḥussain that the state should unify the heterogeneous educational system under one formula and that it should serve the national purposes of the Egyptian state, not the missionary activities of foreigners in the country. Quṭb goes even so far as to agree with Ḥussain that the state should control and direct the religious education of the Azhar for the achievement of national goals, and that the Azhar should be barred from proliferating the types of ideas that are incompatible with the demands of the modern age.[39] In conclusion, Quṭb is in agreement with Ḥussain over those educational policies that promote the national interest and lessen the educational differences between classes and sects. However, Quṭb differs with Ḥussain over the cultural and religious identity of Egypt. Quṭb takes the issue of colonialism and cultural Westernization much more seriously than does Ḥussain. Therefore, he reaches a totally different conclusion about the future cultural policy of Egypt.

One might say that Quṭb's ideas reflect the deep soul of a man in search of cultural identity and intellectual certainty. On the other hand, Ḥussain's ideas reflect the established literary and professional position of a successful public figure immersed in Western culture and education. More importantly, the difference between Ḥussain and Quṭb is a difference between two cultural orientations, social positions, and conflicting alternatives. As a supposedly autonomous intellectual, Quṭb was, in fact, committed to the ideals and social outlook of the masses and their traditional Islamic education and affinities. In this context it is simple to discern the genesis of Quṭb's Islamic ideas.

Artistic Expression of the Qur'ān

Quṭb's ideas in the 1930s, as already expressed, do not represent a uniform attitude, nor do they represent an absolute commitment to religious, social, and ideological issues. Rather, Quṭb was in the process of fathoming the depth of Egyptian culture, and consequently discovered that polarization, tension, and colonialism were more real than imagined.

In response to this perturbed and perturbing situation, Quṭb reaches a new intellectual synthesis in the late 1930s, and begins to discuss such concepts as balance, integration, and aesthetics. Those ideas are best illustrated in his two works on Qur'anic aesthetics. In general terms, he goes beyond preaching art for art's sake at this stage in his life—in the second half of the decade of the 1940s—and argues for a religious, social, and even ideological use of the Qur'ān as an artistic document.

Quṭb maintains that the Qur'ān creates meaning—or establishes a web of meanings—that can be easily detected if one studies its imagery, representation, music, and syntax.

As a young boy, growing up in a traditional village and listening to the recitation of the Qur'ān, Quṭb was in no position to comprehend its epistemological principles and abstract ideas. What mattered was the artistic imagery that the different verses stirred up in the heart of the little boy. "My young and naive imagination," says Quṭb, "magnified the images expressed by the Qur'ān. Although it was a naive imagery, it stirred me and regaled my sensitivities. I would always treasure these images, especially while in states of rapture and animation."[40]

Quṭb laments the fact that the liveliness, dynamism, and engaging images he remembered so vividly from his village life disappeared in his adulthood because of the demanding nature of existence. "Alas! Its signs of beauty have disappeared, and feelings of sweetness and yearning have drawn thin."[41] Quṭb was caught between these two impressions of the Qur'ān. The first was pure, smooth, uncorrupted, and musical; and the second was devoid of insight, complicated, and fragmented (*Mu'aqqad wa mumazzaq*).

In manhood, Quṭb returned to the Qur'ān with a new feeling. "I have returned to my Qur'ān by reading it, but not in the books of exegesis. And I have rediscovered my beloved and beautiful Qur'ān, and found [again] my sweet and longing images—images without the original naivety [I attached to them]. I have come now to comprehend its purposes and goals."[42]

Quṭb argues that it is true that the charismatic personality of the Prophet of Islam had a major effect on converting the first followers to Islam, but that the Qur'ān was the decisive factor in the process of conversion. Quṭb gives the examples of two leaders of Quraysh, 'Umar Ibn al-Khaṭṭāb and al-Walīd bin al-Mughīrah. The first converted after listening to the recitation of the Qur'ān, while the second persisted in his aversion to Islam. However, in spite of their conflicting orientations and temperaments, both of them fell under the spell or were charmed by the Qur'ān as an aesthetic and moving work. In short, the sweeping spiritual presence of the Qur'ān, coupled with its ontological and existential characteristics, left a marked effect on believers and non-believers alike.

How was the Qur'ān able to captivate a public as poetic as the Arabs—people renowned for their deep sensitivities and breadth of imagination? The only possible answer is that they fell under the influence of the mystery and charm of the Qur'ān. Quṭb argues that there were several reasons for the conversion of people to Islam at the beginning of the Islamic revelation: (1) the Prophetic influence; (2) the patience and sacrifice undertaken by Muslims; (3) the victories of

Muslims; and (4) the justice and tolerance of the *Sharī'āh*, especially after it was applied in the Medinan and post-Medinan phase. These reasons—which are historical, social, and religious—cannot in their totality, according to Quṭb, replace another major reason: the *siḥr* (charm) of the Qur'ān. The root of this mystery takes precedence over metaphysics and predictions about the future. This *siḥr* resides in the realm of the Qur'anic system. It is characterized by an intuitive, imaginative, and magnifying expression.

Quṭb also argues that the history of Qur'anic exegesis has failed to present a comprehensive theory of Qur'anic aesthetics. Exegetes were busy elaborating the linguistic, juristic, legal, historical, and grammatical meanings of the text. Thus, the matter of artistic expression in the Qur'ān was never adequately discussed by early scholars. Quṭb says that only two Muslim exegetes—al-Zamakhsharī and al-Jurjanī—came close to conveying the aesthetic meanings of the Qur'ān. Both discussed the inimitability (*i'jāz*) of the Qur'ān, and they laid the foundations of a general, although unsystematic, theory of Qur'anic aesthetics. Generally speaking, however, the main artistic features of the Qur'ān remained hidden and unexpressed.

What is an artistic representation? Quṭb argues that artistic expression of representation is the preferred method of the Qur'ān. It expresses in a concretely imagined way an abstract mental meaning, a psychological state of mind, a concrete event, a lively scene, or a human representation. Furthermore, the Qur'anic method of representation conveys a concrete sense of life, giving it an almost real personality. In this manner the Qur'ān converts abstract ideas into shapes or movement, transforming psychological states of mind into mental paintings or scenes, and thereby magnifying the abstract and unseen truths of human nature.[43]

On the other hand, Qur'anic representation is multidimensional. It is a representation of color, movement, and rhythm. The interrelatedness of description, dialogue, and rhythm in many Qur'anic verses conveys a panoramic scene, full of life and energy. What are the examples that Quṭb gives to prove his main thesis? He contends that the Qur'ān (1) transforms words into concrete images; (2) magnifies abstract meanings, psychological and emotional states of mind; and (3) portrays, through impressive imagery, different human types and their psychological states of mind.

It is clear that Quṭb does not elaborate on the Qur'ān as a doctrinal, social, and ethical document. He is more concerned with its aesthetic value and the meanings which one might derive from it than he is with any other aspect of the Qur'anic revelation. In my view,

Quṭb's utilization of the Qur'anic text as aesthetics paves the way for a more general and perhaps imaginative use of the text as an ideological document in the 1950s and 1960s. As we shall see in the following two chapters, Quṭb begins to understand the Qur'anic *Weltanschauung* as a belief system which is made up of the three interdependent categories—Metaphysics or/and theological doctrine; community or *ummah*, and legal and social regulations and behavior. Metaphysics addresses the question of God as the Supreme Being, while the latter two principles address the Islamic community in history and society. The relationship between God and man is one of the key concepts in the Qur'ān. This relationship is followed by another significant dimension—namely, the relationship between man and man. At this stage, however, Quṭb does not aim at discussing the Qur'ān in this fashion. His goal is to prove, in an artistic way, the inimitability of the Qur'anic text.

Quṭb does not have much to say about the epistemological foundations of knowledge in Islam, neither does he ponder the relevance of reason and revelation. It is true, as Leonard Binder ably shows, that Quṭb of the 1940s considers

> consciousness and not knowledge upon which truth, or reality, or Being, is to be grounded. In particular, Quṭb is to be associated with those who have argued or intimated that the aesthetic is the appropriate form of discourse on religious, social, and historical matters. An important difference is to be found in the fact that Quṭb is not referring to the role of the artist as an interpreter of the cultural consciousness of a particular era. Quṭb writes rather of the role of revelation which conveys, by means of a divine art, a transcendent religious consciousness—and by transcendent I mean the conveying of a universal truth (Being) in a manner which touches without mediation on the human condition (being, in the lower case). But the teaching of the Qur'ān is not merely meant to affect the emotional attitudes of Muslims toward Islam, it is also meant to convince them that external social experience is to be brought into conformity with the aesthetically defined inner experience of truth. This conclusion is, in effect, the reverse of the usual existential argument that takes historical experience as the measure of human goals.[44]

I have shown so far that Quṭb's goal was not to discuss the Qur'anic theory of knowledge, but to focus on the artistic expression found in Qur'anic verses.

In *Mashāhid al-Qiyāmah fi'l Qur'ān*, Quṭb discusses a particular theme—namely, the artistic portrayal by the Qur'ān of the Day of Resurrection. Quṭb says that this is the second book, after *al-Taṣwīr*, in which he aims at rediscovering the charm of the Qur'ān as it was felt by its first recipients, the Arabs who understood it in a pure and simple fashion. Quṭb declares,

> The far-reaching goal is to represent the Qur'ān; revive its pure and artistic beauty; salvage it from the ruins of interpretation and complexity, and [thus] distinguish it from other goals and purposes mentioned in the Qur'ān, including the religious goal. Thus, my objective here is purely artistic, influenced only by the sense of an autonomous art critic. If the end result [of this work] were the meeting of sacred art with sacred religion, this would not be my intention and it would not influence me. Rather, this would be an implicit characteristic of the Qur'ān.[45]

Quṭb discusses the origins and evolution of the doctrine of the Afterlife as it appears in the writings of ancients Egyptians, Greeks, and Romans. He then moves on to discuss the genesis of this idea in the Eastern traditions, especially in Hinduism and Buddhism. He contends that, although the doctrine of the Day of Judgement was not a major principle of the Old Testament and early Judaism, it played a crucial role in the New Testament and the life of Christianity in general. Christian theology is elaborate in its distinction among the Kingdom of God, eternal life, hell, and heaven. Quṭb was not interested in discussing the similarities or differences between the Islamic perception of the Afterlife and that of the Christian. However, he contends that, although there were many Jews and Christians in the Arabian peninsula before Islam, the whole doctrine of the Afterlife was alien to the pagan Arab. Quṭb wrote that Islam portrayed the Day of Judgement in a dynamic way, and made the Arabs believe in the Afterlife, heaven and hell, absolute justice and mercy. Consequently, Islam revolutionized their terminology, principles of cognition, and practices. While, I agree with Quṭb that the Qur'ān led to far-reaching changes in personal, social, and ideological conditions in seventh-century Arabia, we must also note that *jāhiliyah*, the pre-Islamic period, was characterized by the promotion of all manner of moral virtue, such as *ḥamāsah* (bravery in battle or protection of the weak); *muruwah* (manliness and courage); *karam* (hospitality and generosity), and *ḥilm* (forbearance and moral reasonableness).[46] These virtues, however, were not justified by a metaphysical doctrine. Instead, harsh conditions in the desert made of these virtues a basic necessity for survival.

The Qur'ān, however, was revealed as a divine response to the commercial and nomadic problems of Arabian society and, as a result, it emphasized the role of the Divine in human history. Seen from this angle, the Qur'ān was a metaphysical, as well as a moral revolution, that reinstituted the positive values of pre-Islamic Arabia in a new and dynamic ethical and social code that fit the needs of the newly emerging Muslim community. Furthermore, through its emphasis on a new code of behavior, Islam transformed the limited, pre-Islamic notion of religion to the following meanings: (1) religion as a belief system (epistemological construct), which means that religion has universal and ideal rules and principles which define the theological sophistication and abstraction of a religion; (2) religion as rites and rituals; (3) religion as a nation or *ummah*; and (4) religion as a human translation of universal principles and rules. Hospitality, for example, occupied a central place in this ethical and social translation. Quṭb refers to these themes only in his *Ẓilāl* exegesis.

To conclude, once again in his *Mashāhid*, Quṭb does not discuss the historical or political relevance of the Qur'ān. As it has been suggested earlier, he is not interested, for example, in the Qur'anic understanding of knowledge, cognition, vocabulary, or how they might relate to history as a human endeavor. His sole concern, at this stage, resides in elaborating a significant characteristic of the Qur'ān that had been intentionally or unintentionally neglected by Muslim scholars and jurists. However, in his later work on the Qur'ān—especially in the *Ẓilāl*—Quṭb tackles the epistemological foundations and ideological orientations of the Qur'ān in light of what he sees as the needs and demands of Muslims in the twentieth century.

Social and Religious Themes in Sayyid Quṭb's Works: 1948–1952

Social Justice in Islam should be viewed as a critical commentary on the social, economic, cultural, and educational conditions and policies of the Egyptian state in the interwar period.[47] In this book, Quṭb lays down the theoretical framework of proper conduct in social, legal, and political affairs. Notwithstanding his normative analysis and his idealistic solutions, Quṭb's main goal is to dissect socio-economic and political problems in the light of what he perceives as "genuine Islam." In a sense, he takes it for granted that there is a widespread malaise in Egyptian society, and he offers the "true" Islamic solution to the situation.

Here, Quṭb's categories of thought shift from the realms of literature and poetry to those of society and Islam. This conceptual shift reflects a deep ideological alteration in Quṭb's thought that took place in the late 1940s and left him more committed to the plight of peasants and workers. William Shepard, for instance, is correct in pointing to a radical ideological shift in Quṭb's writings at this stage. His description of this shift, however, seems inappropriate. "Sayyid Quṭb appears to have moved from a Muslim secularist position in the 1930s to a moderate radical Islamism (if I may use such an expression) in the late 1940s and then to an extreme radical Islamism during the last years of his life."[48] Instead of "moderate radical Islamism," I prefer to speak of Quṭb's newly discovered Muslim social commitments to the plight of the poor in society.

In this new role, Quṭb, once again, wears the hat of the engaged critic—the detached quality of his thought, analyzed earlier, disappears totally. Although he does not claim to be part of any social or political movement at this stage in his life, Quṭb appears as an organic intellectual in the Gramscian sense. Quṭb is not an ecclesiastic intellectual because, as will be clearly shown later on in this chapter, he attacks the privileges and power-dynamics of the *'ulamā'* class in Egyptian society. In other words, he opposes their static interpretation of tradition and the power they wield by basing themselves squarely within the fold of the great Islamic tradition.

Can we then say that Quṭb, who is not a member of any party or religious organization, defends the interests of a particular social class in Egyptian society? Does Quṭb also talk on behalf of the urban intelligentsia or the masses of peasants in Egypt? We know from his autobiography, *Ṭifl min al-Qaryah*, that Quṭb grew up in a peasant-oriented community, and that the traditional peasant culture, with its superstitions, myths, and folk traditions, never left him completely, not even after he had received a secular education in Dār al-'Ulūm in Cairo. Gramsci, for instance, maintains that every social class creates within itself, organically, one or more groups of intellectuals who give it homogeneity and consciousness of its function in the economic, social, and political fields.[49] Therefore, every class in society has its own organic intellectuals. But Gramsci hastens to add that,

> the mass of the peasants, although they carry out an essential function in the world of production, do not elaborate their own "organic" intellectuals, and do not "assimilate" any class of traditional intellectuals, although other social groups take many of

> their intellectuals from the peasant masses, and a great many of the traditional intellectuals are of peasant origin.[50]

Therefore, Gramsci's contention is that, although the peasantry is able to generate intellectuals, these intellectuals end up providing mental services to other classes in society. In my view, Gramsci's theoretical insight, however original it might be, does not apply to the intellectual formation of Sayyid Quṭb. This is because Quṭb had already identified himself with the social and religious concerns of the peasantry in Egyptian society. Quṭb's intellectual characteristics developed against his peasant background, and his personal and moral identification with the peasant community was unshakable. In that sense, he could be considered as an organic intellectual who expresses the concerns of the peasants and who, in the late 1940s, begins to articulate the concerns of the working class people in Egyptian society.

Undoubtedly, Quṭb offers a theoretical program of Islamization based on his identification with and understanding of the Great Islamic Tradition.[51] Quṭb contends, implicitly at least, that traditional social organization in Egypt—unlike in the West, for instance—occurs in a society in which religious consensus continues to exist among the great majority of the people. From the standpoint of his ontological orientation, Quṭb, with his complex personality and his literary and social background, constantly tries to bridge the gap between the normative and the real, or between the greater and the lesser tradition. His mission is that of expressing the meaning and symbolism of Islam at the social level. Quṭb's Islam never views itself apart from the world or outside of the sphere of history. As an Idea, in the Hegelian understanding, Quṭb's Islam is a self-conscious and willing religion.[52] It is a continuous tradition which is full of theological and social directives about the meaning and end of man's life. The preceding idea is indicative of the deep shift in Quṭb's thought—thought that began by glorifying the present and was later transformed to thought which glorifies the past by seeking to establish an organic link with it.

It is a historical given that the underlying components of the peasants' culture, as with any other human culture, are subject to continuous historical and social change. Quṭb's strong sense of engagement created his later religious *Weltanschauung*. One method that might help us adequately understand the depth of Quṭb's cultural experience is to consider his yearning to fulfill the call of history and society. In many ways, one can conclude that Quṭb's inner and personal transformation ran parallel to the social and economic transformation of Egyptian society itself.

What is Islamic social justice, and what social and political conditions are required to warrant the application of this notion?[53] Quṭb's arguments, although grounded in idealistic solutions as previously noted, reflect the thoughts of a complex man in transition, as well as a complex situation in flux.[54] Furthermore, Quṭb's arguments laid the foundations for many theoretical arguments in Ikhwan circles in the 1960s and 1970s. No doubt, Quṭb's *Social Justice* is a major work that significantly influenced a generation of Arab and Muslim intelligentsia in the post-World-War-II period.

Committing himself to issues of social and economic justice, Quṭb speaks like a traditionalist and asserts that the criteria of modern thought and behavior should be derived from the past. He asserts that, as a guiding principle and salvation from the current malaise of society and religion, it is necessary to move back to the stored-up Islamic and Arabic tradition of the Egyptian people, and not to the European tradition. In a sense, he invokes the past, which he had totally neglected a few years earlier, as a key concept in analyzing the present and its problems. At this stage, Quṭb does not argue that the solution lies in the past, but rather that a fresh look at the past is inevitable in dissecting the complex issues at hand. In other words, Quṭb takes it upon himself to delve into a complex reconstruction of the past as a means of deconstructing the present and rendering it meaningful. Quṭb leaves no doubt about his new sense of the Islamic past. "Here in Egypt and in the Muslim world as a whole, we pay little heed to our native spiritual resources and our intellectual heritage; instead we think first of importing foreign principles and methods, or borrowing customs and laws from across the deserts and from beyond the seas."[55] Quṭb argues against the wholesale Westernization of Egyptian society and against the symbols of this Westernization—namely, the Westernized intelligentsia, missionary schools, and the British influence that was synonymous with Western colonialism. It is no surprise, therefore, that Quṭb turns to a more thorough and serious analysis of the whole notion of cultural colonialism at the end of *Social Justice*.

Turning to "our spiritual and intellectual tradition," in Quṭb's words, is not a matter of personal or religious pride, as some could argue. It is rather a question of historical continuity with the past heritage and, better still, the integration of the present with the past. Here Quṭb stands against any epistemological rupture with, or spiritual alienation from, the past. The past witnessed the harmony of faith and practice. At this moment, however, "we profess Islam as a state religion; we claim in all sincerity to be true Muslims—if indeed we do not claim to be the guardians and missionaries of Islam. Yet we have divorced our faith from our practical life, condemning it to remain in ideal isolation, with no jurisdiction over life, no connection with its affairs, and no remedy for its problems."[56] Religion is not mere faith and salvation. It should be understood as *this-world*-oriented, and it is to be sought in works. Thus, the believer must translate faith into meaningful social action. This "divorce between faith and life" is unjustifiable in the view of Islam. However, it is a concrete condition, and the *'ulamā'* in Egypt do not seem to mind this state of affairs. In this regard, Quṭb refers, in order to prove his point, to the social milieu in which Islam emerged.

> Islam grew up in an independent country owing allegiance to no empire and to no king. It grew up in a nomadic society that was not subjected to the type of conditions and laws prevalent in the Roman Empire (when Christianity became the official religion of the state). This was the most fit condition for the religion (of Islam) in its initial growth, so that it could establish its true social system without any hindrances, while building its laws and organizational pillars, and taking care of its conscience, spirit, behavior and action.[57]

The past independence of Islam as a socio-religious and political system stands in sharp contrast to its present manifestations. In other words, the current secular state's monopoly on religion must be dismantled. For Islam to regain its vigor, it has to be emancipated. However, emancipated from what? One should notice here that Quṭb labors under the context of a nation/state that partially, at least, suffers from colonization by the British. Under those circumstances, the emancipation of the state is synonymous with the emancipation of the individual.

In comparison with the autonomous beginnings of Islam, Christianity, as another world religion "grew up in the shadow of the Roman Empire, in a period when Judaism was suffering an eclipse, when it had become a system of rigid and lifeless ritual, an empty and unspiritual sham. The Roman Empire had its famous laws, which survive as the origin of modern European legislation; the Roman public had its own customs and social institutions. Christianity had no need then—nor, indeed, had it the power—to put before a powerful Roman government and a united Roman public rules and regulations for government or for society."[58] Quṭb applies critical reason to the origins of Christianity for the purpose of showing its inferiority vis-à-vis the origins of Islam, or even Islam itself. However, his argument is far more extensive than a comparative consideration of the historical origins of two universal traditions. Quṭb is obsessed with the present make-up of Islam and the reasons for its historical retardation and decline. Can we find the answer, at least partially, in the present state of western Christianity?

Notwithstanding the historical differences between Islam and Christianity, to Quṭb's mind, they possess a common Hegelian bond—they take seriously the personal relationship between man and God. Likewise, the behavior of clergy in Christianity is not different from that of those in Islam. He asserts that, "[T]he churchmen, the priests, the cardinals, and the popes were unable thus to guarantee their own prosperity or to preserve their influence, so long as the church remained isolated from the economic, social, and administrative life."[59] In the post-Renaissance phase of European history, a major battle raged between the doctrines of the church and scientific ideas of the new secular intelligentsia. Quṭb implicitly argues that, although Islam is against this type of division between the affairs of Heaven and those of this world, the tension between the secular intelligentsia of the Muslim world and the *'ulamā'* has nevertheless been a historical reality. He, therefore, reminds the reader that Islam is a unity, and that there is no division between faith and deed. "Islam does not prescribe worship as the only basis of its beliefs, but rather it reckons all the activities of life as comprehending worship themselves—so long as they are within the bounds of conscience, goodness, and honesty."[60] Yet, why does he need to remind us of this unity, integration, and oneness in Islam? It seems to me that this attitude is a response to and a direct criticism and rejection of a social rupture, a religious malaise, and a power differential.

Quṭb holds the opinion that Islam does not prescribe any priesthood or intermediary between God and man, and that every Muslim can and, as a matter of fact, must approach God without any mediation. In theory, no religious hierarchy exists in Islam. Therefore, a Muslim ruler or administrator should derive his political authority and legitimacy from the masses and the religious law (*Sharī'āh*) that is there to represent their interests. Consequently, in Quṭb's view, there should not be any "churchmen who can have the right to oppress; nor [should] the administrator [have] any power other than that of transmitting the law, which derives its authority from the faith."[61]

What about the religious reality of Egypt in Quṭb's time and even today? Quṭb's theoretical assumptions run counter to an actual situation that centers around a religious hierarchy, saturated with political and economic oppression and injustice, and caught in the web of power dynamics that have robbed the poor of their social prestige and economic growth. Islamic history has known such *'ulamā'* who exploited religion for their worldly benefits. "As for churchmen [i.e. *'ulamā'*] associating themselves with the power of the state or with the power of wealth, and thus keeping the workers and lower classes drugged by means of religion, there is no doubt that this did happen in some periods of Islamic history. But the true spirit of faith disavows such persons."[62] A different type of *'ulamā'*, who were committed to promoting the welfare of the masses and elevating the truth of Islam, also existed. They "encouraged the underprivileged to demand their rights, giving them leadership; and they attacked the oppression of governors, they attacked the denial of privileges, and they fought the persecutions."[63] Quṭb invokes the bright side of Islamic history and indicates that history is borne out by the committed religious intelligentsia who are faithful to the true image of Islam.

Quṭb's thought, at this stage, is subject to creative change. A fusion of the subjective/psychic with the objective/social conditions is at work. It is a moment of intensity that reflects the author's inner perplexity and the bitter social milieu in which he labors. This sort of hardening social experience is often the mother of creative thinking.

After a historical treatment of the origins of Islam and the role of the clergy in both Muslim and Christian history, Quṭb turns to a more precise definition of social justice in modern Muslim society. He contends that the Islamic notion of social justice is all embracing. It takes account of the material as well as the spiritual dimensions of man's well-being. Quṭb enumerates the following principles as the foundations of the Islamic theory of social justice: (1) absolute freedom of conscience; (2) complete equality of all men; and (3) the permanent mutual responsibility of society.[64] The individual is the supreme example of social justice. The individual, according to Quṭb, has to place his trust in Divine and not human authority. To him, divine authority is indivisible. Therefore, man has nothing to fear in this life. He should not allow anxiety to run his life, neither should he be scared of transient matters in life. Yet, in spite of all this encouragement, Quṭb draws our attention to an important aspect in man's life—namely, the material need for food and shelter. He contends that "the empty belly cannot appreciate high-sounding phrases. Or else he is compelled to ask for charity, and all his self-esteem leaves him lost, forever."[65] Therefore, the main conclusion Quṭb reaches is that social justice cannot prevail in a society if the material foundations of that society are not sound, and if there is a minority of people exploiting the majority. One way, then, of ensuring the material well-being of the members of society is through mutual responsibility. The individual who is supposed to be free has to care for the community at large. However, the community, from its side, is responsible for feeding the poor and destitute members. That is why Islam has instituted *zakāt* as an individual as well as a collective social responsibility in the face of poverty.

Quṭb does not divorce social conditions from political theory and practice. He sees society as a comprehensive whole, and an indissoluble unity. Therefore, he argues, Islamic political theory rests on the basis of justice on the part of the rulers, and obedience on the part of the ruled. Even so, if the first condition is nonexistent, the second cannot be met. The ruler has no divine or spiritual authority. Rather, the only authority he possesses is legal and political. The ruler must "derive his authority from his continual enforcement of the law. When the Muslim community is no longer satisfied with him, his office must lapse; and even if they are satisfied with him, any dereliction of the law on his part means that he no longer has the right to obedience."[66] In addition, "a ruler therefore has no extra privileges as regards the law, or as regards wealth; and his family have no such privileges either, beyond those of the generality of Muslims."[67] The well-being of the individual and community are at the heart of Islamic social justice, and the current alliance between state and religion is a betrayal of this condition.

Although Islam, according to Quṭb, respects the individual's property, "justice is not always concerned to serve the interests of the individual."[68] The individual is, in a way, a steward of his property on behalf of society. Therefore, "property in the widest sense is a right which can belong only to society, which in turn receives it as a trust from Allah who is the only true owner of anything."[69]

Thus, although the individual has the right to possess property, the community's interest is supreme. Quṭb argues that the concept of communal property is a distinguishing mark of Islam. He says that communal wealth "cannot be restricted to individuals, a wealth of which the Messenger enumerated three aspects, water, herbage, and fire."[70] One honest way of gaining money is through work. Therefore, Islam, according to Quṭb, is against monopoly, usury, corruption, wastefulness, and dishonest commercial practices. Above all, Islam stands against luxury-loving people, because "the Qur'ān characterizes luxury-loving people sometimes as those whose ambition fails, whose strength disappears, and whose liberality vanishes."[71] Luxury is not only an individual evil, but a social one as well. "The community will be held responsible for this evil which existed in its midst; for luxury must inevitably lead to evil by reason of its very existence in the community . . . Here in Egypt we have excessive wealth, which is a resource. We have also an excessive physical vitality, which is again a resource. We have an excess of spare time, not filled by work or thought, and this too is a resource. Accordingly, young men and women who love luxury, who have youth and leisure and wealth inevitably go astray and seek extra outlets for their excess of resources in body, wealth and time."[72]

Therefore, prevailing social and economic conditions in Egyptian society betray real Islamic principles. It is a story of exploitation, dehumanization, and alienation; it is the story of the Egyptian working class.

> For when the American working man, for example, has his radio set and his private automobile, when he may, if he is able, make a weekly excursion with his family, or visit a cinema; when these things are so, it is not luxury that the White House should be the home of the President. But when millions of a nation cannot find a mouthful of pure water to drink, it is undeniably luxury that some few people should be able to drink Vichy and Evian, imported from overseas. And when there are millions who cannot afford the simplest dwelling, who in the twentieth century have to take tin cans and reed huts as their houses; when there are those who cannot even find rags to cover their bodies, it is an impossible luxury that a mosque should cost a hundred thousand guineas, or that the Ka'bah should be covered with a ceremonial robe, embroidered with gold. And it makes no difference that it is the Ka'bah, or that it is a mosque. For it is the public who have to provide the money which is spent in this way.[73]

In his search for a historical foundation of what he calls "the true spirit of Islam," Quṭb finds that Abū Dharr was the true embodiment of this spirit. He says that "Abū Dharr's protest was one of the reactions of the true spirit of Islam, but it was unpopular with those whose hearts had been corrupted; in the same way such protests are still resented by the modern equivalents of these, the present-day exponents of exploitation."[74] According to Quṭb, Abū Dharr stood against the system of preferential treatment instituted by the third caliph, 'Uthmān, and he was for a complete system of justice similar to the one instituted by 'Alī. When Mu'āwiyah came to power, he used public money for bribes and gifts, and buying the allegiance of others. Very few rulers distinguished between their private funds and public money. In short, social and political corruption is an old story. Quṭb traces it all the way down to the early Islamic state, and the deviation from the Islamic ideal begins early on. Quṭb, in a sense, considers present history to be the culmination of all that complexity beginning with early Islam. Present Muslim history is unfaithful to its origins. The pious have always been the steadfast few, from Abū Dharr in the first century of Islam to Quṭb in the present century. Is most Muslim history, then, just a story of deviation from and betrayal of the ideal?[75] What about the creative tension throughout Islamic history?[76]

Quṭb's utopian vision is sharpened by the plight of the poor—a plight that cannot be justified in the eyes of Islam. He therefore envisions a number of solutions to this situation: (1) The poor and average people should have access to public funds; (2) Islam is opposed to excessive wealth and private manipulation of that wealth; (3) Taxes should be paid on the basis of income—the higher a person's income, the higher the tax; and (4) Families should be supported according to need, social security, universal liability to pay *zakāt*, and mutual responsibility.[77]

When discussing the present state and the prospects of Islam, Quṭb concludes that Islam is at a crossroads. He argues that "It is not sufficient that Islam should have been a living force in the past; it is not enough that it produced a sound and well-constructed society in the time of the Prophet and in the age of the caliphate. Since that distant time there have been immense changes in life, mental, economic, political, and social; there have been material changes in the earth, and in the powers relative to man. All these things must be carefully considered before an answer can be given to our question."[78]

Quṭb comments on the general decline in Islam by saying that there has been a partial halt of the spirit of Islam since the first centuries of Islam—politics overshadowed the religious aspects of society. It is true that there have been social revolutions against exploitation and arbitrary power, but they were never successful. Quṭb hails the renaissance of the Islamic spirit in the form of the Muslim brothers who fought the war in Palestine in 1948. "The recent war against the Jewish settlers in Palestine has revealed the penetration of the Islamic spirit."[79]

Quṭb discusses the long-standing antagonism between what he calls the spirit of Islam and Western colonialism. He says that:

> European imperial interests can never forget that the spirit of Islam is firmly opposed to the spread of imperialism . . . Islam is at once a spiritual power and an incentive to material power; it is

> at once a form of opposition in itself, and an incentive to a still more forcible opposition. Therefore European imperialism cannot but be hostile to such a religion. The only difference lies in the fact that the form of that hostility varies according to the imperialistic methods of each nation, and according to local conditions.[80]

Quṭb expresses his opposition to the liberal intelligentsia and its educational association with Europe by discussing the cultural imperialism of the West. England, he says, took a more devious road in colonizing the Egyptian mind through educational means. The aim of England was "to encourage the growth of a general frame of mind which would despise the bases of Islamic life, and even of Eastern life; when this was accomplished there would be a generation educated in this frame of mind, ready to go into the schools and educational offices to imbue the coming generations with the same ideas."[81] Quṭb follows a pragmatic line of analysis when he says that we cannot neglect the contributions of the West, nor can we follow an isolationist path of development, because our interests are interwoven with the West which is "at the present moment stronger than we; we do not have today the control over it, or the strength equal to its strength, that we had in the first age of Islam."[82]

To Quṭb Islam and the West are two incompatible civilizational entities. The historical intervention of colonialism has damaged the religious and mental well being of many a Muslim. Therefore, Muslims must be persistent in liberating themselves from the emotional, spiritual, and intellectual clutches and residues of colonialism. Quṭb offers a general solution to the problem of colonialism that prescribes an alternative state of mind based on a new cultural and educational system. He maintains that, "No renaissance of Islamic life can be effected purely by law or statute, or by the establishment of a social system on the basis of Islamic philosophy."[83] Therefore the only way is "the production of a state of mind imbued with the Islamic theory of life."[84]

Therefore, the key to renaissance lies in education—the creation of an authentic and indigenous philosophy of education that meets the need of the Egyptians. Although Quṭb here shares a similar premise to Ḥussain's—namely, that education is a guarantee against backwardness and mental deterioration—he differs sharply from Ḥussain in many aspects. Faithful to his premise that the epistemological and cultural foundations of colonialism in Egyptian and Muslim societies must be deconstructed, Quṭb advocates a more aggressive role for indigenous and national culture. That is when isolation from the achievements of mankind is warded off, and that is why Quṭb emphasizes that "isolation from human life, then, is not our aim."[85] Borrowing from Western or exogenous sources is therefore inimical to the spirit of national and indigenous independence. Quṭb asserts emphatically that "when we borrow Western methods of education, systems of training and curricula, we borrow also a general scheme of philosophy and a mode of thought which underlies these methods and systems and curricula, whether we like it or not."[86] Quṭb does not oppose the teaching of Western philosophy in Muslim schools, but this should come only after the inculcation of the Islamic spirit of education in the youth.

Quṭb says that Islamic social justice is justified by religious standards and necessitated by human conditions. That is to say that Islamic metaphysics should be the source of social and economic justice. "We cannot comprehend the nature of social justice in Islam until we have first studied the general lines of the Islamic concept of Divinity, the universe, life and humanity. For social justice is only a branch of that great principle on which all Islamic teachings are based."[87] Because the main teachings of Islam are derived from the basic concept of *tawḥīd*, "a knowledge of this universal Islamic concept will enable the student to understand the principles and laws of Islam and to relate the particulars to the fundamental rules. This will also help him study its features and directions with interest and with depth of perception."[88] Quṭb attempts only partially here to reconstruct what he considers as the Islamic concept (*al-taṣawwur al-islāmī*), and, thus, he prepares the ground for a thorough examination of the Islamic foundations of metaphysics, knowledge, and human action, a job that he carries out in the late 1950s.

Quṭb sees the principle of harmony operating in all spheres of life, between the Creator and created, God and man.[89] Therefore, he says that

> the fundamental thing is this cooperation, mutual understanding, acquaintance, and harmony along the lines set by the Divine law, and whoever deviates from this principle must be brought back to it. For the Divine law is worthier to be followed than the desires of individuals and societies. Such mutual responsibility among all is in keeping with the purpose of the unified universe and the aims of its Creator.[90]

The principle of harmony in Islam stands against any kind of polarization, be it physical, material, spiritual, doctrinal, or practical. "Islam came to unify all powers and abilities, to fuse together spiritual aspirations and bodily desires, to harmonize their directions, and thus create a comprehensive unity in the universe, life, and man."[91]

In Quṭb's view, Islamic social justice is more comprehensive than economic justice. The Islamic view has two considerations. First, man is looked upon as one unity, both spiritual and physical, and the body is not shunned on behalf of the spirit. Second, social life should be based on mutual love and respect. There is, in society, the absolute and just, coherent unity and mutual responsibility (*takāful ijtimāʿī*).

The Islamic theory does not recognize social stratification, and it stands against the cult of personality in matters of its political philosophy. "According to the Islamic theory, just as the encroachment upon society by the cupidity and ambition of the individual is a kind of social oppression which is inconsistent with justice, similarly the encroachment upon the nature and ability of the individual by society is also a kind of injustice. It is an injustice, not to the individual alone, but to the society also."[92]

To conclude, *Social Justice* contains the theoretical principles and foundations of Quṭb's pre-Ikhwan Islamic thought.[93] This work is a radical departure from Quṭb's early work in literary, Qur'anic, and social criticism. Quṭb emerges as a social critic with a radical Islamic agenda. He takes an inward look at what he considers to be the indigenous sources of Egyptian culture and thought—namely, Islam—and maps out the terrain of contemporary Egyptian society.

Although grounded in idealistic solutions, Quṭb's line of analysis dispels the notion of social and human harmony in Egyptian society. It is a society torn between feudalists and exploiters, including the professional men of religion on the one hand, and foreign imperialists on the other. A radical criticism of this state of affairs, therefore, necessitates criticism of two parallel, but equally hegemonic mentalities and forces, one indigenous and the other foreign.

In Debate with the Enemies of Islam: Indigenous and Foreign

Sayyid Quṭb's criticism of social conditions in Egyptian society as outlined here portrays the agonies of a committed social critic in search of his Islamic roots. Quṭb realizes that the ideal is far from being realized, and that a concerted effort is needed to salvage the social sanity of Arab and Muslim societies. Therefore, Quṭb points out, in a general way, the enemies who are, in his view, the real hurdle to achieving social justice for the poor masses. These enemies are classified as both indigenous and foreign. The indigenous include capitalists, journalists, dark-skinned Britishers—or Egyptians with white mentalities—politicians, and a good number of *ʿulamāʾ* who sold out their religious allegiance for wretched worldly interests. The foreign enemies include imperialists, capitalists, crusaders, and missionaries, and they are tireless in their efforts to preserve social conditions in the country.

In this phase—the most critical one in pre–1952 Egypt—Quṭb uses sociological categories to express his concerns and criticisms. His *Maʿarakat al-Islām wa'l Raʾsmāliyah* (*The Battle Between Islam and Capitalism*) is a condemnation of the prevailing social conditions, and is a diagnosis of the plight of modern Muslims who are, in Quṭb's view, victimized by a ruthless alliance of traditionalist *ʿulamāʾ* and heartless capitalists. He is more expressive in this work about the social situation than in *Social Justice*. "The deterioration in social conditions from which the masses of Egypt suffer cannot continue indefinitely . . . This is a fact that should be known by all."[94] Corruption, laziness, exploitation, and wastefulness form the backbone of this condition.

Quṭb's notion of civil society stands in direct opposition to the political, social religious, and ideological forces that control the Egyptian state and society.[95] His point of departure is the welfare of the masses (*al-jamāhīr*) and their integration into a society that protects their political and religious rights and privileges. Quṭb maintains that civil society is in deep crisis because the state has given rise to a well-knit "coalition of regression" that aims at stifling any emancipatory measure taken by the masses who are the backbone of civil society.[96]

This "coalition of regression" that violates basic human rights and values without hesitation, is made up of the following forces: (1) oppressors-exploiters (*tughāt wa mustaghilīn*); (2) professional men of religion (*rijāl al-dīn al-muḥtarifīn*); (3) mercenary writers (*kuttāb murtaziqīn*); and (4) hired journalists (*ṣaḥafiyīn maʾjūrīn*).[97] In analyzing the nature of this alliance, Quṭb points to the seemingly unshakable bond existing between the powers-that-be and the ideological bloc in society which is composed of the men of religion and the writers, and journalists. It is true that Quṭb, as Joel Beinin argues, "is acutely conscious of the link between capitalism and British imperialism and denounces the alliance between Egypt's 'dictatorial ruling class' and imperialism."[98] However, his point of departure is criticism of the prevailing ideology and its main representatives, especially the official

ʿulamāʾ. In his vociferous condemnation of the religious hierarchy and mentality, Quṭb approximates the radical Marxist critique of religion and the religious hierarchy which, at that time, was best represented by the life and thought of the Egyptian radical critic Salāma Mūsa, a Quṭb contemporary. Mūsa, for instance, narrates in his autobiography that, as a young man, he came to a shocking discovery. "British imperialism was not our people's only enemy. A reactionary mentality characterized by a permanent clinging to traditions, a hatred of the modern spirit in politics and social affairs and beliefs—these were the elements that together made another enemy of the people, and a formidable obstacle on its road to progress."[99]

As mentioned above, Quṭb was suspicious of the "men of religion" since childhood. In Cairo, Quṭb faced a much more complex situation than that in the countryside. Nevertheless, he saw the same mechanism in action, although it was more subtle. The urban religious intelligentsia, in Quṭb's view, had been long used to the luxury of city life and were not about to change it if social conditions were bad. Actually, such people thrive on these ill conditions. Quṭb therefore vents his frustration and anger at this powerful ideological bloc because of its manipulation of both religion and people.

It is interesting that Quṭb launches a severe attack against the *ʿulamāʾ*, not in the name of liberalism nor modernization nor socialism, but in the name of Islam and the poor masses. Although he invokes Islamic history here and there to assist him in his task, he lends his support to and is actively engaged in a counterideological and religious movement that aims at weakening the traditional hold of the established and official *ʿulamāʾ* over the masses, and at dismantling the coalition of regression in society. Quṭb finds the *ʿulamāʾ* powerful because (1) they have been the guardians and custodians of the sacred text; (2) they have derived authority and legitimacy from their unique positions as the preservers and interpreters of the central Islamic traditions; and (3) they have enjoyed the respect, however, falsely accorded or ill-deserved, of the rulers and the masses alike.[100]

It is true, as Musallam maintains, that "Quṭb attacks the religious hierarchy in Egypt for having been indifferent to these [socially unacceptable] conditions rather than adopting a proper Islamic stand against them,"[101] but it is equally true that Quṭb considers this hierarchy to be part of a larger scheme or conspiracy to maintain this intolerable state of affairs. The professional men of religion, in Quṭb's view, do not represent the real spirit of Islam because they "have sold out to the devil and to those who pay the cheapest price,"[102] and because they, just like parasites, live off the "mutilated, wretched human debris" (*al-ḥuṭām al-ādamī al-mushawwah wa'l dhalīl*) that makes up the majority of the Egyptian populace. "I indict these current social conditions for diminishing human dignity and destroying human rights . . . Who could dare to say that these millions of barefoot, naked, and hungry peasants, whose intestines are eaten by worms, eyes bitten by flies, and blood sucked by insects, are beings who enjoy the dignity and rights of humans?"[103]

Although Quṭb's primary social concern is the amelioration of the conditions of peasants and workers, he sees the poor to be of a diverse background sharing common deprivation and misery. The poor are made up of the following social strata: (1) peasants; (2) child laborers; (3) servants and door keepers; (4) the elderly; and (5) beggars.[104] In *Ṭifl min al-Qaryah*, as already mentioned, he is committed to the plight of the poor. His commitment expands at this stage to include a larger number of socially undesirable elements who occupy the lower echelons of society. Quṭb likens the "sick social condition" (*al-wāqi 'al-ijtimā'ī al-mariḍ*) to medieval feudalism and its concomitant social and economic polarization between the elite minority and the wretched majority. As the custodians of religious values, the *'ulamā'* do nothing to protest against these conditions. Instead, "a respected and blessed committee of the upper echelon of the *'ulamā'* wakes up from its long and deep slumber mourning the loss of values and the spread of immorality,"[105] and saying "not even a word about the fascist social exploitations or Islam's stand on government or wealth or the unbearable social chasms."[106] From their privileged religious and social position, the men of religion cannot give up their traditional functions of influencing the masses and popular culture, and shoring up support for the status quo, including the colonial one.[107] This influence, Quṭb argues, gives a false picture about the true spirit of Islam.

> The men of religion are the farthest of God's creatures from representing its [Islam's] true image—their education, behavior, and attire do not convey the true picture of religion. What has replaced this image [of the true religion] is ignorance of the nature of this religion, and the system of education left over from the occupation days.[108]

In addition to being allied with the power elite, the Azhar *'ulamā'* maintain reactionary educational policies that do not meet the demands of the age. "The Islamic foundations [of knowledge] do not revolve around the commentaries and subcommentaries studied at the Azhar, which end up killing the youth by devouring the best years of their life, and graduating students who become prey to contradictory attitudes and futile polemic . . . In writing my *ʿAdālah* and *al-Salām al-ʿAlamī*, I was not in need of going back to commentaries, since the original wellsprings of Islam can be found in the Qur'ān, the *Sunnah*, *sīrah* and history which were sufficient in helping me write these two books."[109]

What is the connection between the futile religious polemic and the boring educational methods of the Azhar on the one hand, and colonialism and Westernization on the other? This question is at the heart of the intellectual problematic Quṭb develops in *Maʿarakat*. The answer lies in the realms of history, theology, politics, and international relations. The colonialist block, made up of the United States, Britain, and France, is directly responsible for the pervasive state of exploitation in modern Muslim societies. Muslims have long accepted their peripheral status in international affairs, and have thus been reduced from a proud and independent community to "colonies and zones of interest (*mustaʿmarāt wa manāṭiq nufūdh*)."[110] Contemporary colonialists and capitalists are the crusaders of yesteryear. They consider Islam as the only universal religion that places their interests in jeopardy because Islam "is a dynamic and marching religion (*dīn mutaḥarrik wa zāḥif*)."[111] Alerted to the innate capability of Islam to pose a major threat to colonialism and its cronies, colonialists have adopted the slogan of "in order to defeat your enemy, you have to understand his language." Thus, says Quṭb, colonialists

> are not as oblivious [to the facts of Muslim history] as are our naive and good-hearted intelligentsia, nor are they as dumb as our brilliant rulers. They base their colonialism on comprehensive and detailed studies of the resources and foundations the people they colonize. Their major goal, however, is to annihilate the seeds of resistance [against their rule] . . . Orientalism emerged on this basis as well. It emerged in order to assist imperialism from a scientific point of view and in order to lay down its roots in the [local] mental landscape (*turbah ʿaqliyah*). But we, alas, worship the orientalists stupidly, and we naively think that they are the monks of learning and knowledge, and that they distanced themselves from their [crusading] origins.[112]

It is relatively easy to point a finger at the orientalists and other foreign enemies. The task becomes more daunting, however, when it comes to the dark-skinned Britishers (*al-Inglīz al-sumur*) whose thoughts and souls are manufactured and colonized by their white masters and who are planted in the Ministry of Education to fulfill the educational wishes of the colonialists.[113] In Quṭb's view, Ṭāha Ḥussain and his liberal project are no exception to that.

As previously seen, Quṭb distinguishes between two forms of colonialism: political/military, and spiritual/intellectual. He obviously considers the latter to be much more pernicious and abiding than the former.[114] In addition to orientalism and its indigenous admirers, the men of religion were seen by Quṭb as having conspired to sedate and enslave, wittingly or unwittingly, the intellectual environment of Egypt. "The professional men of religion." Quṭb maintained, "recognize very well that they fulfill a basic function in feudal and capitalist societies, a state-related function that gives them their means of support, and that stipulates that they should intoxicate and deceive the deprived, exploited, and laboring masses."[115] These men of religion fulfill their functions in the context of the native comprador bourgeoisie created and nourished by the forces of occupation. Quṭb admonishes the masses to raise the banner of Islam and to rise against this class of exploiters.

Quṭb diverges from the position on labor and work which he took initially in his *Social Justice*, in which he argued that work is the culmination of the true spirit of Islam. In his *Battle Between Islam and Capitalism*, however, he argues that "those who work in the country go hungry and starve,"[116] explaining that those who perform honest work are not paid enough and yet still refuse to take part in corruption, embezzlement, theft, and exploitation.

Quṭb documents the following social problems in Egypt just before the 1952 revolution: (1) inequity in the distribution of property and wealth; (2) problems of work and salaries; (3) lack of opportunities; and (4) corruption in the workplace and low production. To an extent, Quṭb shares Marx's ideas about surplus extraction and hegemony. He makes the following observations: (1) The city takes precedence over the countryside; and (2) The life-processes of the producers—the peasants and the laborers—are controlled not so much by physical force but by subtle overt mechanisms of control, especially religion and the law. The following statement could summarize some of Quṭb's ideas.

> In the bourgeois mode of power, unlike the feudal, the domination of nonproducers, i.e. capitalists, over the producers, i.e. wage laborers, and the appropriation of surplus-value are assured not by physical force over the life-processes of the producers but by complete control over the labor-process secured by rights of

> property in the means of production and in the product and by the impersonal operation of the market.[117]

Quṭb tackles a major issue in Egyptian society at the time—the complex mechanism of control instituted by the ruling classes. In other words, he dwells on a discussion of the notion of hegemony and its harmful effects on Egyptians, especially the poor peasants.

The modes of exercising power in colonial Egypt become the focus of Quṭb's criticism. He argues that these are a mixture of the subtle and the visible at play against the peasantry, agreeing with the subaltern attitude that "the establishment of bourgeois hegemony over all structures of society requires not so much the abolition of feudal institutions or feudal conceptions and symbols of authority, for these could in fact be appropriated and subsumed within a dominant mode of exercise of power.[118] Quṭb, as an urbanite Muslim intellectual who actually sides with the peasantry and voices their concerns, was certainly a rarity.

ʿAqīdah and Emancipation

The Battle Between Islam and Capitalism prepares the ground for Quṭb's ideological commitment to the Ikhwan movement. In *Islam and Universal Peace*, the commitment to the Ikhwan's thought is conspicuous, and Quṭb begins to develop his notion of Islam as an *ʿaqīdah* (creed) and living doctrine. He argues that the function of *ʿaqīdah* is the conservation of religious belief in times of change and crisis. Quṭb's understanding of *ʿaqīdah* replaces his earlier configuration of poetic theory and its role in the life of the poet. For Quṭb, *ʿaqīdah* is a revolutionary method with such immensely hidden power that it can transform inactive humans into committed and goal-oriented beings. *ʿAqīdah* has both historical and transhistorical properties and faculties. "Only religious belief (*ʿaqīdah*) enables man to communicate with the all-powerful God, and that belief endows the feeble individual with such strength and support that even the forces of wealth and oppression are unable to shake him."[119] Quṭb makes a drastic shift in reliance on the emancipatory power of the masses to a direct retrieval of and reliance upon the divine power as the only means to combat social injustice in society, "Religious belief puts man in close communion with the revealed and concealed powers of this universe and makes his mortality endurable by imbuing confidence in him, and granting him confidence in God's help."[120] *ʿAqīdah* is the motor of life, and it is the only hidden power that a true Muslim in the twentieth century should live for.

> In our country, as in all Muslim countries, we face different kinds of problems and handicaps. Internally, these problems figure as social, economic and moral problems, while externally they figure as international complications. But when we confront these problems, we find ourselves void of energy, foresight, guidance, and goals. In fact, we are in desperate need of a belief which can help us consolidate our powers. We need a unified ideology (*ʿaqīdah*) to confront life and its problems, and ideology that will solidify our strength against our foreign and domestic enemies.[121]

ʿAqīdah and absolute justice are found by Quṭb to be compatible. They furnish the ground for a number of conditions that have to be guaranteed in order to safeguard the well being of Muslim society. Absolute justice, in Quṭb's view, "implies integrity which is above [favoritism] and material influence."[122] Islamic law, when operable, must guarantee the following rights: (1) preservation of life; (2) honor and property; (3) the inviolability of the home; and (4) personal freedom.[123]

One major aim of social justice, as already mentioned, is to achieve social equilibrium (*tawāzun ijtimāʿī*) which is critical to the maintenance of social peace and harmony. All guarantees and securities are means of realizing a lasting social equilibrium. This equilibrium is easily discerned in the Islamic political system, in its legislation, in its judicial structure and in its system of social security. It is most conspicuous, however, in the economic distribution of wealth.[124]

Social equilibrium, as a corollary to social justice, can be attained only if the following principles have been fulfilled: (1) When wealth is not controlled by the minority, but is circulated amongst different groups of society. Quṭb contends that it is the duty of the Islamic state to ensure the application of this principle by levying taxes on the rich to the advantage of the poor. (2) The principle of public or general welfare (*maṣlaḥah ʿāmmah*) whereby the state has the right to take from the money of the rich in order to spend on society. (3) The principle of precautionary measures (*mabdaʾ ṣad al-dharāiʾ*). The Islamic state has the right to take the measures necessary for the prevention of corruption and promotion of the general welfare of society. (4) Prohibition of usury. (5) Prohibition of monopoly. (6) Nationalization of public resources. (7) Prevention of wastefulness and luxury. (8) Prohibition of hoarding (*taḥrīm al-kanz*). (9) Legitimate ownership. And (10) *Zakāt* principle.[125]

Quṭb continues the legal discussion he presents in *Ma'rakat.*

> In capitalist countries, the common man's privilege to elect a candidate to parliament is a very limited freedom. The voter is aware that he is not free to express his opinion as long as the necessities of life are in the hands of the capitalist candidate. Even if we suppose that the voters do have absolute freedom in electing their representatives—which is impossible—the parliament, by virtue of its formation from a certain class, would hardly embrace elements genuinely representing the common man. Accordingly, its legislation must favor the interest of capitalists.[126]

Quṭb maintains that when man's conscience and feelings are governed by a certain law but his life and activities are governed by another, and when the two laws emerge from different conceptions, one from human imagination and the other from the inspiration of God, then such an individual must suffer something like schizophrenia. He would fall an easy prey to the consequences of the conflict between his conscientious feelings and his active material realities, and he would ultimately succumb to anxiety and bewilderment.

Quṭb reflects on the type of Western writing that is critical of Western civilization and culture. Bertrand Russell was well known as a major critic of Western society. Quṭb agrees with Russell on the role of the white man. "It is indeed true that the age of the supremacy of Western man has ended, for Western civilization has served its purpose and become bankrupt. It can now offer nothing to mankind; it is impotent and cannot guide man toward new horizons or rescue him from the present malaise. Since the existence of any civilization is entirely dependent on what it can offer to mankind in the way of remedies for the social ills of humanity, and in the way of opening up new prospects for happiness and prosperity, Western civilization has depleted its stocks and is doomed."[127]

In commenting on the Western mind set, Quṭb does not see much of a difference between communism and capitalism. He points out that

> Communism is the natural continuation of the materialistic outlook on life propounded by Western civilization. This outlook has characterized the civilization of Europe and America since Roman days, and it was intensified in the seventeenth century by

> the emergence of the principle of experimental science propounded by the English philosopher, Sir Francis Bacon, who refused to believe in anything save that which is demonstrated by practical experience through the senses. The difference between the communist way of thinking and the way of thinking now prevalent in the West is not a difference in the nature of the thought itself but in the extent and method of that thought. The materialistic outlook on life is the same in Communism and in the civilization of the West. While in America this outlook takes the form of according the individual absolute liberty to exploit and invest his wealth, in Britain such exploitation and investment is limited and restricted as a result of the nationalization of the major public utilites, and in Russia the state owns everything and the individual is deprived completely of the power to exploit or invest his private resources.[128]

In discussing the challenges of the modern world, including secularization and Westernization, Quṭb says

> This is indeed a stupendous task, and the leaders of Islam must lose no time in preparing and equipping the Muslim world for it. The Muslims must keep paramount in their minds, however, that mankind will not simply be seeking a set of bare metaphysical ideas and theories. It requires a realistic and practical code and system of life; and any theories that are presented to it will be judged on the benefits that are proved to result from their application in the realm of practical life. This has always been the criterion in passing judgement on social ideologies, and it will be the way in which the non-Muslim world will judge the ideology of Islam. It is, therefore, the sacred duty of Muslims to lead such a life as will effectively portray the great merits and healthy attributes of their belief. The social order in the Muslim world must present itself to the non-Muslim world as the practical interpretation of the teachings of Islam, so that the non-Muslim world, when it starts looking in earnest for a way out of its intellectual and spiritual strife, will not fail to be impressed by the beauty and charm of true Islamic ideology in its practical phase.[129]

In his view, Islam was, and should be, rediscovered as a liberation movement for both the mind and soul.

Ideological Commitment to the Ikhwan

In *Dirāsāt Islāmiyah*, a collection of articles written between 1951 and 1953, Quṭb's ideological commitment to the Muslim Brotherhood movement becomes an established fact. He now defends an established sociore ligious movement with a long tradition of political controversy in a politically unstable society.

Examined against the background of Egyptian society of the early 1950s and the social and political turmoil of that period, Quṭb's ideas revolve around such themes as revolution, liberation, Americanization, Arab nationalism, and Islam. Elaborating on his notions of social justice, Quṭb perceives Islam as a "great emancipatory revolution" (*thawrah taḥrīriyāh kubrā*) that led to far-reaching breakthroughs in the spiritual, social, economic, military, and literary realms of human life.[130] Islam is devoted to freeing the masses from atheism, religious fanaticism, racial and ethnic discrimination, social and economic exploitation, and political privileges. However, it is the task of the conscious intellectual, such as Sayyid Quṭb himself, to raise mass consciousness and elevate the masses to the inevitable conflict between them and their oppressive conditions. Quṭb defines Islam simply as a method of confronting averse and oppressive conditions. The birth of a genuine Muslim takes place in the most critical moments of human history. Indeed, a Muslim is empowered with a special mission to fight injustice.

> Those who consider themselves Muslim, but do not struggle against different kinds of oppression, or defend the rights of the oppressed, or cry out in the face of dictators are either wrong, or hypocritical, or ignorant of the precepts of Islam.[131]

Quṭb views Islam as a revolutionary religious system that stands against all passive and quietist manifestations of modern life. Once it touches man's heart, Islam is supposed to cause major changes in feelings, perceptions, and conceptions.

Quṭb also comments on what he perceives as the partial and incomplete attempts of Muslim political leaders to apply Islam in the realms of education and law. He criticizes these attempts on the premise that Islam is a complete and indivisible whole that must be applied in its entirety. Islam, he contends, refuses to be consulted in trivial matters while it is neglected when it comes to basic issues.

> Islam is a complete social system which differs, in its nature, conception of life, and means of application, from any Western

> or applied system in today's world. Surely, Islam has not participated in creating the existing problems in today's societies. These problems have arisen as a result of the faulty nature of the applied systems in the modern world, and as a result of banishing Islam from the real context of life.[132]

Sayyid Quṭb's previous critique of Christianity and the West, general as it was, is narrowed down to his critique of Americanization, its symbols, and its intellectual allies in Muslim lands. In a provocative essay entitled "Americanized Islam" (*Islām Amerikānī*), Quṭb accuses America of being patronizing of Islam and Muslims because of its perceived need to combat the communist threat in the Middle East. America does not oppose Islam per se. However, the type of Islam it nurtures is the castrated one.

> The Americans and their allies in the Middle East reject an Islam that resists imperialism and oppression, and opt for an Islam that resists only communism. They neither desire nor tolerate the rule of Islam. This is the case because, when Islam begins to rule, it will mold the people anew, and instruct them that it is a [legal] duty (*farīḍah*) to both prepare for assuming authority and expelling the colonialists.[133]

Quṭb goes on to argue that 'Americanized Muslims' control the most sensitive posts in society, and their decisions are likely to affect the future course of the Muslim world. "Americanized Muslims" are always ready to render any service, big or small, to their imperialist masters.

In Quṭb's view, the most dangerous of "Americanized Muslims" happen to be certain famous Egyptian authors, journalists, and professional men of religion who become aware of the significance which imperialism attaches to their position, and thus subscribe to ideas inimical to Islam. He argues that there is a lot of talk in Egyptian journalism about Islam, and

> Discussion of religious matters floods many pages of those newspapers that had never shown any love of, or knowledge about, Islam. The publications houses, some of which are American-owned, discover suddenly that Islam must be the subject of its monthly publications. [In addition], a number of famous authors, known for their propaganda on behalf of the Allies, return to writing about Islam . . . And the professional men of religion gain heaps of money, prestige, and authority.[134]

Consequently, the favorite subjects of these people do not revolve around issues of economic and social justice, but the means to fight communism and socialism. These scholars of religion get invited every year to conferences sponsored by American foundations where they reiterate dull themes and reawaken new negativities. "It is permissible to take the legal opinion of Islam on [such matters as] contraceptives, women becoming members of Parliament, and the conditions that lead to the cancellation of ablution [for prayer]. But Islam is never consulted in matters relating to our social and economic conditions, or our financial system."[135] Those who consider religion as a form of business and commerce [*al-mutājirūn bi'l dīn*] are just like that froth that dries up in the air.[136] In short, Quṭb concludes grimly that Islam is being invaded from within, and that a purification of the rank and file of Islam is long overdue.

This important observation of Quṭb's has been overlooked, perhaps for the best of intentions, even by many Islamist writers. Many Arab writers on the Left today—such as Fu'ād Zakariyyā,[137] Maḥmūd Amīn al-ʿĀlim,[138] and Halim Barakat[139]—are unconsciously using the same Quṭbian phraseology—such as, Americanized Islam—without referring whatsoever to this important article of Quṭb's.

For instance, Halim Barakat, in his highly acclaimed, *The Arab World*, highlights the function of religion as a source of legitimacy in what he calls "the authoritarian state" in the modern Arab world. He contends that the ruling families, especially in the Gulf region, have resorted to a complex mechanism of control made up of wealth, power, religion, and army support, and that there has been "an American-Saudi strategy to use Islam as a counter force against nationalist and progressive forces."[140] As Quṭb rightly points out, the question is far more ominous than just an American-Saudi plot to use Islam to delegitimize forces on the Left or those of Arab nationalism. Quṭb reiterates emphatically that the enemy is within and is perpetually fueled by American money and prestige in order to undermine the Muslim personality, home, and world.

In another important article entitled, "The Principles of the Free World," Quṭb reacts strongly to claims that the Western world is the locus of freedom and equality. "The Free world," he maintains, "is just a name that British, French, and American colonialists use to describe that imperialist block [*al-kutlā al-istiʿmāriyah*] which has been fighting against [the progress of] time, humanity, and freedom."[141] In Quṭb's view, the following characteristics distinguish the so-called Free World: (1) killing real freedom in the world, especially in North Africa and Vietnam; (2) committing crimes in Africa in the name of civilizing black people; (3) dislocation of nations and creating permanent refugees, such as in the case of Palestine; and (4) pouring millions of dollars into the control of the minds of the indigenous people.[142] Quṭb maintains that all these characteristics are expected from the so-called Free World whose self-appointed mission is to civilize and enlighten. What is hard to expect, perhaps, is the utter silence "our nations, governments, thinkers, writers, poets, communities, and organizations" have shown in dealing with both the covert and overt dangers and activities of the imperialist world.[143] The most dangerous thing facing the indigenous people of the Third World is the attempt of the Western world to brainwash and mind-control.

> The Free World does not fight us with tanks and guns except for limited periods of time. Instead, it wages a battle against us with tongues and pens . . . It also fights us through the [charitable] societies and organizations it establishes, revives, and supports for the sake of controlling the most sensitive centers in our land.[144]

Quṭb takes his analysis a step further and develops the concept of "intellectual and spiritual colonialism [*istiʿmār fikrī wa rūḥī*]."[145] Colonialism is of two kinds: manifest and latent. Intellectual and spiritual colonialism, or latent colonialism, drugs out the spirits and minds of the people and turns them into obedient slaves. Revolution is a necessary outcome of colonialism. "Holy war against colonialism today necessitates the emancipation of the conscience of nations from spiritual and intellectual colonialism, and the destruction of those systems that drug out the senses, and being cautious of any tongue, pen, society, and group that concludes a truce with those colonialist camps which are bound by common interests and principles."[146] The best way to get rid of imperialism is to destroy its image within us, and destroy its residues "within our feelings."[147]

Quṭb becomes aware of the position of the United States as a leading world power in the wake of his study tour in the country in 1949–1950. Here, he begins to distinguish between the waning imperialism of western Europe and the potential danger of a new power such as the United States. Addressing this novel situation, Quṭb wrote a series of articles in the *Risāla* in 1951 under the title "The America I Have Seen."[148] Quṭb compares the United States to a huge machine that produces unceasingly and then grinds up all the hopes held by average people of ever becoming emotionally healthy and spiritually sane. Quṭb argues that the American is primitive in terms of feelings and social behavior, and that it is this primitiveness that has placed the American, unwittingly, in a race to fulfill his sexual, physical, and other material desires.[149]

Quṭb moves on to describe the nascent American power in the Muslim world and concludes that "the white man is our primary enemy."[150] The white man, declares Quṭb, exploits us to the fullest, and any mention of modernization by the colonizer and his numerous "intellectual slaves" is a travesty of justice.[151]

Quṭb points to a major concept of intellectual imperialism in the Third World, which, in retrospect, has not received much attention from the modern Muslim intelligentsia. It is pertinent, therefore, to pursue this theme in Quṭb's thought and to see how it developed, especially in his writings of the 1950s and 1960s.

In *Dirāsāt Islāmiyah*, Quṭb is sensitive to some of the national issues facing Egyptian society on the eve of the 1952 revolution. One such issue is the proper connection between Islam and Arab nationalism. Quṭb reiterates al-Bannā's position on Arab nationalism.

> The sole banner that binds us in our struggle [against imperialism] is that of Islam. Some amongst us prefer the banner of Arab nationalism [to that of Islam] . . . I do not object to a temporary marshalling of forces if its sole aim is to obtain a larger gathering. There is no serious contradiction between Arab nationalism and Islam as long as we perceive the former as a step on the road [to establishing the Islamic state]. The whole Arab land is a part of Muslim territory.[152]

Seen in the light of the pervasive influence of imperialism, Quṭb, the writer and critic, launches a severe criticism against those writers who belong to his profession but who espouse "imperialist ideas." He calls them "morally loose writers . . . traitors [*khawana*]" and mercenaries.[153]

Quṭb points out that the colonized are a large mix of people who belong to different religious and cultural traditions. Colonialism, he argues, marshals its forces in order to hinder the process of freedom of these different nations, "But it [colonialism] has paid special attention to Islam and the lands of Islam for a while now. Colonialism has not neglected to notice, even for a second, the innate power of the Islamic *ʿaqīdah* [*al-quwwah al-kāminah fī al-ʿaqīdah al-islāmiyah*], and the danger this power poses to all [sorts of] foreign imperialism."[154]

Quṭb enumerates the following characteristics of the concept of *ʿaqīdah*: (1) It is the real spirit of Islam. Quṭb defines Islam as "an awesome emancipatory power [*al-islām quwwah taḥrīriyah hā'ilah*].[155] If *'aqīdah* is reawakened in a nation, freedom will be its inevitable outcome. (2) *'Aqīdah* is superiority [*isti'lā'*], pride [*i'tizāz*], and grandeur [*kibriyā'*]. *'Aqīdah*, therefore, stands against both enslavement and blind obedience. (3) *'Aqīdah* is based on the premise of the total unity of the Muslim world. It seeks to protect the universal concept of Islam against its communist as well as capitalist enemies.[156] Sayyid Quṭb's notion of *'aqīdah* is based on the metaphysical premises of Islam and is, in many ways, similar to Ibn Khaldūn's notion of universal *'aṣabiyah*. It is worthy to note that Quṭb develops the concept of *'aqīdah* against the background of historical and intellectual colonialism in Muslim society. *'Aqīdah* arises in opposition to a number of objective conditions surrounding Egyptian society. Therefore, the final goal is to abolish, go beyond, and replace these conditions by new ones.

The foregoing discussion illustrates a major question in the historiography of Islamism in the modern Middle East—that is, hegemony and the colonialist project. The colonialist moment in modern Egyptian history, especially between 1882 and 1952, was reinforced, not only by the modernization of the infrastructure of Egyptain society, but also by the mental services of the religious class. In other words, hegemony was secured by both coercion and consent. Quṭb's critique of the religious class in Egyptian society must be understood against the larger background that he reacted to—namely, British hegemony. This hegemony was substantiated by many factors, some of which were contributed by the ulama class.

Hegemony and dominance are two key elements in the mechanism of colonialism. As Antonio Gramsci, Partha Chatterjee, and Ranajit Guha, among others, have conspicuously shown, in order for hegemony to be complete, dominance must be secured by overtly peaceful means.[157] In other words, for the colonialist project to achieve utter success in a Muslim society, the active participation of the *'ulamā'*, or a portion of the *'ulamā'*, must be guaranteed. In that sense, "Hegemony . . . critically involves ideological domination. However the balance between coercion and consent in the exercise of hegemony varies historically. Generally, the weaker the engineering of consent, the stronger the repression by the state has to be."[158] As we shall see later, a similar process of hegemony took place in the context of Arab nationalism. The *'ulamā'* were co-opted, and coercion was used by the state.[159]

At the heart of colonialist hegemony, as Quṭb understands it, is the relationship between religious knowledge and power.[160] Quṭb has problems with this formulation because (1) what the *ʿulamāʾ* define as religious authenticity while referring to the metaphysics and absolute values of Islam is defined by Quṭb as the politicization of religion. Orthodox Islam becomes a tool of legitimizing the status quo. (2) The thrust of Islam is the dynamic *ʿaqīdah* already referred to. *ʿAqīdah* means the spirit as well as the practical application of Islam. It is a movement that grows in opposition to, and not in conformity with, colonialism.

Conclusions

Sayyid Quṭb's ideas matured against a complex literary, social, and political background. His literary criticism fermented into political, religious, and social criticism. Infatuated with modernist theories of literature and psychology, and following the examples of Ṭāhā Ḥussain and ʿAbbās al-ʿAqqād, Sayyid Quṭb's passion for ideas led him to the realm of praxis and the turbulence of real life. There, Quṭb rediscovered a bruised, mutilated, and exhausted Muslim *ummah*. That is when his passion was reawakened—a passion to rectify, direct, lead, and die for a cause. Delving deeply into matters, the issue for Quṭb was more than a tormented soul searching for its roots in an alien world, or a strategy for applying an ideal system in an imperfect world. For Quṭb, the question was how to present a viable system of education, of social and economic justice that would stem from Islamic metaphysics.

In his pre-Ikhwan phase, and far from considering revelation and reason to be antithetical, Sayyid Quṭb believes that it is possible to unite the two elements in the historical context of the twentieth century. Revelation, rationalism, and history might suffice to fulfill the religious quest of the modern Muslim. Mental schizophrenia, crisis of identity, historical retardation, and conflict of interests would have to come to an end for the sake of perfecting the *ummah* in a still treacherous societal and political terrain.[161]

In the muddy environment of political and social ideologies, Quṭb had to find an answer to the crisis of Islam and Muslims. The answer is not given but sought after, rediscovered, and re-presented in a realistic form. The answer begins with the central problem of society, which is social justice. After discovering that the answer alone is insufficient, Quṭb ponders the means. One possible and, perhaps, easy way is to join an already established organization that reflects, more or less, the concerns of an agonized intellectual who stands at a juncture, both in his own as well as in his country's life. In short, for the Movement to salvage modern Muslims, Islam must rule. Islam can no longer be a stranger in its homeland.

Finally, Quṭb posits a complex view of the West, which could be summarized as (1) The West is a reflection of Christianity and its history; (2) the West is also renaissance and the rebellion against the authority of the church; (3) the West is colonialism; (4) in its advanced stage, the West is both socialism and capitalism; (5) the West is secularism and the separation of church and state, and (6) the West is a method and an intellectual orientation.

Chapter 5

Sayyid Quṭb's Thought between 1952 and 1962: A Prelude to His Qur'anic Exegesis

*We must make it clear, however, that we do not desire to seek the truth of the Islamic concept (*al-taṣawwur al-Islāmī*) merely for the sake of academic knowledge. We have no desire to add still another book to the shelves of Islamic libraries under the heading of "Islamic philosophy." Never! Indeed, our purpose is not merely cold knowledge which deals only with intellectual issues and adds to the stock of "culture." For us this sort of activity is somewhat trivial and cheap and not worth the effort. Rather, we want to bring about the movement which is beyond knowledge. We want the knowledge of the Islamic concept to lead people toward the realization of its contents in the real world.*

—Sayyid Quṭb, The Islamic Concept and Its Characteristics, *tr. Mohammad M. Siddiqui (Indianapolis 1992) 5*

As shown in the preceding chapter, the literary, cultural, and social oeuvre of Quṭb, developed mainly between 1938 and 1952, represents the thought of a Third-World intellectual who ends up expressing his thinking in religious terminology while trying to come to grips with a volatile and a highly changing socioeconomic, political, and intellectual situation. As such, one must examine the Quṭbian discourse—the pre- as well as the post-1952 discourse—as a comprehensive whole that reflects the thought processes of a religious intellectual in transition. In other words, the Quṭbian discourse, in its totality and diversity, offers a multifaceted conceptual expression and is distinguished from the very beginning by the critical method which Quṭb employs. Thus, one can clearly delineate Quṭbian literary criticism, Quṭbian social criticism, Quṭbian religious criticism, and so on. In this context, I agree with Muḥammmad Ḥāfiẓ Diyāb's criticism of the disjointed and mechanical treatment by many a scholar of the Quṭbian discourse. Diyāb criticizes scholars such as Nabīl ʿAbd al-Fattāḥ and Ḥasan Ḥanafī who employ the "young-mature Quṭb" dichotomy in studying his thought, without shedding any real light on the inner connection and continuities of Quṭb's thought.[1]

To elaborate on this point, we could say that Ḥasan Ḥanafī divides Quṭb's thought into four phases: (1) the literary, (2) the social, (3) the philosophical, and (4) the political phase. We also maintain that the longest of the phases was his first.[2] In Ḥanafī's assessment, Quṭb's thinking between 1952 and 1962 represents his philosophical viewpoints, and Quṭb, at this stage, turns his back on his previous social and economic commitments, and instead prefers "an abstract and pure presentation of Islam."[3]

While it is helpful to discuss the different phases in a scholar's thinking, it is also important to keep sight of two other factors—namely, the inner continuities of thought, and the historical context in which thought is produced. Quṭb's phase of thought during the period of 1952–1962 is an extension, and not a negation, of the previous phase. It is an elaboration on new themes during a unique historical era (the Egyptian revolution of 1952 and its aftermath). In this light, the thesis that many a scholar proposes concerning Sayyid Quṭb's dependence on external sources for his thought is untenable. For instance, such scholars as Yvonne Haddad,[4] Olivie Caree,[5] Muḥammad Aḥmad Khalafallah,[6] Emanuel Sivan,[7] and William Shepard[8] argue that the most distinguishing mark of Sayyid Quṭb's thought in the 1950s is that it fell under the influence of such diverse personalities as Ibn Taymiyah, Muḥammad Asad (Leopold Weiss), Abū al-Ḥasan al-Nadwī, and Abū al-ʿAla Mawdūdī. While no one can deny these external influences on Sayyid Quṭb, who was an avid reader, it must be stressed that they were secondary, and that both the historical situation of Egypt while he was writing and his understanding of the Qur'ān were the primary influences upon his intellectual life and its development.

ʿAqīdah, Faith, Action, and the Islamic System

Quṭb's *Hādha al-Dīn* (originally published in the mid-1950s) develops the ideas of *Social Justice in Islam*.[9] This work and others in this period indicate the extent to which Quṭb goes in his Islamic activist commitment, and reflect a major shift in his ideological commitment from an engaged social and political critic to that of an ideologue and an organized socioreligious and political activist who seeks to change the status quo radically. Here, Quṭb begins to develop the concept of the vanguard, or the followers of the Islamic path who are required to recognize both the hardships of early Islam and the complexities of the modern situation. Quṭb presents an overall critical evaluation of Islamic history, of Western history, and the task of Muslim activists. He warns against complacency and short sightedness, and expects the activist to be a believer in both words and deeds.

> This divine path, represented in its final stage by Islam as entrusted to Muḥammad is not brought into being in the world, in the realm of humanity, simply by virtue of its revelation by God. It is not brought into being by being preached and proclaimed to the people. It is not brought into being by divine enforcement, in the same way that God enforces His will in the ordering of the firmament and the revolution of the planets. It is brought into being by a group of people undertaking the task, believing in it completely and conforming to it as closely as possible, trying to bring it into being in the hearts and lives of others too; striving to this end with all they possess.[10]

Quṭb maintains that revelation (*waḥy*), as the self-disclosure of God in human history, cannot be complete without the active participation of a group of people in fulfilling the divine message on earth. In this context, he highlights two major concepts at this stage: action and struggle. He refers to the Qur'anic maxim, "truly God does not change the state of a people until they change that which is within themselves," in order to show that struggle is a necessary element in establishing the faith of Islam on earth,

> The truth of the faith is not fully established until a struggle is undertaken on its behalf among people. A struggle against their unwillingness and their reluctance, a struggle to remove them from this state to that of Islam and truth. A struggle by word of mouth, by propagation, by exposition, by refuting the false and baseless with a statement of the truth proclaimed by Islam. A struggle to physically remove obstacles from the path of right guidance when it is infested by brute force and open violence. In this struggle misfortune and suffering will be encountered, and

> patience will be necessary. In times of victory too patience is needed: it is then perhaps more difficult. Then one becomes steadfast and unwavering pursuing the path of the faith righteously and unswervingly.[11]

Struggle is the hallmark of Quṭb's thought in this transitional phase. Complementing the notion of the struggling vanguard is another of significant importance, that of servitude (*'ubūdiyah*) to no other system or being except God. Servitude to God—one of the main conceptual terms which Quṭb employs in the *Ẓilāl* discussed in the following chapter—implies true human emancipation which, in turn, stipulates that Muslims must derive their identity and legitimate political existence from no other power except the eternal authority of God. "It is only Islam that liberates man from servitude to other than God, and hence too we are obliged to attempt its implementation, and that of no other path."[12]

Quṭb theorizes that alienation, in both its existential/social and spiritual/emotional senses, pervades the entire world, and is all the more conspicuous in Muslim societies that do not heed the word of God. "Present-day humanity," he argues, "is afflicted with misery, anxiety, bewilderment and confusion; it flees from its true self by taking refuge in opium, hashish and alcohol, to a craze for speed, to idiotic adventures. All this, despite material prosperity, high productivity, and a life of ease with abundant leisure. In fact, the emptiness and confusion increase in proportion to material prosperity and convenience."[13] Quṭb addresses the issue of alienation in subjective terms, and offers Islam as a solution to the subjective needs of man. Islam liberates "the individual from perversions that have latched onto his essential nature; permit the virtuous and constructive forces within him to appear and establish their supremacy; and remove the obstacles which prevent true human nature from striving toward the good in which it was created."[14]

To Quṭb, Islam is not rites or individual religious practices, but an organic religion that links the individual to a healthy environment, "Without this environment, the life of the individual becomes impossible, or at least extremely difficult. Therefore whoever wishes to be a Muslim should know that he cannot devote himself to his practice of Islam except in a Muslim environment dominated by Islam. He is mistaken if he imagines that he can realize his Islam as an individual lost in the midst of a society ignorant of divine guidance."[15] Here, Quṭb gives a solution to the problematic of secularization faced by modern Muslims, and he does that in strict obedience to the original

Islamic principles. He contends that *Jāhilī* systems are characterized "by partial cures and solutions for human problems. They will solve one aspect, but aggravate another, and this is a direct result of their deficient vision, a vision which fails to grasp all facets simultaneously. When they cure the illness arising from their cure of the first illness, yet another illness will arise, and so on, indefinitely."[16]

Quṭb argues that Islamic history, although full of deviation from the true Islamic spirit, has witnessed the rise and the tenacious resistance of the Islamic system (*al-Niẓām al-Islāmī*) which continued to resist all the catastrophes that beset it, and all the attacks to which it has been exposed, for more than a thousand years. Although the basis of the Islamic system or its metaphysics has been infiltrated by all sorts of corrupting historical factors—especially orientalism and imperialism—it has not been wiped out completely. However, with the passage of time, this system "has become weakened and seriously threatened. Nonetheless, up to the present day they have been unable to distort its doctrinal foundations, and these doctrines are available for fresh investigation, to be embraced by a new generation."[17]

As has been argued above, Quṭb considers Islam as a simple religion that rejects any intermediary between the human and the divine. Furthermore, one can comprehend the doctrines that make up this religion without any sophisticated theological or intellectual arguments or explanations. Quṭb invites modern Muslims to ponder the early experience of the Prophet and his companions who, in his view, were the vanguard who dared to challenge the formidable historical condition of seventh-century Arabia, although they arose in the poorest of environments, in the middle of the desert. The vanguard were a unique generation because they endured so much hardship and suffering and were able to create a unique example in human history with no equal parallel. Therefore, it becomes the duty of modern Muslims, who suffer in the desert of the nation/state, to emulate this unique generation and to rise above the tide of division and handicap. Quṭb reminds modern Muslims that Islam did not fold its hands in surrender to the challenging reality of seventh-century Arabian society. "It abolished it, or changed it, and erected in its place its own sublime and unique structure, on its firm and profound basis."[18] Islam is a new moral, doctrinal, social, and political system.

The true hope in liberating modern Muslims from political chaos, alienation, loss of faith, and economic and social injustice resides in the vanguard. The callers to the path of God must possess unique qualities of endurance, understanding, and complete faith. These qualities are essential in an age when "mankind in its entirety is today more distant from God than it used to be. The clouds which weigh over man's nature are thicker and denser than before."[19] The new Muslim vanguard must realize the dangers awaiting them and the potential dangers emanating from a phase that is more learned, deceitful, and complex than any other phase of history.

What is the nature of the Islamic system that Quṭb seeks to apply? What are the fundamental principles of Quṭb's understanding of Islam? And what is the proper connection between this Islam and secularization?

These questions preoccupied Quṭb in the 1950s. This was because, while Nasserism represented the most concrete challenge to his formulations, Quṭb did not perceive Nasserism as a radical departure from the conditions prevailing in Egypt in the pre-1952 phase. Therefore, Quṭb took up the argument that Islam is a social and political system, and not just a metaphysical idea, that ought to be applied and emulated.

> Islam is a system for practical human life in all its aspects. This is a system that entails the ideological ideal—the convincing concept which expounds the nature of the universe and determines the position of man in this universe as well as his ultimate objective therein. It includes the doctrines and practical organizations which emanate from and depend upon this ideological ideal, and make of it a reality reflected upon the everyday life of human beings.[20].

Quṭb points indirectly to the enemies of Islam who strenuously exert themselves "to confine Islam to the emotional and ritual circles, and to bar it from participating in the activity of life, and to check its complete predominance over every human secular activity, a preeminence it earns by the virtue of its nature and function."[21]

Quṭb argues that the complete secularization and possible Westernization of Turkey at the hand of Atatürk is just the beginning of the battle to attack Islamic symbols all over the Muslim world.[22] He is convinced that a final offensive is taking place in "an effort to exterminate this religion as even a basic creed, and to replace it with secular conceptions having their own implications, values, institutions, and organizations. These conceptions were expected to fill the vacuum of faith with faithless dogma."[23] That the Turkish experiment of secularization is taken as a symbol of the secularization of the entire Muslim world is clear from the sheer emphasis which Quṭb and other Islamists have placed on Turkey. Quṭb objected in the late 1930s to

Ṭāhā Ḥussain's theoretical propositions concerning the Westernization and secularization of Egyptian society. Now, in the 1950s, Quṭb sees this to be a reality, and witnesses the attrition of Islamic symbols. Quṭb maintains that the social and political order is a reflection of the ideological domain and of the theoretical realm. The new order of Nasserism in its political and social senses is no reflection of the Islamic ideal, but of the secular one.

Faced with this formidable predicament, and the lack of Islamic values and symbols on the side of the powers-that-be, Quṭb resorts to finding the solution in the theoretical realm of Islam. In a sense, he, as the master theoretician of Islamic resurgence at this stage, is challenged at his conceptual and ideological roots by Nasserism and all of its meanings and symbols. The answer to, "What is to be done?" lies in the epistemology of religion and religious belief. To Quṭb, religion revolves around the question of God. Far from being confined to people's emotions and rituals, or limited to a personal relationship between God and man, Islam is a *Taṣawwur I'itiqādī (doctrinal concept*), that leads to a permanent revolutionary attitude in real life. In other words, *'aqīdah* is a necessary radical method of change in the absence of a religious political system. In theory, *'aqīdah* is the yardstick by which true belief in God and His commands are measured.

Toward an Islamic Theory of Knowledge

The Quṭbian theoretical response to the emerging challenge of Nasserism is the subject of two volumes which Quṭb wrote on what he calls "the fundamental components of the Islamic concept" (*Khaṣā'iṣ al-Taṣawwur al-Islāmī*).[24] Quṭb's main objective in these works is to record what he perceives to be those fundamental principles that constitute the basic foundations of the religious structure of Islam. In other words, Quṭb's aim is to explain in a clear and simple fashion the basic epistemological principles of Islam, as outlined in the Qur'ān and Sunnah, without the unnecessary complications of philosophy, exegesis, and other types of speculative thought.[25]

Quṭb's discussion of the Islamic conception of life is a thorough attempt at reconstructing the basic principles of Islam in a modern setting. Quṭb, for a moment, turns away from abstractions, a priori judgements, closed systems, pretended rationalism, and fixed systems and, instead, advocates a rebirth of the Islamic foundations, a resurgence of its pristine raison d'etre, which is its dynamic interactive capability with the process of human history. Defining the parameters of this reconstruction at this day and age is necessary for the following reasons:

(1) A modern-day Muslim is in need of a comprehensive understanding of the universe as a means of coming to grips with what Quṭb calls two archetypal realities or facts: (a) the fact of lordship (*ḥaqiqat al-ulūhiyah*), and (b) the fact of servitude (*ḥaqiqat al-'ubūdiyah*) and the necessary connection between them.
(2) The position, function, and aim of human existence must be delineated in that context. In other words, man's way of life; his conceptions, and has social, economic, and political system must be derived from the fact of lordship.
(3) The reconstruction of Islamic principles is also necessary because Islam's original mission was to build a unique community endowed with a sense of justice and clear thinking, and it further aimed at liberating other people from the shackles of deviating worldviews and leaderships. This is still a must even today, especially in view of the loss of guiding principles. "Doctrinal conception is the medium of thorough orientation [which exists] alongside the realistic system that results from it."[26] Doctrinal and intellectual refinement is the *modus vivendi* of a moral and concrete life on earth.

In attempting to define the doctrinal conception, Quṭb raises a number of interesting questions about the problem of knowledge as an immediate concern for contemporary Muslims who, in his view, have been assailed, right and left, by all sorts of theories and ideologies. Instead of advocating an epistemic rupture with revelation, he calls on Muslims to treat the Qur'ān as the locus of a thorough reconstruction of the "correct" Islamic notion of the "foundations of knowledge," and to interpret the early experience of Islam afresh. How can modern Muslims approach the Qur'anic text? What is the best way to interpret it as a "foundational document?" The real problem of understanding the Qur'ān as "theory of knowledge," and "epistemology transformed into ideology," lies,

> in our capacity to reconstruct and relive the abundance of the feelings (*mashā'ir*), comprehensions (*mudrakāt*), and experiences (*tajārib*) accompanying the revelation (of the Qur'ān) and the first generation of Muslims, who received the Qur'ān in the thick of the struggle. Theirs was an environment of *jihād* (striving)—*jihād* against the self, temptations, and people. . . . The ambiance

of the emerging Muslim community and its nascent social system was a reflection of a lively friction (*iḥtikāk ḥayy*) between feeling, interests, and principles.[27]

Quṭb contends that theory and action acted in unison in early Islam and generated a true revolutionary wave that has refused to fade away. In other words, early Muslims did not treat the Qur'ān as a text—as a passive book of reading or rhetoric—but as a dynamic conceptual and experiential entity. Quṭb's understanding of the Qur'ān is neither esoteric nor metaphysical, but conceptual and ideological. The aim, therefore, is to change reality in accordance with the basis of the religious and ideological precepts of the sacred text. That is to say, the main aim of modern Muslim activists should not lie in accumulating more knowledge, be it cultural or philosophical, because this type of knowledge is "cold knowledge."[28] The goal must lie in integrating knowledge with both dynamism and action. Consequently, Quṭb translates knowledge as praxis, a way of life, and a vehicle that propels man to carry out the divine instructions.

What is the relation of action-based Islamic revelatory knowledge to philosophy in general and Islamic philosophy in particular? Quṭb questions the basic presuppositions and conceptual contents of, especially, Western philosophy, and disavows the so-called "Islamic philosophy" of medieval Islam. He claims that Muslims lost the original dynamic and experiential meaning of knowledge in the wake of Muslim expansion and as a result of the nascent Muslim culture coming into contact with a mixed bag of foreign cultures, philosophies, and mentalities.[29] Owing to historical circumstances, Muslims in the medieval period ushered in a new phase of life that was distinguished by wealth, leisure, and loss of the pristine values of Islam. The translation of Greek and Roman philosophy, and the theological corpus of Christianity into Arabic "introduced deviations and foreign trends of thought not conforming to the original Islamic concept."[30] Quṭb *contends that mental leisure (*taraf ʿaqlī*) was the distinguishing mark of Muslim intellectual life under the ʿAbbasids.*

Quṭb does not discuss the ideological engineering of ʿAbbasid society and the role that Islam, as religion and ideology, played in the construction, preservation, and maintenance of that society. Neither does he discuss the role of the ideological blocs which were at play in ʿAbbasid society. He contends that the philosophical doctrine developed by Muslims on the basis of Greek and Roman philosophy runs counter to the Islamic method. "Some Muslim thinkers were infatuated by Greek philosophy, especially the commentaries on

Aristotle (the first teacher as he was fondly referred to), and by scholastic and metaphysical studies. They presumed that Islamic thought could not have reached maturity, perfection, greatness, and glory without its first being dressed in the garment of scholastic philosophy."[31] A fundamental incompatibility exists between Greek philosophy and the Islamic conception. The former is "a cold discourse poured in a speculative logic," whereas the latter deals with society in a realistic and direct way.[32] Quṭb presumes that philosophy was an autonomous and self-propelling discipline in medieval Islam. It is the opinion of this writer, however, that the intellectual environment of the formative phase of Islam never separated religion from philosophy, nor philosophy from logic. This type of separation is a modern phenomenon which appeared in nineteenth-century Western thought when philosophy was established, in the words of Richard Rorty, "as an autonomous, self-contained, 'scholastic,' discipline."[33]

Therefore, Quṭb theorizes that

> The search for the components of the Islamic conception (*muqawimāt al-taṣawwur al-islāmī*) cannot be theological, metaphysical, philosophical, cultural, or theoretical in general. Rather, it is a pragmatic, realistic and concrete search for the basis on which that system of human life, which God desires for man, rests.[34]

Thus, Quṭb concludes that philosophical method and doctrinal method are incompatible, and that what has been traditionally termed as "Islamic philosophy" is foreign to the doctrinal system of Islam.[35] European thought, likewise, cannot serve as a model for the revival of any religious doctrine, because it has taken an inimical stand against religion in general.[36] In Quṭb's view, it is a historical and religious duty to salvage Islamic thought from all sorts of corruption and, above all, from mental rigidity (*jumūd 'aqlī*), loss, annihilation, and negativity (*ḍiyā', fanā', wa salbiyah*).[37] The revival of such a pure conception of life, as understood by the Prophet and the early companions, can be done only by those "who labor today and tomorrow under similar circumstances, who alone can grasp the meanings and allusions (*ma'ānī* and *'ihā'āt*) of the Qur'ān. It is they alone who taste the realities of the Islamic conception as presented by the Qur'ān."[38]

Those who labor under similar circumstances are the vanguard who are in touch with the mystery of the Qur'ān, the original environment in which the Qur'ān was revealed, and who undergo suffering, alienation, and exile for the sake of re-establishing the foundations of the correct Islam. The conceptual chaos of the modern age is similar to that in Arabia of the seventh century that necessitated the Islamic revelation in the first place.

> Islam appeared while the world was dominated by a huge multitude of doctrines, conceptions, philosophies, myths, thoughts, illusions, rites and traditions, situations and circumstances in which falsehood was mixed with truth, wrong with right, religion with superstition, and philosophy with mythology.[39]

The vanguard are to ponder this pristine situation of Islam, especially in an age that pays little heed to religion. In this context, Quṭb also shuns the attempt of modern historians of religion at dividing the history of mankind—especially that of the West—into (1) medieval, in which religion was dominant, and (2) modern, in which religion is not. He says that the religious quest is a natural and permanent human quest that cannot be hindered by history.

Likewise, Quṭb explains the emergence of Islam as an answer to two facts: (1) human and existential requirements, and (2) social and historical necessities. Therefore, religion is far from being peripheral or contingent. Man cannot live meaningfully without a doctrine (*ʿaqīdah*) capable of explaining the universal character of man and the universe. Also, a strong connection exists between the doctrinal/ideological attitude of man and his social system. Quṭb, however, does not believe that man's consciousness and conceptions, which constitute his worldview and concepts, are the reflection of his social position in society. He says that any "social system is [a mere] dimension of the overall interpretation of [human] existence, man's centrality and role, and the ultimate purpose of his existence."[40] A social system that is not based on divine foundations is superficial and temporal. In sum, for the vanguard to re-establish the correct foundations of Islam, they must free their minds from all sorts of intellectual rubbish (*rukām ʿaqlī*) that may have accumulated over the centuries, and they must view with suspicion the modern achievements of the Western mind.[41]

The salient features of the Islamic conception (*al-taṣawwur al-islāmī*), which Quṭb attempts to salvage, are the following: (1) lordship, (2) constancy, (3) permanence, (4) comprehensiveness, (5) balance, (6) realism, and (7) divine oneness. The principle of lordship (*rabāniyah*) cannot be subject to permutation, evolution, addition, or change. It is essentialistic with eternal and absolute foundations.[42] Quṭb's *rabāniyah* shares the same basic qualities of Hegel's *geist*.[43] The whole question of man's existence begins and ends with God, while the

Spirit exists in an infinite condition of freedom and inspiration. It is only the consciousness of man that can grasp this possibility of freedom. In both cases, humanity exists in a dialectical relation to the Ideal, which must be emulated and sought after all the time.

In the context of *rabāniyah*—and its historical outcome of revelation—Quṭb elaborates on his understanding of reason as a human faculty par excellence which is endowed with a unique mission: spreading and abetting the divine revelation. Notwithstanding this unique role, reason is limited and is, thus, unable, in Quṭb's view, to provide eternal foundations for the human and religious quest. Although man can transcend the universe with his mind and spirituality, "he is limited in his function—that of viceregency whose purpose is to realize the servitude of man to God."[44] In other words, man cannot play the role of God. Revelation must be his guide in the complexity of life. Consequently, man-made principles of knowledge and practice have always run in contradiction with the pure essence of religion and lordship. Quṭb discusses the intellectual history of modern Europe by saying that man's conceptions have replaced the divine ones as a result of deviations in the meaning of lordship. Such philosophies of life as idealism, rationalism, pragmatism, and dialectical materialism have resulted from human intervention in the divine vision.

Thus, Quṭb's basic theological question is that of God. Revelation and reason constitute a secondary level of investigation. The question of human being and ontology is derivative of the primary concern. Theological conception is a priori, while human thought is contingent. A complex dialectical relationship exists between God and man, and the self-relatedness of man is implied in this experience. There is an explicit relationship between the divine doctrine and human/historical dynamics. In the Quṭbian context, dynamics (*ḥarakiyah*) is a very complex term. It implies activity, work, action, becoming, revolution, transition, suffering, struggle, *jihād*, patience, servitude, and human liberation.

Quṭb claims that the Renaissance view of man, as a basis of the contemporary Western conception of man and the universe, was born in the wake of deviation from the divine.[45] The Renaissance premises rested on the unlimited innate ability of man to rationally transcend the human predicament.[46] Quṭb maintains a notion that is familiar to many a European thinker—namely, that the Renaissance, as a collective ideological and social phenomenon, was responsible for the annihilation of preindustrial social structures, and especially the intellectual underpinnings of these structures. The traditional ambience of harmony between man and nature was no longer viable after the eruption of the Renaissance. Quṭb summarizes what he sees as the conceptual fluctuations or ruptures in European thought in the following manner:[47] (1) Renaissance thought replaced the traditional Biblical concept of the supremacy of scripture by a new concept, the supremacy of human reason. (2) By the end of the nineteenth century, the Enlightenment gave rise to positivism and the rule of the senses and factual matters over religion. Technical reason became more valued than anything else. The end result, according to Quṭb, is the prevalence in contemporary Western thought of notions, categories, and ideas that are solely derived from facts, senses, and experiments. Knowledge is the product of the human mind, which is limited by nature, and which cannot surpass revelation.[48] It should be noted, however, that Quṭb does not underestimate the technical dimensions of Western modernity, nor does he minimize the possibilities unleashed by the progressive nature of nineteenth-century European modernity.[49] What he cannot accept, however, is the *èlan vital*, to use Bergsonian language, of the philosophical project of modernity which, to his mind, has confined human vitality and capacity for self-transcendence to the realm of human history. The guiding principle of this modernity, according to Quṭb, is reason, and the argument of the best European philosophers is that even God can be grasped and manipulated rationally.

Constancy (*thabāt*) is another essential quality of the Islamic conception. Human history revolves "around a constant axis (*miḥwār*)"[50] which is lordship. Lordship is not subject to change and evolution. That is, "it does not change when the phenomena of life and its practical conditions change."[51] Likewise, in his relation to the divine, man must preserve two essential facts which do not change: viceregency and servitude. Quṭb argues that a pervasive sense of malaise surrounds the modern world, because the primary relationship between God and man has been obliterated or lost. Modern life is distinguished by a lack of constancy, mutation of principles, and rejection of the ideal. Once again, Quṭb connects this situation to real social factors. There is a multitude of usurpers, bankers, film-producers, journalists, and writers who benefit from this state of affairs.[52] Here, he reiterates themes similar to those discussed in *The Battle Between Islam and Capitalism*, already referred to.

Quṭb maintains that the Islamic vision cannot be subject to reform, evolution, and change. It is not medieval in character, neither is it backward. He further argues that the polarization between progressive and backward is not a mark of Islamic thought. In other words, Quṭb proposes the revival of indigenous Islamic concepts and terms needed to account for Muslim society and history. In this regard, Yvonne Haddad contends correctly that "the doctrine of constancy in the Islamic worldview is proposed by Quṭb as a dam against Westernization and the appropriation of European values, ideas, customs, and fashions. It also functions as a refutation of the basic intellectual premise of Darwin's theory of progressive evolution, as well as that of dialectical materialism."[53]

A third distinguishing feature of the Islamic conception is comprehensiveness. God is behind this universe, and divine oneness is a basic fact. The theological premises of the Qur'ān deal with the following facts of lordship, servitude, universe, life, and man. Behind all these facts, there is one comprehensive will, and a common source or origin of man. The main goal is to marshall all human forces into fulfilling the goal behind human existence—servitude, which is an essential component of vicegerency. Islam possesses "a comprehensive and well-integrated approach to life and the universe. This approach includes [human] conceptions of conscience and planning in life."[54] In other words, man's external actions should necessarily follow his inner beliefs and thoughts which are, in turn, a reflection of the principle of lordship. Quṭb says that the distinction which Islamic law draws between *'ibādāt* (acts of worship) and *mu'āmalāt* (social relations) is in theory only. In real life, this distinction must not exist, because it has led to an unnecessary polarization between thought and practice in Muslim societies, to the extent that some Muslims have exaggerated thought and downplayed the importance of practice. Any human activity, Quṭb contends, falls in the realm of *'ibādah* or worship. Quṭb says that "this division, with the passage of time, has led people to consider themselves 'Muslims' on the basis of *'ibādāt*, while at the same time they carry out their *mu'āmalāt* activities along the lines of another approach—a nondivine approach which legislates for them in matters of life."[55] To Quṭb's mind, "Islam is an indivisible unity. Any division (into *'ibādāt* and *mu'āmalāt*) is against this unity."[56] In conclusion, Islam's basic premise, besides legislating for the relationship between God and man, is to legislate for the relationship between man and man as well.[57]

Equilibrium, as a main feature of the Islamic conception, points to what Quṭb perceives as the norm between the absolute Divine will and the laws of the universe. A balance also exists between the dignity of man and his role as a vicegerent of God on earth. "There is no contradiction, from an Islamic point of view, between man's greatness, dignity, and participation and his servitude to God."[58] In other words, there is a balance to be struck between the divine sources of knowledge and the wordly ones.

Equilibrium implies positiveness. God is positive, active, willing, and dominant. Positive religion—or positive Islam—rests on authority higher than human authority. The Prophet and his companions grasped and applied the positive dimension of lordship, and were thus able to revolutionize the whole world. "This fact [of positiveness] dwelt in the conscience of the early Muslim community who were shaped in a unique and distinguished way over all other groups in human history. They lived by this fact."[59] One of the main Qur'anic premises, argues Quṭb, is that "man is an active and positive force in life . . . [And] that he is the vicegerent of God so that he realizes God's method in a realistic way: to build, change, and reform."[60] Man is responsible, and he is required to act. Action can take different forms, one of which is *jihād* on behalf of the Muslim community. Positiveness, although resting on divine authority, can be verified, and its competence can be shown only by the dynamism and action of a community of people.

Realism, as another basic feature of the Islamic conception, denotes two basic facts, previously referred to: (1) divine, and (2) human. The divine fact proclaims the active participation of God in the creation and preservation of the universe and the lives of humans. Quṭb stands against the Hindu and anthropomorphic view of God as one unity with the universe. He reiterates the monotheistic view that God is the source and that everything else in this world is contingent upon God. The human fact, according to Quṭb, is what constitutes the realm of society and human history. "The Islamic conception of life looks at man as a realistic element (*kāi'n waqi'ī*), distinguished by certain traits, who possess influence and emotion . . . Man is not looked upon as an abstraction or a thesis which has no reality."[61] Man is that complex structure of body, emotions, passions, fears, and hopes that are subject to social conditions and relationships. Quṭb warns against treating man as an abstraction or as a speculative construct. Man should be taken as a complete whole and, above all, should be considered within a historical and social context. In this, the Islamic method is substantially "different from 'rational idealism' (*mithāliyah 'aqliyah*) which deals with purely rational theses, and which [consequently] has no connection whatsoever with those acting elements in life and the universe."[62]

Tawḥīd or divine oneness is the thrust of the Islamic conception. On the basis of divine oneness, Quṭb concludes that the true "Muslim believes that God is the [supreme] ruler, legislator, and planner of people's lives, relationships, and connection to the universe and life in general."[63] Quṭb warns the followers of the Islamic method against complacency, inactivity, and narrowness of vision. The mission awaiting the believers is imposing because the notion of man's servitude to God has been lost and replaced by that of man's servitude to man. The liberation of man can only take place when the relationship between God and man is restored to its original state of affairs. The restoration of this role is what would make the believers pioneers in leading humanity toward a new future.

Modern Muslims, contends Quṭb, "cannot offer humanity scientific achievements, or civilizational conquests . . . But they can offer something greater that all of that: the liberation of man or the birth of man."[64] Quṭb does not address social differences at this stage, neither does he give a practical solution to the grim state of affairs he describes. His effort has been that of explanation, diagnosis, and reconstruction. He is more a teacher here than a revolutionary strategist.

Thus, the constituent elements of the Islamic conception of God, universe, and life are stable and unchanging. As a universal mission, Islam has come to show people how to realize these essential components. "Islam appeared in order to change the reality of humanity [as a whole]. It is not here to change humanity's beliefs, conceptions, terminologies, feelings, and rites only, but instead to create a new reality above and over that of the *jāhiliyah* in which humanity lived and to which it may return . . . *Jāhiliyah* is one condition of life (*waḍʿ ḥayā*) which is not restricted to a certain phase, and it starts with the servitude of man to man . . . which means that *hākimiyah* and legislation are left to the people."[65]

Quṭb says that the Islamic interpretation of history takes into account the role of man as guided by the divine revelation. The Islamic society established by the Prophet attests to this fact, representing, as it did, the transition from a tribal, mutilated, and divided society to "a homogeneous, universal society."[66] Quṭb makes his point clearer when he says that

> It is not in the nature of this religion to deposit knowledge in the refrigerators of frozen mentalities. In view of this religion, knowledge must be transformed into an instant dynamic (*ḥarakah*) . . . When the Qur'ān was revealed the intention was to carry out the rules right away, so as to become a dynamic element in a dynamic society. Every Qur'anic proclamation (*naṣṣ*) was a living response to a realistic situation.[67]

Quṭb shows that knowledge and action are two inseparable entities that are destined to address the modern problems of Islam. It is true that Quṭb examines, in an albeit philosophical way, the faculty and contents of reason and the positive relationship that might exist between reason and revelation. However, Quṭb does not stop there. He shuns any form of speculative thought that does not prove the positive or pragmatic side of religion.

In his examination of reason, Quṭb makes it clear that human consciousness contains elements that transcend, but not necessarily contradict, reason, such as emotions, feelings, and intuitions. The ultimate and highest sphere of human consciousness is religion. To Quṭb, man is capable of self-transcendence, which is the locus of his true freedom.[68]

Quṭb argues that corruption has occurred in this conception (*fasād fi'l taṣawwur*). This is why there must be pioneers who possess clear vision (*ru'yah wāḍiḥah*). The epistemological foundations of modern civilization have gone astray. No compromise is possible between the Islamic conception and any other *jāhilī* conception. Any such compromise would constitute a psychological defeat (*hazīmah nafsiyah*), a defeat of confidence and, above all, "a defeat of the Islamic conception and the pristine human nature."[69]

Islamic Political Philosophy

In dealing with the Qur'anic philosophy of politics, Quṭb discusses the terms which constitute the main elements of Islamic political philosophy: *sulṭān* (power), *ḥākimiyah* (sovereignty), and *'ubūdiyah* (servitude). He maintains that, "The Meccan Qur'ān revolves around the topic of *'aqīdah* or *fiqh al-uṣūl*, and it does not deal with derivatives or rules because the *Dār al-Islām* had not yet been established."[70] Although the Prophet began his real political authority only after the migration to Medina, the foundation of Islamic political philosophy came as a response to the turbulent environment of Mecca. In other words, Quṭb theorizes that "the elucidation of the issue of government in Islam was a question of *'aqīdah* before it was a question of founding a political system."[71] What that means is that, aside from establishing religion as the basis of the modern Islamic state, Quṭb exhorts people to find certainty in religion, to reject man-made law and injunctions, and to admonish others to follow the precepts of Islam. Put succinctly, the external foundations of the Islamic political system will be erected in the moment when religious philosophy occupies the consciousness of people. Consciously or subconsciously, Quṭb, follows the Hegelian notion of the insoluble bond between religion and (theocratic) state. In an interesting piece on the relation of religion to the state, Hegel argues the case of monotheistic religions in his *Lectures on the Philosophy of Religion*, and concludes that

> In a general sense, religion and the foundation of the State are one and the same; they are in their real essence identical. . . . Religion is the knowledge of the highest truth, and this truth more precisely defined is free Spirit [*taṣawwur i'tiqādī* in Quṭbian terminology]. In religion man is free before God; in that he brings his will into conformity with the divine will, he is not in opposition to the supreme will, but possesses himself in it; he is free, since in worship he has attained to the annulling of the division. The State is only freedom in the world, in the sphere of actuality. . . . There is but one conception of freedom in religion and the State. This one conception is man's highest possession, and it is realized by man. A nation which has a false or bad conception of God, has also a bad State, bad government, bad laws.[72]

To Quṭb as previously noted, Islam is the religion of true emancipation from servitude to other than God. The foundations of the state must be identical with those of the creed. Any deviation from this type of thinking would create havoc in society, and annihilate true freedom.

Quṭb's Doctrine of Man

Up to this point, we have been looking at Quṭb's first systematic attempt at reconstructing the fundamental Qur'anic and doctrinal principles of Islam for the purpose of redirecting the modern Islamic effort at building a new nation and a new social and political system. In other words, Quṭb's reworking of Islamic principles is not a theological construct undertaken in a vacuum, but a necessary task designed to meet an urgent situation. In many ways, Quṭb considered the situation of modern Muslims to be analogous to that of Muslims when Islam initially encountered the *jāhiliyah* of the seventh century. It is true, he argues, that that situation was very complex—ideologically, religiously, and socially. Both situations, however, share something in common—complexity. In other words, the situation to which Quṭbian epistemology responds is that of rupture between *jāhiliyah* and Islam. This rupture is also the culmination of a complex multitude of factors. Quṭb's formulation of Qur'anic doctrines is, besides being creative and comprehensive, an act of challenge in which the status quo is subverted, at least theoretically.

Quṭb does not pose the Islamic set of problematics as a mere encounter between Islam and the contingencies of the modern world. Neither does he perceive any possibility of Islamic adaptation to the modern world. He does not, for instance, ask the question of "Can the Islamic message be adapted to the modern world without losing its essential meaning and character?" Rather, he poses the question of "How can one dismantle the modern bases of intellectual and political power and establish the Islamic order?" From this latter question, Quṭb starts his complicated journey into the maze of Islamic and Western histories; Islamic and Western thought; and Islamic and Western philosophy.

The primary question of Quṭbian discourse is that of God's and man's places in the order of things. We may presuppose—by way of invoking the legacies of Hegel and Tillich—that Quṭb's basic theological formulation rests on the notion that God, and only God, is the answer to the question implied in man's finitude.[73] Complementing that premise is Quṭb's historical formulation of the Divine role as an active agent in human history as well as consciousness. Therefore, one can assume that Quṭb defines religion as a divine manifestation in human history. Man, as an active historical agent, must also be conscious—not of his particular truth per se, but of the Universal, All-Encompassing, and One Truth which must, if followed correctly, bridge the gap between the sacred and the profane and obliterate the dichotomy between the affairs of God and those of man.

Quṭb is acutely aware of this chasm between God and man in the postcolonial, nation/state phase. The modern Egyptian—and, for that matter, the modern Muslim—has not done his best to realize the question of God in his being and life. The vanguard, therefore, must accomplish this difficult task and try to overcome any chasm that might exist between the divine and the human. In a sense, Quṭb relativizes metaphysics and metaphysizes history. It is a dialectical process whose other major agent is the vanguard, the elite, the unitarians, the sacrificers, and the martyrs.

Therefore, besides being concerned about the divine fact, Quṭb is committed to explicating the way in which this fact is connected to human existence and the necessity of coming to terms with it at different human levels. Islam is a historical religion—that is, a particular type of religion. However, this is an incomplete thesis as far as Quṭb is concerned. Islam is both historical and metahistorical, particular and universal; absolute and relevant.

One of the interesting things that Quṭb does in the 1950s is that he attempts to rob the *'ulamā'* of their inherited religious power to preserve, protect, and disseminate the Muslim Creed. He declares the failure of the Muslim hierarchy in his 1940s writings, and in the 1950s, he takes practical steps by offering an Islamic activist alternative, the legitimacy, of which is derived from (1) the original sources of Islam, and (2) the call for a practical application of Islamic principles in a modern setting. In belittling the religious role of the *'ulamā'*, Quṭb comments on them as producers of state-oriented *fiqh*, a type of *fiqh* that is irrelevant to contemporary Muslim societies. "Islamic *fiqh* cannot evolve and grow and face the problems of life except in a Muslim society—in an actual society."[74] Therefore, the problems generated in Egyptian society by the unequal relationship between the West and the Muslim world do not reflect the real nature of Muslim society simply because this society was not yet born. Then, asks Quṭb, "Why do the *'ulamā'* waste their energy on *fiqh*?"[75] The *'ulamā'*, Quṭb argues, are not serious about bridging the unnecessary gap between the Shari'ah and *fiqh*, and between the divine notion of authority and the secular authority reigning in Egyptian society.

Quṭb exercises philosophical thought in his *Islam and the Problems of [Modern] Civilization*,[76] in which he discusses what he considers to be the plight of modern man from an Islamic doctrinal perspective.[77] To prove his point, Quṭb quotes lengthy versions from Alexis Carrel's, *Man the Unknown.*[78] Evidently, Quṭb was impressed with the author's insight into the meaning of man's existence, and especially man's situation in Western civilization.

Carrel contends that the West has not paid sufficient attention to the study of man—his consciousness, spiritual and mental activities, whims and desires—and that the West is far more advanced, in general, in the spheres of technology and hard sciences than it is in the field of psychology. Quṭb and Carrel invoke an oft-repeated thesis currently in early twentieth-century Western thought, and best represented by the American philosopher William James. "For a hundred and fifty years past the progress of science has seemed to mean the enlargement of the material universe and the diminution of man's importance."[79] Although men and women have joyfully welcomed modern civilization, because of the material comforts it has to offer, modern man is not as well-balanced, emotionally and intellectually, as was classical man. In Carrel's view, "modern civilization seems to be incapable of producing people endowed with imagination, intelligence, and courage. In practically every country there is a decrease in the intellectual and moral caliber of those who carry the responsibility of public affairs."[80] Thus, Carrel contends that the predicament of modern civilization lies in its inability to produce men of sufficient intelligence and audacity to guide it along the dangerous road on which it is stumbling. "Modern civilization," he argues, "finds itself in a difficult position because it does not suit us. It has been erected without any knowledge of our real nature. It was born from the whims of scientific discoveries, from the appetites of men, their illusions, their theories, and their desires. Although constructed by our efforts, it is not adjusted to our size and shape."[81]

Quṭb follows in the footsteps of Carrel and contends that the polarization of man into the spiritual and the material is the result of the victory of science over religion. Man must be treated as an indivisible whole. Alas, this is not the situation of man in advanced technological societies. Modern society ignores the uniqueness of the individual and his strong commitment to freedom. Quṭb agrees with Carrel and assumes that modern man lives in a state of spiritual, mental, and psychological chaos, and in uncertainty about the future. Opposed to this ignorance about man, Quṭb contends that the Qur'anic conception of man treats every individual as a unique being endowed with a divine mission.

Quṭb claims that the reason behind the ignorance concerning the nature of man in the industrial world is simple. It was brought about by the historical conflict between the Church and the men of science.[82] The principles of scientific research, Quṭb tells us, developed in Muslim Spain, and the pragmatic scientific method originally developed by Muslims was borrowed by European scientists, such as Roger and Francis Bacon.

Assimilating the Muslim scientific methods, the European mind excelled in natural, geographical, and cosmic discoveries. The Church, from its standpoint of defending the myths and superstitions of the Middle Ages, opposed these discoveries in the name of God and the sacred. In fact, the Church moved to protect its own interests—interests that were closely associated with the environment of the Middle Ages. As a result, the men of science moved away from the religious domain and its spiritual mysteries, so that their science was set apart from the absolute. Quṭb thus blames the Church for driving the men of science away from God.

In the light of this polarization between science and religion in the West, Quṭb investigates three major issues in the life of man: (1)

man's nature and temperament; (2) gender issues; and (3) the question of social and economic systems.[83]

In discussing the doctrine of man, Quṭb relies more, at this stage, on Carrel's theses than he does on the Qur'ān. He says that there are three basic facts underlying the meaning of man: (1) Man is a unique creation in this universe; (2) He is a complex being; and (3) He is a microcosm of the universe. Seen in this light, man is unique in his nature, function, purpose of life, and his future.[84] In terms of Quṭb's treatment of women, he is not explicit about a number of issues. However, he thinks that—at least, normatively speaking—Islam has defined the boundaries of ideal relationships between men and women at the psychological, emotional, social, and educational levels. Quṭb's real concern, here, is that Muslim societies should not follow the path of Western societies whose definitions of the relationship between men and women are distinguished by "confusion and chaos."[85] Quṭb thinks that nineteenth-century Western thought facilitated a tripartite attack on the humanity of man launched by Darwin, Freud, and Marx. These three had something in common. Each attempted in a different way to prove the material nature of man, and to suppress his spiritual side. "Darwin, Freud, and Marx appeared in the nineteenth century. Their implicit assumptions, and [intellectual] predilections focused on dehumanizing man in different ways: Darwin [claimed] that man has absolute bestial qualities; Freud [claimed] that man was muddled in absolute sexuality, and Marx [claimed] that man plays a tiny and negative role in the material and economic conditions of life."[86]

Quṭb tackles methodological problems devoted to the study of man and history. He argues that Islam has devised "a human interpretation of history" which is fundamentally divergent from the Marxist materialist interpretation of history.[87] He continues with the Marxist view that the means and relations of production constitute the infrastructure on which the superstructure of morality, religion, and philosophy rests is infeasible.

He also argues that the Marxist view of economic factors determining the future of man's social movement is useless. To Quṭb, Marxism as a method has followed in the footsteps of those secular ideologies and methods that ignore the religious factor in man's life. In addition to taking the economic infrastructure as the determining factor in the movement of society, Marxists—just as the capitalists of Europe—are Eurocentric. "Marxists consider the history of the world to be that of Europe, and the god of economy that has ruled over the history of Europe is in control of the history of the world. They also presuppose that what has happened in Europe is inevitable in the history of the world—all factors in the history of man are determined by the economic side."[88]

Quṭb attempts a comparative study of European and Islamic social history from the Middle Ages on. He argues that the salient features of European social history are Roman slavery, feudalism, capitalism, Marxism, and Nazism. All of these systems share one thing in common. They have exploited and undermined the humanity of man.[89] Quṭb maintains that feudal conditions in Europe preserved European social and economic integrity until contact was made with the Muslim East during the Crusades. In their encounter with Muslim society, Europeans were alerted to a new social and religious system in which man was respected as an active member of society, and in which the Shariʿāh ruled supreme. The Islamic political system, in Quṭb's view, allowed average people to confront rulers and discuss with them all aspects of the Islamic polity. In the economic sphere, Europeans witnessed the free movement of people from one place of work to another, and even from one town to another. "Perhaps it is true that large estates existed in Muslim society, but no feudal system similar to that of Europe existed there. Certainly, no lords or servants existed there either."[90]

Quṭb argues that the reasons behind the European bourgeois revolution against the feudal system were, in addition to the creation of towns, the emergence of merchant and middle classes, and the Islamic influence on Europe. Capitalism emerged as a result of the dehumanization of man and individual freedom in the feudal age. Bourgeois commercial culture cultivated mechanical and impersonal relations that reduced man to a trivial and undignified status in society. "The capitalist system emerged on the basis of emancipating the individual, making of individual freedom an ideal, and giving the upper hand to individual interest."[91] Thus, the interest of society was subservient to that of the individual, and social ethics were reduced to accommodate individual competition and consumerism. It is true, Quṭb says, that the capitalist system has freed man from the inhuman behavior and economic injustices of feudalism, and that it facilitated individual creativeness, movement, and dynamism, and aided man in general to exploit the natural resources of the world. However, the capitalist system has created a major problem "interest."[92] The capitalist system has protected the interest system, under whose banner it flourished and prospered. Furthermore, it has belittled the role of social, human, and ethical qualities, and prohibited any intervention in running the economy. This capitalist philosophy not only leads to capital accumulation at the expense of social classes, but it adds another dimension, which is that the workers, merchants, and producers become an appendage, under capitalism, to the banking system. The capitalist system, therefore, has taken advantage of the entire society and the state as well. Quṭb goes further, agreeing with Marx implicitly, that the capitalist class, which creates classes of producers and consumers and manages a complex network of social and industrial activities, creates with it a class of propagandists who are "composed of the established university professors."[93] This class of university professors hides behind loads of economic theories. The far-reaching goal of the capitalist system is the creation of a class of bankers whose goal is to accumulate more and more money. "Interest is responsible for this malaise—the malaise of allowing a tiny minority of financial institutions to suck blood out of the whole system"[94]

In addition, a moral disintegration (*inḥilāl khuluqī*) has accompanied the capitalist system. To Quṭb's mind, the major disaster facing the European systems—capitalist and socialist alike—is their attempt to annihilate the existence of the individual as a unique human being. "Individualism (*fardiyah*) is deeply entrenched in the psychological, mental, and biological constitution and make-up of man."[95] Individualism, however, must be in conformity with the interests of society. In other words, Islamic individualism, as opposed to bourgeois individualism, emphasizes the uniqueness of the individual only in relation to group or collective solidarity. In a sense, Quṭb welcomes technological civilization, but without its presupposed enslaving mechanical interdependencies and collectivities. In sum, Quṭb proposes that modernity—with all its accessories such as progress, enlightenment, freedom, equality, and brotherhood—can be fine as long as it does not lead to enslavement, injustice, nihilism, and atheism.

What solutions does Quṭb offer to the crisis of man and society in modern Western culture? Throughout his writings of the 1950s, Quṭb proposes the following solutions: (1) Man, as the vicegerent of God, should be the measure of all things. (2) Modern man should not be so certain of, nor arrogant about, his rational capacities. (3) Moral and mental degeneration must come to an end. (4) The balance between man and technology must be restored. (5) Material and technological factors should not take precedence over man. (6) The only possible remedy for the alienation and spiritual malaise of modern societies lies in a much more profound knowledge of ourselves. (7) Hope may be restored by limiting the disadvantages created by modern civilization. And (8) true freedom lies in strict attention to the needs of our primordial nature.

Quṭb postulates that the paradox of man as a servant to God, and as a free human agent, is a necessary religious presupposition that is strong enough to maintain itself against the pressures of atheism, secularism, and nationalism. As a universal religion, Islam can be the real solution to the problems of modern man. "The proponents of the Islamic method (*aṣḥāb al-manhaj al-islāmī*)," he argues, "are the only ones who are duty-bound to carry the burden, to point out the road of salvation to humanity, and to build the road as well."[96] Our system (*niẓām*), according to Quṭb, does place man, his energies and creation in a safe context—that of progress, dynamism, and love for life. Unlike that of Carrel, our method (*manhaj*) translates spiritual activity into an indivisible religious system which, in turn, shapes and forms every aspect of life. To Quṭb's mind, Carrel cannot be innovative enough in terms of a solution because he, like other honest Westerners, is still the victim of his environment and civilization, in the sense that he has to use its language and follow its logic.

Quṭb contends that the Islamic method (*al-manhaj al-islāmī*) formulates a new position for man in society, and determines afresh his duties, rights, and needs. He says, "Our method realizes the establishment of well-integrated educational, ethical, economic, social, and political systems which, in turn, help in creating man with a complete personality—a man who has been weakened by contemporary life and its followed criteria."[97] Basically, Quṭb notes, the *al-manhaj al-islāmī* and industrial civilization are compatible, especially if the following conditions are met: putting an end to the dehumanization of man; and the abolition of unjust social, political, and economic practices.[98]

Conclusions

As already shown, the discourse of Islamic resurgence in the Arab world was nurtured by charismatic lay personalities who were greatly influenced by the peasant milieu in which they grew up. The series of transformations in Quṭb's intellectual life—from a secular *adīb* (man of letters), to a romantic visionary, and then to a committed member and ideologue of the Muslim Brothers—is but a witness to the great variety of early Ikhwan thought and the complex components that went into its structure. Thought does not arise in a vacuum, and the charge that Ikhwan thought is fundamentalist, narrow-minded, and dogmatic does not hold water. On the contrary, it is as complex as the conditions that gave birth to it.

There is a tendency among some scholars to distinguish between different phases in Quṭb's development; such as Quṭb the poet, Quṭb the man of letters, and Quṭb the Muslim ideologue. Although this type of analysis is helpful in that it sheds light on the external influences that led to changes in Quṭb's intellectual life, it is worthwhile to remember that Quṭb never forsake some of those qualities that were part of his formative phase, especially his quality of criticism.

In this regard, it is necessary to ask who Sayyid Quṭb was! Was he an author, a writer, a critic, an intellectual, an ideologue, or all of the above? There is no doubt that, in the 1950s, he was indeed, all the above. We should see his work at this stage against his complex professional and continuously evolving background as a writer and a critic, as well as against the background of Egyptian political and intellectual life. He tries, in the 1950s, to find a new way of making the "Qur'anic fact," to use an Arkounian terminology, foundational—that is, to make a new way of formulating the underlying bases of modern Islamic thought. The different terminologies—such as fundamentalism, fanaticism, and reactionism—used to describe the foundations of modern Islamic resurgence in popular Western discourse—be it of the mass media, popular journals or books—fail miserably in comprehending, let alone interpreting, the unique tradition of Quṭbianism. Where does one find rigorous essays and articles on, let us say, "Islamic resurgence and Western theories of knowledge," or "the Islamists' invention of tradition and the future of Islam?" As far as our media or popular experts on Islam are concerned, these questions are, in a large measure, irrelevant!

Quṭb remained faithful to the discipline of criticism to the end of his life. His profession as a critic was a leading mark of his life, and he was quick to apply it to all manner of discourse, from the literary, to the political, and to the religious.

In this phase, Quṭb raises the question of knowledge in reference to its object, foundations, and aims as a problematic. He expands on it in his Qur'anic exegesis, as will be seen in the next chapter of this book. Here, Quṭb dismisses philosophy in general—and Islamic philosophy in particular—because of the perceived contradiction between philosophy, as a rational human endeavor, and revelation, as divine parole. Quṭb's argument about the incompatibility of religion and philosophy—that is, Islam and Islamic philosophy—creates a problem for the modern Muslim mind. In order to elucidate this question, let us turn to the following important definition of philosophy. For example, according to Hegel,

> The object of religion as well as of philosophy is eternal truth in its objectivity, God and nothing but God, and the explication

> of God. Philosophy is not the wisdom of the world, but it is knowledge of what is not of the world; it is not knowledge which concerns external mass, or empirical existence and life, but it is knowledge of that which is eternal, of what God is, and flows out of His nature.[99]

This appraisal of the role of philosophy can, in some measure at least, characterize the object of philosophy as understood by the Muslims in the formative phase.

In this period, the Quṭbian religious project takes a definite shape. It is a project that aspires to reestablish religious foundations that seem, if scrutinized correctly, to contradict directly the cultural and intellectual project of Nasserism which was in the making at the time, and which reached its peak with the reform of the Azhar and the different socialist laws enunciated in the famous 1962 *mīthāq*.[100] Before us stand two cultural projects. The first is represented and sanctioned by the state and was consequently promoted for popular consumption. The second is represented by the master theoretician Sayyid Quṭb and, pushed to the secret recesses of Egyptian culture, it was, therefore, not available for mass consumption. Quṭb poses the question of God mainly as (1) a response to the loss of the religious certainties in Egyptian society, and (2) a result of the peripheralization of religion by the nascent nationalist and socialist thought of the Egyptian revolution. In a very real and ominous sense, the Nasserite project posed a direct threat and challenge to the revivalist project of Quṭb.

Quṭb laments the serious deviation of doctrine and rule witnessed in Islamic history. One can read this cry against deviation as either criticism of a communal consciousness that wore itself out, or as a response to a loss of collective imagination in an age of uncertainty and secular rationality. It is also a call for the establishment of a new dynamic community-consciousness, a new imagined community, and a new vanguard that can shoulder the pain and the suffering of Islam in the modern age. In Quṭb's mind, the formulation of this new consciousness runs counter to the limited and limiting Arab nationalist consciousness.

In spite of the divergent views of the Nasserite project and the Quṭbian one, they surprisingly share a number of things in common. Both were born, to a large extent, in the shadow of colonialism and Westernization, and both opposed these two factors, especially in their capitalist expressions.

Seen against this background, the argument that the Quṭbian discourse of the 1950s is a pirated copy of either the Mawdūdī movement or Ibn Taymiyah's of the thirteenth century is unjustifiable. This argument cannot be supported by the foundations that gave rise to the Quṭbian problematic in the 1950s—Nasserism in particular, and the challenges posed by Arab nationalism and socialism in general. The Quṭbian discourse developed dialectically against the background of Nasserism and its hegemonic proliferation in Egyptian society. Challenged by Nasserism, Quṭb, in the words of Yvonne Haddad, "moved from a stance of an observer and interpreter of society, reflecting on its currents of thoughts and goals, to a revolutionary who charted the vision of a new order to which he wanted to lead all people. Having been disillusioned by all other solutions he formulated his own, grounded in the Qur'anic vision yet relevant for the everyday life of Muslims in the Arab world."[101]

Chapter 6

Qur'anic Contents of Sayyid Quṭb's Thought

The person, writing these lines, has spent forty years of his life reading books and researching almost all aspects of human knowledge. Then he turned to the fountainhead of his religion and doctrine. He discovered that whatever he had read so far was indeed minute in comparison with the colossal stock [of the Islamic heritage]. He does not, however, regret spending forty years of his life in the pursuit of these sciences. He became cognizant of the nature, deviation, minuteness, pomp, and noise of jāhiliyah. *He now realizes that no Muslim should combine these two sources-divine and* jāhilī- *in his education.*

—*S. Quṭb,* Mā'alim fī al-ṭarīq *(Beirut 1973) 143–144. See also, Quṭb,* Milestones, *tr. M. Siddiqui (Kuwait 1989) 210–211*

The intention of the present chapter is to prepare an analysis of the main principles, foundations, and questions of Sayyid Quṭb's Qur'anic exegesis. A comprehensive analysis of those principles has become necessary in light of the controversy surrounding the intellectual underpinnings of Islamic revivalism, its political inclinations in general, and the Quṭbian discourse in particular. It has already been established by other scholars that Quṭb is the main ideologue of contemporary Muslim resurgence in the Arab world. Therefore, it is necessary to embark upon a systematic explanation and critique of his Qur'anic ideas.[1]

One must see Quṭb's Qur'anic exegesis as a unique attempt to give a consistent and exhaustive answer to the malaise of Islam and

Muslims in the modern period. In other words, the Quṭbian project takes its mature conceptual shape with the *Fī Ẓilāl al-Qur'ān*[2] (hereafter referred to simply as *Ẓilāl*), and he gives to the question "What is to be done?" intellectual as well as organizational responses.[3] His thought, which was subject to a complex set of influences, attempted a definite break with what was perceived to be secular and nationalist patterns of thought and culture. Whether that was successful depends on the alternatives given by Quṭb, and the degree to which they have been followed by his disciples and admirers. Further, to give an indication of Quṭb's intellectual bearing, one might point out that a good deal of the radical Islamist organizations and groups that were mushrooming in Egypt in the post-Nasser era, drew their inspiration and derived their theological or Qur'anic interpretations from Quṭb's *Ẓilāl*, especially from specific excerpts published under the title of *Mā'alim fī al-ṭarīq* (*Signposts* or *Milestones*).[4] Although his life came to a tragic end as a result of the encounter between the Muslim Brotherhood and the Egyptian state in the 1950s and 1960s, the same problems and questions raised by Quṭb in his different works—and especially in *Ẓilāl*—have, by no means, been eradicated or ameliorated. On the contrary, they have gained a new presence in the intellectual and cultural landscape of the contemporary Arab world, especially in light of the recent Western encroachment upon the Middle East.

Finally—and in retrospect—Quṭb's execution proved to be a continuous embarrassment to the Nasser regime mainly because Quṭb was challenged, not so much intellectually and religiously, as psychologically and physically. In certain ways, Quṭb is more feared in his death than he was in his life.[5]

Questions of Method in *Ẓilāl*

A complicated work often begs the question of how to interpret it both effectively and fairly. This question becomes specially pivotal and more urgent in view of the fact that the text before us is not a simple literary work, but a multifaceted one dealing with a great variety issues and questions of social, political, religious, and cultural concern. In other words, as an interpreter of the text, I am not concerned with the autonomy of the work per se, but with the proper historical context in which it was written, and the aim or aims that it purported to achieve.

In explicating a text, and "[i]n order to know what degree or kind of exactness is required for the understanding of a given writing, one must therefore first know the author's habits of writing."[6] From a careful reading of his earlier writings, and as previously noted, Quṭb made a rare transition in the modern intellectual history of the Arab world from a secular man of letters to a committed religious ideologue and critic. Also, to a large extent, after his conversion to Islam, he labored under the burden of a number of fundamental questions, including imperialism, nationalism, religion, and more. The heart of the *Ẓilāl* is an elaboration of the same questions, but in a totally different era—that of ascendant nationalism and descendant Ikhwan. Here, the Quṭbian project faces a formidable challenge at the level of its conception of knowledge, the meaning of the *ummah*, the function of religion, and the role of the Islamically engaged person under the gradually spreading umbrella of nationalism.

In a large measure, the Quṭbian project is formulated in negation to the hegemony of Nasserism at this stage. It is an elaboration of why the Islamic ideology must take a different course, and how to achieve major objectives in uncertain and critical times. In that sense, one would agree with the following formulation of a Quṭbian disciple who maintains that "the principal goal of the Qur'ān as understood by Quṭb is dynamic, pragmatic, and alive. It purports to rebuild the Muslim personality, the Muslim community, and the Muslim society."[7] This rebuilding, however, is done in negation to a certain status quo.

Quṭb's driving force behind writing the *Ẓilāl* is an obsession with method, doctrine, or *'aqīdah* that must, in his view, pave the way for the reconstruction of Islam, and find the solution for the malaise of modern Muslims. "Sayyid Quṭb," said Ṣalāḥ al-Dīn al-Jourshī, a contemporary Tunisian critic of the Quṭbian legacy, "immersed himself completely for a period of ten years in unlocking the meanings of the Qur'anic texts, while in a state of total distance from his environment. The fact that he spent that time in prison and the prison's hospital was instrumental in enabling him to get rid of all the deposits of his early [secular] culture."[8]

The same view is corroborated by Emmanuel Sivan. "Quṭb's [Qur'anic] ideas matured during his nine years in prison. The prison experience was to be, in effect, crucial in the making of most of the other New Radicals as well."[9]

Prison seems to have exerted a double effect of incarcerating the person physically but emancipating him religiously—making him discover the pure source of his religion. That is exactly what happens with Quṭb who develops a strong critique of society on the basis of his Qur'anic vision, which is distilled from his painful prison experience.

Quṭb's habits of writing change dramatically with the *Ẓilāl*. He no longer refers to Western or secular sources, but stresses the need for undergoing a major process of training in the footsteps of the first generation in Islam. It is necessary, he declares, to drink solely from the spring of the Qur'ān. Thus, the Qur'ān, and not Western sources of knowledge, becomes the criterion. Quṭb recounts a story in *Milestones* of an Algerian writer, Malek Bennabi, who used Western criteria to judge Quṭb's writings. Quṭb was prey to the same influences.

> Until then [perhaps the early 1950s], I had not gotten rid of the cultural influences which had penetrated my mind in spite of my Islamic attitudes and inclinations. The source of these influences was foreign—alien to my Islamic consciousness—yet these influences had clouded my intuitions and conceptions. The Western concept of civilization was my criterion; it had prevented me from seeing with clear and penetrating vision.[10]

As mentioned earlier, Quṭb's active intellectual career spanned a period of at least thirty four years, during which he lived in the shadow of two distinct political regimes, each of which had a unique relationship with Western colonialism: (1) The Fārūq monarchy, and (2) Nasserism. In his long intellectual career, Quṭb went through a systematic transformation in his literary interests, philosophical arguments, and religious objectives. It is clear however that Quṭb's main objective behind writing the *Ẓilāl* is not to elevate Arabic literary criticism to the status of a discipline, or Qur'anic studies to a mere hermeneutical field. Rather, as the main ideologue of the Ikhwan in the 1950s and 1960s, what Quṭb had in mind was committing the religious text to certain objectives. In general, what one witnesses is an overall shift in emphasis from the literary and aesthetic forms of expression to the social and idoelogical dimensions of Islam. In line with the basic arguments of modernist Muslims exegetes such as Muḥammad ʿAbduh and Rashīd Riḍā, Sayyid Quṭb pursued a double intention of (1) interepreting the Qur'ān as the sacred text par excellence, and (2) advancing his religious claims and views which, to a large extent, conflicted with those of the status quo.

As already suggested, the *Ẓilāl* is shaped by the experience of a tormented, agonized, alienated, yet committed social and religious critic. The relationship between religion and society, therefore, takes a primary importance. The heart of this relationship reflects the often painful debates in the modern Arab and Muslim cultural scene about the proper relationship between the intelligentsia, on the one hand, and the state, religion, politics, freedom, and social justice on the other. In essence, Sayyid Quṭb is an intellectual in search of ultimate values and guiding principles in times of crisis. In the process of this search, he becomes committed to a religious and political organization that has immediate and less universal goals than might have been thought.

Quṭb proved to be a lonely intellectual with a tragic personality, perhaps much more so than was Ḥasan al-Bannā before him. Just like al-Bannā, Quṭb was an unceasing critic of society and state, on the one hand, while, on the other, he was the mirror that reflected the pain and suffering of all that had gone wrong in modern Muslim societies.[11] Quṭb delcares philosophy unfit to execute the necessary task of critique and deconstruction, taking religion and society as the new ground of political and cultural criticism. In this context, he pursues the question of his cultural identity while lending his intellectual authority to the political leadership of the Ikhwan.

That the text is political in nature is a given, because most of it was written while the author was in jail resulting from his disapproval of the post-1952 Egyptian nation/state.[12] Then, what does that say about the nonpolitical ideas of the text? Is there an asymmetrical relationship between purely political ideas, for instance, and purely literary, social, or religious concepts and thoughts?

Following in the footsteps of Fredric Jameson,[13] Edward Said,[14] and Robert D'Amico,[15] I would argue that knowledge cannot be produced in a vacuum. It must be subject to historical, social, and political influences and tastes. Frederic Jameson, for instance, argues that, in interpreting a certain text, one must give priority to "political interpretation." Edward Said, on the other hand, contends that the distinction between pure and political knowledge is a shallow academic adventure. "What I am interested in doing . . . is suggesting how the general liberal consensus that 'true' knowledge is fundamentally not political (and conversely, that overtly political knowledge is 'true' knowledge) obscures the highly if obscurely organized political circumstances obtaining when knowledge is produced."[16]

That the Quṭbian discourse at this stage is political in nature must not elude any intelligent observer. At the heart of this discourse, however, is Quṭb's theological and philosophical formulations that concern the question of knowledge, as referred to in the previous paragraph.

In order to gain proper understanding of Quṭb's political and religious objectives, one must examine in great depth the key terms and concepts which Quṭb employs in his Qur'anic exegesis. To do so, we must take the following factors into account: (1) the semantics of

Quṭb's Qur'anic exegesis, and (2) the relationship of semantics vis-à-vis the cultural and political environment.

To start with, what is semantics? Is it also a necessary factor in explicating the Quṭbian Qur'anic discourse? According to Izutsu, semantics is inescapable in treating any Qur'anic exegesis. He maintains that "each individual word [of the Qur'anic text], taken separately, has its own basic meaning or conceptual content on which it will keep its hold even if we take the word out of its . . . context."[17] Furthermore, key words possess a relational meaning, which, in turn, presupposes a constellation of relationships in the Qur'anic text that must be investigated in order to acquire the intended meaning or meanings. This semantic and conceptual framework can elucidate the meaning of key concepts that very often have multiple relations.

> Vocabulary, far from being a homogeneous plane, consists of a great number—or rather, we should say, an indefinite number—of strata of associative connections or spheres of conceptual association, each one of which corresponds to a predominant interest of a community in a given period of history and thus epitomizes some aspects of its ideals, aspirations and preoccupations . . . Vocabulary, in short, is a multi-strata structure.[18]

The semantics of Quṭb's exegesis do reflect the conceptual foundations of his *Weltanschauung*, aims, and methods. Therefore, one possible method would be to isolate the key terms underlying Quṭb's Qur'anic terminology. This is necessary, as a primary stage, because Quṭb's exegesis revolves around a multiplicity of key terms such as *jāhiliyah*, revolution (*thawrah*), dynamism (*ḥarakiyah*), migration (*hijrah*), state (*dawlah*), and so on. One must stress that Quṭb's interpretation is based primarily on the following factors: (1) philological understanding; (2) the primary social and political situation of the verses or conditions of the revelation; and (3) the present meaning that can be derived from the other two factors. As such, Quṭb's theoretical reflections gain a new significance. Far from restricting himself to philology and past meaning, he is concerned about the relevance of the Qur'anic text to the present.

Quṭb is preoccupied, more or less, with four broad objectives in the *Ẓilāl*: (1) correct interpretation of the nature of God; (2) proper understanding of the role of man as the vicegerent of God; (3) the viability of the Qur'ān as a comprehensive system of guidance and knowledge for the modern Muslim; and (4) the necessity of establishing a just and ethical social order.[19]

Quṭb's method rests on a number of interdependent principles, including theology, philosophy, sociology, politics, and hermeneutics. Experience also plays a significant part in his methodological construct. Therefore, one must relate to the expressions which he puts forward as part of a whole stream of consciousness emanating from the historical experience of such a religious figure in a highly diversified intellectual context. Hence, once and again, Quṭb emphasizes his oft-cited dictum, of "contemporary Muslims will perceive the essence of the Qur'ān only through reflection and experience." This is primarily because of the intersection of the personal and the epistemological from his early work, and his late experience.

Quṭb's Understanding of the Origins of Islam

As noted in the previous section, the single most important intellectual influence on Quṭb's life and thought in the Nasser era is the Qur'ān. Quṭb sees the present as pregnant with possibilities similar to those which gave birth to Islam in seventh-century Arabia. The Qur'ān was the conceptual vehicle of a universal revolution. It is necessary to retrieve this potential and amalgamate the revolutionary message of Islam into current conditions. Quṭb makes no attempt at all to compromise with the current social order.

Quṭb maintains that pre-Islamic Arabian society was characterized by social injustice, religious diversity, immorality, and lack of social solidarity in general. He believes that the Qur'ān was a revolutionary document that transformed the nomadic Arab from a primitive social, religious, and intellectual state to that of urban civilization.[20] The first Muslim generation, in both Mecca and Medina, refused to accept defeat, as have the Muslims of modern times.[21]

Quṭb draws a comparison between the Islam of Mecca and modern Islam. What are, therefore, the major characteristics of Meccan Islam, and how are they relevant to the present situation, according to Quṭb?[22] In both cases, he argues, Islam is under siege—the building of *'aqīdah*, a distinguishing mark of the early phase of Islam, is incomplete. Olivier Carre points out that, according to Quṭb, "Meccan Qur'ān is nothing more than a revolution (*thawrah*) of conscience, and doctrine which was an introduction to everything that followed: the ethical, political, legal and social order."[23] The Medinan phase—although fundamentally distinguished from the Meccan one in that Muslims were able to secure political power and social prestige—was an expansion of the Meccan phase in terms of doctrinal and religious preparedness. While in Mecca, Muslims were not in a position to imagine themselves as a secure and strong *ummah*. They were still swimming in an ocean of ignorance and uncertainty.

What helps Muslims in Meccan Islam to overcome their fear and stand steadfast facing the ocean of ignorance was a divine miracle in the form of the Qur'ān. Quṭb is emphatic in pointing out that the Qur'ān presented Islam as a serious, dynamic, and pragmatic doctrine.[24] Muslims were "given a doctrine, and an ethic which was a reflection of this doctrine."[25] Therefore, the initial edifice of the Muslim *ummah*—its raison d'etre, so to speak—was its ability to imagine itself both doctrinally and ethically. That imagining, however, stood in a dialectical relationship to the reality of pre-Islamic Arabia. It was, to a large extent, an outcome of negation. In this regard, Quṭb notes, "Indeed the very nature of this Religion demanded that the Holy Qur'ān should limit its message to the question of faith during the Meccan period. Quite ostensibly, the entire religion hinges on the concept of the Unity of God."[26] However, Quṭb does not argue on behalf of static faith or mere remembrance in Sufi manner, for example, of the bounties of God and the day of judgment. His call transcends the ethical boundaries of Islam, and, instead, we find him totally absorbed in the revolutionary aspect of both the Qur'ān and the dynamic historical gestation of Islam.

Likewise, the only way for the modern Muslim *ummah*—which has been extinct for a few centuries—to revive itself and rebuild its religious foundations is to take itself back to that initial Meccan phase, before any legislation was given. Therefore, "The supporters of the modern Islamic Movement must understand that when they summon people to reestablish this religion, they have to summon them first to commit themselves to *ʿaqīdah*."[27]

In its thirteen years of the Meccan state, the Qur'ān did not treat *ʿaqīdah* as a theory, nor as an eccelesiatical argument, but as a pragmatic need, because the Qur'ān was waging a battle in an actual situation. "In the process of building the *ʿaqīdah* in the conscience of the Muslim community, the Qur'ān was waging a huge battle (*maʿrakah dakhmah*) against *Jāhiliyah* and its surroudings."[28] Building the *ʿaqīdah* and establishing the community went hand in hand. In Quṭb's opinion, a theoretical and ideological growth, if not translated into practice, does not reflect the spirit of Islam as a practical religion.[29] Further, he maintains that *ʿaqīdah* should be the weapon of the modern movement.

> It is necessary that those who are behind the Islamic movement should comprehend the nature of this religion and its method of

> dynamism as we have already shown. They should also know that the long process of building the *'aqīdah* in the Meccan phase was integral to another process—that of the practical build-up of the Islamic movement.[30]

Therefore, *'aqīdah* and dynamism constitute the basis of early Islam. These thoughts of Quṭb resonate with what Fazlur Rahman had to say, years later, about Meccan Islam.

> The early Islamic literature strongly suggests that the Prophet was not a pan-legist. For one thing, it can be concluded a priori that the Prophet, who was, until his death, engaged in a grim moral and political struggle against the Meccans and the Arabs and in organizing his community/state, could hardly have found time to lay down rules for the minutiae of life. Indeed, the Muslim community went about its normal business and did its day-to-day transactions, settling their normal business disputes by themselves in the light of commonsense and on the basis of their customs which, after certain modifications, were left intact by the Prophet. It was only in cases that became especially acute that the Prophet was called upon to decide and in certain cases the Qur'ān had to intervene. Mostly such cases were of an ad hoc nature and were treated informally and in an ad hoc manner.[31]

Quṭb argues that the real battle facing Muḥammad and his disciples, in the process of building the *'aqīdah* in the hearts of early Muslims, revolved around the notion of *ḥākimiyah* (God's sovereignty).[32] It is important to point out that Quṭb treats this whole issue in the context of the prevailing social classes in Mecca at the time. Meccan society was made up of the following classes: (1) merchants; (2) a religious hierarchy controlled by priests, who belonged to the first class; and (3) commoners who did not control their destinies.[33] This class structure, besides being unequal and oppressive, stood en masse against the proliferation of the Divine notion of life, and persecuted the early generation of Muslims.

What made the transition so impressive was Islam, which "transformed them into a rightly guided, wise, learned, and experienced leadership leading the whole humanity."[34] With little awareness of complex societies and civilizations, nomadic Arabs were only fit to lead a tribal-based desert life. Islam was a religion of transformation using the Qur'ān as its conceptual and ideological weapon, and the Mosque as its concrete and central place of learning. "The Prophet's Masjid, where the Qur'ān and the Qur'anic guidances were recited, became the large university that trained and graduated that [distinguished] generation of Muslims who led humanity in a wise and guided way—this leadership which the whole human history has not created yet."[35] Islam, therefore, interacted with a grim situation, and that interaction led to fantastic results—namely, the expansion of the social, political, and intellectual consciousness of the Arabs.

'Aqīdah, translated into *'ibādah* (worship of God), summarizes, in a nutshell, the foundations of early Islam. In this regard, Quṭb comments sadly on the later evolution of Islamic jurisprudence which, in his view, blurred the central position of *'aqīdah* in Islam. Jurists of the second and third centuries of Islam, he argues, developed a juridical system which divided social life into (1) forms of worship (*'ibādāt*) and rites, and (2) social transactions (*mu'āmalāt*). This division became an anomaly because some Muslims, blinded by the wealth which they accrued in this life, inevitably forgot the orginial menaing of *'ibādah* as the culmination of *'aqīdah*. Worse yet, others tended to draw a clear-cut distinction between *'ibādāt* and *mu'āmalāt*. "This divison, with the progress of time, has made some people think that their Islamicity would be decided on the basis of *'ibādāt* alone, while they are engaged in *mu'āmalāt* on the basis of another system."[36]

Medinan Phase

As noted in the previous section, Quṭb's thought, as displayed in *Ẓilāl*, is preoccupied with genesis, gestation, process, and transition. In this context, he discusses the importance of the *Baqarah* chapter in the Qur'ān, revealed in the aftermath of migration, and its relevance to the then-present conditions of the Muslim community. Quṭb contends that this chapter contains principles and guidelines which reflect the Muslim community in transition and struggle. Essentially, this chapter revolves around one axis, although it contains many themes. On the one hand, there is the attitude of Jews toward the Islamic revelation. On the other, the chapter discusses the circumstances of "the nascent early Muslim community, which was being prepared to carry the trust of calling and vicegerency."[37] Quṭb emphasizes the notion that these circumstances of hardship and conflict which accompanied the Muslim message, "have always manifested themsleves under different circumstances and times, which make the Qur'ānic guidelines the constitution of this eternal call."[38] Quṭb says that the decision of the Prophet to send his early followers to Medina led to a de facto "freezing of the *da'wah* (call) in Mecca, although a number of people continued to accept Islam."[39] The Prophet's major priority and preoccupation was to locate a new place where *'aqīdah* is given a free hand, thus liberating it from the political and social constraints which it faced in Mecca. Furthermore, the small-scale *hijras* attempted by Muslims before the large-scale emigration to Medina represented the repeated efforts of early Muslims to "find an independent and secure base of operation."[40] As a result of facing this formidable set of circumstances, a distinguished class of Muslims (*Tabaqā mumtāza min al-muslimīn*), both immigrant and native allies, was created.

The essential difference between the Meccan phase and the Medinian one is a matter of emphasis. The Meccan is distinguished by its doctrinal revolution, while the Medinan is marked by its legislation and application of the primary concepts of the *'aqīdah*. The *Baqarah* chapter—the first chapter to be revealed to Muḥammad after the *hijrah*—contains a number of legislative acts. In this regard, Quṭb affirms that the Qur'ān is "a dynamic and lively document,"[41] aimed, from the beginning, to create an Islamically based society through establishing "a unique conception (*taṣṣawur khāṣṣ*), a unique system, and a unique society. . . . [further] its aim was to establish a new *umma* on earth, an *ummah* who possesses a special function in leading humanity and who would establish a unique societal model unparralled in history."[42] Theory had to become practice, and dynamism had to become the real soul of this society. "The Qur'ān establishes dynamism (*ḥarakiyah*) in the Muslim consciousness and life."[43] Furthermore, it is the source of both Islamic intellectualism and Islamic activism.

Muslims in Medina could conceive of themselves as one *ummah* on the basis of their bond and new environment. They did distance themselves from the sea of *jāhiliyah*, only as a prelude to dismantling it. Their true guide to life, once they are settled in Medina, is the Qur'ān that "faces a real situation . . . and thus moves the Muslim community forward."[44] In the Meccan phase, Muslims were restrained from waging *jihād* against the enemies of Islam only as a precautionary step—Muslims needed time to secure their belief and install the *'aqīdah* in their hearts. In addition, Muslims had both the time and freedom to spread their message.[45] According to Quṭb, the Qur'ān gave a similar restraining order not to wage *jihād* during the first few years in Medina after the migration. Commenting on the reasons behind this, Quṭb makes the following points: (1) no *jihād* was ordered at this stage because of the no-war pact that Muhammad had signed with the Jews and others; (2) Muslims could spread their message freely; and (3) the Prophet and his military leaders chose to face the military might of Quraysh, the heart of real *jāhiliyah*, without any distractions on the home front.[46]

It should be noted, however, that Quṭb's assessment of both the Meccan and Medinan phases contrasts sharply with that of classical orientalism. Ignaz Goldziher, for instance, offers an opposite view about doctrine, state building, and *jihād*.

> Islam extended itself into the larger world by means of external power before its fundamental doctrines had crystalized and taken on definite form, before even the first lines of its practical life had been given definite shape. Those who participated in this expansion of Islam (or, more accurately, this effort to conquer the world) were Muslims who had not yet incorporated Islam into their consciousness to any substantial degree. Islam for them was a battle cry more than it was a doctrine. The Qur'ān itself was known only to a small minority of those who fought so successfully for the victory of the word of God in Syria, Babylon, Persia, and Egypt.[47]

In Quṭb's opinion, the migration of the Prophet and his companions to Medina is not a culmination of an arduous journey, but the beginning of one. Here, Quṭb portrays the Qur'ān as an ideological text that meshes with the concrete day-to-day activities of Muslims and shapes their lives to a large extent.

> And since the Muslim community (*al-jamā'ah al-muslimah*) in Medina is on the verge of undergoing a hard *jihād* in order to realize God's system (*minhāj*) on earth . . . the Qur'ān initiates a process of spiritual build-up . . . and establishes correct criteria by which it can estimate accurately the values of this battle.[48]

However, life, even at its best, warns Quṭb, is a form of *balā'*, or plight. Life is a dialectical process,

> It is necessary to train humans against the backdrop of plight (*balā'*). The believers realize the costs of their adhering to *'aqīdah* only after they undergo the test of insistence upon the battle for justice, and after they undergo fear, hardship, hunger, poverty, and a loss of [their] selves.[49]

In addition to paying high costs for raising the banner of the *ʿaqīdah*, the intention of the Qur'ān during the early formation of the Muslim *ummah*, in both its Meccan and Medinan sides, is to create a determined and strong leadership, and to elevate this leadership above any human desire, worldly pursuit, wealth, fame, or success. In short, the goal was to build "absolute devotion, commitment, and devotion to God and His call."[50]

In this context, Quṭb comments with great insight on the battle of Uḥud, which the Muslims lost. In explaining the causes of Muslim defeat, he concludes that, at the time the battle took place, the process of psychological and doctrinal preparedness was uncomplete. Failing to obey the Prophet's orders, some Muslim fighters fell prey to "a movement of psychological retreat (*ḥarakat irtidād nafsiyah*)."[51] Therefore, Quṭb reminds us that the Qur'ān's emphasis upon long and arduous education is one of the features of the Medinan Qur'ān. By the time the process of divine training was complete, "The new call moved their souls deeply and seeped into their depth, and led to a complete emotional and psychological coup (*inqilāb shuʿurī wa nafsī*). The end result was that they cut off themselves completely from the *jāhiliyah*."[52] Therefore, on the basis of the Qur'ān, Quṭb defines Islam "as a complete divorce (*insilākh*) from *jāhiliyah*."[53]

What are the problems facing the newly emerging Muslim society in Medina? The early Muslim community, according to Quṭb, was not immune to facing an inevitable conflict with (1) "the deviant doctrines of the Arabian Peninsula,"[54] and (2) the Medinan Jews, as a representative of another monotheistic tradition. Quṭb claims that it was in the interest of Medinan Jews to wage a fierce campaign against Islam because of their prestigious social position. They used a multitude of tactics to "shake off [the Muslim] belief and destroy the Muslim ranks."[55] Quṭb discusses the objective economic, social, and religious circumstances which led to conflict between Muslims and Jews at this early stage of the Islamic community. The first was that Arabian Jews occupied a distinguished place in the tribal system of Medina, especially because of their feeling of superiority vis-a-vis the illiterate Bedouin who did not possess any sacred book. The second circumstance was that they started to feel threatened by the initial victories achieved by Muslims and, consequently, felt isolated from a society in which they had practiced "their commercial and intellectual leadership."[56] Quṭb believes strongly that the conflict between Jews and Muslims—in the past as well as in the present—has revolved mainly around issues of doctrine and belief.[57]

Because of its tremendous emphasis on establishing a novel creed (*'aqīdah jadīdah*), a new knowledge of God, and a new conception of life, and additional emphasis on internalizing them in the early Muslim generation, it was inevitable that Islam would engage in a head-on conflict with the foundations of *jāhiliyah*, both inside and of outside of Arabia.[58] In Quṭb's view, one must see early Muslim expansion as a reflection of the strength and inner formation (*binā' dākhilī*). "It was a doctrinal, cultural, and civilizational expansion"[59] and, thus, it was a culmination "of complete human superiority . . . It was a declaration of a new birth of man: the birth of a new man never seen before."[60]

Mecca and Medina and the Imagination of Today's Islamists

One must not mistake Quṭb's discussion of early Islam for a futile intellectual exercise, nor merely a religious piece of propaganda. Quṭb's point of departure is the troublesome question of "What is to be done?" in order to rectify the malaise of modern Muslims, and face the challenges of nationalism and secularism. Integral to this problematic of the Quṭbian project is a certain consciousness of history, and a selective way of seeing the early history of Islam. History is the product of doctrine more than it is of human beings and environments. Doctrine is the single most important instigator of events, peoples, and ideas.

In light of the previous discussion, one is tempted to raise a number of questions. What constitutes a Muslim *ummah*, nation, and society in the modern time, and what is the difference between the Muslim *ummah* and *jāhiliyah*? What methods must be used to uplift the status of the *ummah*? Who will carry out this revival? Finally, what happens if revival is not achieved?

Quṭb's bone of contention—and the gist of his thinking on the predicament of modern Muslims—revolves around the fundamental question of what constitutes a Muslim *ummah* or a nation in the modern sense of the term. This Quṭbian formulation of "what constitutes a nation?" is deeply steeped in history—namely, in the modern history of the Muslim world—which, in his understanding, had been in a state of pervasive decline for centuries. As the ex-secular thinker and the risk-taking ideologue, Quṭb is torn by the implications of this decline, and what it means to reconstitute the *ummah* from a state of nothingness. To a large extent, the state of decline he describes is synonymous with *jāhiliyah*. In other words, in his evaluation of the meaning and historical implications of *jāhiliyah* in the *Ẓilāl*, Quṭb refers to the spread of political and social division, the ascendance of the tribal and regional mentality, and the prevalence of social and moral malaise in modern Muslim societies.[61] He acknowledges that he faces a *muhimmah dakhmah* or a huge task in a literal sense. This colossal task centers around freeing the Muslims from a mountain of wrong notions, man-made values and traditions, false laws and constitutions, and the ocean of modern *jāhiliyah*.

Condemning all secular and nationalist ideologies—for they "base their sovereignty on the servitude of man to another man"—Quṭb defines the central pieces of his imagined *ummah*, *ʿaqīdah*, and its historical agent, the Islamic shariʿāh. One must not apply the components of the modern nation/state—as in territoriality, ethnicity, and sovereignty—to the Islamic *ummah*, "The fatherland is that place where the Islamic faith, the Islamic way of life, and the Shariʿāh of God is [sic] dominant."[62]

As a thought developing in negation to the status quo, and examining afresh the early historical experience of the Prophet and his companions, Quṭb's thesis refuses to give credence to the crushing pressure of modern *jāhiliyah*, and the fact that it permeates every aspect of modern Muslim society. It strikes an optimistic note in that a diagnosis is offered, and a certain technical solution is found for the predicament of decline. Quṭb's courageous diagnosis of *jāhiliyah* is the first step that led him to face the gallows. He comments with brutal, shocking, and perhaps unrealistic sarcasm on the contemporary state of Muslims.

> We are also surrounded by *jāhiliyah* today, which is of the same nature as it was during the first period of Islam, perhaps a little deeper. Our whole environment, people's beliefs and ideas, habits and art, rules and laws—is *jāhiliyah*, even to the extent that what we consider to be Islamic culture, Islamic sources, Islamic philosophy, and Islamic thought, are also constructs of *jāhiliyah*.[63]

What a brutal condemnation! What a rift between revolutionary Nasserism and revolutionary Islam! The incompatibility and the collision are more than real on the theoretical plane. Modern *jāhiliyah* is a little more pernicious and deeper than the pre-Islamic one.

Quṭb's answer is perhaps simpler than his diagnosis of the grim situation of modern Muslims. A vanguard, as seen in the preceding chapter, must emerge. It must cut itself off from the modern *jāhiliyah*, its norms, and theory of knowledge. The vanguard must go back to the Qur'ān to quench its thirst for knowledge. It must train itself with patient perseverance while alerting itself to the dangers and difficulties posed by *jāhiliyah*. *Jāhiliyah* will fight us. The price will be extremely high. We must be ready to pay the price so that we can carry the banner of Islam and free society from all sorts of servitude—except that to God and oppression.

Quṭb believes that the *ummah* has always been under pressure by all sorts of enemies, and that the only solution for the predicament of the modern *ummah* is to use the Qur'ān.

> The battle, like the one [faced by early Muslims] is still going on since the human self is unchanging and the enemies are the same as before. The Qur'ān is present in our midst, and there is no salvation for the human soul and the Muslim *ummah* except when employing this Qur'ān in the battle, so it can wage in a live and complete way as it did in the past. If Muslims do not realize this fact, no success will ever take place.[64]

The pure Muslim vanguard is a must in a sea of competing philosophies and doctrines. To establish this notion, at least theoretically, Quṭb insists on a certain formulation of early Islam—that of Mecca and Medina, and that of trial and error, hardships and migrations, fights and ordeals, and failure and success. The Qur'ān must be understood, not for the sake of accumulating more knowledge or its artistic beauty, but for the sake of a personal and political revolution. There is no room for a defeatist mentality. There is no room for more *uḥuds*, more retreats, and more resignation to the current state of affairs. The construction must follow this ideological diagnosis.

What sort of people is the vanguard made up of? Quṭb devotes a section of the *Ẓilāl* to answer this question. Like a true liberation theologian, Quṭb exhorts the weak, both men and women, to discover the immense sources of power which they possess, and to rise against the oppressive status quo. He reminds the poor of the early phase of Islam when the poor of Mecca and Medina joined the new religion, and he admonishes them to cease being "an appendage to the arrogant and the oppressors."[65] However, did not Nasser's nationalism address the same social forces in society? Did it not speak in the name of socialism and egalitarianism? Quṭb has no answer. Instead, he elaborates on the role of the oppressors in Muslim history, and he stipulates that oppression and arrogance have been intertwined. The arrogant have always rejected the Qur'ān as the truth. Instead, they associate it with mythology (*khurāfa*).[66] Also, excessive wealth leads to moral and sexual corruption in society and to more abuse of power. The poor have always taken the initiative and joined new religious movements, because they have nothing to lose.[67]

To summarize these points, in his call for revival, Quṭb is critically engaged in a two-dimensional process of deconstruction and reconstruction. This complex process is characeterized by three main notions.

(1) His call for the dismantling of the sources of non-Islamic knowledge in Muslim societies is accompanied by a call for the rejuvenation of the primary sources of Islamic knowledge—namely, the Qur'ān and the *Ḥadīth*. Quṭb argues that Prophet limited his companions to one source of knowledge, so that they would be united in intention, direction, and telos.

(2) Because the Qur'ān prescribes praxis in addition to theoretical knowledge, it is necessary that the new Muslim vanguard should be aware of the practical applications of Islam as a way of life.

(3) Finally, as a consequence, the pioneers must sever any ties they may have with all aspects of *jāhiliyah*.

Toward a Philosophy of a Counter Movement: *Fitnah* and Oppression in the *Ẓilāl*

One can easily notice a disquieting trend of analysis among a significant number of authors writing on the social, ideological, and intellectual history of the Ikhwan in the 1950s and 1960s, especially when dealing with the thought of Sayyid Quṭb.[68] All these authors rush to the argument that the fountainhead of Quṭb's arguments in this period is *jāhiliyah* and his condemnation of modernity. They simply and inconclusively reduce a whole complex process of thought, developing against many variables and facing many challenges, to the Islam/*jāhiliyah*/modernity trichotomy. In brief, Quṭb's thought is seen to be antiestablishment, be it religious or secular.

Although Quṭb knows that, at this stage of the late 1950s, his ideal of establishing an Islamic political system is far from realization—mainly because of the ideological hegemony of the Egyptian nation/state—he nevertheless posits the rules for Islamic activism. He argues that a Muslim has a right of political resistance. The *'ulamā'* are anxious to preserve an archaic Islam which is no longer compatible with the process of modern history. The *'ulamā'* inculcate political and intellectual passivity, and promote a false sense of security in face of the dangers surrounding modern Muslims.

The Qur'ān is replete with verses treating the subject of *fitnah* and its impact on early Muslims. Fully aware that the nationalist and secularist system which he is seeking to abolish will fight back, Quṭb sheds some light on the meaning of *fitnah* for the modern Muslim activist.

The notion of *fitnah* permeates the entire text of the *Ẓilāl*. In the words of Olivier Carre, "The notion of *fitnah*, which means seduction, sedition, and persecution, plays a major role in the *Ẓilāl*."[69] In the preceding section, we discussed the uniqueness of the Islamic doctrine and how Quṭb warns Muslims against emulating others both conceptually and behaviorally. The most pernicious form of *fitnah*, Quṭb maintains, constitutes accepting the worldview of others, while forgetting the Islamic sources. This is the inner *fitnah*. It is the disease of the Muslim heart, soul, and mind, and it is total inner-defeat and submission to rules other than those of God.[70] Quṭb is troubled by *fitnah* because it is unavoidable in the process of building the Islamic community. The answer that he gives is awareness of the dangers of this *fitnah*, and perseverance. Therefore, Quṭb emphasizes the step-by-step process of building the Islamic state.

In addition to sedition, seduction, and persecution, *fitnah* is reflected in arrogance, worldly pride, and material success. *Fitnah* could be caused by members of one's family, close relatives, and neighbors.[71] *Fitnah* is also understood as deviating Muslims from their straight path, and the consequent ossification of their belief-system.[72] Carre observes correctly that "external *fitnah* consists of deviating Muslims from their belief and their definite ideal of Islamic society. This is the role of the traditional enemies of Islam from the beginning."[73]

Quṭb defines political and social oppression as *fitnah*. He says that *fitnah* is one of the major sicknesses facing any society. Belief is also a form of *fitnah*, especially in hard times. Life is mainly an internal battle against any manifestation of evil. "*Fitnah* is a permanent pattern whose purpose is to examine hearts and purify ranks."[74] Any community that overlooks *fitnah*, and does not stand up to oppressors and the corrupt, deserves the evil of the oppressors. As a positive and sustaining system (*manhaj takāfulī wa ijābī*), Islam incites believers to face up to oppression and injustice. The major *fitnah*, in Quṭb's view, is the rejection of shari'āh as the supreme source of legislation in the land.[75] In this, he invokes the Qur'ānic verse, "O ye that believe! Betray not the trust of Allah and the Messenger, nor misappropriate knowingly things entrusted to you. And know ye that your possessions and your progeny are but a *fitnah*; And that it is Allah with whom lies Your highest reward." (Qur'ān 8: 27–28)

In commenting on these verses, Quṭb argues that wealth, progeny, social prestige, and power can distract believers if belief is not made a priority. Any good life presupposes certain duties and costs, and the failure to fulfill those duties that pertain to the healthy survival of the Muslim *ummah* is but "treason to God and His Prophet."[76] Carrying out these duties becomes a religious neccesity when one understands that the Islamic movement of the Prohpet underwent two distinct phases: (1) patience, persistence, and mere survival; and (2) political formation, expansion, and strength. This distinction is important for the modern Muslim movement, because it means that history repeats itself, and that any current stage of preparedness would definitely culminate in the establishement of the Islamic order in the twentieth century. The Islamic camp (*mu'askar islāmī*), in Quṭb's view, must be in a permanent state of preparedness, and must take note of the following things when facing an enemy: (1) Anyone who makes a pact with Muslims, but abrogates it later, should be disciplined; (2) The Muslim camp has to be prepared all the time; (3) Peaceful pacts are cautiously encouraged; (4) *Jihād* is a religious duty even if the camp of the enemy is stronger; (5) Muslims are encouraged to destroy the foundations of the enemy's power; and (6) *'Aqīdah* is the basis of the Muslim camp.[77]

However, Quṭb falls prey to a dialectical formulation. On the one hand, he exhorts Muslims to *jihād*, and to permanent revolution against those conditions that are deemed to be un-Islamic. On the other, he voices his bitterness and deep frustration regarding the spread of *jāhiliyah* in the Muslim camp.

The Islamic *da'wah* is a culmination of a long historical process begun in the early history of man to acquaint man with God and his commandements. Therefore, the contemporary Muslim movement must discover the theological and historical axis in which the *da'wah* appeared and reformulate its position on the basis of this past model. Quṭb hastens to add that because the modern day *jāhiliyah*—as with any other one in the past—is not a mere theoretical formulation or a philosophical tendency, no theoretical or philosophcial alternative can become viable. What is needed, instead, is a practical movement, or "an organic and dynamic gathering (*tajamu' ḥarakī 'uḍwī*)"[78] in order to face this situation.

> Islam cannot be represented in a pure theory . . . [especially] when its believers constitute an organic part of the existing *jāhilī* gathering. Any such existence will never lead to an actual existence of Islam, since those "theoretical Muslims" who are part

> of the *Jāhilī* community will definitely have to respond to the exigencies of this society, and they will have to act, willingly or unwillingly, consciously or unconsciously, in order to fulfill the basic needs of this society and ensure its survival . . . In other words, those theoretical Muslims who are supposed to dismantle the bases of Jāhilī society do in fact strengthen it and they remain living cells giving it life and expansions.[79]

In a nutshell, the new Islamic community should be distinguished by autonomy, strong doctrinal orientation, pragmatism, historical vision, and theological sophistication.

Quṭb says that the Islamic movement was born against the background of hardship and suffering. Once Quraysh was aware of the ideology of the Islamic movement, its cohesion, and commitment to fighting evil, the *jāhilī* society was awakened to this danger and started to fight the Islamic leadership and its followers. The next phase was marked by torture, ostracism, suffering, and variegated ordeals faced by the nascent Muslim group. Those elements who could not take this suffering reconverted to the *jāhilī* society. Thus, the early Muslim group was formed by a process of selection. Only the fittest survived the ordeal and renewed their commitment to the Islamic camp.[80]

Because the battle with *jāhiliyah* is universal, Quṭb reiterates the need of contemporary Muslim activists to learn from the lessons of the past.

> Those who are engaged in such a battle [with *jāhiliyah*] are the only ones who can have a taste of the Qur'ān, which has, in turn, faced these challenges and directed them. Meanwhile those who grope for a rhetorical or aesthetic study of the Qur'ān, trying to understand its meaning and significance, can hardly discover its fact in such a passive and frozen situation which is distant from the battle and action.[81]

One major challenge facing the modern Muslim movement is the immense political and social divisions prevalent in Muslim societies since colonialism. Any battle with *jāhiliyah* is considered by Quṭb to be a phase of trial and trepidation (*fatrat ibtilā'*).[82]

In his evaluation of the foundations of a countermovement, Quṭb is constantly informed by the Qur'ān as well as the events in early Islamic history of schism. In the formative phase of Islam, many sects arose competing for power, resorting to various texts of the Qur'ān to justiify their claims. Quṭb is well aware of the early use of the religious text for the sake of worldy interests and prestige. These divisions have marked the religious history of Islam until the modern period, and he argues that today's nationalism is but another *fitnah* in religion.

FURTHER THOUGHTS ON *'AQĪDAH* AND *DĪN*

It is the assumption of many a Muslim theologian that Islamic faith has taken a fixed and well-defined form as a system of doctrine since the early phase of Islam. The contents of this system define God as substantiality and actuality, and determine the relationship of man to God. Without these contents, the foundations of Islam as a creed become meaningless and historically irrelevant. Although Islam, unlike Catholic Christianity, does not possess an eccleiastical structure—at least in a theoretical sense—its *'ulamā'* and lay people alike have always guarded it against heresy and innovation.

In elaborating on the nature of the Islamic religion, Quṭb distinguishes among three distinct meanings of the term *dīn* (religion.)

(1) *Dīn* as a belief system or epistemological construct, means that *dīn* possesses universal and ideal rules and principles, such as theological abstraction. Hegel argues that the immediate form of religious certainty is that of faith.

> Faith, indeed, directly involves an antithesis; and this antithesis is more or less indefinite. It is usual to put faith in contrast with knowledge. Now, if it be wholly opposed to knowledge, we get an empty antithesis. What I believe, I also know; it is contained in my consciousness. Faith is a form of knowledge, but by knowledge is usually understood as mediated knowledge, a knowledge involving clear apprehension.[83]

In like manner, Quṭb does not see any contradiction between rational knowledge and belief. In fact, he, calls Islam the religion of reason. This, of course, may sound apologetic. However, taken as an immediate object of mediation between God and man, the primitive elements of belief are rationally grasped while, at a more sophisticated level, belief can mean an inner transition from the particular to the universal, or the physical and concrete to the abstract and unknown.

(2) Quṭb understands *dīn* as rites and rituals, and as a concrete expression of the faith.

(3) He maintains that *dīn* forms the backbone of the *ummah*.

(4) Finally, *dīn* must undergo a process of interpretation of

its universal principles in light of changing circumstances and times. Without this ability to lend itself to interpretations, it would be impossible for it to be dynamic and pragmatic. It is only those people who have a real grasp of *'aqīdah* who can fulfill this task. What is important here is that Quṭb transcends one of the *'ulamā's* major prerogatives—their historical privilege of interpreting the *dīn*. This is revolutionary, in a sense, because he does not restrict the right of interpreting the text to a special class of people, but can imagine every capable person, especially the vanguard, doing so.

This argument gives Quṭb the opportunity to claim that *'aqīdah* is a necessary method of belief in the absence of a theocratic state. In a chaotic or spiritually stagnant situation, *'aqīdah* must assume the role of a dynamic approach that elevates society to the degree expected by God.

As a reflection of the infallible Divine commands, in Quṭb's view, *'aqīdah* becomes a historical agent for real change. That is to say, far from being static, neutral, ahistorical, and asocial, *'aqīdah* can translate itself into a dynamic social and historical movement, whose major objective must be to transform the world of man. Commenting bitterly on the state of scholarship in the Muslim world, Quṭb maintains that "Defeated [Muslim] scholars have basically accepted the Western understanding of religion as a mere doctrine in man's conscience having no relation to realistic programs of life."[84]

Throughout the *Ẓilāl*, Quṭb seems to juxtapose two underlying assumptions: (1) that the progressive secularization of life in Egyptian and Muslim societies is diminishing the function of religion as the principal instigator of events; but (2) that religion ought to take the lead in giving an ultimate meaning to human existence. Quṭb approximates the gist of Clifford Geerts's definition of religion, especially if the term "symbols" is substituted by *'aqīdah*.

> Religion is: (1) a system of symbols which acts to (2) establish powerful, pervasive, and long-lasting moods and motivations in man by (3) formulating conceptions of a general order of existence and (4) clothing these conceptions with such an aura of factuality that (5) the moods of motivations seem uniquely [to be] realistic.[85]

To summarize, in attempting to come to grips with Muslim ontology in the twentieth century, Quṭb develops universal or abstract and specific or practical concepts, categories, and principles. It is impossible to understand Quṭb's general method if one does not delineate these universal and particular ideas and concepts. Quṭb's universal principles are derived from the following: (1) metaphysical qualities; (2) primordial human qualities; (3) historical principles; and (4) social relatedness. Quṭb perceives man as a responsible being who is related ontologically to other beings, and who has a sense of social responsiblity.

One can say that, in erecting his ontology, Quṭb—besides studying the semantic meaning of the key concepts of the Qur'anic *Weltanschauung* and the changes the Qur'ān introduced to the semantic structure of the Arabic language of the *jāhiliyah*—discusses these basic formulations against the socioeconomic, cultural, and political background of early Islam. Connected closely to this is the major preoccupation of Quṭb which is the relevance of the Qur'anic *Weltanschauung* to the modern conditions of Islam. As such, one might have to study Quṭb's ontology as dynamic, relational, and concrete. Furthermore, this ontology must be studied in its totality—as a comprehensive whole. In other words, one must dissect the multilayered relationship of meaning developed by Quṭb. Therefore, it would be erroneous to study Quṭb's key concepts in isolation from one another, precisely because this level of study would obscure the real meanings of the author and the interrelationships of these meanings. As we shall see, it would be erroneous to assume that one word, such as *jāhiliyah*, could carry the whole weight of meanings intended by Quṭb. One must look at this term—which is frequently used by Quṭb as has already been seen—in relation to other key terms used, as well as in relation to the transformation of Islamic epistemology in the past few centuries.

Therefore, the ontological system of an author gains importance only if seen in its totality. The constitutive factors of Quṭb's Qur'anic discourse are the following:

(1) Ummatic versus tribal entity. Here, the individual owes allegiance to something more abstract and universal than a specific tribe. Human bondage is based on divine principles that, ideally speaking, culminated in the historical experience of the Prophet and his companions. The Muslim individual is perceived as an innovating, laboring, patient, and dynamic being. He also must have achieved total emancipation with the rise of Islam. Therefore, the Muslim's self-consciousness is a consciousness of the ultimate concern, of God, and of his own place in relation to the community at large. In an abstract sense, the Muslim is responsibile to no one except God. Practically speaking, however, he should represent the conscience of the group or the *ummah*.

(2) Ideal versus real. Quṭb's *élan vital* is the dynamism of doctrine. At the heart of both sacred text and doctrine is a method of transfor-

mation, revolution, and reconstruction. Method awakens the *ummah* to its responsibilities, the essence of which is to ponder the "sea of *jāhiliyah*" for the sake of changing it. Thus, action, vitality, commitment, initiative, sacrifice, relatedness, and universalism are the qualities of an authentic Muslim.

Islam and Its Current Enemies

Quṭb claims that Islam has been always opposed by three forces that have become almost universal—namely, international Zionism, international Crusaderism, and international Communism.[86] To his mind, the enemies of Islam have always attempted to undermine the significance of *ʿaqīdah* as a bond of unity among Muslims, regardless of race, class, language, and geographical location. The distinguishing mark of Islam in the modern period is a fierce battle between Islam and its enemies. Although the enemies of Islam do raise different banners today and speak different languages, they are all fighting *ʿaqīdah*. The modern fight against Islam is not taking place in the name of religion, but in the name of "territory, economy, politics, and military locations. The enemies of Islam have deceived the naive by claiming that the waged battle today is not over *ʿaqīdah*, and that the question of *ʿaqīdah* is an anachronistic and useless one. But they know that they wage a battle to destroy this strong rock that of *ʿaqīdah*."[87]

The enemies of Islam have resorted to lifting the Islamic banner as a means of camouflaging their real intentions. Quṭb does not fully identify who the enemies are, but says that "they are fully aware of the nature of the human self and of the history of the Islamic movement alike."[88] These enemies have successfully dismantled the Islamic caliphate in Turkey, and although this caliphate was, according to Quṭb, merely a show, on the symbolic level, it was crucial to the state of Islam.

Islamic Conception of Human Reason

Because doctrine is the tree from which branches of knowledge and activism arise, a question comes to mind. "What is the relationship between doctrine and human reason?"

To Quṭb, one distinguishing mark of the Islamic conception (*al-taṣawwur al-islāmī*) is the belief in the Unseen. "Belief in the Unseen is the juncture of man's elevation above the world of animals. Today's

Materialists, as ever, desire that man regress to the world of bestiality where materialism is abundant."[89]

Man occupies a previleged position in the world of creation. His distinguished role in this world derives from (1) the "contract of viceregency" (*ʿiqd al-istikhlāf*), and (2) knowledge (*ʿilm*). God guides man, through revelations, in the fundamental principles of life. The good/evil duality is an essential foundation of this life.[90] Although man is distinguished from animals by his immense knowledge, his mental capacity is by no means unlimited. Human reason cannot fathom the world of the Unseen, since "this is not one of the conditions of vicegerency" as stipulated by God.[91]

Quṭb establishes what is believed to be a Qur'anic maxim—"To the extent that God has placed the secrets of nature under the mercy of man, He has hidden from him the secrets of the [world of the] Unseen, since it is useless to comprehend these secrets."[92] Man is responsible with his knowledge, and this responsibility leads to action. Therefore, Islam rejects the concept of predestination. Sin is committed on an individual basis in the context of society, and man must bear the responsibilities of his actions.

Quṭb stresses the immutability and onenness of the Islamic doctrine in view of the fact that God, the One, has always revealed consistent messages. "Islam—the submission to God alone—has always been the original message and the last message."[93]

Therefore, as an eternal and essentially unchanging doctrine, one must detect fundamental differences between the Islamic and *jāhilī* views. "The *jāhilī* conception does not distinguish between one generation and another in the same race since the bond of race and blood is the basis, whereas the Islamic conception draws the line between a believing generation and an unbelieving one [even if they belong to the same race]."[94]

Quṭb's point of departure in matters of doctrine is his analysis of the Baqarah Sūra, whose main objective, he says, is laying down the basic conceptual criteria of Muslim thinking, and setting forth the rule of social action. Muslims, therefore, constitute a distinguished nation if they follow the already outlined criteria.

Quṭb hastens to admonish those Muslims who have fallen prey to the philosophy and social behavior of others. Imitation of others means taking both mental and social forms, both of which constitute inner defeat.

> The Prophet, in his capacity as a pragmatic leader, spoke against inner defeat (*hazīmah dākhilīyah*) before others did. Inner defeat

seeps into the self and gets people [Muslims] transformed by imitating others. The Muslim *ummah* emerged, however, in order to assume the leadership of humanity, and, therfore, it must derive its belief from the source that wanted it to play a leadership role.[95]

Quṭb takes the *qiblah* as a measure of the *ummah*'s maturity, and as a sign that the structure of its society and the foundations of its government are well-laid-down, "The Muslim community, which faces a distinguished *qiblah*, must comprehend the real meaning of this direction. The *qiblah* is not a mere place or corner that the community faces while in prayer. Place or direction is a symbol—that of distinction and specificity. It is a distinction in conceptual attitude, personality, telos, interests, and place."[96] Instead of being at the periphery, the Muslim community (*ummah*) must be an example and must play the role of the universal leader. That is when its *muhimmah ḍakhmah* (immense task) gets realized.[97]

The Muslim *ummah* cannot realize the tasks it bears without the full use of reason. Human reason, in addition to occupying a privileged position in the thought of Islamic resurgence, relates to revelation in an intricate way.

> The content of the Qur'ān revolves around man himself, and it includes [man's] conceptions, beliefs, feelings, ideas, behavior and practice, connections and relationships. As for physical sciences, and innovation in the world of matter, these fall in the realm of man's reason, experiences, discoveries, theses, and theories, and constitute the basis of man's vicegerengy on earth. The Qur'ān heads off man's primordial nature [*fiṭrah*] from deviation and corruption, and rectifies the system in which he lives so as he can take advantage of those capacities granted to him. [Further, the Qur'ān] provides man with a general conception of the nature of the universe and its relationship with its Creator, the harmony of its constitution, and the nature of the relationship between its constituent parts.[98]

In a sense, revelation deals with the a priori foundations of man, and reason deals with the consequences, a reflection of the premises. Both are integral to each other, and, in this sense, there is no truth to the claim that the fundamentalist freezes reason or makes reason an appendage to revelation. Both revelation and reason are complementary in terms of their functions and outputs.[99]

If revelation and reason are complementary, what does Quṭb say about the relationship between revelation and science? Quṭb follows the premise that the Qur'ān, as the locus of the Islamic revelation, contains a priori principles and rules; and science, which is an extension or a consequence of the human mind, is somewhat peripheral to the Qur'ān. In this context, Quṭb points to the impact of secularization on the modern Muslim mind.

In his view, secularization permeates every aspect of life, culture, and mentality of modern Muslims. Consequently, secularization, as the direct outcome of Western modernity, has planted what came to be believed a priori rules of thinking and conduct in the Muslim environment. In Quṭb's view, it is therefore normal that some Muslims, including the most educated and intelligent, would take science as the criterion and measure of every truth. This inevitably leads to a conflict between the Qur'anic view and the secular, scientific one. Further, those in the Muslim world who attempt to prove the compatibility of the Qur'ān and science have fallen into a methodological error because they do not share a basic orientation. At the same time, these Muslims have fallen prey to a pernicious psychological defeat that compels them to assume that science is basic and the Qur'ān is contingent.

In the words of Quṭb, "The Qur'ān is thematically complete, and final in terms of its revelationary facts. The conclusions of science, on the other hand, . . . are not final or absolute, mainly because science is tied down to man's reason and tools which cannot naturally give a final and absolute fact."[100]

After this abstract elaboration, Quṭb moves on to the plane of prophecy and history. In this regard, he comments on the following verse: "Messengers who gave good news as a warning, that mankind, after [the coming] of the Messengers, should have no plea against Allah: for Allah is Exalter in Power, Wise." (Qur'ān 4: 165)[101]

Quṭb argues that human reason, although important and celebrated in Islam, cannot unlock the mysteries of the universe and grasp the meaning of life if unassisted by revelation.[102] According to Quṭb,

> The function of reason is to receive guidance from revelation, and to grasp what the prophet says. Furthermore, the function of the prophet is to announce, elaborate, and salvage the primordial human nature from debris. Prophecy must draw the attention of reason to ponder the signs of guidance and belief in the souls and the horizons, and to help it locate the sources of guidance, and the system of correct vision, and to establish the basis from which the system of pragmatic life is derived.[103]

Reason must be bound by both text and prophecy. Quṭb notes with regret that in Islamic intellectual history, two different trends of thought, each of which did not estimate the position and value of human reason, emerged. The first, represented by the Muʿtazilites, overestimated reason and placed it above revelation. The second, represented by conservative and rigid *ʿulamā'*, attempted to abolish the role of reason, thus greatly underestimating its significance and value. Quṭb says there is a middle path that sets a proper relationship between revelation and reason, and thus it frees the *ummah* to practice "the freedom of thought (*ḥurriyyat al-naẓar*)."[104]

Quṭbian Conception of *Jihād*

Many have debated the pros and cons of *jihād*. The question seems to be raised at every juncture, in the media as well as in the public consciousness. However, a precise understanding of *jihād* is still lacking. That the question is at the basis of modern Islamic resurgence goes without saying. Generally speaking, modern Islamists have affirmed *jihād* as a principal aspect of the Qur'ān, and have interpreted it in a way to fit their overall objectives.

Quṭb uses the term *jihād* to denote several interdependent meanings, including doctrinal, spiritual, military, political, and social *jihād*. However, his definition of *jihād* stems from his understanding of Islam as a revolutionary *ʿaqīdah* or ideology that seeks to dismantle the status quo and rebuild anew on the bases of the sovereignty of God and the freedom of man from the servitude of other men. *Jihād* is, then, a reflection of this desire, and the Quṭbian doctrine of *jihād* assumes, in the final analysis, a sharply differentiated universal aim. "This religion is really a universal declaration of the freedom of man from [the] servitude to other men and [the] servitude to his own desires."[105] In addition, *jihād* possesses two forms, external and internal.

Quṭb is quite alarmed by the decline of Islam, the plight of its people, and the apologetic and defeatist mentality of its scholars and intelligentsia. Nationalism, secularization, and orientalism have all compounded the problem by blurring, in different ways, the fine distinction that Islam establishes between physical war and *jihād*. The supreme aim of *jihād* is to preserve the *ʿaqīdah* and to defend it in case danger befalls it. There is nothing defensive about the expansion of Islam. It was a logical consequence of the spread of the Islamic message.

> Those of our contemporary Muslim scholars . . . defeated by the pressure of the current conditions and the attacks of treacherous orientalists, do not subscribe to this characteristic of Islam. The orientalists have painted a picture of Islam as a violent movement which imposed its belief upon people by the sword. These vicious orientalists know very well that this is not true, but by this method they try to distort the true motives of Islamic *Jihād*. But our Muslim scholars—these defeated people—search for reasons of defense with which to negate this accusation. They are ignorant of the nature of Islam and its function, and that it has a right to take the initiative for human freedom.[106]

Quṭb criticizes vehemently those Muslim scholars who become apologetic and defensive while discussing *jihād*. He ascribes to them both spiritual and mental defeat (*mahzūmoun rūḥiyan wa ʿaqliyan*).[107] He contends that these scholars cannot draw a proper distinction between two principles in Islam: (1) noncoercion in religion; and (2) the determination to annihilate all those forces of *jāhiliyah*, which act to destroy the Muslim entity. Far from being a defensive war, *jihād* is necessary to elevate the divine banner.

We must free ourselves, contends Quṭb, from modern conceptions and criteria when defining the notions of *religion* and *nation*. Islam is not a religion in the conventional sense. It is not a mere relationship between man and God, and it cannot be limited to the narrow definitions of the nation/state. Islam, says Quṭb, is not a "homeland" in the modern, secular sense of the term. It is *ʿaqīdah* lived and practiced freely. In Quṭb's mind, *ʿaqīdah* is distinguished by realism, dynamism, and submission to God. Muslims must fight if these characteristics are blurred or barred, "The function of *jihād* is to protect *ʿaqīdah* from siege, *fitnah*, and to protect its method and system in life."[108]

According to Quṭb, Muslims are duty-bound to fight any power that attempts to block the peaceful spread of the Islamic message. In other words, the principle of *jihād* is conditioned on the emancipation of man from the slavery of other men. Every Muslim man and woman must fight to preserve the *ʿaqīdah*, "God's sovereignty cannot be established and maintained by a few dedicated men—the priests as was the case with the Church, neither by those who claim to speak on behalf of the divinity, as was the case in theocracy."[109] Muslims must relate to *ʿaqīdah*, not as a defensive doctrine, but as a necessary mechanism. "*Jihād* is a necessary companion for *daʿwah*."[110]

Quṭb proclaims that the final aim of *Jihād*, besides the protection of doctrine and society, is to address man in general. Every human being must listen to the message of the Qur'ān.[111] In treating *jihād*, Quṭb shows his indebtedness to Abū ʿAla Mawdūdī, and draws heavily on his *Jihād in Islam*.[112] Quṭb agrees with Mawdūdī that Muslims must not rely on orientalist literature to understand their own history and doctrine. Orientalists have propagated two major views about Islam, neither of which is true. First, they define religion as a system of rituals and rites only, and then, they think of Muslims as belonging to various nation/states, thus obscuring the essential bond of *ʿaqīdah* that underlies Muslim life.[113] Therefore, Islam is not a scholastic nor didactic attitude nor a metaphyscial doctrine only. Instead, it is a call for a social revolution. Quṭb echoes the words of Mawdūdī closely. "This *daʿwah* is not a philosophical elucidation of a scholastic doctrine, or an explanation of a metaphyscial proposition, but a call for an international social revolution."[114]

I have argued in this chapter that one must understand Quṭb's remarks about *jihād* as a response to the state of decline of modern Islam. Quṭb expresses his frustration with the current state of Islam throughout the pages of the *Ẓilāl*.

First, he bemoans the fact that modern-day Muslims have not understood the Qur'ān as a dynamic and moving force, and as a battle-oriented document.

> We need, more than ever, to perceive the Qur'ān as a propelling, dynamic, and lively document. There is a great distance between us, on the one hand, and the Islamic movement, life, and reality, on the other. The Qur'ān became disjointed in our consciousness (*ḥiss*) to the extent we lost its dynamic historical reality. Alas, it no longer represents in our consciousness that type of life that actually took place on earth in the history of the Muslim community. We do not remember anymore that the Qur'ān was the daily preoccupation of the recruited Muslim from which guidance for action and execution were derived. The Qur'ān has met its death-bed in our consciousness (*māta al-qur'ān fi ḥissinā*). . . . And it no longer maintains the same image in our consciousness as it did in the past . . . What is required is for the Qur'ān to establish in the Muslim consciousness and life.[115]

Second, he admonishes the leaders of the contemporary Muslim community to study the current objective conditions of Muslims at the personal, social, and political levels, and examine them both against the background of the Qur'ān and the harsh reality of early Islam.

Third, he maintains that the nature of people does not change, and the battles that modern Muslims have to wage are in essence the same as before.

Fiqh and *Sharī'āh*

As a Muslim thinker and a critic, Quṭb's discussion of questions pertaining to *sharī'āh* and *fiqh* is unavoidable. However, one must note that the whole discussion is situated in the context of Quṭb's reaction to the nation/state in the modern Muslim world. Quṭb opposes the nation/state because of its lack of Islamic symbolism, and the peripheral role which religion plays in it. Quṭb does not consider the nation/state to be a historical given, but an anomalous reality that must be overcome.[116] Far from being a theological or philosophical system only, religion is a way of life. As such, legislation should also be an integral part of religion. "The nature of any religion should organize the life of people on the bases of legislation, and should not be limited to the ethical side alone."[117] Historically speaking, Quṭb argues, there has been a major difference between Islam and Christianity in matters of legislation. Christianity was born with a separation between religion and legislation as a result of the antagonism between the rabbis and Christ. Consequently, Quṭb states that Christianity has failed to legislate in the social and economic spheres, which has led its followers to separate instinctively between their spiritual and material values and attitudes. This separation has had disasterous consequences, and this is the reason for the wretchedness, confusion, deviation, abnormality, and malaise in today's civilization.[118]

Basing his argument on the notion that the principal source of Islamic legislation is the Qur'ān, Quṭb criticizes those *fuqahā'* who take tradition (*'irf*) as a principle. How does he, then, explain the continuous presence of *jāhilī* ideas in Islam? Islam is a comprehensive religion which transformed life entirely and, therefore, any *jāhilī* principle or conception was abrogated by the new religion. Any consideration given to *'irf* by *fiqh* is not Islamic because the Islamic source is the Qur'ān.[119] *'Irf* should be rejected as a principle of Islamic legislation. Quṭb argues that *jāhiliyah* in its different manifestations has always used *'irf* as a principle. He gives the parallel example of racism in the United States in the 1950s when it was justified as a form of tradition.

One of the principal terms which Quṭb uses in his discussion of *sharī'āh* is *fiqh ḥarakī* (dynamic *fiqh*). There is a tremendous difference, in Quṭb's eyes, between dynamic *fiqh* and paper *fiqh* (*fiqh awrāq*).

Quṭb argues that dynamic *fiqh* is the criterion for the dynamism and pragmatism of Islam.[120] In his view, this term is significant for the following three reasons.

First, it has been forgotten for centuries as a result of the malaise in Islam.

Second, the *'ulamā'* have also been negligent. Because of their support of the status quo, they have given preference to static *fiqh*, "Dynamic *fiqh* is totally different from the *fiqh* of paper (*fiqh awrāq*), although both share the same text and source."[121] The *'ulamā'* are to be blamed squarely for their blind espousal of the current state of affairs. For them, "the work in the field of Islamic *fiqh* is a comfortable venture indeed. It does not contain any danger. But this kind of work goes against the grains of this religion, its method, and its nature. It would be more useful for these *'ulamā'* to deal with literature, the arts, or commerce. Dealing with *fiqh* in this fashion is a major waster of time and effort."[122]

Third, in order to revive the Qur'anic text and make it relevant to the modern world, one must stress *fiqh ḥarakī*. Quṭb maintains that the text cannot be understood in a vacuum, but in a dynamic relation to action, activism, and movement. The human component should not be the source of *fiqh*, as many jurists have mistakenengly assumed. However, it should be related to the essence of foundation of Islam which is doctrine or *'aqīdah*.[123]

As a pragmatic system, Islam refuses to argue in a vacuum about themes and issues that are not part of reality. In a sense, Quṭb maintains that the modern arguments of many a Muslim scholar about *fiqh* and *sharī'āh* application are futile because a true Muslim community has not yet existed. It is when we have Islam in practice that we can delve into *fiqh* questions in order to find solutions to the needs of the emerging Muslim community.[124] "Islamic *fiqh* did not emerge in a vacuum, neither does it live or can be understood in a vacuum. It [instead] arose in a Muslim society responding to the realistic needs of the Islamic life. Also *fiqh* did not establish Islamic society; on the contrary, Islamic society established *fiqh*."[125]

Islam is a comprehensive, dynamic movement and is highly distinguished by its inner organicity and coherence. Therefore, theory and practice are inseparable. Quṭb argues that the *fiqh* distinction between *aḥkām al-'ibādāt* and *aḥkām al-mu'āmalāt* is static and does not reflect the dynamism and inner organicty of Islam as a doctrinal movement. Any deviation from one fundamental principle of Islam is a deviation from the doctrine.[126]

Fiqh emerges against the backdrop of religious, sociopolitical, and economic backgrounds. As such, *fiqh* is needed in order to dislodge *jāhiliyah* and to provide answers for the Islamic movement. Quṭb argues that a new *Ijtihād* in *fiqh* is necessary because of the new circumstances, needs, and challenges facing modern Muslims. A new *Ijtihād* is needed in dynamic *fiqh* in order to tailor the modern situation with its needs and conditions to the tastes of historical precedents in Islam.[127]

Toward an Islamic Theory of Imperialism, Colonialism, and Orientalism

As seen in chapter four of this study, Quṭb develops his views on imperialism in a manner that is, more or less, consistent with the reality of pre-1952 Egyptian society.[128] In the *Ẓilāl*, he takes his ideas far afield and discusses colonialism and its political and cultural expressions as a problematic in modern Arabic/Islamic thought.[129]

Quṭb develops a highly sophisticated Islamic theory of imperialism, and he sees a clear connection between the economic and political machinations of imperialism and the culture of the periphery—the indigenous one. His main concern, however, is the impact of the new cultural dynamics which the colonized—for example, Muslim world—might have had on Islam, as a universal religious phenomenon. As a result, Quṭb theorizes on the state of the indigenous intelligentsia under colonialism and assesses their cultural and intellectual role under the novel conditions imposed by Western hegemony. Quṭb argues that cultural imperialism is a much more dangerous phenomenon than an outward military occupation and subjugation of a nation by another—in this case, Europe versus Muslim nations—because of the transplanation of its values into those of the colonized society—a type of activity that will transfer these values to the newly independent countries afterward.

Therefore, the main issue in Quṭb's eyes is colonial culture. What is the nature of cultural colonialism? What were the religious and social changes also brought about as a result of this encounter? Does the cultural clash, which Quṭb and other Muslim thinkers describe, contain elements of cultural fusion, and vice versa? Did cultural colonialism confront Muslim societies uniformly and in parallel historical phases? Was the response of the Muslim intelligentsia homogeneous? If not, which Western cultral elements were assimilated, and which were repressed or Islamized?[130]

As seen in chapter four, Quṭb first expressed his ideas on colonialism as a young Egyptian man of letters who was searching for a place in the literary world. At this point, he was thinking more as an Egyptian nationalist rather than a Pan-Arabist or Muslim intellectual. In a revealing article, entitled "The Language of Slaves," he criticizes an emerging trend in Egyptian intellectual life favoring Western ideas and ways of life, especially as exemplified by Ḥussain Fawzī. Quṭb says, "Slaves are not to be encountered in the United States only . . . In Egypt, a new form of slavery is emerging: it is of those slaves whose attire is that of free men but in whom slavery [of the mind] is deeply engrained."[131] He further argues that these so-called "mental slaves," who have been brainwashed by the West, cannot even admit the atrocities committed by the French in North Africa and the British in the Middle East. Quṭb contends that the West survives in the Arab world on propaganda and deceit. He says that the British, as master colonialists, "have spread the myth that they differ from Germans in that the latter are liers and savages, whereas they [the British] are the civilized protectors of humanity . . . British gold and money was pouring on the centers of propaganda which, in turn, was given to [indigenous] journalists and writers whose job was to bless and praise the protectors of democracy and freedom."[132] From the start, Quṭb sees a direct link between what he calls a "class of collaborators" and the Western powers.

Our discussion of Quṭb's views of colonialism can take on a historical significance because a number of Third-World intellectuals have been trying to arrive at an indigenous view of themselves and the world around them. This process has been known as cultural decolonization.[133] Quṭb argues that the crisis of identity in the Muslim world is very pervasive, and, as a consequence, it has inhibited the Muslim intelligentsia from finding the right solutions to the ever-emerging problems facing their countries after independence. He also argues for a national identity to be broadly based on the consciousness of the Muslim past—thus, he places in a historical context present-day problems. Although many Muslim lands fell under the direct colonial hegemony of the British and French, they did not succeed in totally wiping out the cultural influence of Islam, neither did Muslims become *tabula rasa* in their hands. What they succeeded in doing, however, was to create a distorted Muslim identity that is cut off from its historical mission of Islamization. Thus, the modern Muslim is caught between the glories of the past and the agonies of the present. Some have sought refuge in Westernization, while others have been ossified with stagnation, unable to bridge the gap between past and present.

Quṭb's writing of the *Ẓilāl* takes place mainly in the context of newly gained independence which was, however, still amenable to colonialism. He carefully utilizes the material at hand to show that colonialism is part of the problem, and that the solution to all problems encountered lies in Muslim hands. He also sets forth to distinguish between external colonialism and internal receptivity to colonialism, or, in Malek Bannabi's terms, "colonizibility," as an inherent attitude.[134]

According to Quṭb, colonialism does not manifest itself as an inhibiting mythological construct, but as a tangible movement capable of forging lasting intellectual and political alliances in the Muslim world, even after independence. The disease in the Muslim world is not wholly attributable to colonialism, but colonialism has taken great strides in fostering a total cultural and mental dependence of Muslims on the West. Quṭb argues that colonialism is methodic. It used systematic methods to fabricate scholarship about all aspects of the Islamic sciences in the form of orientalism. Above all, as a political movement, colonialism has shifted the social and political alliances in Muslim societies to its advantage, and has always attempted to co-opt the Muslim clergy in order to assist it in furthering its plans in the domains of culture, ideas, and religion. Quṭb would agree with Bennabi that colonialism has adopted "the technique of disorientation [which] adapts itself continuously to new situations, sabotaging all initiative."[135]

The most disquieting situation for Quṭb is the deep effect which colonialism has left on the Muslim intelligentsia. He sees intellectual confusion rampant in educated Muslim circles, and he raises the banner of "mental and spiritual purification," or what Mohammed Arkoun would call authenticity.[136]

In a perceptive manner, Quṭb reflects on the modern situation of Islam, in which he falls short of calling it "malaise." What troubles him the most is, perhaps, not Western colonialism and its political, military, economic and social effects, but the apathy of Muslims and their double standard in thought, action, law, and even morality. Quṭb's critique of the present conditions of Islam could be taken as a reflection of his anguished spirit or as an imprisoned man who deserves to be free. He sees a pervasive attitude of thought/action polarization and criticism/passivity, Western mind and Islamic soul. All these phenomenon are troubling, to say the least.

In his search for authentic Islamic principles and doctrines as a means of reconstructing an Islamically sound theory of knowledge, Quṭb battles against the orientalists as the main enemies of Islam. Quṭb argues that the distinctive mark of the Islamic religion is the notion of *ʿaqīdah* which cannot be adulterated by foreign ideas, because it is a Qur'anic fact. Muslim life has to be distinguished by the originality of its thinking and behavior. In this sense, Quṭb warns modern-day Muslims against learning about Islam from orientalists. We have consulted orientalists, he says, in matters of our religion, studied our history under them, and trusted them in our tradition, and have done nothing to prevent them from distorting the Qur'ān and the *Ḥadīth*.[137] He claims that, even in matters of *'aqīdah*, Muslims are attracted to the orientalist scholarship.

> We, who claim to be Muslim, receive our principal knowledge about the Qur'ān and the *Ḥadīth* of our Prophet [PBUH] from the Orientalists and their disciples. We receive our philosophy and doctrine of existence and life from this or that philosopher and thinker: Greek, Roman, European and American. [We also] receive the organization of our life, legislation, and laws from these foreign sources.[138]

Quṭb perceives orientalism as a European intellectual enterprise whose objective is to subvert Islam from within. In that sense, he shares with Edward Said the notion that orientalism is a type of knowledge constructed for the purposes of dominating the Orient, which is, in this case, Islam. Said defines the term as a number of interdependent factors: (1) It is an academic tradition. This refers to institutions and scholars who study the East, be they historians, philologists, or theologians; (2) It also refers to a style of thought based on distinctions made between the Orient and the Occident—that the Orient is the "other"; and (3) It is also used as a Western type of knowledge for dominating, restructuring, and wielding authority over the Orient.[139] Quṭb, as well as Said, views orientalism as a European cultural enterprise whose final aim is the subordination of East to West. Further, Quṭb would agree with Said's thesis that "[t]he relationship between Occident and Orient is a relationship of power, of domination, of varying degrees of a complex hegemony."[140] However, Quṭb goes further than Said in exploring the indigenous cultural and political arrangements of orientalism, and the heavy intellectual load the indigenous intelligentsia carries on behalf of orientalism.

It has been already noted that Quṭb is mainly interested in the intellectual and cultural modes created by colonialism in the Muslim world. He considers colonialism as a cultural and educational tool of hegemony, and the only way, in his mind, to counter such a hegemony is by creating an educated and conscious Muslim intelligentsia which would be capable of transcending colonialism with new categories of thought and practice. Although Quṭb is aware of the social distinction between Muslims—meaning between intelligentsia and poorer classes—he is far from using Marxist categories in his analysis of Western domination. He shies away from using such terms as the "bourgeoisie" and "working classes" as he did earlier in *The Battle Between Islam and Capitalism*. To his credit, however, Quṭb sees culture as humanly produced. That is to say, he considers Western culture to be the creation of the dominant class in Europe which, in its own way, expanded to the Third World and spread its intellectual and cultrual fruits persistently. Therefore, Quṭb's consistent search for cultural autonomy reflects his desire to create an Islamic theory of imperialism with which one can explain the prevailing political, economic, and cultural attitudes in the colonized Muslim world. Quṭb's own thinking reflects the thesis that is current among many leading Third-World intellectuals that the

> culture of the coloni[z]ed in these circumstances, represented cultural domination and backwardness. To the extent that imperialism could not allow the colonial people to develop the productive forces to the full, it also hindered the advance of the cultural life of the woppressed people. Neo-colonial culture as expressed in the writings of the neo-colonial intellectual reflected this depressed culture.[141]

Quṭb argues strongly that the enemies of Islam—especially Jews, Christians, and Westerners in general—have shown a systematic antagonism toward Islam in that their goal is to mutilate and finally destroy the Islamic *'aqīdah*. Based on this premise, Quṭb argues that, throughout the past fourteen centuries, there has been a universal conspiracy against Islam in which orientalists have injected foreign, inauthentic material into the original Islamic sources, especially in Qur'anic exegeses and *Ḥadīth* commentaries.

> [Orientalists] have injected new material as a means of obscuring the real events and facts. In addition, they have obscured real events and added new facts and even new personalities. They have injected (new material) and obscured Qur'anic exegeses to the extent [that] they have left like a waste land for a reasearcher.[142]

Quṭb argues strongly that the prominent intellectual leaders of the Muslim world today have been produced by orientalists and their image is dominant.

> A huge army of collaborators in the image of teachers, philosophers, doctors, and researchers follow in the footsteps of these powers—[the orientalists] and sometimes writers, poets, artists and journalists who carry Muslim names . . . And some of them are even *'ulamā'*[143].

Therefore, Quṭb sees a direct link between the source and its consequence. He mainly comments on the postcolonial Third World and the status of knowledge in this world—how knowledge is still being manipulated by Westernized elites in Islamic societies:

> This army of collaborators is instructed to shake the foundations of *'aqīdah* in souls by all means necessary. [This shaking] has taken the form of research, science, literature, art, and journalism. [In addition to] weakening its foundation, the intent is to belittle the importance of *'aqīdah* and *Sharī'āh* alike, and to interpret it in an unsuitable manner, and to emphasize its "reactionary character," and to call for leaving it aside.[144]

Therefore, Quṭb believes that orientalist understanding and formulations of Islam are explicitly anti-Islamic. Theirs is a two-pronged attack: epistemological (intellectual or doctrinal), and political. However, instead of destroying the foundations of the Islamic belief, the Qur'ān remains not only doctrinally intact, but spiritually superior to the writings of those orientalists. In terms of the political attack, Quṭb claims that the West was behind the dismantling of the Ottoman caliphate and the establishment of secular Kemalism in modern Turkey, and whose principal goal was to establish secularization and Westernization.

> Orientalists [the intellectual tools of crusading and zionist imperialism] have exerted extreme effort in distancing the Kemalist experiment of the accusation of atheism, since the discovery of its atheism has given it a limited role to play (in the Muslim world). . . . But it has failed to fulfill the other role—which other experiments try to fulfill in the area—which is emptying religious formulations and commitments of their meaning and giving them *Jāhilī* forms and conditions.[145]

One conclusion is that orientalism, according to Quṭb, has been formed in response to the political triumph of Islam in the seventh century, and its main goal, ever since, has been to drive a wedge between doctrine and politics in Islam. Therefore, the main enemy of Quṭb is not atheism per se, because this has never been a major danger in Islam. Instead, it is Jews and Christians who have always sought to destroy Islam and Muslims. Quṭb makes a connection between the Crusades and the Inquisition on the one hand, and the present treatment of Muslims by Westerners.

> The followers of other religions slaughter those who belong to Islam, and they wage a war [as] ugly as the that of the Crusaders and the Inquisition in Spain—either through their direct apparatuses in the colonies of Asia and Africa or through the conditions that they create and support in [the so-called] independent countries. [The goal of this war] is to substitute secularist doctrines and systems for Islam . . . And which call for evolution in Islamic *fiqh*, and orientalist conferences are celebrated for the purpose of its evolution.[146]

Unfortunately, states Quṭb, some Muslims seek the comprehension of their Qur'ān and *Ḥadīth* on the basis of orientalist scholarship.

> What a shame! Those Muslims, who emulate the orientalists, pass on as the high brow intellectuals and masters of Islamic thought, while at the same time they are produced according to the models provided by zionists and crusaders.[147]

Therefore, it is a priori dangerous to consult the orientalists in matters of true Islamic doctrine. In other words, Quṭb bemoans the intellectual environment of modern Islam because of its sterility and inability to produce authentic Islamic philosphers and thinkers who follow in the footsteps of the traditional Islamic intellegentsia instead of the West.

Orientalist scholarship has asked some of its most serious scholars to devote themselves to the study of Islam. "Why?" asks Sayyid Quṭb. His answer is blunt. It is because they are busy searching for the secrets of this religion, so that they can destroy its foundations. Westerners produce on average one book a week about Islam, which indicates that they know every little detail about it.[148] The historical movements that fought against colonialism were mainly "based on religious consciousness or at least religious emotions."[149] However, this battle is far from over, because the attacks of orientalism have not yet wavered.

Quṭb evokes some of the themes he had discussed earlier in *Social Justice*. One such theme is the orientalist charge that Islam and politics are incomaptible. "This is the tone used by the orientalists and their disciples in the Muslim world as a prelude to the claim that Islam is not fit to govern nowadays."[150] Islamic political theory, to Quṭb, does not admit secularization. This is because Islam is an inseparable unity.

> W. C. Smith has written a whole book on "Islam in the Modern Age," whose main objective is to prove [that] the Atatürk's Turkish secularism is Islamic in nature, and that it is the only successful Islamic movement in the modern period. Those Muslims who care about the existence of Islam have to follow this unique and correct experiment.[151]

He continues by arguing that, "But the final overthrow of Islam took place only in the present age, when Europe conquered the world, and when the dark shadow of colonization spread over the whole Islamic world, East and West alike. Europe mustered all its forces to extinguish the spirit of Islam, it revived the inheritance of the Crusaders' hatred, and it employed all the materialist and intellectual powers at its disposal."[152]

In sum, Quṭb considers orientalism to be an intellectual and social movement. It has always fabricated, controlled, and manufactured knowledge. Therefore, there should be a clear opposition between the Islamic theory of knowledge and the orientalist one. However, does that mean that one has to reject orientalist scholarship out of hand?

The unavoidable contradiction in the theory of knowledge between orientalism and Islam underlies another significant contradiction—the way in which Islam and orientalism view Islamic history. Quṭb focuses on the need to rewrite Islamic history, and suggests a new type of methodology. In his important essay, "History: Concept and Method," he makes the following points:

First, imperialism could have triumphed intellectually and spiritually during the age of Muslim decline had it not been for the staunch survival of the Muslim doctrine (*ʿaqīdah*). Rather, the Muslim world "shook itself alive just like an almighty giant dismantling its chains, breaking off from its weight, and challenging the aging colonialism."[153] What preserved the living spirit of the Muslim *ummah* was its deep doctrine, which "imperialism, despite its intellectual, spiritual, social, and political efforts, could not kill."[154]

Second, the Qur'ān, as already shown, was translated as a dynamic text by the early Muslim community. In Quṭb's understanding, "Islam is an innovative and creative movement," and not just rites and rituals.[155]

Third, orientalism's treatment of Islamic history is marred by biased scientific and experimental methods that obscure the role of the divine in human events; Eurocentrism which relegates non-European history to a peripheral stage, and imposes on other nations and histories Western epistemological formulations, concepts, ideas and modes of thinking; and an antagonistic attitude to Islam because of the long history of conflict between Islam and the West.[156]

Therefore, argues Quṭb,

> Islamic history must be rewritten according to new principles and a new methodology. This history exists today in two forms; the form of ancient Arabic texts . . . The other place it is available is in the European sources, especially the works of the orientalists . . . [This European version of Islamic history] generally depends on the old Arabic sources, it does not, despite the organization and ordering, serve to assure those who are aware of it.[157]

Muslims must begin to rewrite their own history, and stop looking at themselves through Western glasses. Quṭb points out that

> in our schools and colleges, we study, in a specific manner, distorted Islamic history and blown-up European history. This error is not unintentional; it is rather a reflection of a hidden desire on the side of imperialism that does not want us to be proud of our history. Instead, it wants us to consider Europe as the only prime mover of human history. Once we have given up on our past showing appreciation of the European role [in history] and giving allegiance to the White Man, our control by imperialism would be made easy.[158]

Quṭb charts out the history of colonialism in the Muslim world. He places Zionist Jews and Crusading Christians in the same camp—that of fighting Muslims. He says that they failed to convert Muslims all over the Muslim world into atheism by using materialistic doctrines (*madhāhib māddiyyah*), or through missionary activity and cultural imperialism. After this failure, they resorted, he argues, to more benign methods of establishing social and political systems which adopt the attire of Islam while rejecting its essence, and under this false veil, they have been active in carrying out the recommendations of missionary and orientalist conferences.[159] These Western-produced systems in the Muslim world "lift the banner of Islam, or, at least, declare their respect of religion, while refusing to rule in the name of God, thus dismissing God's *shari'āh* from life."[160] Also, these powers have constantly created false enmities between those systems as a means of preserving Western influence. Quṭb here talks about political, economic, cultural, and intellectual dependency. He says clearly that there is an overall program to preserve a mutilated and wretched status quo in the Muslim world, and the most dangerous part of this "conspiracy" is the amount of manipulation, intimidation, and propganda provided by those "religious apparatuses which have been bought to falsify the parole [of God], and infidelity, an Islamic description, and present corruption, immorality, and promiscuity as evolution, progress and renewal."[161]

Colonialism has taken different shapes, and, to Quṭb, both colonialism and Islam are incompatible. He sees missionary activity as one facet of colonialism, and, consequently, he does not forsee any possibility of rapprochement between Islam and the West.

Quṭb stands against cooperation between Muslims and Westerners, mainly because of the inferior position in which Muslims have found themselves in relation to the West. Quṭb does not "otherize" the West as much as he rejects its conceptions and ways of life. His aggressive views are based on what he sees as historical facts, meaning, Western colonialism in Muslim land and their agencies. The most dangerous of all is the battle over ideas and philosophies and conceptions. The West, he says, still maintains "collaborationist agencies in the colonies in Asia and Africa, and has created new conditions in the so-called independent states in order to replace Islam with secular creeds and doctrines which negate the Unseen on the basis of its scientificity, and they call for the development of morality so that is becomes that of animals . . . and calls for the "development" of Islamic *fiqh*, where orientalists convene conference for its development."[162]

In addition, a whole reductionist attitude prevails. Because of the control of the mass media and the production of culture at the hands of the colonialist and the colonialist-minded, simple-minded Muslims tend to think that the whole battle is sectarian or individual in nature. The enemies of Islam, Quṭb says, are delighted at the success of their recent program, especially after the failure of missionary activity.

So far, the Ikhwan, as an ideological movement, has been characterized as a socioreligious movement that seeks a fundamental change in the status quo. This is clear enough. What is less clear, however, is the intellectual climate in which the Ikhwan grew and the role of the intellectuals in the movement. Has an intellectual community been created by the Ikhwan—a kind of community endowed with a philosophical and critical spirit? Perhaps the answer to this question lies in the general context of Egyptian society, and whether an influential Egyptian intellectual class emerged during that period. The answer in general is in the affirmative. There was a major Egyptian class of intellectuals, both secular and religious, which exerted a major influence on Egyptian cultural life, and the Ikhwan intellectual class was not oblivious to the main social, economic, and political problems with which the Egyptian intelligentsia grappled.[163]

The Ikhwan was able to produce a community of intellectuals who were entrusted with the difficult task of bridging the gap between the diverse intellectual (and elite) tradition of Islam, and the culture of the illiterate and semiliterate masses. Sayyid Quṭb is a fine example of that tendency. Quṭb is a lay religious intellectual who labored through the principal problems of the Ikhwan movement and attempted to find solutions to the abstract theoretical problems and immediate concerns of that movement.

In his assessment of the role of the indigenous intelligentsia, Quṭb argues that they have betrayed their mission on two counts: (1) the clerics have become the betrayors of their people, *La trahison des clercs* in Julien Benda's words,[164] and (2) they—meaning the *ʿulamāʾ*—not only collaborated with the state and the elite in society, but have accepted the orientalist and Western forms of knowledge.

To conclude this section, it is revealing that Quṭb is highly engaged in critiquing orientalist thought and imperialist claims during the same time when the nation/state of Nasser appropriated to itself that privilege unhesitatingly. It is also interesting that the Islamist discourse on orientalism and colonialism was emerging in the 1950s and 1960s, not so much in response to the nationalist critique, but parallel to it. What is remarkable about the Quṭbian discourse is that it emerged during a time when its political side is being marred, if not totally damaged, by a state that claims to be fighting colonialism both intellectually and politically.

Criticism of a Counter-State Ideology: Contemporary Debates Concerning Quṭb's Qur'anic Exegesis

Quṭb's versatile thought and his ideological orientation have not gone unnoticed among a number of observers, both lay and academic alike, who were concerned about the impact which Quṭb's ideas might have on the post-1966 generation of the Ikhwan. In examining the current debates briefly, I endevor to shed more light on the contemporary intellectual landscape of Arab Islamic resurgence in an attempt to answer the following questions: "Has Islamism in the Arab world reached a deadlock?" and "Is there a new intellectual crisis facing the contemporary Islamic movement in the wake of the execution of Quṭb?"

Quṭb's critics—both Muslim and non-Muslim, academic and nonacademic—agree on the following points: (1) Quṭb's Qur'anic ideas matured against a background of prison conditions, and were, therefore, unoriginal, emotional, unrealistic, and antimodernist; (2) To the question, "Who is a Muslim?" Quṭb's answer does not meet the basic conditions set by the Qur'ān and the Sunnah; (3) Likewise, Quṭb, considering the modern Muslim world to belong to "the House of War," or to the *jāhiliyah* system, has condemned all modern Muslims to apostacy, and declared that they were committing a sin because they did not rise against the status quo; (4) His call for isolation from the affairs of Muslim societies and a retreat from all sorts of social and political intercourse with it is a contradiction with the social message of Islam which stipulates that man is a social being; and (5) His argument that all other societies are steeped in *jāhiliyah*, and that it is the duty of the vanguard to fight this situation, is also unwarranted in view of the early history of Islam when the Prophet and his companions made pacts with nonbelievers.[165]

The charge that Quṭb's Qur'anic exegesis of the 1950s and 1960s is unoriginal, and that he is indebted in his basic Qur'anic formulations to outside sources, permeates the work of such scholars as Muḥammad Ḥ. Diyāb, Ḥasan Ḥanafī, Emmanuel Sivan, and Kenneth Cragg. These people suggest that there is a clear connection between Quṭb's *Ẓilāl* thinking and that of Mawdūdī, Nadwī, and Ibn Taymiyya, especially in relation to such concepts as *jāhiliyah*, *ḥākimiyah*, and *hijrah*.[166] I consider this criticism as highly developed in Emannuel Sivan's *Radical Islam: Medieval Theology and Modern Politics*. Sivan's point of departure is the earlier critique of Quṭb's ideas leveled by Ḥasan al-Huḍaybī, the supreme Guide of the Ikhwan, in *Preachers and not Judges*.[167] Huḍaybī was weary of Quṭb's condemnation of all contemporary Muslims, and he adheres to the oft-cited Islamic principle that, "We must consider any one who proclaims that 'there is no God but Allah and that Muḥammad is the messenger of Allah,' to be a Muslim . . . And we must treat him on the basis of the *sharīʿāh* since he is a Muslim."[168] As did Huḍaybī, Sivan bases his whole argument throughout his entire book on the concept of *Jāhiliyah*, but reaches different conclusions from those of Huḍaybī, mainly because of the different methods, audiences, and goals which both have in mind.

Sivan's main goal is to prove that Quṭb's Islamist ideology is not only incompatible with Arab nationalism and socialism, but is, essentially, at odds with Western modernity and its intellectual and historical manifestations. In the words of Sivan, "The core of Sayyid Quṭb's ideas, thus, consists in total rejection of modernity . . . since modernity represents the negation of God's sovereignty (*ḥākimiyah*) in all fields of life and relegation of religion to the dustbin of history."[169] Huḍaybī's main goal, on the other hand, seems to be more modest—namely, the alleviation of the impact of Quṭb's critique of Muslim society. Both Huḍaybī and Sivan, however, agree that Quṭb borrows his ideas from his Indian teachers, especially Abū al-Ḥasān al-Nadwī and Abū al-ʿAla al-Mawdūdī.[170] Both seem to agree, in one way or another, that Quṭb's ideas of the 1950s and 1960s were not original, and that they did not fit the Egyptian or the Arab situation because they were borrowed from Indian sources. However, Sivan goes a step further than Huḍaybī and maintains that "The genius of Quṭb consisted in his grounding his argument in the thought of a prominent medieval thinker, Ibn Taymiyya (1268–1328), and some of his votaries, through an act of creative interpretation."[171] While no one can deny the different influences on Quṭb's thought, one must note three factors.

First, the most single important document affecting Quṭb at this stage is the Qur'ān and the main principles which it contains.

Second, Quṭb discovers gradually through a complex process of transformation and change that Islam, as he understands it, stands in contradistinction to Arab nationalism or any Third-World secular revolutionary idea. Quṭb, had gone a long way, even before the 1952 revolution, in offering Islam as a substitute to the suffering of the masses. Now, he realized, after torturous prison years, that to raise the banner of the Islamic solution would embarass the regime and those associated with.

Finally, it was but logical for Quṭb, under prison conditions or not, to pursue his critical analysis of the state and its associates, especially if its fundamental relationship toward religion did not change. This is what Quṭb harkens to once and again in *Ẓilāl*. The relationship between the *'ulamā'* and the state does not change. The ulama are subservient to a new political system. This is the only change.

The most thorough and systematic critique of Quṭb's Qur'anic ideas is found in Ṣalāh al-Dīn al-Jourshī's *The Islamic Movement in the Whirlwind: A Dialogue Around Sayyid Quṭb's Thought*, referred to previously. Al-Jourshī is a post-1970 Tunisian Islamist who fell, as did many of his generation, under the impact of Quṭb's ideas, and who gradually came to realize the grandiose errors Quṭb commits in his *Mā'alim*. To rectify these errors and to gain a better appreciation of Quṭb's ideas, al-Jourshī compiles and comments on a series of articles published in Beirut in 1973 under the pseudonym Abū 'Izza, a former Palestinian disciple of Quṭb, and which revolve around the central features of Quṭb's *Ẓilāl*.

Abū 'Izza surveys the political and intellectual history of the Ikhwan from 1928 to the early 1970s, and reaches the conclusion that the Movement has long suffered from deadlock, and that it faces a real intellectual and organizational crisis. The predicament of the Ikhwan in its post-Quṭbian period manifests itself in a real lack of any theoretical progress, and an inability to come to grips with the fast changes engulfing the Arab world, especially since the 1967 debacle. Even after these severe years, these

> pregnant years that labored and gave birth to colossal events, rarely seen in the Arab and Muslim world, the Movement is amazingly standing, intellectually speaking, in the same position of the 1950s. Worse yet, oppressive prison conditions led to deviant emotionalism and eccentric thinking. This eccentricity represents a dangerous deviation which is compounded by the intellectual poverty (*faqr fikrī*) the Movement suffers from.[172]

Abū 'Izza argues that two main reasons summarize the current predicament of the Ikhwan .

First, from the beginning, the Ikhwan has fixed its gaze on accomplishing colossal goals (*ahdāf ḍakhma*), such as the reform of Islam in the modern world, and the retrieval of its classical standing and prestige in the spread of social justice. The Ikhwan has simply failed to meet such enormous burdens.

Second, as a movement, the Ikhwan has become a refuge to those fearful of society, who aspire to destroy the foundations of civil society as a means of building it anew. The Movement has developed into a ghetto, which is a symbol of isolation and ostracism. Quṭb's thinking in the *Ẓilāl* is a true reflection of this mentality. His thinking "does not prescribe any Islamic method, but is a culmination of severe protesting cries."[173]

Then, what is the way out of this predicament? One way out is that the Islamic Movement must address the following questions openly and courageously, as a means of achieving theoretical progress and social credibility: (1) It must determine anew the position of the individual member in the Movement, and his/her relationship to the entire society, as well as to the world; (2) The Islamic Movement must redefine its central thesis on society that was declared *jāhilī* by Quṭb, and must be able to find a better way of dealing with the current secular regimes in the Arab world as well as abroad; (3) The Movement must give up Quṭb's violent methods in order to be integrated into contemporary civil society; (4) New ways should be found to achieve Islamic principles without any feeling of coercion and oppression; and (5) the Islamic Movement must be equipped with a modernist outlook that deals with the Islamic tradition of jurisprudence in a way that benefits the contemporary needs of both individual and society.[174]

In his evaluation of Abū 'Izza's critique of Quṭb's intellectual legacy, al-Jourshī agrees in essence with him and sums up the attitude of bewilderment and anxiety which Tunisian Islamists faced in the 1970s as a result of the intellectual and political crisis that preyed on Quṭb's life.

> To us [Tunisian Islamists], the Qur'ān was a non-problematic discourse, and the companions [of the Prophet] were a unique Qur'anic generation unsplit by contradictions and unlimited by time and place. Meanwhile, we both rejected and misunderstood the essence of present reality. In our dreams, the Ikhwan represented the generation of salvation. All we knew about them was what Ḥasan al-Bannā had written in his *Memoirs* and what they had written about themselves. We had often been fascinated by their heroism in the battlefields, in the [Suez] Canal, Sinai, as well as on university campuses. We had always been bewildered by their strong and unweakened patience vis-à-vis all sorts of torture. Alas, our relationship was full of innocence.[175]

Al-Jourshī, as did Abū 'Izza, bemoans the fact that the Ikhwan live in intense crisis, and the crisis is intellectual in essence. However, is it all the error of Sayyid Quṭb? Here, al-Jourshī sounds less condemnatory of Quṭb's legacy than is Abū 'Izza.

> Abū 'Izza has placed the entire responsibility of current paralysis [intellectual and organizational] on the shoulders of Sayyid Quṭb, and offered many a proof. However, I think that it is unfair to do so. Undoubtedly, Sayyid Quṭb has exerted a great deal of influence on the youth of the Movement, and, in effect, he "imposed' himself"—his thought, resistance, straightforwardness, and martyrdom—on the young. Consequently, he became both a

> religious and organizational authority for those workers in the field of Islam. But we must not overlook the heavy legacy Quṭb had "inherited," and the predicament he found the Ikhwan in when he joined the Movement.[176]

Al-Jourshī is basically troubled by Quṭb's indictment of Nasserism, mainly because Quṭb, "in his first stage, struggled against feudalism, imperialism, and capitalism, and the Palace and served the interests of the Free Officers for over a year and accused the United States and its allies in Egypt of plotting to destroy the alliance between Nasser and the Ikhwan."[177] He is also troubled by the fact that Quṭb proclaims that the Muslim world is steeped in *jāhiliyah*. In al-Jourshī's words, Quṭb announces in *Ẓilāl* the absence and death of the *ummah* in both the civilizational and political fields. The pioneers, therefore, must develop in isolation of the *ummah* and society, and reestablish new foundations. Simply put, this is utopian.

It is interesting that both Abū 'Izza and al-Jourshī place their fingers on an essential problem besetting the Ikhwan leadership in the wake of the execution of Quṭb. Fatḥī Yakan, a Lebanese disciple of Quṭb, back in 1967 posed the question of "What is to be Done?" in light of what he termed "the degeneration and failure which have plagued the Islamic Movement [and which] were the result of arbitrary methods of work and negligent planning."[178] In a sense, Yakan prepares the ground for a future critique, such as that of Abū 'Izza or al-Jourshī, of the experience of the Ikhwan. "One of the greatest mistfortunes to have befallen the Islamic Movement," he theorizes, "is the indifference shown by its followers as well as their failure to evaluate the intellectual and political battles they were fighting."[179] In other words, the basic ailment confronting the Islamic Movement, according to Yakan, is as a result of the "intellectual chaos [existing] between the leaders and the members."[180] Yet, where Yakan differs from both Abū 'Izza and al-Jourshī is in his evaluation of civil society, and his basic agreement with Quṭb that the pioneers or Muslim workers "live in a *jāhiliyah* society that has no real connection to religion, a society which has forsaken all principles and values, a society in which the inclination toward good is outweighed by corrupting factors."[181] Yakan also reiterates Quṭb's dictum that "submission to the present reality of *jāhiliyah* is but a form of psychological defeat and surrender," and that what is needed in present Muslim history is courageous, dynamic, and mature members who are armed by Qur'anic methodology, prophetic vision, and tireless espousal of the principles of Islamic *da'wah*. Finally, what distinguishes Yakan from other critics is his firm belief that the current system in the Arab world must be demolished. Compromise is impossible because of dictatorial regimes.

> The ordeal in the life of the Islamic Movement became even more severe [in recent years]. The leadership of the *ummah* was usurped by tyrant rulers who subjected the faithful to the worst of hardships. They killed their men, widowed their women, and subjected them to all kinds of torture. It was inevitable for the Islamic worker to pay the supreme price: blood, sacrifice, and martyrdom. And yet the Islamic Movement would not retreat . . . The enemies as well as the sons of Islam [are] plotting against the Movement.[182]

Conclusions

Quṭb constantly shifts from the theological to the ideological or from the doctrinal to the world of realpolitik in his Qur'anic exegesis. Whereas he praises the early Muslim generation for its unique commitment and understanding of Islam, he shows his frustration—and sometimes his despair—at the contemporary Muslim generation which has forsaken Islam and forgotten its original message of revolutionary activity, commitment, social justice, and social change. He says that the liberation of Palestine cannot come from those who claim to be Muslim because "they have disassociated themselves completely from the religion of God . . . thus rejecting it totally, and they do not refer, in matters of their legislation, economy, socialization, ethics, and mores, to the book of God."[183] In a way, Quṭb documents, perhaps faithfully and painfully, the tragic eclipse of Islam in the modern world as a result of the state of apathy prevalent in the Muslim world. Just as did ʿAbduh and many modern Muslim theologians and thinkers, Quṭb sees the West in highly doctrinal and religious terms.

Quṭb's Qur'anic discourse was developed, to a major extent, in response to three major formations: (1) Quṭb's intellectual preoccupation up to the Egyptian revolution of 1952; (2) the historical and social conditions preceding the 1952 revolution; and (3) the dramatic changes taking place in Egyptian society in the wake of the revolution, especially those changes that pertain to the ever-changing relationship between religion—or Islam—and society.

That Quṭb's Qur'anic discourse developed in the context of, and in response to, the development of Nasserism was but normal in a society in transition. The political, economic, and consequently ideological disintegration of the *ancien régime* left a clear ideological vacuum. Quṭb was highly aware of this sensitive moment in Egyptian history and the possibilities implanted in Islamic ideology to offer an alternative to this state of affairs.

Quṭb was speaking on behalf of a social movement that had planted roots in Egyptian society, a movement that found itself competing for ideological hegemony and domination with the Free Officers. Nasserism exercised hegemony because of its control over the state and social institutions. "Hegemony," in the words of Antonio Gramsci, "critically involves ideological domination. However, the balance between coercion and consent in the exercise of hegemony varies historically. Generally, the weaker the engineering of consent, the stronger the repression exercised by the state has to be."[184] Nasserism's physical repression of the Muslim Brotherhood in the 1950s and 1960s reflected, to a certain extent, its shaky ideological control over all sectors of society. Nasserism was in the process of shoring up its ideological hegemony, and its conflict with the Brotherhood won it the support of two major elements in society: (1) the secular classes, and (2) the Azhar's *'ulamā'*. On the one hand, the secular classes saw a clear contradiction between secularization and Islamization. On the other, the *'ulamā'*, as representatives of official Islam, detested the popular appeals of the Brotherhood as a mass-oriented movement. The new regime, especially between 1952 and 1962, moved to secure the support of the *'ulamā'*—who still functioned as traditional holder of power over the masses—in order to acquire the support of the people for its nationalist and future socialist programs. This historical development in a Third World supports the observation of Antonio Gramsci, who was writing in the 1920s in Italy.

> One of the most important characteristics of every class which develops toward power is its struggle to assimilate and conquer "ideologically" the traditional intellectuals. Assimilations and conquests are the more rapid and effective the more the given social class puts forward simultaneously its own organic intellectuals.[185]

For all sorts of political and social reasons, the Muslim Brotherhood failed to articulate the interests of the disaffected classes which they claimed they represented because either (1) they had no clear and cohesive program, or (2) Nasserism prevented them from doing so.[186]

Against the preceding background, Quṭb's Qur'anic ideology developed. He was totally disillusioned by the failure of the Ikhwan to assume power after the collapse of the monarchy. Ḥasan Ḥanafī portrays a moving image of the agony and suffering of the leadership of the Ikhwan, including Sayyid Quṭb.

> After that time [1956], the Brethren became an underground movement, living in Egypt as a persecuted community. A prison psyche began to develop and to impose itself on their minds. Their deep motivation was a hatred of reality, a need to revenge what nationalism, Arabism, socialism, secularism, and all that Nasser and the Ba'th party stood for. It was a desire to destroy everything and to build anew, a rejection of the other, a refusal of dialogue, a denial of all compromises, etc. All this had culminated in Sayyid Quṭb's Signs on the Road (*Mā'alim fī al-Ṭarīq*). The vanguard, the elite, the new generations of the Prophet's companions were destined to inherit and rule the whole world. The actual world was a world of disbelief, a *jāhiliyah* world which had to be destroyed completely and totally in order to build a new world of belief where everyone could live and practice his own faith. This division of the world into white and black, good and evil, right and wrong, belief and disbelief, pure and impure made the Brethren mind highly Manichaean. They lived in permanent internal and external war. Sayyid Quṭb paid for it in his life in 1965. . . . Even the socialist trend in Quṭb's thought had disappeared.[187]

This lenghty quotation has been only a cursory presentation and analysis of the major themes in Sayyid Quṭb's Qur'anic exegesis. As previously shown, Quṭb's Qur'anic project rests on three interdependent principles or categories or ultimate notions: (1) Metaphysics or/and theological doctrine; (2) Community or *ummah*; and (3) Legal and social regulations and behavior. He is preoccupied with the correct method of interpretation because of the immediate relevance that he sees for the Qur'ān to our modern situation. Quṭb addresses the theological assumptions of the Qur'ān while stressing the inner unity and coherence of its pronouncements as a living *Weltanschauung*. As such, his Qur'anic exegesis is based on key ideas and notions that he derives from the metaphysics of the Qur'ān. In a sense, the structure of his ideas is drawn from the Qur'ān. The method of his interpretation is based on a double movement, moving from the present to the past and back to the present.

From a careful reading of the text, one can conclude that Quṭb's method expresses four broad objectives: (1) Correct interpretation of the nature of God; (2) Proper understanding of the role of man as the vicegerent of God; (3) The viability of the Qur'ān as a comprehensive systm of guidance and knowledge; and (4) The necessity of establishing an Islamic society based on the preceding presuppositions.

Quṭb's understanding of social, political, and economic conflict is essentially doctrinal: it is a conflict between Islam and non-Islam. Consequently, the concept of *jāhiliyah* plays a pivotal role in his thought-structure. In this context, he also realizes that the vanguard or the elite leadership, and not the masses, are the movers of history and revolutions.

Far from being a passive thinker in his last years in prison, Quṭb is painfully aware of the social and economic contradictions in society, and calls for the development of a coherent Islamic discourse that could answer the intellectual and social needs of the moment. The following is a brief outline of Quṭb's main ideas: (1) Islam and *Jāhiliyah* are incomapatible; (2) The modern world, including the Muslim world, is subject to neo-*Jāhiliyah*; (3) Islamic doctrine is a priori superior to other doctrines, be they secular or religious; (4) Islam is the solution to the social and religious malaise in human society; and (5) Islamic doctrine, besides being theoretical, is also social and ideological and (6) The overall goal of Islam is to establish a truly Islamic society.

Although it is somewhat inaccurate to speak of "Islamic theology" in the manner that one speaks of Christian theology, Quṭb understands Islamic theology as a dynamic system whose objective is to create reflective praxis. In other words, theology is not understood as abstract or static metaphysics, but as a dynamic belief system, a critical and reflective epistemological system, and a way of life. As such, theology has a practical function, and this function is not entrusted to a special and privileged class of intellectuals. In other words, Quṭb does not perceive theology to be the privilege of the *'ulamā'* alone, and, in that, he robs the *'ulamā'* of one of their almost sacred roles which they have held over the centuries—the preservation, systematization, and dissemination of religious ideas and concepts.

Theology then serves the needs of every class in society, and its goal should not be to defend Islam rationally but to explicate its general and universal rules against the changing circumstances or situations of Muslims. By "situations" is meant the social, economic, cultural, and intellectual conditions of Muslims that vary from time to time and place to place. Here, Quṭb subjects the contemporary situation of Muslims to a creative interpretation whose sole purpose is to awaken in them the vitality and dynamism of early Islam when Muslims had to labor under hard circumstances.

Quṭb's theological project is not concerned with the often sterile arguments about the compatiblity or incompatiblity of revelation and reason. He does not see any tension between the two. On the contrary, Quṭb perceives reason as aiding revelation in elucidating truth in a human milieu. Furthermore, Quṭb is very rational and logical in his understanding of doctrine and its practical applications in society. He combines rational analysis with theological vision. He also downplays the role of myth and superstition in Islam, and perceives Islam as a "rational religion." Thus Quṭb goes beyond any apologetic defense of the Islamic revelation, and he does so without losing the essential and unique character of this message.

Quṭb's theological discussion is situated in a divine a priori that is, by definition, not amenable to scientific experiments or arguments. This a priori is the main criterion of the Islamic doctrine. As such, he also tries to abstract valid concepts from this formula and create valid concepts and arguments. As a theologian, Quṭb is committed and alienated at the same time. He is committed to the Islamic message and its spread in modern-day Islamic societies, but he is alienated from the prevalent systems of thought and practice in the Muslim world. His committment, though, surpasses his sense of alienation. Quṭb's ultimate concern, however, is to bridge the gap between the ideal and the real. Therefore, his theological presuppositions are ontological in nature. They deal with the social situation of Muslims as well as with the best manner to remedy this situation. From this vantagepoint, Quṭb delves into the structure of Muslim societies, the social meaning of contemporary Muslim life, and the aim or *telos* of existence.

Quṭb also transforms theology into an ideological weapon, an existential reality, and a revolutionary message. Yvonne Haddad sums up this orientation.

> The most advocate of the interpretation of Islam as revolution is Sayyid Quṭb, the late popular Qur'ān interpreter, especially in his revised edition of the first thirteen volumes of *Fī Ẓilāl al-Qur'ān* . . . For humans to participate in this endevour, to bring about the Islamic revolution, it is necessary to harmonize their goals with those of God.[188]

Finally, the real point in question for Sayyid Quṭb is not whether the elite culture of the *'ulamā'* or the secularized intelligentsia will survive, but whether a new cultural expression, based on a novel interpretation of the Qur'ān, will emerge. Quṭb has declared once and again the stagnation of the *'ulamā'* and the sterility of its intellectual, legal, and cultural formulations. Therefore, the question becomes how to bypass this astonishing product of centuries of decline and enfeeblement to effect a renaissance without any recourse to the *'ulamā'* and their culture.

Quṭb agrees with the Muslim modernist on three basic points. (1) The problems of modern Islam are self-generating, on the one hand, and are caused, on the other, by the great gap existing between the Muslim world and the West, which ensued from the technical advancement of the West; (2) A fresh reappraisal and reintepretation of the Qur'ān is needed; and (3) A new pioneering elite needs to emerge.

However, Quṭb and Muslim modernists differ fundamentally in the way in which they view the West and Westernization. This, in turn, highlights another crucial difference, which is the direction that the Muslim world must next take. For Sayyid Quṭb, the direction is to summon the Muslim past, as it were, to the present, and use the context of early Islam as a faithful model to combat modern *Jāhiliyah*. For the modernist, the question of modernity in its Western form is not only unavoidable, but it is a historical given that is inescapable in these times. A Muslim must not only coexist with modernity, but must also realize that its problems are his. Also, to be part of the modern world, Muslims must contribute—along with the West—to solving problems caused by modernity. Quṭb clearly takes a different approach, which can be summarized as the best way to deal with modernity—or *jāhiliyah*—is to dismantle it.[189]

Much has been said about the thought of Quṭb in the *Ẓilāl* as being a product of prison conditions. While this thesis is tenable, in view of the many years that Quṭb spent in prison and the repression of the Ikhwan during the Nasser regime, his *Ẓilāl* must also be seen as a continuation of a strong trend in modern Islam that seeks to dismantle the status quo.

Chapter 7

Toward an Islamic Liberation Theology: Muḥammad Ḥusayn Faḍlallah and the Principles of Shiʿī Resurgence

We [liberals] are continually tempted by the urge to sit back and grasp our time in thought rather than continuing to try to change it.

—*Richard Rorty,* Essays on Heidegger and Others: Philosophical Papers, vol. 2 *(Cambridge 1991) 184*

The philosophers have only interpreted the world in various ways; the point, however, is to change it.

—*Karl Marx, "Theses on Feurerbach." In Karl Marx and Frederick Engels*, Collected Works, *vol. 5 (New York 1976) 8*

Concomitant with this immobile posture is the pervasiveness of fear. We fear the new and the unaccepted and the unfamiliar. That is why when new ideas proposing new approaches to our problems are presented, there is immediately a revulsion on our part because we have been trained to recoil from the unorthdox.

—*Renato Constantino*, Dissent and Counter-Consciousness (*Quezon City, Philippines 1970) 5*

It is for this reason that I am convinced that the greatest, most urgent and most vital task confronting us today is to speak-to speak out correctly, to speak out of a sense of suffering, yet at the same time precisely and scientifically, and thus to analyze what afflicts us.

—*Ali Shariʿati*, On the Sociology of Islam, *tr. Hamid Algar (Berkeley 1979) 41–42*

The purpose of this chapter is to delineate and discuss critically the main ideas of Muḥammad Ḥusayn Faḍlallah, a contemporary Shiʿī *ʿalim*, born in Iraq in 1936 and who has been living in Lebanon since 1966.[1] The study of Faḍlallah's ideas can shed a great deal of light on the following factors: (1) the crisis of civil society in the contemporary Arab world; (2) the meaning of violence in a transitional and volatile political situation; (3) the relationship between violence and the sacred; (4) the nature of the role of the *ʿulamā'*, who have traditionally played the role of the guardians of the faith; and (5) the reconstruction of indigeneous, and, in this case, religious culture in response to the immediate danger of colonialism as seen in the state of Israel.

These questions define, more or less, the parameters of Faḍlallah's thought and his emergence, in my view, as the foremost liberation theologian[2] in contemporary Arab Islam, especially after the untimely death of Muḥammad Bāqir al-Ṣadr in 1979.[3] From reading between the lines, one could deduce clearly that Faḍlallah, in addition to being influenced by the ideas of Khomeini, Montazari, Shariʿati, al-Bannā, and Sayyid Quṭb was also influenced by Fanon, Freire, and even Marx. As a post-Quṭbian thinker, Faḍlallah develops many ideas of Quṭb in relation to some contemporary issues facing the Muslim world.

Religious Critique of the Status Quo and the Role of the *ʿUlamā'*

Perhaps one of the major differences between Sayyid Quṭb and Muḥammad Ḥ. Faḍlallah is that, whereas the former developed his Islamist project against the background of an aggressive and ideological Arab nationalism, the latter has developed his liberation theology project against the background of a gradually disintegrating nation/state, such as Lebanon, the rise of sectarianism, and an increasing external intervention, be it Western, Israeli, Syrian, or Iranian. Faḍlallah's project of liberation theology rests on the premise that decline, backwardness, laziness, apathy, and loss of dynamism have been so embedded in the Muslim psyche for many centuries now that the only plausible answer is a permanent intellectual and cultural revolution stemming from a certain reading of the Islamic principles.

The key to unlocking the hidden and numerous variables in Faḍlallah's thought is, perhaps, found by looking at his complex religious journey as an *ʿālim*, who grew up in a Shiʿī theological school in Najaf and received his educational training at the hands of the most preeminent Shiʿī *ʿulamāʾ* of his day.[4] How does he envision the concept of *ʿilm* in terms of its relevance to the contemporary Islamic situation? And, what function must the *ʿulamāʾ* fulfill during conditions of misery and oppression? The answer to these questions might enlighten us to the critical possibilities which Faḍlallah invests in modern Islamic education as revolutionary pedagogy and to its possible use as a weapon by the oppressed in order to liberate themselves from objective and subjective conditions of oppression and injustice.

To start with, it is obvious that Faḍlallah does not confine his analysis of knowledge to an abstract and irrelevant dogma, but is persistent in presenting a form of religious intellectualism that is both comprehensible and revolutionary. In other words, he theorizes that the conditions of injustice in the modern Muslim world have been humanly constructed over the years by concrete and objective historical and social forces of oppression, and the prelude to dismantling these conditions is through the dissemination of a counterconsciousness ideology and movement spearheaded by the committed *ʿulamāʾ* and *duʿāh* (preachers). He considers those committed and engaged *ʿulamāʾ* and preachers to be just like the pioneers in Quṭbian terminology, to be the intelligentsia par excellence of modern Islam.

How then can the *ʿulamāʾ* achieve a revolutionary status in society without jeopordizing the main principles of their religion? Faḍlallah, the *ʿālim*, discovers that there is much sacred knowledge being disseminated throughout the Muslim world, but that it does not result in any appreciable impact on the daily life and practice of people. He asks the question "Why are the *ʿulamāʾ* so degraded and their position so depreciated?" That is why Faḍlallah's point of departure is not *ʿilm* nor sacred knowledge in its metaphysical, theological, and exegetical aspects, as mentioned previously, but the role of the *ʿulamāʾ* as an engaged segment of society that is committed to moving society forward. In this sense, he reminds us of the famous words of al-Ghazālī who was equally troubled by the depreciation of the *ʿulamāʾ*'s position in twelfth-century Muslim society.

> I am no longer obliged to remain silent, because the reponsibility to speak, as well as warn you, has been imposed on me by your persistent straying from the clear truth, and by your insistence upon fostering evil, flattering ignorance, and stirring up opposition against him who, in order to conform to the dictates of knowledge, deviates from custom and established practice of men.[5]

Faḍlallah, in the same vein, is compelled to speak out against social and political oppression, simply because it is a sacred duty to speak out. He does realize that the twentieth-century situation of Islam is fundamentally different from that of al-Ghazālī's, but that the mechanisms of injustice and oppression are operating in exactly the same way as before. In that sense, he considers *'ilm* as a sacred duty only if it is committed to the problems and issues that the larger society faces.

Faḍlallah is aware of the Qur'anic verse, "Allah raises those of you who believe and those who have been given knowledge whole degrees." (Qur'ān 58:11)[6] However, he considers his function as a simple servant of the masses. *'Ilm* does not gain any meaning unless it is transformed into a critical theory of action. In a sense, the true intellectual is the one who combines both *'ilm* and critical perception. Faḍlallah, in his course of commenting on the education and acculturation of the *du'āh* (preachers) in the contemporary Muslim scene, postulates that the *dā'iyah*, as a true intellectual, must combine in his personality the following foundational principles and criteria: (1) *'ilm* (sacred knowledge); (2) *ma'rifah* (quantitative and practical knowledge); (3) *wa'y* (consciousness); and (4) *ḥiss* (perception).[7] To him, "The question of ignorance and knowledge is that of intelligence and consciousness before it is a question of quantitative knowledge."[8] These four elements must be interchangeable in the personality of the preacher as revolutionary intellectual. In this sense, Fadlallah reminds us of the famous distinction drawn by Richard Hofstadter between intelligence and intellect.

> Intelligence works within the framework of limited but clearly stated goals, and may be quick to shear away questions of thought that do not seem to help in reaching them. Finally, it is of such universal use that it can daily be seen at work and admired alike by simple or complex minds. Intellect, on the other hand, is the critical, creative, and contemplative side of mind. Whereas intelligence seeks to grasp, manipulate, re-order, [and] adjust, intellect examines, ponders, wonders, theorizes, criticizes, [and] imagines. Intelligence will seize the immediate meaning in a situation and evaluate it. Intellect evaluates evaluations, and looks for the meanings of situations as a whole.[9]

The preacher, as true intellectual, is an ideologue with a critical intellect and sharp vision. The preacher must always be on the move against oppression, backwardness, and fear. A perceptive preacher is a man distinguished by an inner ability to feel and see through things, and even predict things before they happen. Above all, critical perception depends upon compassion, mercy, and identification with sorrowful events. It also indicates patience, guidance, and direction.

Faḍlallah worries that the intelligence of the men of religion might be tainted by miseducation and centuries of decline, as well as Western education and ideas. Even the social perception (*ḥiss ijtimāʿī*) of the common people has been formed against this background of oppression. "We [Muslims] have perceived or ascertained the abominable crimes that the capitalist System has generated since we are still going through the [bitter] experience of economic and political imperialism."[10] This is only one side of the picture which can be explained through the lenses of social and economic conditions. What is more poignant, however, is the inability of the modern Muslim to translate *ʿilm* into creative theory and progressive action.

Against this background, Faḍlallah does not look at *ʿilm* as an isolated sanctuary, and the *ʿulamāʾ* are not its isolated priests. Drawing on the Qur'anic verse that "Only the knowledgeable of His slaves [*ʿulamāʾ*] fear Allah," Faḍlallah makes a connection between the *ʿulamāʾ* and the Prophets. The *ʿulamāʾ*, to his mind, are the trustees of the prophets over the masses.[11] He takes the following *ḥadīth* to heart. "The *ʿulamāʾ* are the trustees of the prophets as long as they [the *ʿulamāʾ*] do not cherish this world. They [the companions of the Prophet] asked, 'What does cherishing this world mean?' He [the Prophet] answered: it means being a slave to the Sulṭān [or authority]. If you see them [the *ʿulamāʾ*] doing this type of thing, beware lest they destroy religion."[12] To Faḍlallah, the *ʿulamāʾ* are not just the heirs of the Prophets, in a material or religious sense, but the overseers of their prophetic mission. In other words, they are entrusted with the mission of ameliorating the social and political conditions of the people.[13] An ecclesiastical hierarchy does not exist in Islam, and everyone in the final analysis is responsible. The *ʿālim*, especially when he wears religious garb, is a symbol of the preservation of the message. The message is that one refuses to be contained by authority, that one preserves one's independence and autonomy, and that one remembers all the time that the *ʿālim* is the heir of the prophets in that he must be willing to sacrifice even his blood for the sake of the cause. To Faḍlallah, "The question is not that of a man who shows up at the doorsteps of the mosque so that others pray behind him . . . The question is the destiny of the Qur'ān, and the message, and this movement."[14] The *ʿulamāʾ* are not the ones who simply, "enjoin what is right and forbid what is wrong"[15] by words, but the ones who act as models in transforming their existing conditions. Many have used Islam for certain material purposes. Faḍlallah differentiates between martyrdom and the commercial use of Islam or the commodification of Islam. There is certainly a major difference between these two situations. To be concerned about the daily social and political problems of people leads to perpetual sacrifice and meaningful existence, and perhaps final martyrdom. On the other hand, to use Islam as a medium to reach a material benefit is in the final analysis to be obedient to the whole social and political structure that is maintined by the powers-that-be.[16]

Based on his premise that man's commitment to a cause is the question, Faḍlallah draws attention to the Western infatuation with the danger of Islamic fundamentalism. He argues that "They claim in their Western mass media as well as in the collaborationist media here at home, that, far from lying in Israel, colonialism, and the system of injustice at home, danger lies in Islamic fundamentalism." The West, in the words of Faḍlallah,

> wants everyone to fight this new brand of Islam, this type of Islam that does not lend itself easily to both imperialism and arrogance, and that refuses to be a servant in the palaces of kings and princes, and that refuses to be a mouthpiece for the Sultans so that it calms down the masses for the sake of the rulers. Do you know why this Islam is a danger? It is so because it draws open the eyes of the people to freedom as it does to the worship of God. To be a servant of God means that you stand a free person before the world. And the meaning of you becoming the servant of God alone is that you fear no one except God . . . [What the enemies are] after is the head of this Islam, not the official Islam that moves freely in the sectarian and royal places. They are after the Qur'anic Islam. That is why the Western media compels people to believe that these believers are extremists, radicals and terrorists. In our eyes, they are committed Muslims.[17]

Parallel to al-Bannā's and Quṭb's discussion of the role of the official *'ulamā'*, Faḍlallah sees a strong connection between some *'ulamā'* and the oppressive agents in society. Nevertheless, he seems to appreciate the predicament of the great majority of the *'ulamā'* who do not give a helping hand to the forces of oppression, but who are, at least, the product of oppressive conditions themselves, and, consequently cannot comprehend their own predicament. Many of these *'ulamā'* criticize certain forms of ethical and social deviation in society. Meanwhile, however, they neglect to discuss the fundamental social and political issues, such as political and social injustice, and social crimes. Faḍlallah relies in his arguments on the legal tradition in Islam and agrees with modern Islamic activism that Islam is not only a religion of worship, but a dynamic social and cultural force that is inseparable from the daily concerns and problems of people. He theorizes that it is essential to distinguish between two presences of Islam.

> To my mind, Islam has two presences: (1) in the context of the state, and (2) in the context of the individual and society. Islam differs from the current social and intellectual movements in regards to the idea that a Muslim cannot wait to apply Islam to his individual and collective life until the establishment of the Islamic state. . . . The existence of an Islamic political system is not an essential condition for the application of Islam in individual and collective realms.[18]

This is perhaps one of the main differences between Quṭb and Faḍlallah. Above all Islam is "the religion of ongoing *jihād* at all fronts. It seeks to realize the principles of [Muslim] majesty, pride, and freedom from all kinds of imperialism and slavery."[19] The problem with a great number of *du'āh*, according to Faḍlallah, is that they do not grasp the *shari'āh* emphasis upon *jihād* as a great principle in Islam. The situation becomes even more critical when these *'ulamā'*

> stand against the principle of change in society, and oppose explicitly the movement of revolution against the oppressive System and evil powers in the world. They consequently represent the greatest reserve force of counter-revolution that supports the interests of the conservative groups and the allies of the *ancièn régime*. In the this sense, the believers (*du'āh*) change to become scared elements (*'anāṣir khā'ifa*) that are ambivalent toward the factors of change. Consequently, belief gets transformed into an element of rigidity (*'unṣur jumūd*) instead of becoming an element of forward movement and expansion.[20]

Faḍlallah warns against ambivalence toward corrupt conditions and lack of determination that characterizes the Muslims of the age of decline. The following statement of Jean-Paul Sartre is very apt: "To understand is to change, to go beyond oneself."[21] Faḍlallah's project is based on fighting dominant ideas in society by creating an alternative revolutionary thought structure. It is a call not to remain within the compass of dominating ideas, or even within the compass of that recent colonial tradition that "weighs like a nightmare on the minds of the living."[22]

Although he does not use Marxist vocabulary, Faḍlallah calls for dismantling the hegemonic ideas of the *ancièn régime*, apparantly echoing the following famous words of Karl Marx.

> The ideas of the ruling class are in every epoch the ruling ideas, i.e., the class which is the ruling material force of society is at the same time its ruling intellectual force. The class which has the means of material production at its disposal, consequently also controls the means of mental production.[23]

Faḍlallah, fully aware of the impact of modern historical conditions on Muslims, which he views as a perpetual cycle of decline and repression, challenges the Muslim intelligentsia, especially the *ʿulamāʾ*, to reconstruct the basic concepts of Islam in a way that sheds light on the contemporary situation. He maintains that the Muslim intelligentsia have been besieged by cloudy concepts (*afkār ghāʾima*) precisely because they lack "a solid conceptual base" (*qāʿida fikriyya ṣaliba*).[24] From this angle, Faḍlallah tackles the issue of the cultural formation of the *ʿulamāʾ* and what it means at present. Although he argues that it is the responsibility of every Muslim to shoulder the responsibility of *daʿwa* in all walks of life, he basically places the responsibility on the shoulders of the *ʿulamāʾ*, who, in his view, must be engaged in the life of their people. From this angle, he, like Sayyid Quṭb, attacks the *fiqh* of the dark ages, or that type of jurisprudence produced during the age of decline. He considers it to be the *fiqh* of ignorance, backwardness (*jahl wa takhalluf*), and compromise that denies the existence of problems, and that considers that, as long as Islam is practiced, there is no need to criticize the status quo nor the oppressive behavior of the privileged in society. To Faḍlallah the real question is that of the Islamic glory (*al-ʿizza al-islāmiyya*).[25] Faḍlallah invokes the event of Karbalāʾ and the martyrdom of al-Ḥussain and members of his family as an indication that martyrdom in difficult times is necessary to the preservation of Islamic glory.

To Faḍlallah the *ʿālim*, in addition to being the preeminent guardian and interpreter of the sacred texts, is the conscience of the community.[26] He moves with its pains and sorrows and feels the pulse of his people. Because he perceives the community to be under imminent danger of, not only persecution, but extermination—especially as a result of the Israeli occupation of South Lebanon, where a substantial number of Lebanese Shiʿīs reside—Faḍlallah's simple answer is resistance. It is the answer, "for the sake of man before land and nation. As long as man is humiliated and enslaved, land has no value at all. And as long as the enemies invade and settle in man's psyche and emotions, nation has no value."[27]

The answer is to destroy long-lasting fears. For this purpose, he writes a concise but important treatise on the nature and function of resistance to foreign military power and the ramifications of this type of situation on a relatively small Shiʿī community. In *al-Muqāwama al-islāmiyya* (*Islamic Resistance*), Faḍlallah considers the resistance against Israel as part of a larger confrontation between the *ummah* and the Israeli enemy. To him, the question of the Lebanese south is not sectarian—neither Shiʿī nor Sunni nor Christian, but symbolic of the larger problems facing the *ummah* nowadays. In this regard, Faḍlallah believes in constant revolution and change. Revolutions, in his view, should not be restricted to a certain region or country of the current Muslim world.

> Revolution cannot be limited to a particular region. Revolution is the expression of a dynamic thought that reflects the deep pain, oppression, and exploitation of man. In this regard, revolution is a universal human phenomenon . . . that cannot be a commodity subject to export and import. Revolution is debate, dialogue, challenge and movement, and once these are achieved, it becomes a natural phenomenon in the world.[28]

In his view, "oppression is evil, colonialism is evil, and zionism is evil."[29]

Islamic Theory of Oppression

Faḍlallah develops his Islamic theory of oppression on the basis of both his understanding of the Qur'ān and his reading of the objective, social, economic, political, and cultural conditions surrounding the masses of the oppressed in the modern Muslim world. Essentially, Faḍlallah perceives oppression as a process of dehumanization that negates the freedom given to man by the Qur'ān. The oppressed (*al-mustaḍaʿfoun* in Qur'anic terminology) suffer from social and economic exploitation and, above all, self-depreciation.

Faḍlallah considers the rich and power elite to be responsible for this state of affairs. In a sense, he argues that both oppression and fear are humanly engineered.[30] Moreover, the power elite is capable of politically thwarting the freedom of the poor who, according to Faḍlallah, fall under the sway of the rich who possess the economic means of production. Therefore, they are perpetually denied the ability to become self-sufficient. In other words, the poor are made to be dependent upon the economic structure of wealth, and they are robbed of their independent decision-making. Simply put, they are alienated. Here, Faḍlallah agrees with Marx that the poor are denied their creative quality, because the outcome of their labor is taken away from them. This is more than simple dehumanization. Economic power becomes a strong "element of [external] pressure that paralyzes or abolishes the autonomous will of man."[31] Although Faḍlallah does not believe in the Marxist method of class analysis, nevertheless, he argues that, like the proletariat in Marxist terminology, the oppressed are alienated because they are robbed of their essential values.[32]

What defines man's identity is his ability to attain freedom without any internal or external impediment. Faḍlallah agrees essentially with Paulo Freire's formulation that real freedom is "thwarted by injustice, exploitation, oppression, and the violence of the oppressors; it is affirmed by the yearning of the oppressed for freedom and justice, and by their struggle to recover their lost humanity."[33] However, he does not go so far as Freire in proclaiming that the great historical mission of the oppressed is to liberate both themselves and their oppressors. Faḍlallah does not see this link at all. On the contrary, he is of the mind that, if the conditions of oppression must be dismantled, it logically follows that the power elite must be destroyed. As has been mentioned, it behooves the *'ulamā'*, as the leading and committed intelligentsia in society, to intervene critically on behalf of the masses in order to map out the way to salvation. They must help the masses transform their situation of oppression to that of liberation. Freedom recognizes itself in anguish, and the oppressed, in order to attain their emancipation, must go through much suffering, which, in turn, is a requirement of this type of life.

Furthermore, Faḍlallah maintains that, because of the tribal and semitribal nature of many a Muslim society, family ties and presitge still play a crucial role in fostering conditions of oppression. The rich always rely on their family tradition or their understanding of it. It is no surprise, therefore, that those who stood against the prophetic messages belonged to the highest families in society.[34]

In addition to economic power and family ties, Faḍlallah argues that the rich resort very often to military power in order to maintain their power and prestige. What that means is that, all over the Muslim world, there is a minority of power holders who have access to the army, which is in the service of the power elite.[35] Externally speaking, Faḍlallah is of the opinion that the indigenous power and military elite forges ties and alliances with international imperialism in order to limit and paralyze the autonomous freedom of smaller nations. This relationship of power is not limited to economic or social exploitation, but also to a cultural and intellectual dependency as well. Faḍlallah reaches the important conclusion that different modes of exploitation, both latent and manifest, exist in the modern Muslim world. Human history is the summation of "the perpetual tragic conflict between the powerful and the weak, between the arrogant and the oppressed, and between injustice and justice."[36]

In addition to these forms of exploitation, Faḍlallah introduces the term, "doctrinal oppression" (*istidh'āf fī al-'aqīda*), in order to describe the impediments that shape the current intellectual landscape in the Muslim world. He describes the preceding terms as man lacking "the flexible and strong thought that enables him to open up to Truth, and, consequently, he lacks the intellectual methods that enable him to possess either detailed or comprehensive knowledge as a means of discerning different views."[37] In other words, Faḍlallah believes that the powerful and oppressors prefer that the oppressed live in a perpetual situation in which they are not even aware of their conditions. He postualtes that "at the level of both doctrine and life, no difference exists between the cases of individual oppression and those cases of oppressing communities and nations. From this we conclude that confronting the power of evil and intransigence, represented by imperialist power that promotes economic and political imperialism, is an Islamic responsibility that has to be carried out within the context of the means [Muslim] masses possess."[38]

Faḍlallah maintains that the Qur'ān, as a sacred document, speaks aginst oppression and encourages man to rebel against it. He notes that the Qur'ān makes a distinction between two categories of the oppressed: (1) those who have the means but lack the will to change their conditions, preferring fear, comfort, and laziness, unwilling to sacrifice their sense of safety and personal gains and prestige; and (2) those who are born in objective oppressive conditions, and who are encouraged by the Qur'ān to emigrate as a means of breaking down the circle of fear and oppression. The first are punished because they do not heed the Qur'anic advice of migrating. "When angels take the souls of those who die in sin against their souls, they ask, 'In what [plight] were ye?' They reply, 'Weak and oppressed were we in earth.' They say, 'Was not the earth of Allah spacious enough for you to move yourselves away [from evil]?' Such men will find their abode in hell—What an evil refuge!" (Qur'ān 4:97).[39] Faḍlallah maintains that there is more than one way of confronting oppression, one of which is emigration in order to practice religion freely, away from any oppression.

Toward an Islamic Theory of Power

As shown in the previous section, Faḍlallah embraces a revolutionary Islamic worldview that does not shy away from resisting oppression and injustice. His point of departure in treating the issue of power is the handicapped situation of the Muslim *ummah* and the increasing external pressure on Muslims, according to him, to resort to self-defeatism and apathy to the challenges surrounding them. Faḍlallah poses the question as to why one should devote so much energy and time to discussing the issue of power. He asserts that both power and weakness are two key dynamics that define the relationship between "the oppressed nations" (*al-shū'ūb al-mustadh'afa*) and "the arrogant powers" (*al-qiwa al-mustakbira*).[40] This is a dialectical situation, no doubt, that weighs heavily on the daily lives of the oppressed, and makes them totally dependent on the oppressors in their economic, cultural, social, and even conceptual lives. In order to achieve a correct understanding of Islam, as "a social and political religion"[41] (*dīn ijtimā'ī wa siyāsī*) that is highly entertwined with all aspects of life.

> The Islamic theory of power must be transformed into a comprehensive educational process, with curricula and programs that move in all directions. It is very hazardous indeed for weakness to impose itself on the *ummah* against the background of backwardness, the pressure of the arrogant powers, and the negative and apathetic attitude prevailing amongst Muslims in face of challenges.[42]

For *jihād* to become an ever-growing and dynamic process, Muslims must present Islam "as an independent economic, political, and conceptual equation that faces the infidel and arrogant equations [of foreign powers]."[43] In a sense, Faḍlallah does not treat *jihād* in the way understood by, to quote Bernard Lewis, "The overwhelming majority of classical theologians, jurists, and traditionists . . . [who] understood the obligation of *jihād* in a military sense, and have expounded it accordingly."[44] *Jihād* is an all-embracing concept that covers the spiritual and the physical, the concrete and subtle. Faḍlallah agrees with Quṭb that *'aqīdah*, as an abstract theological doctrine, is useless unless it provides a guiding light to the issues besetting contemporary Muslims.

Faḍallah defines power as both a material force and a spiritual energy. Material force alone does not suffice to preserve the well-being and the territorial integrity of a nation. Basing his argument on the well-enunciated premise that "the weak have the right to make a different set of rules for themselves,"[45] Faḍlallah stipulates that the poor nations need inner and spiritual power in order to face the continuous propaganda, which is, in the opinion of Faḍlallah, the hallmark of the West, waged by the arrogant powers. Neocolonialism becomes institutionalized as a result of the psychological defeat of the oppressed. To lack power does not only mean losing the will to struggle and the desire to become alive, "but that you become a carbon copy and shade of another human being,"[46] and the weak nations become carbon copies of the strong ones.

In countering the argument that Islam, as a monotheistic religion, robs man of his essential freedom of choice vis-à-vis the mighty power of the Divine, Faḍlallah asserts that the relationship between God and man, as explained by the Qur'ān, is essentially emancipatory. "It is a basic source of power that energizes man continuously, and propels him to an autonomous movement of perpetual growth and renewal, so that he can renew life around him and push it forward."[47] However, Faḍlallah acknowledges that, throughout Islamic history, a number of philosophies and worldviews emerged to justify social injustice and the oppression of the poor by the rich in the name of predestination and the abstract power of God.[48]

Faḍlallah sees history as a perpetual struggle between the oppressors and the oppressed. Injustice, at the deeper level, involves the annihilation of man's humanity and the obstruction of his autonomous will by the exploitative, hegemonic, and dominating forces existing in a society. Faḍlallah is indeed conscious of the social dimensions of oppression and freedom. While his point of departure is a certain understanding of the Qur'anic text and the affirmation of individual freedom, he tries to come to grips with the debilitating situation of his community in Lebanon and the larger situation of the *ummah*. In a sense, Faḍlallah grapples with the painful breakdown of civil society in Lebanon and the debilitating impact which this breakdown may have had on the ordinary people. What is painful, further, is that violence is not only masked or latent, but is explicit, appearing in daily loss of life perpetuated by internal as well as external forces. Violence is initiated, as it has been for centuries, by a power elite that does not take the masses into account, except to inflict suffering and pain upon them. The response to this tragic situation is, by definition, tragic. However, this tragedy perhaps provides some sort of salvation to the community at large.

Faḍlallah is not oblivious to the deep impact which the feudal mentality might have had on the modern Muslim mind. He stresses that the bourgeois revolution—or the nationalist revolution in the modern Muslim world—has failed to shake off highly entrenched feelings and concepts of slavery, submission, and exploitation that still define the cultural parameters of the modern Muslim world. Therefore, Muslims must understand Islam as a radical rupture from all these entrenched modes of slavery. Islam becomes a social and historical agent of great transformation and change.[49]

Faḍlallah is obsessed—and understandably so—with the sectarian, economic, and social divisions in Lebanese society. He is uncomfortable with the divisions and in-fighting of the Muslim community. He spends a great deal of time trying to reconstruct the Islamic ideology of social cohesiveness as one important step toward combating collective weakness and dependence on outside forces. Social unity that translates itself as a counterforce to sectarianism and disunity can be achieved only if certain conditions are met. First, the Qur'anic components of unity—that is, mercy and compassion among believers—are actualized under the current conditions. Second, the historical examples of unity are studied carefully. And third, the historical agents of oppression are uncovered and defeated. Not surprisingly, Faḍlallah considers the last condition to be a high point of priority. He argues that three modes of power in Islamic history have always been responsible for the institutionalization of the philosophy of weakness and backwardness: (1) the social and economically privileged elite that fights any revolution in the name of the preservation of the status quo; (2) those men of religion, rulers and politicians, who thrive on division and who follow the maxim of 'divide and rule'; and (3) proponents of deviant ideologies which are mainly instigated by outside forces to destroy the coherence of the *ummah*.[50] Social cohesiveness presupposes doctrinal unity. Faḍlallah warns against conceptual disunity because any "difference in general doctrinal issues would pave the way for real gaps in the social and conceptual skeleton of society."[51]

Faḍlallah maintains that the Qur'ān sanctions the use of power in Islam, and considers it as an ethically- and socially-bound issue. Historically speaking, however, the rich have used power as a mechanism to distinguish themselves from society, and as a mode to both exploit and oppress the poor and weak in society. The historical use of power in such a fashion has always constituted a problem for the oppressed. Faḍlallah maintains that the oppressed were prevented from transforming themselves into independent and participant beings, and are always made to feel dependent on powers higher than themselves. The negation of their humanity, in a sense, led to self-depreciation and blindness to the real possibilities that they might possess. To Faḍlallah's mind, it has been the sacred duty of the responsible *'ulamā'* and thinkers of Islam to alert the silent and oppressed majority to their plight, and to the doctrinal and ethical Islamic attitude that opposes such exploitation and misery. Also according to Faḍlallah, the *'ulamā'* must maintain a dialogical relationship with the oppressed as a means of helping them express their long-embedded suffering. In a sense, he reminds us of the words of Freire that "the only effective instrument [in liberating the oppressed] is a humanizing pedagogy in which the revolutionary leadership establishes a permanent relationship of dialogue with the oppressed."[52] Faḍlallah maintains that the use of power by the oppressed is justified for the following reasons: (1) to ward off inner defeat and apathy; (2) to relate to the message of Islam in a dynamic and clear way; and (3) to fight neocolonialism as a social, economic, and political reality in the contemporary Muslim world. Both classical and modern colonialism, according to Faḍlallah, has used its military and political powers in order to coerce nations into submission and slavery. This situation has resulted in racial superiority of the colonizer, and a dependent economic relationship between the colonizer and colonized in which "the weak and colonized nations have to provide raw material to support the industry of the colonizer."[53] This is, however, the first stage of colonization that precedes a more pernicious form of slavery in which

> industrial civilization leaves its stamp on the lives of nations, and fashions their personality in its own way so that the oppressed fix their gaze on it in their general and specific endevours. Against this background, [colonialism] has always created distress (*fitnah*), invented wars and problems, and prevented the growth of industrial movement in the developing countries that had been for long trying to reach self-sufficiency in consumer products. Imperialist countries have succeeded to convert the economy of

> the developing countries into a military-oriented one, . . . thus forcing these countries into bankruptcies as a result of heavy military duties and much debt.[54]

In this, Faḍlallah reminds us of what Franz Fanon had to say about colonialism.

> Colonialism and imperialism have not paid their score when they withdrew their flags and their police from our territories. For centuries, the capitalists have behaved in the underdeveloped world like nothing more than war criminals. Deportations, massacres, forced labor and slavery have been the main methods used by capitalism to increase its wealth, its gold or diamond reserves, and to establish its power.[55]

Islam, as previously mentioned, does not eschew propagating power as an instrument for liberation. The main goals of the use of power can be summarized as: (1) reconstruction of Muslim life, and ensuring that power, if used in a proper doctrinal and ethical sense, is a major positive dynamic in society; (2) protecting the *'aqīdah* from the oppression of its enemies, thus entailing distress among the believers; (3) aiding the oppressed and exploited against the oppressive powers represented by internal and external enemies; (4) weakening the infidels and destroying their power; and (5) seeking self-defense and the preservation of the people, sacred places, and the country against any aggression.[56] Thus, Islam has, both legally and ethically, justified the use of power against any wrongdoing and deviation from the path of justice. This brings up the issue of the interest (*maṣlahah*) of the Muslim community. The *maṣlahah* necessitates fighting against oppression at this stage in Muslim history.

Power is also necessary to respond to the critical challenges of the contemporary situation. Faḍlallah makes the point that his contemporary Muslim world suffers from a loss of positive energy, on the one hand, while on the other, its local and international enemies have eaten up a great chunk of its resources, both material and human. Faḍlallah gives the example of the oil industry that is virtually controlled by a minority of rich people whose destiny is greatly intertwined with that of colonialism.[57]

Faḍlallah considers the West to be the enemy par excellence. He argues that the West is responsible for creating a violence-laden environment in the Middle East in general, and Lebanon in particular. Violence, to him, emanates not from a state of mind, but from given social and political conditions imposed by the oppressive power of the West. He warns against seeking any form of alliance with imperialism in order to get rid of domestic oppressors. He argues that the collaboration of the Arab leadership with the British on the eve of World War I was a great historical mistake. It led to the creation of a new form of colonialism that was far worse in its oppression than was the Ottoman era.[58] In the final analysis, power is an essential component of human life. The only way to prevent the abuse of power, and the corruption that could result from it, is by applying strict Islamic criteria. Revolution under the prevailing conditions is a must. This is the paradox, and this is the price that Muslims must pay in order to preserve their doctrine and themselves.

As mentioned already, Faḍlallah does not deny the link that might exist between Islam, as a revealed religious phenomenon, and violence. On the contrary, he seems to think that this relationship is, not only necessary and urgent, but is at the heart of the Islamic religious quest. Faḍlallah translates violence into a self-defensive act of resisting the enemy and martyrdom.[59] The latter key term, of course, is embued with the heavy symbolism of Shiʿī history. Martyrdom has assumed a sacred place par excellence and, from this perspective, it is perhaps easy to discern the complex objective and subjective history of Shiʿism in Lebanon through the lenses of predicament and martyrdom. According to Rene Girard, "Sacrifice contains an element of mystery."[60] Sacrifice can give meaning to a meaningless world in which things must be smashed so that a new order can be reborn.[61] To Faḍlallah, the situation facing Muslims in Lebanon in particular, and the Muslim world in general, contains a great deal of pain, deviation from the true path of Islam. Only a mysterious act might be able to dislodge its harsh components.

Rene Girard also argues that

> the sacrificial process requires a certain degree of misunderstanding. The celebrants do not and must not comprehend the true role of the sacrificial act. The theological basis of the sacrifice has a crucial role in fostering this misunderstanding. It is the god who supposedly demands the victims; he alone, in principle, who savors the smoke from the altars and requisitions the slaughtered flesh.[62]

The *ʿālim*, as the interpreter of the Sacred Text, carries the burden of offering a theological explanation, if not justification, of the sacrifical process. Muḥammad Ḥussain Faḍlallah has done just that. In a sense, the believers who wish to achieve martyrdom in order to advance the collective cause of Islam and Muslims must, in principle, meet the approval of a theological body. They cannot sacrifice themselves on their own, lest they summon the wrath of the divine. Therefore, Faḍlallah defines martyrdom as a mechanism that helps to alleviate suffering, draws Muslims closer to each other, and alerts the world to the plight of the downtrodden.

Mission and Commitment: Role of *Dā'iya* in Times of Crisis

Faḍlallah uses three interdependent key terms in order to illustrate his concept of a dynamic Islamic movement—*du'āh* (preachers), *ḥarakiyyoun* (activists), and *'ulamā'* (learned men of religion). We have already dwelt at some length at the *'ulamā'* and their function as deliverers of the poor and oppressed in society. A discussion of the first two terms is in order.

Faḍlallah grapples with the historical application of Islam and especially its relevance to the contemporary situation. As did Sayyid Quṭb, he believes in the dynamism of the Islamic mission and the necessity of the emergence of preachers who might be able to practice this mission. Unlike Quṭb, however, he does not believe that Muslim society lives in *jāhiliyah*, although he acknowledges that there is a sense of acute predicament that permeates the whole psychological attitude of Muslims. He highlights the motif of oppression at the expense of *jāhiliyah* and prepares the ground for a thorough critique of the state of affairs that, to his mind, had been saturated by oppression for many centuries. He believes that change is the solution to the condition of oppression. For the Muslim *ummah* to grasp the overall meaning of doctrine and its various implications in life, it must be prepared psychologically to accept change, and, therefore, gradual change is necessary. Faḍlallah stresses over and over again that the leaders of *da'wa* must come to grips with the objective social and economic conditions in which the *ummah* exists, analyze the basic features and problems, and offer diagnoses that befit the situation.[63] He bemoans the fact that a large number of Muslim youth carry a distorted understanding of Islam because of the prevalence, according to him, of incorrect concepts brought forth by adverse social and economic conditions and erroneous practices of some men of religion.[64]

Faḍlallah's understanding and presumption of Islam as a practical religion (*dīn 'amalī*) underscores his pragmatic goal as a theologian.

He is concerned with obtaining concrete results through the efforts of both the community and the preachers at large. The community must be compelled to grasp an understanding of its state of affairs and meet the challenges which it is facing. Faḍlallah notes that Islam is withdrawing from the life of society gradually. He asks, "How is it conceivable that we draw back and languish in carrying out our responsibilities, in a way that invokes a lazy and defeatest logic? How can we justify our submission to despair, denying that there is ever a problem, or not believing that there are stormy challenges that shake the universe around us?"[65] In Faḍlallah's view, the situation is so critical that it does not admit of any isolation, inaction, laziness, fear, and ambivalence. Those who subscribe to such notions are on a par with the enemies of Islam, he claims.

Against this background, the preachers must feel the pulse of the community. Broad-mindedness in religious and cultural formation is the key to revolutionary pedagogy. In addition to learning the Qur'ān and the *sunnah*, the preacher must acquaint himself with all manner of disciplines from literature to psychology and science. It becomes urgent, therefore, that the preachers study other cultures, and even learn the techniques and methods of Christian missionaries in Muslim lands. The genius of Christian missionaries, according to Faḍlallah, is that they were able to practice their mission work through all sorts of disciplines, including medicine, business, law, and so forth. Preachers must be selective in their knowledge. They should choose practical knowledge that lends a helping hand to their situation. They should also avoid mental leisure and empty rhetoric. Islamic mission work must revolve around the cultural aspects of society, in that preachers should be the builders of a new and modern Islamic culture. To be able to do so, the temperament of the preacher must be stamped by both his mission (*risālah*) and the concrete conditions in which he lives.[66]

To be in tune with the cultural side of society, it is necessary that the preachers face and surmount the difficulties with an open perception (*iḥsās munfatiḥ*) mainly because of the predominance of despair, defeatism, naivete, apathy, and cynicism in the contemporary situation. Many a *dā'iya* has lost this social perception and, consequently, the *du'āh* "cannot face reality with intelligent feelings, open perception, and comprehension of the surrounding environments, conditions, and events. Knowledge for the *du'āh* turns into naive and fragile conclusions, missing and severed information, and limited experiences."[67] The preachers must come to grips with the imperialist problematic. Faḍlallah maintains that imperialism has always taken advantage of sectarian and political divisions, and historical malice and enmity to promote its domination and hegemony, particularly in Lebanon. However, the worst aspect of the whole matter is that those who lack social perception among the Muslims have gone along with these imperialist conspiracies. Faḍlallah is highly critical of what he terms the emotional outbursts and naivete that characterize the workers for Islam. Because they lack both "a deep and broad conceptual base and an intelligent and critical sense,"[68] they have become an easy prey in the hands of imperialism. In a sense, Faḍlallah reaches a point of despair when discussing the various limitations and handicaps of the preachers, and he says that it is perhaps impossible to achieve the goal of deliverance because of (1) the ignorance of the fighters, and (2) the enmity of the enemies.[69]

Contrary to his wishes, perhaps, Faḍlallah believes that only a few dedicated and trained preachers and activists can fulfill the mission he has in mind. One major aspect of this mission is the reconstruction of modern Islamic thought, which requires, in his view, a complete immersion in both Islamic and Western sources. One must not be oblivious to the great Western achievements in science and civilization. Also, authentic Islamic concepts and values should be invoked in order to understand the modern situation. In a sense, Faḍlallah refuses to escape into a rosy and ideal past. Instead, he is so obsessed with the modern situation to the extent that he challenges all Muslims to grapple with Western civilization in an objective and somewhat constructive way.

It is true that Faḍlallah warns against the hazards of colonialism in the Muslim world, but, surprisingly enough, he thinks Muslims can derive a great benefit from the intellectual and cultural achievements of Western civilization. To his mind, Muslims must employ a correct method to understand the West, and this method should account for the intellectual foundations of Western civilization and its broad human and social goals. One problem of modern Muslim thinkers is their failure to understand Western civilization because they merely emphasize one issue at the expense of others—namely, the issue of the spiritual malaise of the West.[70] Faḍlallah argues that this should not be the only yardstick by which to understand the West, especially as Muslims themselves have been, historically speaking, under the spell of the modern West. In other words, Faḍlallah argues that one must come to grips with the internal dynamics of Western civilization and must try to understand it from within. On the other hand, it behooves the same Muslim intelligentsia to apply Muslim criteria to the Islamic civilization. That is to say that Islam, as a civilization, has its own logic, and it is hazardous to "rationalize or modernize Islam so it can enter through the wide gate of modern life."[71] Although Faḍlallah attacks both colonialism and capitalism as two products of Western civilization, he does not envision any clash of civilizations between Islam and the West in the aftermath of the disintegration of the Soviet system and the emergence of the United States as the leading superpower in the world.[72]

The solution that Faḍlallah gives to the predicament of modern Muslims calls for the application of the Prophet's method of change at the following levels: (1) a gradual dissemination of Islamic ideas; (2) a peaceful method of dissemination without gaining the wrath of the status quo; (3) a personal method of dissemination; (4) emigration in case religion is under siege and attack, with emigration meaning safety, metamorphosis, and general breakdown of society; and (d) a determined and committed attitude that has a breadth of patience and knowledge. One must realize mobile and practical conceptual bases (*qawāʿid fikriyya wa ʿamaliyya mutaḥarrika*).[73]

Islam and the Problem of Israel

As a Shiʿī scholar residing in Lebanon, Faḍlallah displays a unique view on the Palestine question, and he shares the concern with many an Islamist thinker that the Arab nation/state has utterly failed in finding a lasting solution to the Palestinian question mainly because of the narrow foundations of Arab nationalism. Worse yet, Faḍlallah argues that the Muslim *ummah* at large has turned a deaf ear to the Palestine question, and treated the Palestinian as a heavy burden and an insoluble problem.[74] Faḍlallah says that the Palestinian is always under heavy scrutiny in almost every Arab country, and the only lasting solution to the Palestine question must flow from Islamic unity, which can be achieved only if regionalism and political divisions are dismantled in the modern Muslim world. He contends that the Palestine question is at the heart of modern Islam.

> To my mind, the question of Palestine, as a result of its unique nature, position, allusions, and the political impact it has had on the Muslim world, summarizes in a nutshell the movement of Islamic history in this age. In its genesis, the Palestine question represents the conflict between Islam and British colonialism, that was intersected by a conflict between Islam and the Zionist movement. The Palestine question has led to a general conflict between Islam and the West.[75]

Faḍlallah, following in the steps of the ideology of modern Islamism, considers Israel as an extension of Western colonialism. To his mind, Israel is not a settler colonial/state in the classical sense, but a Western outpost.

> That Israel has emerged as a comprehensive plan to co-opt the area politically, militarily, economically, demographially, and culturally is a question that does not need any scrutiny. Any reading of the history of the Zionist movement and the Israeli military and political reality will inform us that Israel always attempts to create new favorable conditions so it can expand. Israel cannot satisfy itself to occupy some land, but it wishes to occupy the whole region, if not militarily, politically and economically.[76]

Faḍlallah maintains that, as a result of Israeli hegemony and Western penetration in the area, the Islamic presence is under severe threat. Israel, of course, cannot do all of this without, especially, the full support of the United States. He mocks the narrow outlook of American foreign policy and its lack of appreciation of Islam as a dynamic force in contemporary Muslim societies, "America wishes to conquer any Muslim spirit that raises the banner of Islam or freedom. It [America] senses that the Islam of Truth, not that of sectarianism, but that of the Qur'ān cannot compromise with an imperialist or an arrogant person."[77] He equates any indigenous collaboration with either Israel and the United States as a form of *fitnah*—a deviation from the true path of Islam and a split within Muslim ranks. He calls on men, women, and children to mobilize against those who might try to create *fitnah*, because "the question is that of our existence, our future and life. This is the question that we must be responsible for."[78]

Against this background, Faḍlallah resorts to Shiʿī symbolism as a means of coming to grips with the present. He invites modern Muslims to contemplate the tragic event of Karbalā', and postulates that this tragedy must be transformed "to a new form of heroism in order to prevent any new tragedy."[79] Faḍlallah draws a comparison between Yazīd, the Umayyad caliph responsible for Karbalā', and the modern state of Israel. Both have attempted to humiliate and kill Muslims. "Israel gives us the option of either dying under the wheels of its tanks or dying alive under the wheels of its political, economic and cultural policies and maneuverings."[80]

From Faḍlallah's perspective, martyrdom, just like revolution, is a constant necessity. Resistance is not a transient episode, but is a continuous event as long as its goals are not achieved. "Death for a resistant Muslim does not constitute a tragedy or a fake psychological condition. Death for him is a thought-out condition that is not instigated by passing feelings. The resistant Muslim lives for the goals as long as they exist."[81] To his mind, the choice of martyrdom and death is in agreement with the spiritual and doctrinal foundations of the believer. Death becomes a self-willed process instigated by internal factors. Also, "death is a step that leads to reaching the martyr's goals. That is why the believer, when he achieves self-martyrdom, lives through spiritual happiness."[82] Faḍlallah contends that self-martyrdom is not the result of brainwashing, nor is it irrational or immoral. Those who interpret martyrdom in such a way are guided by the premises of psychology.

> The problem with the discipline of psychology is that it attempts to study the phenomenon of martyrdom from the perspective of pragmatic vocabulary and laboratory results. They refuse to admit that certain things can be understood only through labor and pain. You can never be capable of appreciating freedom if you do not come to grips with enslavement. You can appreciate the cries of the starved only when you come to grips with the pangs of starvation.[83]

What gives the martyr the right to die is not merely a cause in a theoretical sense, but the practical conditions that give rise to that cause. In a sense, Faḍlallah seems to be saying that the *'ulamā'* must sanction martyrdom only when the situation requires self-martyring acts. In a sense, what Kramer has to say is somewhat true in that the self-martyring operations "could be made Islamic only by sanctification, which takes the form of reconcilation between the act and the abstract principle, done by those qualified to interpret sacred law."[84] But the *'ulamā'*, in Faḍlallah's view and as has been said earlier, are the conscience of the suffering community. Suffering is mainly caused at the hands of Israelis, and the only answer to this suffering is martyrdom.

In addition to Shi'ī symbolism, Faḍlallah stresses the importance of national (such as Lebanese) unity in face of what he terms Western aggression. He reiterates the notion that colonialism is the only beneficiary of sectarian conflicts, and Israel is the immediate entity to benefit from: (1) sectarian divisions; (2) religious and doctrinal Muslim divisions; and (3) political differences. He adds that all communities in Lebanon suffer from the same divisive political and social reality, and that Israel is the common denominator to all these divisions.[85]

In his treatment of Israel and the West as the enemy, Faḍlallah contemplates the current political regimes in Arab countries and comes to the conclusion that most of them are more pernicious and even harsher in their treatment of their subjects than external enemies. He says that

> The Arab regimes, in their alliance with either [the capitalist] West or [the communist] East have benefited greatly from the Palestine problem by oppressing their people and claiming that they were waging war against Israel, and that the situation of war necessitates emergency rules. Thus, the [Arab] regimes have succeeded in appropriating the *ummah* by expropriating its freedom of expression, and cancelling out its right in political maneuvering and movement.[86]

Also, some Arab regimes, especially in the Gulf, claim that "the real enemy is not Israel but the Palestinians. We know that the intention of such a plan is to drive a wedge between the Arab and Muslim *ummah* on the one hand and the Palestinian question on the other."[87] Faḍlallah also argues that the majority of the Arab regimes, Israel, and the United States seek a solution to the Palestine question at this juncture in history for the following reasons: (1) the Arab world is ready to be rid of the Palestinian situation; (2) Israeli society has fallen under the impact of the *intifāḍa* and is unable to deal with it socially or psychologically; and (3) the United States stands to benefit a good deal from the new World Order, this being an opportune moment to exert the American version of peace. He also argues that Israel plays an insignificant role in confronting the Islamist danger mainly because "the Arab regimes have done a marvelous job in confronting the Islamic movement."[88] The Arab regimes themselves have replaced Israel in importance by delivering a valuable service to the Western interests in the area.

Faḍlallah modifies this position only slightly while commenting on the PLO/Israeli agreement, signed in September of 1993 under the auspices of the United States. He says that this agreement is likely to lead to two main results: (1) a state of political and ideological loss and chaos in the Arab and Muslim world, and (2) "to an American, Arab, and Israeli alliance against the Islamic movements and all movements of national liberations."[89] In a sense, the Arab world is entering a new critical phase distinguished by a new form of political hegemony and a novel condition of economic and technological dependency on both Israel and the West. In face of this newly emerging and complex situation, Faḍlallah resorts to *jihād* as the only solution. "Although some people consider *jihād* to be violence and violence to be useless, the Israeli experience has undoubtedly proven that violence was the sole bridge on which the Jews trod in order to reach Palestine."[90] The executioners of this type of *jihād* are committed *du'āh* and *'ulamā'*, who, in Faḍlallah's view, must deal with the current situation intelligently.

> We appeal to the Islamic activists (*al-ḥarakiyyeen*) once more to come to grips with the current situation that poses a challenge to all of them. They must face the common challenges and problems from the perspective of their Islamic unity. However, if they desire to raise differences of doctrinal and legal nature, they must do so from a position of unity and not division. . . . We feel that many of the existing regimes in the Muslim world act as the guardians of international arrogance in instigating and courting infighting (*fitnah*) among Muslims. We must learn how to limit the evil of these agents by becoming ourselves guardians of our Islamic reality so others cannot infiltrate and deviate it.[91]

There is no doubt that any peace agreement between the Arab world (including the Palestinians) and Israel is likely to pose a continuous challenge and even threat to the philosophy and future plan of the Islamic movements, especially the ones operating in such countries as Lebanon, Jordan, and Egypt. Faḍlallah is certainly aware of this threat, and like any committed *'ālim* he preaches perseverence and struggle.[92]

Conclusions

As the spiritual and intellectual leader of Ḥizbollah, Faḍlallah develops his liberation theology against the background of extremely painful conditions which Muslims, especially Shi'īs, were undergoing in Lebanon. It is true, as Esposito notes, that Faḍlallah "combines traditional religious scholarship with a powerful reinterpretation of Islamic history and belief that emphasizes political activism and social reform,"[93] but it is equally true that the starting point of Faḍlallah's theology is the crushing social and political conditions that must be transformed by the oppressed and their revolutionary agent, the *'ulamā'*. To him, accepting the current social and political conditions is tantamount to accepting decay and paralysis. Faḍlallah considers the situation to be fluid enough to warrant the creation of a novel and openminded Islamic cultural and religious space. He is, thus, able to get nearer to the ordinary man than many other Muslim revivalists because of his commitment to lead a simple life with the masses of the urban poor and refugees in South Beirut. He implores the ordinary individual not to sit down passively, watching things go by, but to transform them into a new situation.

Quite naturally, then, Faḍlallah sees the salvation of the Muslim masses in a social and political movement that represents their aspirations. His dream is that this movement would emerge first in Lebanon, where he resides. Faḍlallah does definitely represent an independent line of thinking and action, although he enjoys the confidence of some top Iranian leaders.[94]

Perhaps the most disturbing factor in Faḍlallah's theology of liberation—in addition to conditions of oppression and exploitation—is the sectarian, social, and political divisions Lebanon was subjected to. To his mind, it was possible to reconstruct the Muslim community against this complex background of internal divisions and external threats. Faḍlallah considered Ḥizbollah as a military and moral force that would lead to that reconstruction. In other words, Ḥizbollah was the culmination of the revolutionary outlook and plan of the *'ulamā'*. He never saw Ḥizbollah, however, as a divisive organization. Here, he would definitely disagree vehemently with the observation made by Martin Kramer, an Israeli scholar, who, in his course of commenting upon the role of the clergy and Ḥizbollah in Lebanon, argues that "Ḥizbollah worked upon these differences, [in the Shi'ī community] splitting families, neighborhoods, villages, and towns along existing lines, and infusing ideas into existing rivalries and feuds. Ḥizbollah raced through Lebanon like a hundred rivers along the dry beds of division that break the Shiite landscape in Lebanon."[95] To Faḍlallah, violence, oppression, and division had been a given in modern Lebanese history, and Ḥizbollah emerged in response to this state of affairs as a means of empowering the Shi'īs and giving them back their self-worth.

Perhaps the major difference between Quṭb's thought and Faḍlallah's is that, whereas the former was shaped and even controlled by a strong nation/state, the latter was shaped by the disintegration of a once glamorous and modernist nation/state. The Nasserite state that controlled the economic means of violence sought to abolish Islam as an indepedent political and cultural actor in society. Bruce Lawrence observes correctly that, to a large extent,

> Islam has ceased to be, if ever fully was, an independent variable in Muslim societies. The dominant rubric for the social as well the political domain is the nation/state. The nation/state not only controls the mechanisms of power [but] it also curtails, without eliminating, the possibility of Islamically induced violence. Muslims may still fight, kill and die, but they do so, with rare exceptions, as members of nation/states.[96]

One of the rare exceptions to this rule is, of course, Lebanon. The disintegration of the Lebanese nation/state led to the flourishing of different groups who were able, in the absence of a strong oppressive political system, to articulate various ideologies that had been repressed over the years. What that means, in effect, is that criticism, as a weapon, can be used under these circumstances to enhance the perceptions of the people to the transience of the situation and to impress upon them the fact that to build up a civil society on the ashes of a crumbling state is possible only through the healthy exchange of ideas and criticism. What Faḍlallah's critique is also telling us is that private space can be restored in the absense of an oppressive nation/state. Whereas the private space of the individual was invaded by the carelessness and oppression of the state, and his critical faculties were whittled down by either his miseducation or the lack of education he was subjected to, he has the opportunity to flourish if he follows the revolutionary ideology of the *'ulamā'*.

Faḍlallah does not employ the legal concepts of *Dār al-Islām* and *Dār al-Ḥarb* so thoroughly analyzed in classical Islamic legal theory. From a careful reading of his work, it becomes apparent that it is almost impossible to extricate the *Dār al-Islām* from *Dār al-Ḥarb*. They are so mixed, and have been so for many centuries, that Faḍlallah uses quasi-mystical language to express the inner and subjective confusion and malaise of the modern Muslim community.

In commenting on the role of the Shi'ī *'ulamā'* in Lebanon in particular, and the *'ulamā'* in general, one pertinent question arises. How do they view their role in society—especially in a society that is divided politically, socially, and religiously? The answer that Faḍlallah gives is reminiscent of many instances throughout Islamic history when the pious men of religion stand with the poor and the downtrodden. Although Faḍlallah relies heavily on the Shi'ī interpretation of history, he, by no means, limits himself to Shi'ī personality. He invokes the role of both 'Ammār bin Yāssir and Abū Dharr al-Ghifārī who stood against oppression and injustice. Although one might argue that Faḍlallah has fashioned in his mind and in those of his followers a revolutionary vision of a new Lebanon, what propels him to action is not "the pure image of a future Lebanon that will regain stability through Islamic law and justice,"[97] as much as the historical oppression of the Shi'īs in Lebanon. This is his starting point, and everything else is a by-product of this vision.

To Faḍlallah's mind, the function of the *'ālim* must be less of imparting knowledge in the traditional sense, and more in the defense of the community from outside dangers. The responsibility of the *'alim* lies, not in the transmission of obsolete culture, but in the manufacturing of a new one, and in modeling culture in the hearts and minds of the new generation, a generation that has been corrupted by bad cultural practices and is ill-informed about the true principles of Islam. In many ways, he approaches the understanding of culture laid down by Lucien Goldmann in many of his writings, especially in *Cultural Creation in Modern Society*.[98] In a sense, both agree that "culture must be fertilized, watered, and given time to germinate."[99]

The disintegration of the political system of the state poses new challenges that had been hitherto unforeseen. One of the consequences of a politically weak state is the disappearance of traditional family bonds. Faḍlallah considers the spiritual ties in the one family or community to be the cementing force of the traditional structure. He says that the current Muslim generation suffers from a severe drought in its human values, and is subject to a loss of feelings and emotions. "Spiritual dryness [*al-jafāf al-rūhī*] and emotional drought [*al-jadb al-'āṭifī*]" characterize the life of the young people who try persistently to escape from their situation and rebel against life.[100]

As has been seen, Faḍlallah invokes a long-standing tradition in Islam—that of resistance and revolution. However, he invokes it to meet a particular situation—the situation of the Shi'īs in Lebanon. He invokes and interprets this tradition in a relevant manner, not so much to create an Islamic order in Lebanon, but to protect the Lebanese, civil society from infighting, defeatism, and external dangers. Faḍlallah proposes a formula of coexistence in Lebanese society that does not overemphasize the Islamic state. He is mainly preoccupied with restoring dignity to the masses, the poor, and the downtrodden. He calls for the establishment of a revolutionary movement spearheaded by the *'ulamā'*, and that, in his view, must be in constant dialogue with both Muslims and Christians in Lebanon.[101]

Chapter 8

Islamic Revivalism: The Contemporary Debate

The intention of this concluding chapter is to shed a new light on Islamism through the lenses of its contempoary secular and leftist critics in the Arab world. This is, by no means, an attempt to belittle the importance of resurgence as a unique religious, social, and intellectual movement. Instead, this chapter concentrates on an awareness of another point of view that does not share the same premises of Islamism.

I have earlier defined modernity as a major philosophical and cultural moment in the history of modern Europe, and I have argued that a basic, but perhaps latent feature, of modernity is its epistemological and rationalist edge. The natural question that has faced a number of scholars writing on Islamic resurgence is whether resurgence and modernity are, indeed, compatible. When examining the philosophical foundations of modernity and the theological principles of Islamic resurgence—one possible and perhaps unavoidable answer—is that, although Islamism has emerged in response to Western penetration of Muslim countries, both draw on two different historical and conceptual traditions and worldviews that cannot be merely reduced to the compatibility/incompatibility dichotomy.[1]

I have argued in the second chapter of this work that Islamism is a modern phenomenon that cannot, in many ways, be understood, except by recourse to hegemonic Western modernity under the context of expansionist colonialism.[2] It is, therefore, worthwhile to examine the recent Arab (secular) criticisms of Islamism against the background of an evolving—and sometimes subtle—Western presence in the area. In light of the rationalist and secularist underpinnings of modernity, we must assume at the outset that these criticisms are launched in the context of a de facto secularization in most Arab countries.

It is possible to advance a number of definitions for the term "secularization." One such definition can be easily explicated when examining the notion of progress. As has already been noted, the secular notion of progress does not derive its cognitive thrust from a divinely ordained relationship between God and man, as much as it does from man's reason and his relative and finite values. In other words, the human mind appropriates the divine foundations, and turns them into progressive and ever-changing foundations and meanings. The stability and security derived from Being are replaced by the flux and the transformation of being. In philosophical terms, secularization, in both its official and subjective meanings, is the emancipation of the human mind from preordained concepts and epistemes. In other words, the intellectual problem of secularization is no longer the centrality of God nor the divine commands in human endeavors, but that of constant transformations which, in many ways, subvert the traditional foundations from within, and make use of man's reason as the foundation of new and changing matters. Whereas religion is about divine parole and foundational epistemology, secularization is about—to borrow a statement from Michel Foucault—"epistemological acts and thresholds."

Most secularist Arab thinkers hold tenaciously to the proposition that the universalization of modernity and its acceptance by the Arab society and the Arab mind in the nineteenth century was inevitable, and that an appeal to traditionalism in the form of authenticity is just an escape from the new conditions created by modernity.[3]

One such thinker is the Egyptian pragmatist philosopher Zakī Najīb Maḥmūd, who, in his controversial *Renewal of Arab Thought*,[4] dwells at length on the following question, "Is it possible to create a compromise between our Arab heritage and the demands and conditions of the contemporary world?" Maḥmūd envisions an overall Arab renaissance that would be possible only if modern Arabs emancipated themselves from the following shackles: (1) the debilitating situation of freedom of expression in the Arab world. Civil society is in a state of perpetual crisis mainly because people are not respected as citizens by the state; and (2) the frozen and historically obsolete categories of the ancestors dominate the collective intellectual environment. He argues that Arabic has remained rhetorical to the extent that it fails to convey modern concepts and terms developing against the background of a historically evolving secular modernity. Maḥmūd suggests that the only road to modernity is "to move from a type of knowledge based on speech and rhetoric to a new type based on machine and science."[5]

Maḥmūd, in the mode of the nihilistic philosophers of nineteenth-century Europe, almost declares that "God is dead," but he is certain that heritage is dead. He maintains that, "in relation to our age, [Arab and Islamic] heritage has lost its stand, mainly because it revolves around the axis of the relationship between God and man. What we search for in nervous expectation is a new axis: the relationship between man and man."[6] In order to grasp modern Arab ontology, Maḥmūd argues, one must be in a position to salvage the "rational dynamics of the collective Arab mind" from the "heap of myths and irrationality" accumulating over the centuries.[7] Maḥmūd contends that a great gulf exists between the masses and the Arab intelligentsia. The masses "find refuge in myths as a means of solving their problems," whereas the intelligentsia have offered a system of rationalism that must take deep roots in the soil of society.[8] Maḥmūd proposes the cancellation of the whole Islamic heritage and following the ways of Western rationalism. Arab intellectuals must emancipate themselves from the discourses of the ancestors.

Perhaps the most critical voice of the complacency of the Arab intelligentsia is that of Yāssīn al-Ḥāfiẓ, a Syrian Arab nationalist turned Marxist. Since the 1967 defeat, al-Ḥāfiẓ argues, the *salafī* past-oriented ideology (read as antimodernity) has dominated the intellectual output of not a small number of the Arab intelligentsia, a sign of the internal defeat of the Arab mind and soul. He further maintains that dogmatic ideologies and conceptions dominate the modern Arab intellectual environment for the following reasons: (1) schools are unable to teach Arabic in the modern spirit; (2) history is taught in an ideological and partisan way; (3) sciences are taught in a rigid manner; (4) religious education is presented in a traditional and secterian way; and (5) no interest is shown in teaching foreign languages. He bitterly criticizes the university experience in many an Arab country, and concludes that university life has been in decline due to the following reasons: (1) liberal thought has been in retreat; (2) free thinking has not emerged as a coherent pattern of thought; and (3) a de facto separation of university and society exists.[9]

One of the best examples of a contemporary secularist critique of Islamism, as an antimodernist phenomenon, is represented by the work of Fu'ād Zakariyyā. Although he does not attempt any definition of secularism in his writing, Zakariyyā stresses that he applies the secular paradigm to critique what he perceives as the pitfalls of the contemporary Islamic movements.[10] In his critique, Zakariyyā takes up the following issues: (1) recent attempts at applying the *Shari'āh*; (2) mass-orientation of resurgence; (3) "petro-Islam"; and (4) science, reason, and revelation.

In discussing his thoughts on the application of the *Shari'āh*, Zakariyyā dwells quite a bit on the possible relationships among religious law, current regimes in Arab and Muslim countries, social justice, and political freedoms. He doubts that the application of religion would produce positive results, mainly because, in his view, many current rulers are appealing to the *Shari'āh* as a last attempt to preserve power. They further pay lip service to Islam, and their main intention is to get the political backing of the Islamic movement that is mass-oriented in nature:

> There is an ocean of difference between the current systems of government [in the Arab world] and the values of freedom, justice, and equality as preached by all religions, philosophers, and reformers throughout history. Nevertheless, the proponents of the application of the *Shari'āh* in our land do not heed the astonishing failure of previous experiments. On the contrary, their voices became extremely loud when the application of the *Shari'āh* in the Sudan [under Numeiri] turned into an international scandal.[11]

The proponents of the *Shari'āh*, Zakariyyā further argues, justify their position on the basis of the Qur'anic text and remain totally oblivious to the historical practice of Islam. We can point to numerous examples throughout Islamic history in which many a ruler practiced absolutist rule and made a mockery of the lives, property, and freedom of Muslims. Zakariyyā reminds the Islamist camp of the distinction that they must draw between textual and historical Islam. He argues that the application of the *Shari'āh* falls in the domain of historical Islam, and that, as a practical issue, "invoking the power of the texts [i.e. the Qur'ān and the *Sunna*] is insufficient."[12] What is dangerous, however, in the opinion of Zakariyyā, is the mass emotional appeal which the Islamic movements exert. As a result of this mass appeal, the discussion around the *Shari'āh* issue "remains generalized and elastic, although, if it is subjected to rational analysis, it remains ambiguous and messy."[13] This leads Zakariyyā, as a secular democractic thinker, to make bold assertions about the role and the function of the masses in the contemporary Muslim scene. He contends that a mass appeal of an idea or ideology does not necessarily make it valid. Since the early 1970s, one major trait permeating Arab societies has been false consciousness, and the masses have suffered loss of consciousness (*in'idām wa'y*) as a result of the deplorable economic and political conditions prevailing in the Arab world. In Zakariyyā's view, "the extensive spread of the Islamic movements in their current manifestations is but a clear reflection of the lack of consciousness among the masses. The spread of these movements becomes inevitable after one-third of a century of oppression, the suspension of reason, and the domination of a dictatorial political system."[14] Perhaps, the worst trait characterizing the modern Islamic movements is their mental poverty. Zakariyyā argues "In my view, their major problem is that they [the Islamic movements] do not take full advantage of their mental faculty, which they often suspend to the point of complete paralysis."[15] The monolithic mind of Islamic resurgence is accustomed to unquestioned premises, and to the belief that "doubt is a mistake, criticism is a crime, and questioning is a crime."[16] In other words, these movements are far from embracing the central tenets of modernity as already defined.

Zakariyyā expands his analysis of what he perceives as the paralysis and monolithism of thinking of Islamism in Egypt to an important phenomenon, especially in the Gulf region—the connection between Islamism and petrol. He surveys briefly the birth of Islam in Arabia and concludes that the economic factor was organically connected to the rise of Islam and the Islamic doctrine (*'aqīdah*) in particular. Islam encouraged pilgrimage as a means of attracting a large number of people from around the civilized world to an impoverished region. "One of the main goals of pilgrimage was the alleviation of poverty in this dry desert, and helping its people to break down their circle of isolation so that their territory becomes, for a specific period of time annually, the gathering place of all Muslims from all over the world."[17] It is a "civilizational irony" (*mufāraqa ḥaḍāriyya*), to use Zakariyyā's favorite term, that the same territory that functioned as a pilgrimage site for all these people is also providing incessant barrels of Black Gold that has turned the rulers of the area into virtual billionaires almost overnight. This civilizational irony has also meant "fundamental and sweeping changes in many areas as well."[18]

The second irony which Zakariyyā discusses is the fact that

petrolum appeared, not in historically stable agricultural and centralized societies such as Egypt, but in tribal desert societies that had been dominated for a while by tribal modes of tradition—and Islam, in itself, had long been tribalized. Zakariyyā maintains that against the background already established, two possibilities arise: (1) either petrolum wealth is placed under the service of Islam; or (2) Islam is placed under the service of petrolum and the rulers of the region where oil has been discovered.

Zakariyyā asserts boldly that one of the main features of contemporary Arab history is the sad fact that, instead of preserving the purity of Islam and the ensurance of the expansion of its ideals of social and economic justice, Islam has been badly used by a few families.

> A specific type of Islam has been gathering momentum of late, and the appropriate name that applies to it is "Petro-Islam." The first and last goal of "Petro-Islam" has been to protect the petroleum wealth or, more correctly, the type of social relations underlying those [tribal] societies that possess the lion's share of this wealth. It is common knowledge that the principle of "the few dominating the largest portion of this wealth" permeates the social structure [of the Gulf region].[19]

Zakariyyā ponders the question of progress that might have resulted from this fantastic wealth and that could have done an unforgettable service to those Arab and Muslim countries that do not possess petroleum by placing them on the path of exceptional modernization. Ironically, what has taken place instead is that these tribal, but wealthy societies, "could not even find long-term solutions to their standing problems."[20] Therefore, the logical solution "to preserve this abominable situation" has been to exploit the religious sensitivities of the masses for the purpose of "spreading a unique brand of Islam never seen before in history: the Islam of the veil, beard, and the *Jilbāb*; the Islam that permits the stoppage of work during prayers' time, and prohibits women from driving automobiles."[21] Zakariyyā bemoans, perhaps in a Quṭbian way, the wedge that "Petro-Islam" is driving between religion and practical life, or between belief and the problems of both individual and society.

Although he bases his arguments on secular premises, Zakariyyā strikes the reader as being as concerned about the predicament of Islam and Muslims as have been the main intellectuals of the Islamic movement. He also seems to revive some of their terminology in his secularist discourse. He bemoans the fact that, in petrolum-dominated countries, "it is in the interest of the ruling elite to preempt Islam and reduce it to shallow formalities so that the problems of poverty, the bad distribution of wealth, the predominance of the consumption mentality, and the loss of the final opportunity of a thorough revival of petroleum societies, would escape the attention of the masses."[22] It is unfortunate, stresses Zakariyyā, that the mass consciousness in these countries has been perniciously invaded by, and drowned in, the ocean of the empty texts and commentaries of the ancient jurists and exegetes who have no real understanding of the fundamental challenges that face contemporary Muslims. In the final analysis, Zakariyyā reminds us that the current state of affairs is ideal for international and exploitative capitalism.

> Would a country like the United States dream of a better condition than the one dominating the new generations of the petrolum-producing countries who are in perpetual fear of the severe punishment of the grave and its snakes that tear to pieces anyone who dares to question, criticize, or rebel against the prevailing conditions and values? Would the West, including Israel, imagine to dream of a better condition than the one in which the most dynamic and active Islamic movements proclaim that the question of Jerusalem and the problem with Israel must be postponed until the establishment of the Islamic political system?[23]

There is definitely, says Zakariyyā, a strong and an unbreakable bond between "Petro-Islam" and the interests of modern capitalism. "In a nutshell, this Islam is placed at the service of protecting the interests of the ruling elite and its allies of exploiting foreign countries."[24] Modernity gets compartmentalized and falls under the control of aggressive capitalism and brutal tribalism.

One can note three points about the secularist camp in the modern Arab world.

First, far from being a dead issue, religion occupies a center stage in the intellectual orientation of Arab secularism. Secularist thinkers are perturbed by the fact that the Secular State has not taken the issue of religion seriously. They address this historical error by examining afresh the complicated relationship between religion and state. Any observer of the secularization debate in the modern Arab world would disagree with the thesis of a noted specialist, Leonard Binder, on the Middle East, that "Islam in its various forms, and categories, and applications, is only a part of Middle East culture, and by itself accounts for little."[25]

Second, Arab secularists are determined, more than ever, to produce a discursive secular approach that poses a challenge to the theological and religious interpretations of social reality and human history. Secularists are convinced that the social and political terrain of Arab society contains the necessary seeds for secularization and modernization, and that what is needed is a proper implementation of secularist philosophy and worldview. In a sense, it is here relevant to introduce the distinction made by Leo Strauss between political philosophy and political theology. According to Strauss, political theology is made up of those teachings that are based on divine revelation, whereas political philosophy is limited to what is accessible to the unassisted human mind.[26] Arab secular political philosophy—such as Maḥmūd's and Zakariyyā's—rejects any divine intervention in the historical and political process. Political philosophy, as advanced by Arab secularists, is based on the notion that the best context for political action is that of a democracy.

Third, Arab secularists push the assumption that only secularism, and not Islamic resurgence, can ensure a smooth transition in the Arab world from the closed to the open society. One can find, more or less, a resemblance between the Arab secularist theory and Karl Popper's famous notions of what constitutes an open, progressive, and future-oriented society. For instance, Popper claims that the main characteristics of a closed society are defined by its organic ties, tribal and collectivist mentality, lack of individuality, and religious rigidity. The open or secular society, on the other hand, is marked by individuality, freedom of expression, rationalism, social mobility, and a critical appraisal of social reality.[27] In other words, secularists assume that the Arab society must be able to maintain a degree of tolerance and openess to outside influences, and that a transition from the closed society to an open one signals a total breakdown of tribalism and religious rigidity. Then, to the minds of the secularists, any reaction against liberalism in the modern Arab world, especially in the form of Islamism or tribalism, is, in fact, a reaction against socioeconomic progress, and the scientific culture of modernity.

Faraj Fūda agrees with these contentions of Arab secularists. As a controversial thinker who had "devoted himself [until his 1992 assassination] to the propagation of secularism,"[28] his thought represents perhaps the clearest example of mature secularist criticism of the religious problematic in the modern Arab world. He shares Zakariyyā's main theses, and argues that, even in its sublime phase, Islamic history was marred by bloodshed, and that the assassination of three out of four caliphs in the wake of the death of Muḥammad was not a historical accident. Fūda says that the Islamist camp—which includes the main stream Ikhwan and its different offshoots—as well as the official establishment as represented by the Azhar, play on people's fears and emotions, and stand against the unity of the citizens (both Copts and Muslims) of the one nation/state.[29] In contradiction to Quṭb and other contemporary Islamists, Fūda argues three points.

First, Egyptian society is basically religious. It does not live in *jāhiliyah*, and it abhors religious extremism.

Second, he further maintains that the call for the application of the *Sharīʿāh* in Egypt is not a goal by itself, but a means to establish an Islamic political system. The real issue, Fūda suggests, is political in nature, and this involves issues such as democracy, human rights, women's rights, and the rights of minorities. Fūda notes that the Islamic movements have maintained a dismal record vis-à-vis all the mentioned issues, and that they have failed miserably "in offering a political program that discusses issues and methods of government, politics, and economics."[30]

Third, Fūda mocks the naive belief—that has become a central propaganda piece in the hands of the Islamists—that an immediate application of the *Sharīʿāh* would lead to immediate miraculous solutions to the problems of society. A righteous Muslim ruler, he argues, has never historically guaranteed the reform of society and the solution of its problems.[31]

Fūda dwells at length on post-Muḥammadan history—especially that of the rightly guided caliphs—and he tackles the assassinations of ʿUmar, ʿUthmān, and ʿAlī in a new light in order to prove four points.

First, these three caliphs, who were the companions of Muḥammad and the closest to the pristine spirit of Islam, fell prey to the dramatic expansion of Islam in the first century, and were unable to contain the logical social, economic, political, and religious contradictions and tensions resulting from this dramatic expansion. Second, although they were adamant in applying the Prophet's commands and example, they were unable to maintain social justice and equal security among the people, especially the new converts to Islam. Third, political assassination is a mark of Islamic history, both classical and modern. Finally, the concept of the religious state is just a utopia which, like communism, has never been historically achieved.[32]

On the basis of this treatment of early Islamic history, Fūda reaches the following conclusions: (1) Justice cannot be achieved by the righteousness of one ruler, and it does not result from the application of the *Shari'āh*.[33] (2) The essence of Islam is something larger than the *Shari'āh* per se. (3) The modern Muslim world has not given rise to a genuine and dynamic Islamic thought. For instance, what is the Islamic perspective on overpopulation, foreign debt, public or private sector? (4) Modern Muslims cannot accommodate modernity and face the challenges of the modern world by "wearing beards and putting on Pakistani dress."[34] The activists of the Islamic movements today are the best example of rigidity and stagnation permeating the contemporary Muslim scene.

> These people have hated society, and it is society's right to express the same level of hatred toward them . . . They have accused it of *jāhiliyah*, and it is its right to accuse them of extremism and narrowness of mind. . . . These people have done harm to Islam, . . . accused it of extremism and rigidity, . . . They have just reflected their psychological diseases, and it is time that this religion and we, Muslims, reject them forever.[35]

Those who call for the return to the origins of Islam, the application of the *Shari'āh*, and the condemnation of society suffer from historical retardation, conceptual chaos, and lack of vision.

> It is a proven fact when reading Islamic history that we live in a [modern] society that possesses higher criteria, including ethical ones, and that is more progressive and humane in terms of the relationship between rulers and ruled [than the early Islamic one]. We are indebted in all of that to the universal human culture that even religion does not reject.[36]

The only way out of the predicament is to be enlightened. "Islam is at the crossroads. There are two alternatives, either we fall prey to bloodbaths as a result of ignorance and narrowness of mind, or Islam and modernity meet. The latter can be achieved through enlightened *ijtihād,* courageous analogy, and visionary horizons."[37]

In short, Fūda, unlike contemporary revivalist thinkers, envisages an Islam that has nothing to do with politics. In his opinion, there are two Islams—that of religion, and that of state or politics. He gives himself the right to criticize the latter.[38] Political Islam has been distinguished by the role of the sword, "The sword has cut off (flown away) more Muslim heads than infidel ones throughout history."[39] The logical conclusion is that violence has been the essence of political Islam. On the basis of the preceding premise, Fūda concludes that violence is endemic to Islam, and he takes this as a way of explaining the violence perpetrated by the contemporary Islamic movements. Violence is their nature.

Fūda disagrees with Sayyid Quṭb and Munīr Shafīq about the symbolism invested in early Islam. Shafīq, in elaborating Quṭb's thesis on the role of Medinan Islam in the life of the contemporary Islamic movements, argues that Islamic doctrine has been removed from the social and political domain of the contemporary state, and that is why Muslims lack the dynamic role of *'aqīdah* in transforming people and their lives in dynamic Islam.[40] The best way for Muslims to prosper is to give *'aqīdah* a chance to fight against colonialism and Westernization, and to affirm their identities and move their nations forward by being culturally, politically, and economically independent of the West.[41]

Just before his assassination in the summer of 1992, Fūda remained pessimistic about the secular possibilities in Egyptian and Arab societies and the triumph of his version of democracy. He enumerates several major dangers that challenge, at heart, the nation/state, its philosophy, and the coexistence between its citizens: (1) the dramatic expansion of the Muslim business sector and the manipulation of the national economy by Islamic banking; (2) the resort to violence by many Islamic groups; (3) legalization of the mainstream Ikhwan; (4) support given by the Azhar as the official religious establishment in the elections to those who call for the application of the *Sharī'āh*; and (5) the co-optation and control of the mass media, as the most powerful means of the modern nation/state, to control public opinion.[42] Fūda argues that the defense lines of the secular state have been exposed, and the only remaining alternative is to repress political Islam by force.

> It is undoubtedly clear that Political Islam has succeeded in coopting and neutralizing the most important defensive as well offensive system of the State—the mass media—not by erecting an antagonistic media system, since this is legally impossible, but by controling the State's media from within through the use of the most dangerous of weapon, that of money.[43]

Fūda admits, however, that most Arab states, including Egypt, committed a grave error, just after they achieved indepedence, by attacking religion and religious authority directly and suddenly, and by imprisoning the religiously oriented people. In the face of the crisis of the nation/state, the shakedown of the economy, and the fact that religion occupies center stage in alleviating the suffering of the masses, the contemporary state has no solution but to watch the Islamic movement either fill the gap or repress it.[44] In short, Fūda considers Egypt as basically a secular nation/state. Most Egyptians are religious by nature. A religious rule is violent and sectarian by nature. The Islamic movements are political in essence, and they manipulate Islam and the religious feelings of the masses in order to achieve their political program.

Both Adonis (also known as ʿAlī Aḥmad Saʿīd) and Burhān Galyoun focus on the secularist critique of Islamism in a philosophical and cognitive way. They both argue that there is a predominance of traditional—also read as "backward," "paralyzed" and "antimodern"—modes of thinking as well as cultural and social patterns in modern Arab society. Traditional modes of thinking are maintained by the family, school, university, and mass media, which are to Adonis—to use a favorite Althusserian phrase—the ideological state apparatuses.[45] Adonis argues that, far from establishing new conditions and new relationships, the dominant ideological system in the Arab world

> reproduces the past exploiting relationships. This dominant ideology is a reembodiment of the past exploiting ideology, and any superficial political change is no more than a replacement of an old exploiting class by a new one . . . Modern Arab family is still in the grip of a theocratic-tribal formation, and Arab education is indeed reactionary in both the contents and method of its teaching. Moreover, religion still dominates the entire civil life, as well political, legal, and cultural life. Class consciousness is hidden under the impact of religious domination.[46]

Adonis maintains that "Arab society still remains in its dominant ideological structure very traditional. Nonetheless, it is led ideologically by a pioneering elite in the direction of modernity."[47] Only a genuine conceptual and systemic revolution that reverses religious and tribal domination would ensure a gradual progression of Arab society toward modernity. In the opinion of many a radical thinker, "revolutionary ideology and religion are essentially contradictory and that religion has not contributed to the Arab struggle against imperialism."[48]

A number of progressive Arab thinkers do not agree completely with the Marxist critics of traditional Arab society, mainly because, in the wake of the 1967 war, public opinion was assailed by all sorts of opinions about the role of Islam in society. Islam came to dominate the intellectual scene as never before. "Many an Arab thinker has been alerted to the fact that we [Arab intellectuals] still discuss the same issues discussed by the early generation of the *Nahḍah*, over a century ago."[49] One can generally argue that European rationalism emerged as a means of freeing knowledge and reason from the domination of an elitist and obscurantist theocracy. In the words of Ghalyoun, "Rationalism is a cultural strategy that aimed principally at dismantling the monopoly of religion over the theory of knowledge."[50]

The Muslim world, whose destiny has become part of European modernity since the early nineteenth century, produced a tiny modernizing elite, educated in the schools of the West. This tiny indigeneous modernizing elite has been given a privileged position by the nation/state. According to Ghalyoun, the process of rationalism unfolded itself through a tiny elite that has remained aloof from the masses, either because of its distinguished and elite religious origins or because of its distinguished social position. In short, Arab rationalism, from the beginning of colonialism, has taken the side of the exploiting classes.

> Western rationalism was a culmination of a long-standing suspicion in all the traditional systems of thought, and was an affirmation of the freedom of man, individual, community, and nation. However, Arab rationalism has affirmed and justified the existing system, the [bipolar] system of modernity and dependency, either in the name of progress or the logic of history, but always against the freedom of the [average] individual.[51]

Western rationalism did not seek to abolish the religious sphere completely, but to neutralize religion or to include it under its rationalizing umbrella. Rationalism is double-edged. First, in the secularism of the mind, reason is no longer under the spell of religion. Second, there is the secularism of politics in which a de facto separation exists between politics and religion.

Modernization, as the practical application, can take roots in society without modernism which, as the consciousness of modernity, is not a necessary condition for modernization. The ideology of modernity has been usurped by a tiny secular bureaucratic elite whose main aim is to preserve the status quo. Ghalyoun argues that the presence of a traditional mentality and the accompanying resurgence of Islam are a balancing agent that prevents the nonmodernized masses from becoming a straw driven by the winds of modernity.[52]

> [Arab] modernists make a drastic mistake when they think that mass resistance [to the process of Arab rationalism] is intertwined with or derived from Islamic resurgence. . . . In the same vein,

> Islamists make the same mistake when they assume that the mass refusal of modernity is a collective plea for the establishment of a religious state.[53]

Ghalyoun argues that modernity is not institutions or concepts that we can accept or reject freely, "Modernity has been a continuous process [in Arab society] for the past two centuries."[54] The central question is, "How can we ensure a smooth continuation of historical modernity without it becoming a tool in the hands of the power elite in Arab society?" This question relates essentially to the notion that backwardness, antimodernism and loss of vitality are not the result of the influence of heritage upon us, but result from the fact that modernity has become an alienating and dividing agent as a result of its monopoly by the Arab elite.[55]

Ghalyoun argues that social science has failed to predict the contemporary resurgence of religion. One of the main assumptions that modern political science has taken for granted, for instance, is that all societies, traditional and modern, are gradually disentengling themselves from the grip of religion, and that political secularization is inevitable. "How come," asks Ghalyoun, "that history has betrayed itself and produced what had not been expected? And how can one explain this 'historical deviation'?"[56]

Ghalyoun agrees with Fūda that one main reason for the rise of Islamism has been the crisis of the modern nation/state. Resurgence presents both a doctrinal and political challenge to the secular elite. Islamism has seen the nation/state to be a historical extension of colonialism, and that both nationalism and colonialism have one goal in common—that of crushing the spiritual and religious foundations of the modern Arabs. The entire cultural space, especially as represented by the mass media, has been entirely controlled by a secular elite that has paid lip-service to Islam. Ghalyoun discusses three discourses, the first of which is the discourse of Islamism. The second is the discourse of the secular technocratic state that finds itself suddenly facing the formidable challenge of Islamism. The state is depending more and more on the official *'ulamā'* establishment as a means of warding off the challenge of resurgence. This idea is best expressed by Ayubi who contends that the Secular State has left a vacuum that enables Islamism to appropriate Islam as its powerful weapon.

> the fact that the contemporary State lays claim to secularism has enabled some forces of political protest to appropriate Islam as their own weapon. Because the State does not embrace Islam

> (except in a "defensive" reactive way), it cannot describe its opponents as the traditional State could as being simply heretic cults. Political Islam now reverses the historical process—it claims "generic" Islam for the protest movements, leaving to the State the more difficult task of qualifying and justifying its own "version" of Islam.[57]

The third discourse is loosely called the "secularist camp." Ghalyoun defines it as a loosely knit and fragile alliance of a group of intelligentsia, party and union members, and leftist thinkers. "This secularist alliance, unlike the Islamic one, is neither based on a strong tradition, nor popular consciousness, which exemplify a strategic depth and a conceptual and political reservoir of the contemporary Islamic movements."[58] Religious capital (*ra's māl dīnī*) has become the banner of the dispossesed, the alienated, and a protest movement against the failed mechanisms of the secular state. Arab modernity has failed miserably in alleviating the suffering of the masses, and, instead, "it has created all the necessary conditions for a novel barbarism—a great majority of people who are alienated both mentally and materially and who live a muddy existence."[59] In the opinion of Ghalyoun, "New Islamism is a clear expression of the metamorphosis of the shacks' inhabitants from a peripheral social group to a complete society."[60]

By Way of a Conclusion

The 1967 Arab defeat with Israel could provide a starting point for the current secularist-Islamist debate about the role of religion in society and politics, the meaning of democracy, and the nature of civil society. One can convincingly argue that 1967 paved the way for various Islamic movements and ideologues to formulate an alternative to the crisis of the nation/state and the social and political vacuum resulting from the defeat.[61] It is not only that "Political Islam" emerged as a viable political force, but that Islam itself, as religion, history, and the central part of the collective subconscious, has assumed a new presence, and therefore, the post-1967 Arab discourse has been filled with religious language.

What that means is, in effect, a number of things, two of which are easily observable.

First, the post-1967 Islamic movements are led by newly formed religious or lay leaders, leaders who grew up in the shadow of defeat and neo-colonization as exemplified by the state of Israel and the support which it receives from the West. Moreover, these leaders have been successful in mobilizing a major segment of the population and in competing for legitimacy with the more established *'ulamā'* that, more or less, form part of the state and its stability.

Second, there is a noticeable tendency in the Arab world—especially in the wake of the Iranian revolution—of an influential number of intelligentsia converting to Islam or resorting to Islamic concepts and language. The clearest example of all is that of the ex-Maoist Palestinian thinker Munīr Shafīq who, since 1979, has seen in Islamic resurgence the only salvation of the crisis of the modern state. Many share this opinion—in perhaps less extreme forms.[62]

The Islamic response to the secularist camp is spearheaded by a number of prominent Islamist thinkers—such as Muḥammad al-Ghazālī, Yūsuf al-Qaraḍāwī, Munīr Shafīq, and Yūsuf al-'Azm—some of whom were discussed earlier in this book.

All the Islamist thinkers start from premises that are essentially different from those of the secularists. The Islamists reject the "death of God" thesis as promoted by Arab secularists. In essence, the argument is that nihilism, the negation of God's role on earth, and the affirmation of the central role of man are rejected once and for all by the Islamists. In the words of Qaraḍāwī, "being Muslim defines our doctrinal position, ideological and civilizational identity, and does not, at all, abolish our historical position or geographical location."[63] What that means is that, to the mind of Qaraḍāwī, Muslims, who have been heirs to a long and glorious civilization, are caught in the web of civilizational and philosophical conflict, especially with the West. The best way, therefore, to retrieve mental equilibrium is to examine afresh the absolutely clear foundations of Islam that have not been marred by historical pitfalls. In other words, Qaraḍāwī's point of departure is doctrinal and Qur'anic (or normative) Islam, whereas the point of the departure of the secularists is, in the words of Qaraḍāwī, "an Islam that carries the burdens of history."[64] Qaraḍāwī's concept of Islam, which is being disseminated today by the "committed, balanced, and enlightened trend of Islamic resurgence,"[65] is dominated by the following characteristics: reason, renewal, *ijtihād*, middle-roadness [*wasaṭiyya*], pragmatism, respect for women and family, belief in education and oneness, rejection of priesthood, belief in the right of the *ummah* to elect its rulers, preservation of private property, taking good care of the poor and dowtrodden, and encouraging the love of nation and *ummah*.[66]

From all of this, Qaraḍāwī reaches the often-quoted conclusion that secularism (*'ilmāniyya*) is a concept foreign to Islam, in that it does not emanate from its "stable foundations." "Secularism," in the words of Qaraḍāwī, "is a 'Western commodity' that did not grow up in our soil, and it consequently does not measure up to our doctrines and conceptual premises."[67] Qaraḍāwī is in agreement with Yūsuf al-ʿAzm, a Syrian Islamist, who considers the domination of secularism in modern Arab society as a mark of defeatism and capitulation. "Defeated thought fights for the separation of state and religion. Then, gradually, both individual and family live in the shadow of a broken society. As a consequence, the defeated Muslim *ummah* forcefully drinks the cups of poison while it is in a state of loss of will, numbness of feeling, and waste of mind."[68]

In the view of the Islamists, the question does not revolve around the recent economic changes in the Gulf States and the exploitation of Islam to preserve the status quo. In view of al-ʿAzm, religiousity has had deep roots in Muslim society.[69] Al-ʿAzm, who perceives Islam as doctrines and rites that cannot be affected by the deviation of the political system, sees Islam to have been intact since the beginning of history. Islamic resurgence is a natural extension of Islamic activism throughout Islamic history. "Resurgence is a natural, logical, and unique phenomenon in the Arab and Muslim world. Resurgence does reflect powerfully the conscience, identity, and hopes and ambitions of the *ummah*. Resurgence is the only trend that is capable to remain, persevere, and triumph against all predicaments."[70]

NOTES

CHAPTER 1

1. See, for instance, the simple analysis provided by J. Miller, "The Challenge of Radical Islam." *Foreign Affairs*, Spring 1993, 43–56. For a critique of this tendency, see A. Al-Azmeh, *Islams and Modernities* (London 1993), especially 18–138.

2. This last observation has escaped the attention of astute commentators on political Islam, such as D. Pipes, who perceives all fundamentalist Muslims to be the real enemy of West. See R. H. Pelletreau, Jr., et al., "Political Islam. Symposium: Resurgent Islam in the Middle East." *Middle East Policy*, vol. 3(2), 1994, especially 5–8.

3. Classical Islamic intellectual history is extremely diverse. Consult the following three works by A. Amīn: *Fajr al-islām* (Beirut 1975); *Ḍuḥā al-islām*, three vols. (Beirut 1976), and *Dhuhr al-islām*, four vols. (Beirut 1976).

4. See, for instance, S. Amin, *The Arab Nation: Nationalism and Class Struggle* (London 1978).

5. F. Gilbert, "Intellectual History: Its Aims and Methods." *Daedalus*, vol. 100(1), Winter 1971, 94. K. Mannheim makes, more or less, a similar observation. "The study of intellectual history can and must be pursued in a manner which will see in the sequence and coexistence of phenomena more than mere accidental relationships, and will seek to discover in the totality of the historical complex the role, significance, and meaning of each component element." K. Mannheim, *Ideology and Utopia: An Introduction to the Sociology of Knowledge* (New York 1936) 93.

6. R. Darnton, "Intellectual and Cultural History." In M. Kammen, ed., *The Past Before Us: Contemporary Historical Writing in the United States* (Ithaca 1980) 337.

7. Ibid.

8. A good example of this method is illustrated in G. Shukrī, *al-Nahḍah wa'l suqūṭ fi'l fikr al-miṣrī* al-ḥadīth (*Renaissance and Decline in Modern Egyptian Thought*) (Beirut 1976). Also, H. Djait comments on the attempts of modern Arab and European authors to study the evolution of classical and modern Arab political leadership as follows: "This idea [studying the historical evolution of Islamic leadership] might prove quite useful, if we sharpened its focus, because it sheds light on the problem of continuity and discontinuity better than the rather hollow dyads of apogee/decline, decadence/renaissance, Arab/non-Arab, orthodoxy/heterodoxy, not to mention the recent dialectic between tradition and modernity." H. Djait, *Europe and Islam: Cultures and Modernity* (Berkeley 1985) 124.

9. H. Gibb, *Modern Trends in Islam* (Chicago 1947) ix. Of course, since Gibb wrote these words, a number of influential studies have appeared on modern Arabic thought. One should mention the following: I. Boullata, *Trends and Issues in Contemporary Arab Thought* (Albany 1990); A. Daher, *Current Trends in Arab Intellectual Thought* (Washington 1969); A. Hourani, *Arabic Thought in the Liberal Age* (Oxford 1970); R. Khuri, *Modern Arab Thought: Channels of the French Revolution of the Arab East*, tr. Iḥsān ʿAbbas (Princeton, 1983), and H. Sharabi, *Arab Intellectuals and the West: The Formative Years, 1875–1914* (Baltimore 1970). For a good bibliography on modern Arab thought, consult P. Khoury, *Traditions et modernité: thèmes et tendances de la penśee arabe actuelle* (Beirut 1983).

10. Islamic biographical literature, according to H. Gibb, was at the basis of classical Islamic culture. According to Gibb, the intellectual history of the community was written by its elite active men and women, "It is clear that the conception that underlies the oldest biographical dictionaries is that the history of the Islamic community is essentially the contribution of individual men and women to the building up and transmission of its specific culture." H. Gibb, "Islamic Biographical Literature." In B. Lewis and P. O. Holt, eds., *Historians of the Middle East* (London 1962) 54. See also, G. Makdisi, "Tabaqat-Biography: Law and Orthodoxy in Classical Islam." *Islamic Studies*, vol. 32(4), Winter 1993, 371–398.

11. Olivier Roy calls these lay intellectuals "The Islamist New Intellectuals." See O. Roy, *The Failure of Political Islam*, tr. Carol Volk (Cambridge 1994) especially 89–107.

12. Of course this is not true in the case of both Iran and Sudan.

13. M. Foucault, *The Archeology of Knowledge and the Discourse on Language* (New York 1972).

14. Ibid., 5.

15. "Foucault's concern is not to provide a transcendental, ahistorical grounding for knowledge, but to understand and evaluate the production of knowledges in their historical specificity, and the way in which acceptable methods of knowledge acquisition come into existence and pass out of it." L. Alcoff, "Foucault as Epistemologist." *The Philosophical Forum*, vol. 25(2), Winter 1993, 121.

16. On the meanings of *nahḍah*, decadence and stagnation, see S. H. Nasr, "Decadence, Deviation and Renaissance in the Context of Contemporary Islam." In K. Ahmad and Z. I. Ansari, eds., *Islamic Perspectives: Studies in Honor of Sayyid Abul A'la Mawdūdī* (Leicester 1980) 35–42. Nasr argues that, "The modernists never tire of speaking of nearly every form of activity in the Islamic world as a renaissance, whose Arabic translation, *al nahḍah*, has become such a prevalent word in contemporary Arabic literature. There is something insidious about the carefree usage of the word renaissance, for it recalls the Renaissance in the West when the rebirth of spiritually deadly elements of Graeco-Roman paganism dealt a staggering blow to Christian civilization and prevented it from reaching its natural period of flowering as a Christian civilization." (Ibid., 37). The modernist attitudes that Nasr criticizes are represented by the following: F. Rahman, *Islam and Modernity: Transformation of an Intellectual Tradition* (Chicago 1982); M. Siddiqi, *Modern Reformist Thought in the Muslim World* (Islamabad 1982); and O. Turan, "The Need of Islamic Renaissance." In M. A. Khan, ed., *Proceedings of the International Conference* (Islamabad 1970) 24–31.

17. A. Laroui, *The Crisis of the Arab Intelligentsia: Traditionalism or Historicism?* (Berkeley 1976) vii. The Tunisian philosopher H. Djait comments on the phenomenon of *nahḍah* by saying that, "It must be acknowledged that the cultural phenomenon of the *nahḍah* (renaissance) paved the way for both these forms of development by reconstructing the Arab heritage, by restoring the connection to the splendors of an age now given classic status, in a word, by spreading an atmosphere and ideology of renascence. The immediate consequence of this movement, whose vital center lay in Egypt and Syria, was the emergence of a modern Arabic language and literature, hence a re-Arabization by the core of the Middle East." H. Djait, *Europe and Islam*, 137–138.

18. Gibb, *Modern Trends*, 1.

19. See J. Crabbs, *The Study of History in Nineteenth Century Egypt: A Study in National Transformation* (Detroit 1984).

20. See N. Keddi, *Sayyid Jamal al-Din al-Afghani: A Biography* (Berkeley 1972). M. Bennabi describes Afghani's achievements as follows: "Al-Afghani found himself, by an accident of history, the incorruptible witness and the implacable judge of a society that slowly attained its decomposition, while colonialism installed itself on its soil. . . . Al-Afghani's impetuous temperament made of him a militant rather than a thinker who would carefully

examine problems and work out solutions. His extraordinary culture was only a dialectical, even demagogic, means of revolutionary action that had a psychological and intellectual, rather political, impact on a still totally apathetic Muslim world." M. Bennabi, *Islam in History and Society*, tr. A. Rashid (Islamabad 1988) 22.

21. On M. ʿAbduh, see C. Adams, *Islam and Modernism in Egypt* (New York 1933); U. Amin, *Mohammad Abduh: essai sur ses idées philosophiques et religieuse* (Cairo 1944); R. Caspar, "Un aspect de la pensée musulmane moderne: Le renouveau du Moʿtazilisme," *MELANGES*, vol. 4, 1957; E. Kedourie, *Afghani and ʿAbduh: An Essay on Religious Unbelief and Political Activism in Modern Islam* (New York 1962); M. Kerr, *Islamic Reform: The Political and Legal Theories of Muhammad Abduh and Rashid Rida* (Berkeley 1966); D. Khalid, "Ahmad Amin and the Legacy of Muhammad ʿAbduh," *Islamic Studies*, vol. 9(1), March 1970; R. Rida, *Tārīkh al-ustādh al-imām al-Shaykh Muḥammad ʿAbduh* (Cairo 1933), and H. Sharabi, *Arab Intellectuals and the West* (Baltimore 1974).

22. H. Sharabi, *Neopatriarchy: A Theory of Distorted Change in Arab Society* (New York 1988) 6.

23. S. G. Miller, trans. and ed., *Disorienting Encounters, Travels of a Moroccan Scholar in France in 1845–1846: The Voyage of Muhammad As-Saffar* (Berkeley 1992) 193–194. As-Saffar's sentiments about "Muslim progress" are shared by another North African thinker and reformer—Khayr al-Dīn of Tunisia (1822–1889). According to Sami Hanna, "Khayr al-Dīn was clearly in advance of his time, as were a few of his contemporaries, all of whom were struggling to conceptualize and crystallize the stirring of regeneration in the Ottoman Empire during the first three quarters of the nineteenth century. They understood what must be done. They perceived the source of European development to be based on three pillars: (1) minds liberated to think critically; (2) wills freed to change policy, to experiment, to achieve self-direction; and (3) scientific technology applied to practical problems." S. A. Hanna, "Khayr al-Dīn of Tunisia: The Impact of his Book *Aqwam al-Masālik* on the Arab and Ottoman Reformers." *Islamic Culture*, vol. 65(2, 3), April–July 1991, 103.

24. A. Hourani, *Islam in European Thought* (New York 1991) 109.

25. W. C. Smith, *Islam in Modern History* (New York 1956) 16.

26. Ibid., 45–46.

27. M. Arkoun, *Arab Thought*, tr. J. Singh (New Delhi 1988) 78.

28. On Islam and modernity, see F. Rahman, *Islam and Modernity: Transformation of an Intellectual Tradition* (Chicago 1982).

29. Arkoun, *Arab Thought*, 79.

30. M. Arkoun, *Essais sur la pensée islamique* (Paris 1977), and *Pour une critique de la raison islamique* (Paris 1984).

31. M. Mahdi, "Islamic Philosophy in Contemporary Islamic Thought." In C. Malik, ed., *God and Man in Contemporary Islamic Thought* (Beirut 1972) 105.

32. S. H. Nasr, *Islam and the Plight of Modern Man* (London 1975) 90.

33. See A. Hourani's discussion of the various Muslim attempts in his, *Arabic Thought*. Muḥammad ʿAbduh defends the role of reason in Islam as "the fountain of certainty and foundation of belief in God, His [infinite] knowledge and capacity." M. ʿImārah, *al-ʿAmāl al-kāmilah li'l imām Muḥammad ʿAbduh*, vol. 3 (Beirut 1972) 325. The concept of stagnation is essential in the thought of Islamic resurgence. There cannot be revival without stagnation. One must not assume, however, that the long Islamic centuries from the fall of Baghdad to the beginning of Western encroachement in the Muslim world were that stagnant.

34. See, for instance, Muḥammad ʿAbduh's arguments on Islam and science in M. ʿImārah, ibid., especially 278–282.

35. Concerning this issue, see, L. Gardet, "*De quelle manière s'est ankylose la pensée religieuse de l'islam*." In G. E. von Grunebaum and R. Brunschwick, eds., *Classicisme et déclin culturel dans l'histoire de l'islam* (Paris 1957).

36. H. Laoust, "*Le Réformisme orthodoxe des 'Salafiyya,' et les caractères généraux de son organisation actuelle*," *Revue des Etudes Islamiques*, 6: 175–224 (1932) 185.

37. M. A. Lahbabi, *Le Personnalisme Musulman* (Paris 1964) 100–101.

38. On Musṭafa ʿAbd al-Rāziq, consult the following: I. M. Abu-Rabiʿ, "Al-Azhar and Rationalism in Modern Egypt: The Philosophical Contributions of Shaykhs Mustafa ʿAbd al-Raziq and ʿAbd al-Halim Mahmud," *Islamic Studies*, vol. 27(2), Summer 1988, pp. 129–150; G. C. Anawati and M. Borrmans, *Tendances et courants de l'Islam arabe contemporaine* (Munchen, 1982), especially pp. 30–35 under the title "Le cheikh Mustafa ʿAbd al-Raziq et son école," and Taha Hussein, "Le cheikh Mostafa ʿAbd el-Razeq tel que je l'ai connu." *MELANGES*, vol. 4, 1957, pp. 249–253.

39. M. ʿAbd al-Rāziq, *Tamhīd li tārikh al-falsafah al islāmiyyah*, 3rd ed. (Cairo 1966) 5.

40. E. Renan, *Averroes et l'Averroisme: Essai historique* (Paris 1882) vii–viii.

41. ʿAbd al-Raziq, *Tamhīd*, 144.

42. H. Gibb, "Whither Islam?" In H. Gibb, ed., *Whither Islam? A Survey of Modern Movements in the Moslem World* (Lodon 1932) 343.

43. Ibid., 335.

44. Compare this to what Marwan Buheiry has to say about the Russian orientalist Eugene de Roberty, "Modernization, to him, was a universal model, and in this respect he wanted Europe 'to work on the Muslim elite . . . by sending Western scholars, artists, engineers, and workers, while keeping strictly at home in Europe the Catholic, Protestant, priests, and missionaries.' The Real task was to build railways in the world of Islam and to proceed with a secular colonization of land and industry." M. R. Buheiry, "Colonial Scholarship and Muslim Revivalism in 1900." In L. I. Conrad, ed., *The Formation and Perception of the Modern Arab World: Studies by Marwan R. Buheiry* (Princeton 1989) 114–115.

45. Gibb, "Whither Islam?", 329.

46. In my view, the most enduring work of Gibb's is his little but influential *Modern Trends in Islam*. Gibb, in the words of William Polk, is the last of the universal Arabists, who "was a man of rare capacity to absorb, digest and translate an extraordinary rich and complex civilization. Few of his successors have even attempted to assay the project, and none has really followed in his footsteps. In this context what distinguished Gibb was his energy, his inquiring mind, and his common sense. Without putting too fine a point on it, one might say that he was the last of the gentlemen scholars, the Orientalists, the generalists who eschewed specialization, almost with contempt, in their emphasis on the single key to a holistic view of culture and civilization." W. R. Polk, "Sir Hamilton Gibb Between Orientalism and History." *International Journal of Middle East Studies*, vol. 6(2), April 1975, 139.

47. One must be careful in using the terms *Arab mind* or *Muslim mind* because of the racist connotations it might carry. For a critical analysis of Western literature on the "Arab mind", see the excellent study by F. M. Moughrabi, "The Arab Basic Personality: A Critical Survey of the Literature." *International Journal of Middle East Studies*, vol. 9(1), February 1978, 99–112.

48. Hamilton Gibb, *Modern Trends in Islam* (Chicago 1947) 7.

49. Ibid., 7.

50. G. Pruett, "The Escape from Seraglio: Anti-Orientalist Trends in Modern Religious Studies." *Arab Studies Quarterly*, vol. 2; 4, Fall 1980, 304.

51. H. Gibb, "The Heritage of Islam in the Modern World (1)." *International Journal of Middle East Studies*, vol. 1(1), January 1970, 3.

52. Ibid., 4. The Italian orientalist Carra de Vaux makes a similar observation around 1900. "Islam is an institution possessing a character of

exceptional fixity . . . which places its adherents in an uncritical frame of mind opposed to progress." Quoted by M. Buheiry, "Colonial Scholarship and Muslim Revivalism in 1900." In L. I. Conrad, ed., *Formation of Modern Arab World,* 113.

53. H. Gibb, *Modern Trends*, 1.

54. E. Said, *Orientalism* (New York 1978) 278.

55. G. E. von Grunebaum, *Modern Islam: The Search for Cultural Identity* (Berkeley 1962) 24.

56. Ibid., 131.

57. Ibid., 171.

58. Originally published in French in 1954, M. Bennabi's *Vocation de l'Islam* has been translated by Asma Rashid under the title, *Islam in History and Society* (Islamabad 1988).

59. Ibid., 20.

60. L. Gardet, "*De quelle manière*," in G. von Grunebaum and R. Brunschvig, eds., *Classicisme et déclin culturel dans l'historie de l'Islam* (Paris 1957) 93–94.

61. Ibid., 97.

62. R. Brunschvig, "*Problème de la decadence.*" In von Grunebaum and Brunschvig, *Classicisme*, 35.

63. A number of scholars challenge the thesis of general decline before the onset of the West in the nineteenth century. See R. A. Abou-El-Haj, *Formation of the Modern State: The Ottoman Empire Sixteenth to Eighteenth Centuries* (Albany 1991); R. Owen, "The Middle East in the Eighteenth Century—an Islamic Society in Decline? A Critique of Gibb and Bowen's Islamic Society and the West." *Review of Middle East Studies*, number one, 1975, pp. 101–112, and William Smyth, "The Making of a Textbook." *Studia Islamica*, vol. LXXVIII, 1994, pp. 99–116.

64. English translation, A. H. al-Nadwī, *Islam and the World*, tr. M. Kidawi (Kuwait 1977).

65. Ibid., 169.

66. Ibid., 95–96

67. Scholars of the Ottoman Empire would disagree with this assessment of Nadwī's. See, for instance, M. F. Koprülü, *The Origins of the Ottoman Empire*, tr. and ed., G. Leiser (Albany 1992); and R. P. Lindner, *Nomads and Ottomans in Medieval Anatolia* (Bloomington: 1983).

68. al-Nadwi, *Islam and the World*, 108.

69. Ibid., 178.

70. Ibid., 196.

71. Ibid., 183.

72. Ibid., 189.

73. Ibid., 193.

74. M. al-Bahiy, *al-Fikr al-islāmī al-ḥadīth wa ṣilatihī bi al-istiʿmār al-gharbī*, 5th ed. (Beirut 1970).

75. For a similar treatment of the "Islamic problematic" and the conditions for renaissance, see A. Aroua, *l'Islam a la croisée des chemins* (Algiers 1969).

76. Ibid., 35.

77. Ibid., 36.

78. See, for instance, M. Khalidī and O. Farrūkh, *Al-Tabshīr wa'l istiʿmār fi'l bilād al-ʿarabiyya* (Beirut 1986), originally printed in 1953. The following summarizes the basic attitudes of many Arab and Muslim thinkers toward the West: "The intensification of western cultural penetration and military domination of Muslim people in the nineteenth century, generally justified in colonial and missionary rhetoric as efforts to elevate Muslims from their decadent conditions, to civilize them, and to make them worthy members of the new world order, hastened the decay and collapse of Muslim empires." Y. Y. Haddad, "The Revivalist Literature and the Literature of Revival: An introduction." In Y. Y. Haddad, et al., *The Contemporary Islamic Revival: A Critical Survey and Bibliography* (New York 1991) 3.

79. M. Asad, *Islam at the Crossroads*, 14th ed. (Gibraltar 1982) 51.

80. al-Bahiy, *Al-Fikr*, 211.

81. Ibid., 207.

82. Ibid., 503–504.

83. On M. Shaltut and the whole question of Azhar reform, consult M. D. Abraham, "Mahmud Shaltut (1893–1963), A Muslim Reformist: His Life, Works and Religious Thought" (Unpublished doctoral dissertation, Hartford Seminary 1976); and K. Zebiri, *Mahmud Shaltut and Islamic Modernism* (Oxford 1993).

84. The term *historicity* or *historicism* is used in two ways. First, it is used by G. Hegel, K. Marx, and K. Popper to deduce historical patterns or

laws on the basis of which future historical events can be predicted. In that, the conflation of both history and metaphysics is involved. Second, the term is used by Marxists to express how the material foundations of a society can determine the historical stage and evolution of that society. See, K. Popper, *The Poverty of Historicism* (New York 1957). In this work, the term is employed in the first sense. There are certain distinct patterns of the *nahdạh* according to which we can predict the rise of several theoretical issues in the future Arab world.

85. K. Marx and F. Engels, *Collected Works*, vol. 3 (New York 1975) 175. Marx maintains the following: "Man makes religion, religion does not make man. Religion is the self-consciousness and the self-esteem of man who has either not yet found himself or has already lost himself again."

86. Laroui, *The Crisis*, 83.

87. For a good analysis of Laroui's ideas, see M. A. Labdaoui, *Les nouveaux intellectuels arabes* (Paris 1993), especially chapter 6, 211–256.

88. A Laroui, *L'idéologie arabe contemporaine* (Paris 1970) 4.

89. Ibid., 8.

90. Ibid., 39.

91. Ibid., 26.

92. Ibid., 27.

93. A. Laroui, *The Crisis of the Arab Intelligentsia*, 153–154.

94. Ibid.

95. A. Hourani, *A History of the Arab People* (Cambridge 1991) 445.

96. Laroui is representative of a major trend in modern Arab thought that can be generally termed Marxist which has pronounced more than once "the death of religion." For other Arab writings on the subject, see: S. J. al-ʿAzm, *Naqd al Fikr al Dīnī* (Criticism of Religious Thinking) (Beirut 1969), and M. A. al-*ʿAlim, al-Waʿy wa'l waʿy al-mafqūd fi'l fikr al-ʿarabī al-muʿāṣir* (*Consciousness and Lost Consciousness in Contemporary Arab Thought*) (Cairo 1986).

97. Paul Tillich, *Systematic Theology*, vol. 1 (Chicago 1953) 108.

98. M. A. al-Jābirī, *Takwīn al-ʿaql al-ʿarabī* [*The Constitution of the Arab Mind*] (Beirut 1988).

99. M. A. al-Jābirī, *al-Khiṭāb al-ʿarabī al-muʿāṣir* (Beirut 1982) 20.

100. In this regard, Jābirī quotes the best representative of modern Islamic revivalism in the Arab world, Sayyid Quṭb, who maintains that today's

Muslims, "are also surrounded by *jāhiliyah*, which is of the same nature as confronted during the first period of Islam, but perhaps a little deeper. It also appears that our entire environment is seized in the clutches of *jāhiliyah*. The spirit of *jāhiliyah* has permeated our beliefs and ideas, our habits and manners, our culture and its sources, literature and art, and current rules and laws, to the extent that what we consider Islamic culture, Islamic sources, Islamic philosophy and Islamic thought are all the products of *jāhiliyah*." S. Quṭb, *Milestones* (Karachi 1981) 61.

101. Jābirī, *al-Khiṭāb*, 181.

102. See M. Foucault, *Les mots et les choses* (Paris 1966); and *L'archéologie du savoir* (Paris 1972).

103. J. Charnay, "*L'intellectuel arabe entre le pouvoir et la culture.*" *Diogenes*, 83, July–September 1973.

104. J. Lalande, *La raison et les normes* (Paris 1963).

105. Jābirī, *Takwīn*, 15.

106. On the Islamic concept of knowledge [*'ilm*] see the following: W. Daud, *The Concept of Knowledge in Islam* (London 1989); Z. Hasan, *Philosophy: A Critique* (Lahore 1988); and M. H. Yazdi, *The Principles of Epistemology in Islamic Philosophy: Knowledge by Presence* (Albany 1992).

107. See M. A. Jābirī, "*Ishkāliyāt al-aṣālah wa al-mu'āṣarah fi'l fikr al-'arabī al-ḥadīth wa al-mu'āṣir.*" In Sayyid Yassin et al., *al-Turāth wa taḥaddiyāt al-'aṣr* (Beirut 1985) 29–58.

108. Jābirī, *Takwīn*, 79.

109. A. Laroui, *Crisis of Arab Intelligentsia*, 156.

110. J. Schacht, *An Introduction to Islamic Law* (Oxford 1964).

111. G. Makdisi, "The Juridical Theory of Shafi'ī—Origins and Significance of *Uṣūl al Fiqh*." *Studia Islamica*, vol. 59, 1984.

112. S. Yāfūt, "Al-Hājis al-thālith fi falsafat Muḥammad 'Azīz al Habābī." In I. Badrān et al., *al-falsafah fi'l waṭan al-'arabī al- mu'āṣir* (Beirut 1985) 261.

113. M. A. Lahbabi, *De l'Etre à la personne: Essai de personnalisme réaliste*. (Paris 1954); and E. Mounier, *Qu'est-ce que le personnalisme?* (Paris 1961).

114. M. A. Lahbabi, *Le monde de demain: Le Tiers-monde accuse* (Casablanca, 1980).

115. See P. Tillich, *On the Boundary: An Autobiographical Sketch* (New York 1966), especially 24–30.

116. E. S. Brightman, "Personalism (Including Personal Idealism)." In V. Ferm, ed., *A History of Philosophical Systems* (New York 1950) 341.

117. M. A. Lahbabi, *Liberté ou libération* (Paris 1956).

118. G. Hegel, *Lectures on the Philosophy of World History*, tr. H. B. Nisbet (Cambridge 1975) 54.

119. Lahbabi, *Liberté*, 16.

120. For a full elaboration of the term *being* in Western philosophical writings, see P. Tillich, *Systematic Theology*, 163–210.

121. Lahbabi, *De L'être*, 12.

122. M. A. Lahbabi, *Du clos à l'ouvert: Vingt propos sur les cultures nationales et la civilization humaine* (Casablanca 1961).

123. Ibid., 15.

124. Lahbabi, *Le personnalisme*, 4.

125. Ibid., 90.

126. Lahbabi's views on Sufism do not stem, in my view, from a real understanding of *taṣawwuf* as an authentic religious science in Islam. The real doctrines of Sufism were developed, to a large extent, against the backdrop of the science of theology [*'ilm al-Tawḥīd*] and the tumultuous events of the formative phase of Islam. For a better appreciation of Sufism as an Islamic science, consult the following: A. J. Arberry, The Doctrines of the Sufis (Cambridge 1935); A. B. al Kalabādhī, *Al-Ta'rruf li Madhab Ahl al-Taṣawwuf*, ed. A. J. Arberry (Cairo 1934); A. T. al Makkī, *Qūt al-Qulūb fī Mu'amalat al-Maḥbūb*, 2 vols. (Cairo 1310/1892–93); A. N. Sarrāj, *Kitāb al-Luma' fi al-Taṣawwuf*, ed. Reynold A. Nicholson. Gibb Memorial Series, no. 22. (Leiden and London 1914); A. Schimmel, "The Origin and Early Development of Sufism," *Journal of the Pakistan Historical Society*, 1958; A. Schimmel, *Mystical Dimensions of Islam* (Chapel Hill 1975); and W. M. Watt, *The Faith and Practice of al-Ghazali* (Chicago 1982). Al-Ghazali (d. A.D. 1111) attests to the genuine character of sufism by saying that, "Among the things that necessarily became clear to me from my practice of the mystic 'way' was the true nature and special characteristics of prophetic revelation. The basis of that must undoubtedly be indicated in view of the urgent need for it." (Watt, *The Faith*, 63).

127. Lahbabi, *Le personnalisme*, 95.

128. Ibid., 99.

129. Ibid., 100.

130. See also H. Djait, *al-Kūfa: Naissance de la ville islamique* (Paris 1991).

131. A. Hourani, *A History of the Arab People*, 444.

132. Djait, *Europe and Islam: Cultures and Modernity*, 119.

133. On the metamorphosis of religious tradition and the transmission of religious knowledge from one generation to another, consult the important work of E. Shils, *Tradition* (Chicago 1981).

134. Djait, *Europe and Islam*, 124.

135. Ibid., 125.

136. H. Djait, *La personnalité et le devenir arabo-islamique* (Paris 1974) 163.

137. Ibid., 271.

138. Abdou Filali-Ansary, "Hichem Djait: *La tyrannie du paradigme*." In Hammadi Safi, ed., *Penseurs Maghrebins contemporains* (Tunis 1993) 106.

139. A. K. Khatibi, "Double Criticism: The Decolonization of Arab Sociology." In H. Barakat, ed., *Contemporary North Africa: Issues of Development and Integration* (Washington, D.C., 1985) 14.

140. See, for instance, A. El-Kenz, *Algerian Reflections on Arab Crises*, tr. R. W. Stooky (Austin 1991).

141. Ahmad Dallal, "Islamic Revivalist Thought, 1750–1850." *Journal of the American Oriental Society*, vol. 113(3), July-September 1993, especially 358–359.

142. See M. Gilsenan, *Recognizing Islam: Religion and Society in the Modern Arab World* (New York 1982). See also D. F. Eickelman, *Knowledge and Power in Morocco: The Education of a Twentieth-Century Notable* (Princeton 1985); and D. F. Eickelman, "Traditional Islamic Learning and Ideas of the Person in the Twentieth Century." In M. Kramer, ed., *Middle Eastern Lives: The Practice of Biography and Self-Narrative* (Syracuse 1991), especially 35–60.

Chapter 2

1. According to Arkoun, *turāth* means "the cultural heritage of the classical period of Muslim history (632–1258)." M. Arkoun, *Rethinking Islam: Common Questions to Uncommon Answers*, tr. R. D. Lee (Boulder, Colo. 1994) 26.

2. Von Grunebaum, *Modern Islam* (Berkeley 1962) 82. Also see, G. E. von Grunebaum, "Some Recent Constructions and Reconstructions of Islam."

In Carl Leiden, ed., *The Conflict of Traditionalism and Modernism in the Muslim Middle East* (Austin 1966) 141–160.

3. W. C. Smith, *The Meaning and End of Religion: A New Approach to the Religious Traditions of Mankind* (New York 1963) 159.

4. Ibid., 169.

5. E. Shils, *Tradition* (Chicago 1981) 94–95.

6. See Henry Corbin, *History of Islamic Philosophy* (London 1993); and K. Zurayk, *Tensions in Islamic Civilization* (Georgetown 1978).

7. Shils, *Tradition*, 97.

8. Benedict Anderson, *Imagined Communities: Reflections on the Origin and Spread of Nationalism* (London 1991) 13.

9. Ibid.

10. Halim Barakat, *The Arab World: Society, Culture, and Change* (Berkeley 1993) 34.

11. Hourani comments on the centrality of Arabic as thus: "More conscious of their language than any people in the world, seeing it not only as the greatest of their arts but also as their common good, most Arabs, if asked to define what they meant by 'the Arab nation,' would begin by saying that it included all those who spoke the Arabic language." Albert Hourani, *Arabic Thought* (Cambridge 1970) 1.

12. Compare to the following: "The new revolutionary spirit of Islam is a feature of well-being which Arabism will gain, in order to seek the resumption of its authentic role. Arabism will bring about the modernization of Islam and will lead the enlightenement of the masses adhering to Islam." Muṭāʿ Ṣafadī, "*al-Qawmiyya al-ʿarabiyya wa'l islām al-thawrī*" [Arab Nationalism and Revolutionary Islam] *al-Fikr al-ʿArabī al-Muʿāsir* (June 1980), 6. Quoted and translated by Bassam Tibi, "Islam and Arab Nationalism." In Barbara F. Stowasser, ed., *the Islamic Impulse* (Georgetown 1987) 69–70.

13. John Esposito asserts that the problem facing the Muslim world, especially under colonialism, is that the development of the Muslim world was based on a theory that equated modernization and development with both secularization and Westernization. One result of this theory was the gradual expansion of a Western-trained indigenous elite that was Westernized, both intellectually and culturally, and that sought to develop society along Western arguments. This resulted in clear dichotomies. Therefore, it is surprising "That the most foreceful manifestations of the Islamic resurgence have occurred in the more advanced and 'modernized' [seemingly] secular countries of the Muslim world." John L. Esposito, *The Islamic Threat: Myth or Reality?* (New York 1992) 10.

14. When Ottoman society began to feel the threat of the West in the nineteenth century, the elite culture of Turkey began to formulate the Islamic tradition in a new way. "The attempts of the Ottomans to claim a position of unique eminence in relation to Islamic tradition also extended beyond the appeal to religious values to include an evocation of the cultural traditions of the Islamic Middle East in the broadest sense." C. V. Findley, "The Advent of Ideology in the Islamic Middle East." *Studia Islamica*, vol. 55, 1982, 154–155.

15. William E. Shepard, "Islam and Ideology: Toward a Typology." *International Journal of Middle Eastern Studies*, vol. 19(3), August 1987, 319.

16. In a moving article on "Islamic Modernism," the late Fazlur Rahman bemoans the predicament of modern Muslim societies, which, in his view, are still largely controlled by the conservative *'ulamā'*. For a variety of historical and social reasons, he also notes the failure of Muslim modernism to accomplish its goals of the nineteenth century. However, Rahman does not examine the impact of the resurgence of Islam on the contemporary intellectual situation in the Muslim world. He reaches the grim conclusion that "Time alone will tell what choice the Muslims will make. For the time being, there exists only a total vacuum of Islamic intellectualism and a proliferation of modern secular institutions, which are ill at ease and largely sterile and unproductive due to a lack of integration with the conservative milieu." Fazlur Rahman, "Islamic Modernism: Its Scope, Method and Alternative." *International Journal of Middle Eastern Studies*, vol. 1(4), October 1970, 333.

17. Issa Boullata, "Challenges to Arab Cultural Authenticity." In Hisham Sharabi, ed., *The Next Arab Decade: Alternative Futures* (Boulder, Colo. 1988) 155.

18. For an elaboration on this theme in the context of Tunisian society, see Abdelkader Zghal, "The Reactivation of Tradition in a Post-Traditional Society." *Daedalus: Journal of the American Academy of Arts and Sciences*, vol. 102(1), Winter 1973, 225–238. On the theoretical side of the meaning of traditionalism and its adaptation, see S. N. Eisenstadt, "Post-Traditional Societies and the Continuity and Reconstruction of Tradition." *Daedalus: Journal of the American Academy of Arts and Sciences*, vol. 102(1), Winter 1973, 1–28.

19. Hobsbawm maintains the following: "Inventing traditions . . . is essentially a process of formalization and ritualization, characterized by reference to the past, if only by imposing repetition." Eric Hobsbawm, "Introduction: Inventing Traditions." In Eric Hobsbawm and Terence Ranger, eds, *The Invention of Tradition* (Cambridge 1984) 4.

20. Contrast the comment in note 19 with the following statement: "Political Islam is a new invention—it does not represent a 'going back' to any situation that existed in the past or to any theory that was formulated in the past. What it keeps from the past is the juridic tradition of linking politics and

religion. But even then, it seeks to transform the formalistic and symbolic link that the jurists had forged between politics and religion into a real bond. Furthermore, political Islamists want to reverse the traditional relationship between the two spheres so that politics becomes subservient to religion, and not the other way round, as was the case historically." Nazih Ayubi, *Political Islam: Religion and Politics in the Arab World* (London 1991) 3. What John Esposito has to say is illuminating as well: "Despite stereotypes of [Muslim] activists as fanatics who wish to retreat to the past, the vast majority share a common call for the traansformation of society not through a blind return to seventh-century Medina but a response to the present. They do not seek to reproduce the past but to reconstruct society through a process of Islamic reform in which the principles of Islam are applied to contemporary needs. Each speaks of a comprehensive reformation or revolution, the creation of an Islamic order and state, since they regard Islam as comprehensive in scope, a faith-informed way of life." John L. Esposito, *The Islamic Threat*, 165.

21. The Iraqi historian ʿAbd al-Azīz al-Dūrī argues that "Islam unified Arabs and provided them with a message, an ideological framework, and a state." Quoted by Halim Barakat, *The Arab World: Society, Culture, and State* (Berkeley 1993) 35. On the interaction of religion and ideology in early Islam, see the following: Talal Asad, "Ideology, Class, and the Origins of the Islamic State." *Economy and Society*, vol. 9(4); Suliman Bashear, "Qibla Musharriqa and Early Muslim Prayer in Churches." *The Muslim World*, vol. 81(3–4), July-October 1991, 267–282; and F. E. Peters, *Muhammad and the Origins of Islam* (Albany, N.Y. 1994). On the relationship between religion and ideology in general, see the interesting analysis of Bruce B. Lawrence, *Defenders of God: The Fundamentalist Revolt Against the Modern Age* (New York 1989), especially chapter three; and Talal Asad, *Genealogies of Religion: Discipline and Reasons of Power in Christianity and Islam* (Baltimore 1993).

22. Shils, *Tradition*, 250.

23. Kamal Abu-Deeb, "Cultural Creation in a Fragmented Society." In Hisham Sharabi, ed., *The Next Arab Decade: Alternative Futures* (Boulder, Colo. 1988) 163.

24. In the words of Hisham Sharabi, "Islamism is no longer represented by a peripheral group but constitutes a mass grassroots movement, while secularism still consists of an internally diverse, largely avant-garde movement of critical intellectuals, writers, professionals, scholars, and students." H. Sharabi, *Neopatriarchy: A Theory of Distorted Change in Arab Society* (New York 1988) 11.

25. For an excellent treatment of the subject, see Marshall Berman, *All That Is Solid Melts Into Air: The Experience of Modernity* (New York 1982).

26. J. Habermas, *The Philosophical Discourse of Modernity* (Cambridge 1987) 4.

27. Berman correctly observes that "Rousseau was . . . a deeply troubled man. Much of his anguish springs from sources peculiar to his own strained life; but some of it derives from his acute responsiveness to social conditions that were coming to shape millions of people's lives." Berman, *All That Is Solid*, 17.

28. Tillich maintains that, as a young man, Luther was going through a great anxiety in his life. Luther's anxiety exemplified the great tension within Christianity that he understood and tried to diffuse. This anxiety was particularly painful because, "he was always in fear of the threatening God, of the punsihing and the destroying God. And he asked: 'How can I get a merciful God?' Out of this question and the anxiety behind it, the Reformation began." P. Tillich, *A History of Christian Thought* (New York 1967) 229.

29. B. Anderson, *Imagined Communities*, 140.

30. Kant was a major symbol of this intellectual movement that came to be known as the Enlightenment. "Kant declares that it is vital to Enlightenment not merely that men should free their thinking from all authority, but also that they should make free public use of their reason, and that all should have unfettered rights to report the results of their thought in speech and writing." L. Goldmann, *The Philosophy of the Enlightenment*, tr. H. Maas (London 1973) 4. For an elaboration on the Enlightenment see P. Rabinow, ed. *The Foucault Reader* (New York 1984), especially Foucault's comments on E. Kant's "What Is Enlightenment?", 32–50.

31. In his comment on the genius of Freud, Althusser says, "Theoretically, Freud set up in business alone: producing his 'home-made' concepts and under the protection of imported concepts borrowed from the sciences as they existed, and, it should be said, from within the horizons of the ideological world in which these concepts swam." L. Althusser, *Essays on Ideology* (London 1976) 149.

32. G. Hegel, *Lectures on the Philosophy of History*, tr. H. B. Nisbet (Cambridge 1975) 8.

33. A. Kojeve, *Introduction to the Reading of Hegel: Lectures on the Phenomenology of Spirit* (Ithaca, N.Y. 1980) 32.

34. This view of modern consciousness and modern man as absolute reason is challenged by a number of philosophers. See P. Berger, *Facing Up to Modernity: Excursion in Society, Politics, and Religion* (New York 1977), especially 186–188.

35. In the words of the Italian philosopher Vattimo, nihilism is one basic element of modernity. "For Nietzsche the entire process of nihilism can be summarized by the death of God, or by the 'devaluation of the highest values.' For Heidegger, Being is annihilated insofar as it is transformed completely into

value." Gianni Vattimo, *The End of Modernity, Nihilism and Hermeneutics in Postmodern Culture* (Baltimore 1988) 20.

36. Reinohld Niebuhr, *The Nature and Destiny of Man*, vol. 2 (New York 1964) 160.

37. R. Rorty, *Philosophy and the Mirror of Nature* (Princeton 1979) 132.

38. For an elaboration on this theme, see D. Shayegan, *Le regard mutilé: Schizophrénie culturelle: pays traditionnels face à la modernité* (Paris 1989), especially section three.

39. Anthony Giddens, *The Consequences of Modernity* (Standford, 1990) 59.

40. Ibid., 176.

41. Sharabi, *Neopatriarchy*, 4.

42. Ibid., 37.

43. Ibid., 64.

44. Muḥammad al-Bāqī al-Hirmasī, "al-Islām al-iḥtijājī fi Tūnis." In Ismā'īl S. 'Abdalallah et al., eds., *al-Ḥarakāt al-islāmiyya al-mu'*āṣira fi al-'ālam al-'arabī (Beirut 1989) 276.

45. R. Ghanoushī, *Da'wa ilā al-rushd* (Tunis 1982) 21.

46. Halim Barakat, *The Arab World*, 130.

47. Khurshid Ahmad, "The Nature of the Islamic Resurgence." In John L. Esposito, ed., *Voices of Resurgent Islam* (New York 1983) 220. Ahmad makes the same point in Ibrahim M. Abu-Rabi', ed. *Islamic Resurgence: Challenges, Directions, and Future Perspetives: A Round Table with Khurshid Ahmad* (Tampa 1994). Some thinkers who take the civilizational approach to Islamic resurgence are also of the notion that resurgence is a major feature of all ancient civilizations. See Anouar Abdel-Malek, "Foundations and Fundamentalism." *Die Welt des Islams*, vol. 28, 1988, 25–37.

48. See Fazlur Rahman, "Revival and Reform in Islam." In Holt, et al., eds., *The Cambridge History of Islam*, vol. 2 (Cambridge 1970) 632–42; and John Voll, "Renewal and Reform in Islamic History: Tajdīd and Islāḥ," In John Esposito, ed., *Voices of Resurgent Islam* (New York 1983) 32–47. John Voll argues that "The contemporary Islamic revival is a special response to the particular conditions of the late twentieth century and must be seen in the context of the conflicts and challenges of the modern world. At the same time it is also part of the historical experience of renewal within Muslim societies over the centuries. The current experience of Muslim revivalists cannot be separated from the heritage which they reaffirm. Both are important to

the contemporary revivalist experience and neither can be ignored if that experience is to be understood." John O. Voll, "The Revivalist Heritage." Yvonne Y. Haddad, et al., eds., *The Contemporary Islamic Revival: In A Critical Survey and Bibliography* (New York 1991) 23.

49. S. Amin, "Is There A Political Economy of Islamic Fundamentalism?" In his *Delinking* (London 1990) 183.

50. J. Voll, "Fundamentalism in the Sunni Arab World: Egypt and the Sudan." In Martin E. Marty and R. Scott Appleby, eds., *Fundamentalisms Observed* (Chicago 1992) 347.

51. This is the point made by Michael M. Fischer in "Islam and the Revolt of the Petit Bourgeoisie." *Daedalus*, vol. 3, Winter 1982, 101–125.

52. Eric Davis, "The Concept of Revival and the Study of Islam and Politics." In Barbara Stowasser, ed., *The Islamic Impulse* (London 1987) 37.

53. Nazih Ayubi, *Political Islam*, 5.

54. Francois Burgat and William Dowell, *The Islamic Movement in North Africa* (Austin 1993) 41.

55. Yūsuf Qaraḍāwī offers this theory in his *al-Ḥall al-islāmī, farīḍa waḍarūra* (Beirut 1989).

56. Philip S. Khoury, "Islamic Revivalism and the Crisis of the Secular State in the Arab World: A Historical Appraisal." In Ibrahim Ibrahim, ed., *Arab Resources: The Transformation of a Society* (Washington, D.C. 1983) 214.

57. An elaborate analysis of Islamic resurgence and science is found in Bassam Tibi, "The Worldview of Sunni Arab Fundamentalists: Attitudes toward Modern Science and Technology." In Martin E. Marty and R. Scott Appleby, eds., *Fundamentalisms and Society* (Chicago 1993), 73–102.

58. John Voll, "Renewal and Reform," 43.

59. On the same subject, see Mark Juergensmeyer, *The New Cold War? Religious Nationalism Confronts the Secular State* (Berkeley 1993); and Conor Cruise O'Brien, *God Land: Reflections on Religion and Nationalism* (Cambridge 1988).

60. Partha Chatterjee, *Nationalist Thought and the Colonial World: A Derivative Discourse* (London 1986) 19.

61. Halim Barakat takes a different approach. "For over three decades following World War II, the religious movement remained dormant and confined to a few narrow circles. Secular nationalist and socialist thought, thanks to the triumph of the 1952 Egyptian revolution, dominated the Arab

world . . . The Islamic resurgence [in the Arab World], however, occured only after the Iranian revolution of 1979." *The Arab World*, 258.

62. Benedict Anderson, *Imagined Communities*, 11.

63. Ibid., 6.

64. Ibid., 12–13.

65. Ibid., 15.

66. Some scholars argue that the West must come to grips with the inner situation in modern Islam and must not see Islamic resurgence as a threat to the new world order. Ibrahim M. Abu-Rabiʿ, ed., *Islamic Resurgence*, 98. See also Mohamed Karbal, "Western Scholarship and the Islamic Resurgence in the Arab World." *American Journal of the Islamic Social Sciences*, vol. 10(1), Spring 1993, 49–59; and James Veitch, "Muslim Activism, Islamization or Fundamentalism: Exploring the Issues." *Islamic Studies*, vol. 32(3), Autumn 1993, 261–278.

67. Anderson, *Imagined Communities*, 116.

68. Ibid., 140.

69. On this phenomenon, see Charles D. Smith, "The 'Crisis of Orientation': The Shift of Egyptian Intellectuals to Islamic Subjects in the 1930's." *International Journal of Middle East Studies*, vol. 4(4), October 1974, 382–410. See also, C. Ernest Dawn, "The Formation of Pan-Arab Ideology in the Interwar Years." *International Journal of Middle East Studies*, vol. 20(1), February 1988, 67–91.

70. "The vision of religious nationalists is appealing in part because it promises a future that cannot easily fail: its moral and spiritual goals are transcendent and not as easy to gauge as are the more materialistic promises of secular nationalists." Mark Juergensmeyer, *The New Cold War*, 24.

71. Abdulaziz Sachedina, "Activist Shiʿism in Iran, Iraq, and Lebanon." In Martin E. Marty and R. Scott Appleby ed., *Fundamentalism Observed* (Chicago 1992) 405.

72. R. Hrair Dekmejian, *Islam in Revolution: Fundamentalism in the Arab World* (Syracuse 1985) 9.

73. Ḥaydar Ibrāhim ʿAlī, *Azmat al-islām al-siyāsī* [*The Crisis of Political Islam*] (Casablanca 1991) 18.

74. Ibid., 21.

75. Ṣalāḥ al-Dīn al-Jourshī, "al-Ḥaraka al-islāmiyya mustaqbaluhā rahīn al-tagayurrāt al-jazriyya" [The Future of the Islamic Movement Depends on

Fundamental Changes]. ʿAbd Allah al-Nafīsī, *al-Ḥaraka al-Islāmiyya: ru'yā mustaqbaliyyā* (Cairo 1981) 124–125.

76. Barakat, *The Arab World*, 143–144.

77. J. Voll, "Fundamentalism in the Sunni Arab World," 54.

78. "[I]t would be wrong to believe that the instigators of Islamist movements recruit their partisans from the illiterate masses alone. It has already been noted that the founder of the Egyptian Takfir wa Hijra was an engineer. In Tunisia, the sources of Islamism are found in the engineering schools, the faculties of medicine and science of the national university. The link between scientific progress and the return to spiritual values is not to be doubted." Habib Boulares, *Islam: The Fear and the Hope* (London 1990) 20.

79. Esposito, *The Islamic Threat*, 23.

Chapter 3

1. See A. Q. Awda, *Islam Between Ignorant Followers and Incapable Scholars* (Riyadh 1991).

2. Muḥammad al-Ghazālī has written more than seventy books on different Islamic subjects. One book of his that created some controversy is *al-Sunna al-nabawiyya bayna ahl al-fiqh wa ahl al-ḥadīth* (Beirut 1989).

3. Some of Qaraḍāwī's ideas are treated in the course of our analysis.

4. See Mustafa al-Sibāīʿ, *al-Islām wa'l ishtirākiyya* (Cairo 1960), and "Islamic Socialism." In Kemal H. Karpat, *Political and Social Thought in the Contemporary Middle East* (New York 1968), especially 122–126.

5. See Saʿīd Ḥawwā's autobiography, *Hādhihi tajribatī wa hādhihī shahādatī* (Cairo 1988), and his major study of the Ikhwan, *al-Madkhal ilā daʿwat al-ikhwān al-muslimīn* (Amman 1979). See also I. Wesmann, "Saʿīd Ḥawwa: The Making of a Radical Muslim Thinker in Modern Syria." *Middle Eastern Studies*, vol. 29(4), October 1993, 601–623.

6. See the following by Ḥasan Turābī: *al-Ḥaraka al-islāmiyya fi'l Sūdān* (Khartoum 1989); "Challenging Times, but Madinah is Our Model." *Impact International*, vol. 23(3–4), 1993; "Islam as a Pan-National Movement and Nation-States: An Islamic Doctrine on Human Association." *Islamica*, vol. 1(2), 1993. See also A. El-Affendi, *Turabi's Revolution: Islam and Power in Sudan* (London 1991); M. A. Ghani, "Practicality and Realism in the Islamic Movement in Sudan, *Inquiry* (Tampa, Florida), vol. 1(4), August 1992, pp. 16–20; Arthur L. Lowrie, ed., *Islam, Democracy, The State and the West: A Round Table with Dr. Hasan Turabi* (Tampa 1993), and I. Riad, "Factors

Contributing to the Political Ascendancy of the Muslim Brethren in Sudan." *Arab Studies Quarterly*, vol. 12(3), 1990, pp. 33–53.

7. For an excellent analysis of Ghanoushī's ideas see François Burgat and William Dowell, *The Islamic Movement in North Africa* (Austin 1993), and M. C. Dunn, *Renaissance or Radicalism? Political Islam: The Case of Tunisia's Al-Nahda* (Washington, D.C. 1992). See also Rashed al-Ghannouchi, *The Right to Nationality Status of Non-Muslim Citizens in a Muslim Nation*, tr. M. El Arian (Washington, D.C. 1990); and, his "People of the State or State of the People in the Muslim Nation-States?" *Crescent International*, 19: 17, 1990.

8. C. Harris, *Nationalism and Revolution in Egypt: The Role of the Muslim Brotherhood* (The Hague 1964) 151.

9. Muḥammad A. Khalafallah, "al-Ṣaḥwa al-islāmiyya fi miṣr" [Islamic Reawakening in Egypt]. In Ismaī'l S. 'Abdallah, ed., *al-Ḥarakāt al-islāmiyya al-mu'āṣira fi'l waṭan al-'arabī(Contemporary Islamic Movements in the Arab World)* (Beirut 1989) 41.

10. Ḥasan al-Bannā's writings and speeches have been translated into most Islamic languages.

11. See the following: A. Z. al-Abidin, "The Political Thought of Ḥasan al-Bannā," *Islamic Studies*, vol. 28(3): 219–237; I. Bello, "The Society of Muslim Brethren: An Ideological Study." *Islamic Studies* 20(2), 1981; H. Enayat, *Modern Islamic Political Movements* (Austin 1982), especially chapter three; R. P. Mitchell, *The Society of the Muslim Brothers*, new ed. (New York 1993), and A. Mouassali, "Ḥasan al-Bannā's Islamist Discourse on Democracy and Shūra." *Middle Eastern Studies*, vol. 30(1), January 1994.

12. Fathi Yakan, *Islamic Movement: Problems and Perspectives*, tr. Maneh al-Johani (Indianapolis 1984) 20.

13. Ḥasan al-Bannā, *Mudhakarāt al-da'wa wa'l dā'iya* (Beirut 1970) 38. The *Memoirs* are rendered partially by N. M. Shaikh as *Memoirs of Ḥasan al-Bannā Shaheed* (Karachi 1982). Because of the inaccuracy of the English translation, I here use the Arabic source.

14. Donald M. Reid, *Cairo University and the Making of Modern Egypt* (Cambridge 1990) 148.

15. See Zahia R. Dajani, *Egypt and the Crisis of Islam* (New York 1990) for an elaboration on this theme.

16. Ḥ. al-Bannā, *Mudhakarāt*, quoted and translated by Harris, *Nationalism and Revolution*, 43–44, 146.

17. Charles Wendell, tr., *Five Tracts of Ḥasan al-Bannā, 1906–1949* (Berkeley 1978) 2.

18. D. F. Eickelman, "Traditional Islamic Learning and Ideas of the Person in the Twentieth Century." In Martin Kramer, ed., *Middle Eastern Lives: The Practice of Biography and Self-Narrative* (Syracuse 1991) 39.

19. Modern leading Arab intellectuals left behind their memoirs which illustrate the complexity of life in the modern Middle East. See the following: M. Bennabi, *Memoires d'un temoin du siecle* (Algiers 1965); and A. al-Fāsī, *al-Naqd al-dhātī* (Rabat 1979); and Taha Hussayn, *The Stream of Days*, tr. H. Waymont (London 1948).

20. The following can easily apply to al-Bannā's description of himself in his *Mudhakarāt*: "Real autobiography is a weave in which self-consciousness is delicately threaded throughout interrelated experience. It may have such varied functions as self-explication, self-discovery, self-clarification, self-formation, self-presentation, self-justification. All these functions interpenetrate easily but all are centered upon an aware self aware of its relation to its experience." Karl J. Weintraub, "Autobiography and Historical Consciousness," *Critical Inquiry*, vol. 1(4), 1974–1975, 824.

21. Al-Bannā records that the first book he read on Sufism was *al-Manhal al-ṣāfī fī manāqib Ḥassanayn al-Ḥaṣafī. Mudhakarāt*, 16.

22. In his *Mudhakarāt*, al-Bannā reports a conversation with the shaykh of the *ṭarīqah* who said to him, "I predict that God will gather many hearts around you, and will cause a great number of people to rally around you." *Mudhakarāt*, 14.

23. Classical Sufi manuals often distinguish between many layers of adepts, such as *khāṣṣa*, *'āmma*, and more. See A. R. A. al-Qashānī, *A Glossary of Sufi Technical Terms*, tr. N. Safwat (London 1991). According to Abū al-Ḥasan al-Shādhilī, the *khāṣṣa* are the people that God has "drawn away from evil-doing and its roots, and employed for well-doing and its branches. He made them love the places of solitude (*khalawāt*) and opened before them the path of spiritual communion (*munājā*). He made Himself known to them and they came to know Him. . . . They are not veiled from Him; rather they are veiled with Him from others. They know only Him, and love none but Him." Ibrahim M. Abu-Rabi', ed. *The Mystical Teachings of al-Shadhili, Including His Life, Prayers, Letters and Followers*, tr. Elmer H. Douglas (Albany 1993) 126.

24. Afaf Lutfi Marsot, *Protest Movements and Religious Undercurrents in Egypt: Past and Present*. Occasional Papers Series (Georgetown 1984) 5.

25. al-Bannā, *Mudhakarāt*, 20.

26. Ibid., 61–14; and I. M. Husaini, *The Moslem Brethren: The Greatest of the Modern Islamic Movements* (Beirut 1956) 3–4.

27. al-Bannā, *Mudhakarāt*, 20.

28. *Wendell, Five Tracts of Ḥasan al-Bannā*, 36.

29. al-Bannā, *Mudhakarāt*, 21–22.

30. S. al-Zayn, *al-Ṣūfiyya fi naẓar al-islām* (Beirut 1976) 5.

31. Ibid., 8.

32. M. Gilsenan, *Recognizing Islam* (New York 1982) 112.

33. Muhammad Bayyumi, "The Islamic Ethic of Social Justice and the Spirit of Modernization: An Application of Weber's Thesis to the Relationship between Religious Values and Social Change in Modern Egypt." An unpublished doctoral dissertation (Philadelphia 1976) 158–159.

34. Ishak Musa Husaini was born in Jerusalem in 1904 and, after an illustrious academic career that took him to England and Beirut, he died in Jerusalem in 1991. Consult Taysir al-Nashif, *Mufakirroun falasṭiniyūn fi'l al-qarn al-'ishrīn* (Baghdad 1981); and Ḥasan Salwadī, *al-Doktor Isḥāk Mūsa al-Ḥusaini, 'amīd al-adab al-'arabī* (Taybeh 1991).

35. Ishak M. Husaini, *The Moslem Brethren*, 30.

36. Christian Harris, *Nationalism and Revolution*, 136.

37. Ibid., 137. On the connection between Ḥasan al-Bannā and Jamāl al-Dīn al-Afghānī, see Francois Burgat and William Dowell, *The Islamic Movement*, 34–36.

38. 'Abdallah al-Nafīsī, *al-Ikhwān al-muslimūn, al-tajriba wa'l khaṭa': awrāq fi'l naqd al-ẓātī* [*The Muslim Brothers, Trial and Error: Readings in Self-Criticism*] (Cairo 1989) 12.

39. Partha Chatterjee, *Nationalist Thought and the Colonial World: A Derivative Discourse* (London 1986) 25.

40. al-Bannā, *Mudhakarāt*, 49.

41. Ibid., 50.

42. Ibid., 52.

43. Rif'at al-Saī'd, *Ḥasan al-Bannā, kayfa wa limādha?* (Cairo 1984) 87.

44. See L. Binder, *Islamic Liberalism: A Critique of Development Ideologies* (Chicago 1988).

45. K. M. Khalid, *From Here We Start*, tr. Isma'il al-Faruqi (Washington, D.C. 1953).

46. Ibid., 32.

47. Ibid., 32. Compare Khalid's ideas to the following from Hegel's *Phenomenology*. "That mental sphere [insight] is the victim of the deception of a Priesthood, which carries out its envious vain conceit of being alone in possession of insight, and carries out its other selfish ends as well. At the same time this priesthood conspires with despotism, which takes up the attitude of being the synthetic crude unity of the real and this ideal kingdom—a singularly amorphous and inconsistent type of being—and stands above the bad insight of the multitude, and the bad intentions of the priests, and even combines both of these within itself. As the result of the stupidity and confusion produced amongst the people by the agents of priestly deception, despotism despises both and draws for itself the advantage of undisturbed control and the fulfillment of its lusts, its humors, and its whims. Yet at the same time it is itself in this same state of murky insight, is equally superstition and error." G. Hegel, *The Phenomenology of Mind*, tr. George Lichtheim (New York 1967) 562.

48. I borrow this statement from Pauline M. Rosenau, *Post-Modernism and the Social Sciences: Insights, Inroads, and Intrusions* (Princeton 1992) 78.

49. Khalid, *From Here We Start*, 33.

50. Ibid., 36. Many a nationalist and secularist Arab intellectual has commented on the role of the Muslim religious establishment in upholding the status quo. For instance, the Syrian historian, Shakir Mustafa, in the course of analyzing what he views as the reasons for the modern cultural crisis in the Arab world, argues that the *'ulamā'* fulfilled the function of providing "values and ideas which would make the exploited classes submissive, and legitimize[d] the rule of the military with their feudal-bourgeois allies: ideas of resignation, fatalism, being content with little. Of the *ḥadīth* (oral tradition) they chose to emphasize sayings like, 'obey those amongst you who retain power.' Their impact is felt indirectly in popular proverbs such as 'If you cannot overcome a hand, kiss it and pray that it shall be broken', or 'He who marries my mother becomes my uncle'." Shakir Mustafa, "Arab Cultural Crisis and the Impact of the Past." *The Jerusalem Quarterly*, 11, Spring 1979, 46.

51. Muḥammad al-Ghazālī, *al-Islām al-muftara 'alyhī bayna al-shuyui-'yīn wa'l ra'smaliyīn* (Cairo 1952) 27.

52. M. al-Ghazālī, *Our Beginning in Wisdom*, tr. Ismai'l R. al-Faruqi (Washington, D.C. 1953) 69–70.

53. I. Husaini, *The Moslem Brethern*, 42–43.

54. Wendell, *Five Tracts of Ḥasan al-Bannā*, 123. See also Muḥammad al-Ghazālī, *al-Islām wa'l istibdād al-siyāsī* (Cairo 1950) 51. Al-Ghazali maintains that "The Islam of the Azhar is the same Islam modern colonialists promote and support."

55. M. Bayyumi falsely argues that "Bannā was able, not only to gain the support of reformers, but also to gain the 'men of religion.' He never attacked al-Azhar, because [he] believed it was a symbol and center for the expression of Muslim solidarity." Bayyumi, *The Islamie Ethic*, 189.

56. al-Bannā, *Mudhakarāt*, 61–67.

57. See, W. M. Watt, *The Faith and Practice of al-Ghazali* (Chicago 1982).

58. al-Bannā, *Mudhakarāt*, 72.

59. In the view of the contemporary observers of Islamic resurgence, the mosque is the most influential place in the spread of the ideas of resurgence. "The mosque . . . constituted the first framework for the gestation of the Islamist discourse and its very first receptacle. It played first of all as protector, a shelter where the first militant trajectories could be elaborated. The government everywhere assessed little by little the danger which existed in tolerating a liberty of association and freedom of speech which was all the more subversive since it contrasted with a civil environment that was still tightly controlled. Very quickly, the mosques' highly symbolic space became one of the principal places for confrontation between Islamism and the government." Francois Burgat and William Dowell, *The Islamic Movement in North Africa*, 87.

60. al-Bannā, *Mudhakarāt*, 127.

61. Ḥasan Bannā, "New Renaissance." In Kemal H. Karpat, ed., *Political and Social Thought in the Contemporary Middle East* (New York 1968) 121.

62. Ibid., 128.

63. Terry Eaglton, *Ideology* (London 1992) 194.

64. Harris, *Nationalism and Revolution*, 157. Ishak M. al-Husaini comments on the same theme by saying that "the Brethren did not propose any solution for the great number of abstruse religious problems which were the deep concern of educated Muslims. The majority of their followers were from the uneducated or semieducated class." I. Husaini, *The Moslem Brethern*, 107.

65. Wendell, *Five Tracts of Ḥasan al-Bannā*, 219.

66. Ibid., 19–20.

67. Johanness G. Jansen, "Ḥasan al-Bannā's Earliest Pamphlet." *Die Welt des Islams*, vol. 32(2), 1992, 258. The pamphlet in question is by Ḥasan al-Bannā, Aḥmad al-Sukkarī, and Ḥāmid ʿAskariyya, and named *Mudhakarra fi'l taʿlīm al-dīnī* (Cairo 1929).

68. Wendell, *Five Tracts of Ḥasan al-Bannā*, 26.

69. Ishak M. Husaini, *The Moslem Brethern*, 95.

70. Wendell, *Five Tracts of Ḥasan al-Bannā*, 28.

71. Ibid., 28.

72. Ibid., 29.

73. See L. Binder, *Islamic Liberalism*.

74. John Esposito notes that, throughout the history of Islamic resurgence, one can notice that "While Westernization and secularization are condemned, modernization as such is not. Science and technology are accepted, but the pace, direction, and extent of change are to be subordinated to Islamic belief and values in order to guard against the penetration of Western values and excessive dependence on them." John L. Esposito, *The Islamic Threat*, 19.

75. Wendell, *Five Tracts of Ḥasan al-Bannā*, 106.

76. I. Husaini, *The Moslem Brethern*, 103.

77. H. al-Bannā, *Da'watuna* (Cairo 1943). This quotation is translated by Franz Rosenthal in "The 'Muslim Brethren' in Egypt." *The Muslim World*, vol. 37(4), October 1947, 284.

78. Ibid., 283.

79. Wendell, *Five Tracts of Ḥasan al-Bannā*, 64.

80. Ibid., 61.

81. I. Husaini, *The Moslem Brethern*, 88.

82. Ḥ. al-Bannā, *Majmū'at rasā'il al-imām al-shahīd Ḥasan al-Bannā* (Beirut 1981) 119–121. English translation, S. A. Qureshi, *Selected Writings of Hasan al-Banna Shaheed* (Karachi 1983) 173–176.

83. al-Bannā, *Majmū'at rasā'il*, 122–123. See also H. Enayat, *Modern Islamic Political Thought* (Austin 1982) 84–85.

84. R. Sai'd, *Ḥasan al-Bannā*, 31.

85. See Daniel Bell, *The End of Ideology: On the Exhaustion of Political Ideas in the Fifties* (New York 1960).

86. On the personality of al-Bannā, see Jābir Rizq, *Ḥasan al-Bannā* (Manṣūra 1986), and 'Abbās al-Sīsī, *Ḥasan al-Bannā: Mawāqif fi'l da'wa wa'l tarbiya* (Cairo 1982).

87. Eric Hoffer's notion of the rise of mass movements is illuminating. "No matter how vital we think the role of the leadership in the rise of a mass movement, there is no doubt that the leader cannot create the conditions which make the rise of a movement possible . . . There has to be an eagerness to follow and obey, and an intense dissatisfaction with things as they are, before movement and leader can make their appearance. When conditions are not ripe, the potential leader, no matter how gifted, and his holy cause, no matter how potent, remain without a following," E. Hoffer, *The True Believer*, 103.

88. Ibid., 21.

89. A. Hourani, *Islam in European Thought* (New York 1991) 107.

90. Ibid., 109.

91. Ibid., 113.

92. Ibid., 112.

93. Antonio Gramsci, *The Modern Prince and Other Writings* (New York 1957) 119–120.

94. Ibid., 118.

95. N. Abercrombie, S. Hill, and B. S. Turner, *The Dominant Ideology Thesis* (London 1985) 13.

96. Gramsci, *The Modern Prince*, 118.

97. A term used by Gramsci. See also N. Abercrombie, S. Hill, and B. S. Turner, *The Dominant Ideology Thesis*, 13.

98. Karl Mannheim, *Ideology and Utopia*, 192.

99. An extensive analysis of these notions is to be found in, D. Macdonell, *Theories of Discourse: An Introduction* (London 1986).

100. For a psychological analysis of al-Bannā and the early Ikhwan's leaders, see Muḥammad Mahdi *al-Ṣaḥwa al-islāmiyyah*: *al-dawāfi' wa'l 'awa'iq* (Manṣūrah 1992).

101. For an elaboration of the question of meaning and history, see Robert D'Amico, *Historicism and Knowledge* (London 1989), especially chapters one and two.

102. On Muslim perceptions of the West in the nineteenth century, see R. R. al-Ṭahṭawi, *Kitāb takhlīs al-ibrīz fī talkhīṣ Bāriz*. In M. 'Imarah, ed., *Al-a'māl al-Kāmila li-Rifa'ā Rāfi' at-Ṭahṭāwī* (Beirut 1973) French translation by A. Louca, *L'or de Paris: Rélation de voyage, 1826–1831* (Paris 1988). See also,

S. G. Miller, *Disorienting Encounters: Travels of a Moroccan Scholar in France in 1845–1846: The Voyages of Muhammad As-Saffar* (Berkeley 1992).

103. S. Amin, *The Arab Nation*, 32.

104. Consult Ibrahim B. Ghānim, *al-Fikr al-siyāsī li'l imām Ḥasan al-Bannā* (Cario, 1992); and Sai'd Ḥawwa, *al-Madkhal ila da'wat al-ikhwān al-muslimīn* (Amman 1979).

105. I. Husaini, *The Moslem Brethern*, 41.

106. M. Gilsenan, *Recognizing Islam*, 217.

CHAPTER 4

1. The most comprehensive bibliography of Sayyid Quṭb's work is to be found in the following: Muḥammad Ḥ Diyāb, *Sayyid Quṭb: al-khiṭāb wa'l idiulūjiyya* (Casablanca 1992) 201–250; 'Abd al-Bāqī M. Ḥussayn, *Sayyid Quṭb: Ḥaytūhu wa adabūhu* (Al-Manṣūra 1986) 401–444; Ṣalāh al-Khālidī, *Sayyid Quṭb: Mina al-mīlād ila al-istishhād* (Damascus 1991) 585–592; Adnan A. Musallam, "*The Formative Stages of Sayyid Quṭb's Intellectual Career and his Emergence as an Islamic Dā'iyah, 1906–1952.*" Doctoral Dissertation (Ann Arbor 1983) 284–296. See also Ahmed S. al-Moussalli's doctoral dissertation which was turned into a book, *Radical Islamic Fundamentalism: The Ideological and Political Discourse of Sayyid Quṭb* (Beirut 1992).

2. Quṭb produced a number of works in the literature genre, including *Muhimmat al-shā'ir fi'l ḥayāt wa shi'r al-jil al-ḥāḍir* (Beirut n.d.) (first published in 1933); *Kutub wa shakhṣiyāt* (Beirut 1974) (first published in Cairo in 1946); and *al-Naqd al-adabī: uṣūluhu wa manāhajihu* (Cairo 1947).

3. See the following by Quṭb *al-Taṣwīr al-fannī fi'l qur'ān* (Cairo 1962); and *Mashāhid al-qiyāma fi'l qur'ān* (Cairo 1966).

4. Quṭb's most distinctive work of this genre is *al-'Adāla al-ijtimā'iyya fi'l islām* (Cairo 1949). English translation, John B. Hardie, *Social Justice in Islam* (New York 1980).

5. The major work in this area by Quṭb is *Ma'arakat al-islām wa'l ra'smāliyya* (Cairo 1974) (originally published in 1951).

6. Quṭb's monumental work of exegesis is *Fī Ẓilāl al-Qur'ān*. 6 vols., rev. ed. (Beirut 1974).

7. Quṭb's writing about Islam and the West is dispersed throughout his various works. Consult *The Islamic Concept and Its Characteristics* (*Khaṣā'is al-taṣawwur al-islāmī wa muqawimātuhu*) (Indianapolis 1992); *Islam: The Religion of the Future* (*al-Mustaqbal lihādha al-dīn*) (Delhi 1976); and *This Religion of Islam* (*Hādaha al-dīn*) (Delhi 1974).

8. Samir Amin offers a precise assessment of the significance of Sayyid Qutb's thought in contemporary Arab society. "The recordings of Ayatollah Khomeini, the long educational talks that the Arab television stations, from the Morocco to the Gulf, offer their viewers, the religious education propagated by the militants, the endless range of books and pamphlets shelved in bookshops under Islamiyat labels, have added nothing to the master's [Quṭb's] thinking. Moreover, at least, half of the work cited has been allowed to fall into oblivion: it is precisely that part dealing with Muslim history and the West. The dogmatic chapters dealing with justice and power in Islam are by contrast more or less faithfully reproduced." Samir Amin, "Is There a Political Economy of Islamic Fundamentalism?" in his *Delinking* (London 1990) 177. See also Samir Amin, *Azmat al-mujtama' al-'arabī* (Cairo 1985); Adnan Musallam, "Sayyid Qutb and Social Justice, 1945–1948." *Journal of Islamic Studies*, vol. 4(1), 1993, 52–70; Yvonne Haddad, "Sayyid Qutb: Ideologue of Islamic Revival." In John Esposito, ed., *Voices of Resurgent Islam* (New York 1983); and Ahmad Moussalli, "Sayyid Qutb: The Ideologist of Islamic Fundamentalism." *Al-Abḥāth* (American University of Beirut), vol. 38, 1990, 42–75.

9. E. Sivan, "Sunni Radicalism in the Middle East and the Iranian Revolution," *International Journal of Middle East Studies*, 21(1), February 1989, 1.

10. For an elaboration, see Muḥammad H. Diyāb, *Sayyid Quṭb*, 28–99.

11. Quṭb did not learn from the Christian systematic theologians. However, there are elements of his work that ar reminiscent of Paul Tillich's magnificent work, *Systematic Theology*. 3 vols. (Chicago 1953–1962).

12. D. Macdonell, *Theories of Discourse: An Introduction* (London 1986) 45.

13. A lot has been written about the influence which 'Abbās al-'Aqqād exerted on the formative phase of S. Quṭb's life. See M. Abubakar, "Sayyid Quṭb's Interpretation of the Islamic View of Literature," *Islamic Studies*, vol. 23(2), Summer 1984, 57–66; Aḥmad Badawī, *Sayyid Quṭb* (Cairo 1992) 9–69; Ṣalāh al-Khālidī, *Sayyid Quṭb: mina al-milād ila al-istishhād* (Damascus 1991) 93-191, and A. Musallam, "Sayyid Quṭb's Literary and Spiritual Orientation (1932–1938)" *The Muslim World*, vol. 80(3–4), July–October 1990, 176–189. Quṭb himself took the side of the more liberal al-'Aqqād against the conservative al-Rāfi'ī. Consult the series of aticles he wrote in al-Risāla in 1938, especially "Bayna al-'Aqqād wa'l Rāfi'ī." *Al-Risāla*, Number 251, April 1938, 692.

14. S. Quṭb, "al-Dalālah al-nafsiyah li'l alfāẓ wa'l tarākīb al-'arabiyah." *Ṣaḥīfat Dār al-'Ulūm*, 3(3), January 1938, 23.

15. Ibid., 27.

16. S. Quṭb, "al-Dalālah al-nafsiyah li'l asālib wa'l itijāhāt al-ḥadithah." *Sahifat Dar al-'Ulum*, 5(1), July 1938, 102.

17. S. Quṭb, *Muhimmat al-shā'ir fi'l ḥayāt*, 23.

18. On the concept of harmony in Quṭb's thought, see Abderrahman Cherif-Chergui, "*El principio de armonia en Sayyid Quṭb.*" In J. M. Barral, *Orientalia Hispanica* (Leiden n.d.) 195–208.

19. S. Quṭb, *Muhimmat*, 15.

20. For an extensive analysis of Quṭb's early attitude on poetry and philosophy, see Badawī, *Sayyid Quṭb*, 12–16.

21. S. Quṭb, *Muhimmat*, 91.

22. Ibid., 91.

23. Ibid., 92.

24. See Taha Husain, *An Egyptian Childhood*, tr. E. H. Oaxton (London 1932).

25. S. Quṭb, *Kutub wa shakhṣiyāt* (Beirut 1974) 5.

26. S. Quṭb, *Ṭifl min al-qarya* (Beirut n.d.) 78.

27. On the complex relationship among *barakah*, religion, and society in the modern Arab world, consult M. Gilsenan, *Recognizing Islam: Religion and Society in the Modern Arab World*, especially chapters 4 and 5.

28. S. Quṭb, *Ṭifl min al-qarya*, 137.

29. Adnan Mussallam, *The Formative Stages*, 74.

30. For an analysis of liberal thought in Egypt in the interwar period, consult Albert Hourani, *Arabic Thought in the Liberal Age* (Cambridge 1970), and Charles Smith, *Islam and the Search for Social Order in Modern Egypt: A Biography of Muhammad Husayn Haykal* (Albany 1983).

31. Ṭāha Ḥussain, *Mustaqbal al-thaqāfa fı miṣr*, vol. 1 (Cairo 1938) 31.

32. Sayyid Quṭb, "Naqd mustaqbal al-thaqāfa fī miṣr." *Ṣaḥīfat Dār al-'Ulūm*, vol. 4, April 1939, 34.

33. Ibid., 35.

34. Ibid., 38.

35. Ibid., 41.

36. Ibid., 45.

37. T. Hussein, *The Future of Culture*, tr. S. Glazer (New York 1975) 13.

38. Quṭb, *Ma'arakt*, 100–101.

39. Quṭb, "Naqd mustaqbal al-thaqāfa," 76.

40. Sayyid Quṭb, *al-Taṣwīr al-fannī fi'l Qur'ān* (Cairo 1963) [originally published in 1945] 7.

41. Ibid., 8.

42. Ibid.

43. Ibid., 34–35.

44. Leonard Binder, *Islamic Liberalism: A Critique of Development Ideologies* (Chicago 1988) 194–195

45. Ibid., 10.

46. See the following works on *jāhiliyah* and Islam: I. Goldziher, *Muslim Studies*, vol. 1 (Chicago 1966); T. Izutso, *God and Man in the Qur'ān: Semantics of the Qur'anic Weltanshauung* (Tokyo 1964); Izutso, *Ethico-Religious Concepts of the Qur'ān* (Montreal 1966), and A. R. Nicholson, *A Literary History of the Arabs* (Cambridge 1953).

47. In my discussion of Sayyid Quṭb's *Social Justice in Islam*, I rely on the original first edition of his *al-'Adālah al-ijtimā'iyya fi'l islām* (Cairo 1949), and John B. Hardie's translation, *Social Justice in Islam* (Washington, D.C. 1953) which is somewhat faithful to the original Arabic. In an insightful article, William Shepard compares the later edition of *al-'Adālah* to the 1949 and finds that some substantial changes were introduced to the later editions, either by the author himself or the person who holds the copyright to this important work. My view is that the latter is true. Shepard maintains that "more than 50 percent of the paragraphs in the first edition havc undergone some change, or have been eliminated or replaced entirely." William Shepard, "The Development of the Thought of Sayyid Qutb as Reflected in Earlier and Later Editions of 'social Justice in Islam'." *Die Welt Des Islams*, vol. 32(2), 1992, 202.

48. William Shepard, "The Development of the Thought of Sayyid Quṭb," 201.

49. A. Gramsci, *The Modern Prince and Other Writings* (New York 1957) 118.

50. Ibid., 119.

51. For a good analysis of the "little" and "great" traditions of Islam, see R. Antoun, *Muslim Preacher in the Modern World: A Jordanian Case Study in Comparative Perspective* (Princeton 1989).

52. See George W. Hegel, *Lectures on the Philosophy of Religion*, tr. E. B. Speirs (London 1895).

53. On the notion of social justice in modern Islamic thought, consult Hmida Ennaifer, "La pensée sociale dans les écrits musulmans modernes." *IBLA: Revue De L'Institut Des Belles Lettres Arabes*, vol. 50(160), 1987, 223–253.

54. Adnan Musallam notes correctly that, "The emergence of the 'social justice' theme in Sayyid Quṭb's thought can only be understood within the context of the prevailing conditions in Egypt." A. Musallam, "Sayyid Qutb and Social Justice," 69–70.

55. S. Quṭb, *Social Justice in Islam*, tr. John B. Hardie (New York 1980) 1. Because there are some marked differences between the Arabic text of *Social Justice* and the English translation, I will be using both sources.

56. Ibid., 2.

57. S. Quṭb, *al-ʿAdālah al-ijtimāʿiyya fi'l islām* (Cairo 1949) 8–9.

58. S. Quṭb, *Social Justice*, tr. J. Hardie, 2.

59. Ibid., 5.

60. Ibid., 9.

61. Ibid., 11.

62. Ibid., 13.

63. Ibid., 13.

64. Ibid., 30.

65. Ibid., 43.

66. Ibid., 95.

67. Ibid., 97.

68. Ibid., 103–104.

69. Ibid., 105.

70. Ibid., 109.

71. Ibid., 127.

72. Ibid., 130.

73. Hardie's translation, ibid., 132–133. (It is strange that these important comments of Sayyid Quṭb are deleted from the Arabic texts printed after 1954.)

74. Ibid., 216. Abū Dharr al-Ghifārī (d. A.D. 652), a companion of the Prophet, was known for his humility and love of the poor. See A. Shari'ati, *On the Sociology of Islam* (Berkeey 1979).

75. S. Amin is of the opinion that, to Qutb, and to the rest of "the Muslim fundamentalists," Islamic history of the past fourteen centuries is "nothing but shame." Amin, "Is There," 179. Samir Amin argues as follows: To the Muslim fundamentalists, "philosophical debates are impious. The [Q]ur'ān is the only source of philosophy; reflection on the basis of Greek philosophy is condemned, and there is vilification of the interpretations of the Arab liberal bourgeoisie who wanted to revive the reputation of the 'centuries of Muslim enlightenment'." Ibid., 179.

76. I borrow the term, *creative tension*, from K. Zurayk, *Tensions in Islamic Civlization* (Georgetown 1978).

77. Quṭb, *Social Justice*, tr. J. Hardie, 221–225.

78. Ibid., 227.

79. Ibid., 233.

80. Ibid., 238–239.

81. Ibid., 239.

82. Ibid., 242.

83. Ibid., 249.

84. Ibid., 249.

85. Ibid., 250.

86. Ibid., 250.

87. S. Quṭb, "The Bases of Social Justice in Islam." *The Criterion: Journal of the Islamic Research Academy*, vol. 3(4), 1969, 5.

88. Ibid.

89. On the notion of harmony in Quṭb's thought, see, Abderrahman Cherif-Chergui, "El Principio de Armonia en Sayyid Quṭb," 195–208.

90. Quṭb, "The Bases," 10.

91. Ibid., 11.

92. Ibid., 15.

93. Unfortunately, Quṭb did not live long enough to witness the tremendous rise of the oil industry in the Gulf States and its impact on such issues as social justice, labor migration, and religious rationalization of the

status quo. In my view, however, Quṭb popularized the issue of social justice and, as such, it has become the backbone of many Ikhwan writings on contemporary Muslim issues. Al-Qaraḍāwī, for instance, comments on the extremism of the youth in Muslim countries and points to one of its salient causes. "Furthermore, the young constantly witness clear social injustices and great disparity between the poor and the rich, between those who can hardly exist and those who waste millions on gambling and women; they see mansions which cost millions but are occasionally—if ever—used while millions of Muslims remain unsheltered; they hear of fortunes smuggled abroad to be kept in secret foreign accounts, while millions of Muslims are content with the little that is still denied them, those who can hardly feed their children or buy medicine for the sick and old. Yet, if those who usurp oil revenues, or those who have benefited from the policy of economic cooperation withthe West, or the agents of big international companies, donated but a portion of the wealth thrown away on gambling or on women, it would relieve a great deal of poverty as well as feed and shelter tens of thousands. Countless riches and public funds are being usurped in broad daylight; bribery and favoritism are deeply rooted. Those who commit these thefts always escape justice, but those who commit relatively insignificant misdeeds are harshly and severely punished. Such injustice has created bitter feelings of envy, hatred, and malice between the various sectors of the community." Yūsuf al-Qaraḍāwī, *Islamic Awakening Between Rejection and Extremism*, tr. A. S. al-Shaikh Ali and Mohamed Wasfy (Herndon, Va. 1991) 84–85.

94. Sayyid Quṭb, *Ma'arakat al-islām wa'l ra'smāliyya* (Cairo 1974) 5.

95. The relationship between *'ulamā'* and the state is a major theme in contemporary Ikhawn literature. Al-Qaraḍāwī, for instance, maintains that one of the main reasons for the current extremism of the Muslim youth is the lack of religious guidance which the youth receive from reliable *'ulamā'*, and that "Most of the eminent *'ulamā'* who are entrusted with leadership and guidance have become mere pawns in the hands of those in authority, who direct them as they wish." Yūsuf al-Qaraḍāwī, *Islamic Awakening*, 72. In a book, the eminent Ikhwan scholar Muḥammad al-Ghazālī argues that "Islam is being misused in the name of Islam . . . It is misused by authority-serving ulama, *fiqh*-lacking youth, and confused crowd." Muḥammad al-Ghazālī, *al-Ghazw al-thaqāfī yamtadū fī farāghinā* (*The Cultural Invasion Expands through Our Vacuum*) (Amman 1985) 8.

96. Salāma Mūsa, an Egyptian Leftist journalist and a contemporary of Quṭb, shares similar views. "Much of what I had to endure in my own life in the way of bad accidents that tended to frustrate my energies and dissipate my forces was due to this personal alliance between the Egyptian reactionaries and the British imperialists. Their combined efforts to keep us in shackles compelled me to creep along slowly where otherwise I might have flown, and on many occasions it compelled me to sit back instead of moving forward however

slowly." Salāma Mūsa, *The Education of Salāma Mūsa*, tr. L. O. Schuman (Leiden 1961) 186–7.

97. S. Quṭb, *Ma'arakat al-islām*, 6.

98. Joel Beinin, "Islamic Responses to the Capitalists Penetration of the Middle East." In Barbara F. Stowasser, ed., *The Islamic Impulse* (Georgetown 1987) 100.

99. Salāma Mūsa, *The Education*, 33.

100. In an interesting piece on, "The Men of Learning and Authority," Michael Gilsenan analyzes the theological function and social position of the *'ulamā'* in the modern Arab world and reaches similar conclusions to Quṭb's. Gilsenan contends that the *'ulamā'* have been the keepers of the Qur'ān because of its metaphysical, historical, and symbolic values. In his word, "The text becomes an instrument of authority and a way of excluding others or regulating their access to it. It can be used to show that others are wrong and we are right; what is more, we have the right to be right and they do not! We know. So revelation is controlled and becomes a potential mode of control." Michael Gilsenan, *Recognizing Islam: Religion and Society in the Modern Arab World*, 31.

101. Musallam, *Sayyid Quṭb*, 214.

102. S. Quṭb, *Ma'arakat al-islām*, 6.

103. Ibid., 10.

104. Joel Beinin notes that, "Quṭb's analysis of the Egyptian ruling class, its institutions, and its alliance with imperialism has much in common with the Marxist analysis of these questions that was widespread and popular in Egypt at this time." Beinin, "Islamic Responses," 101. One must understand the preceding statement in light of Quṭb's religious and social engagement with the plight of the poor in Egyptian society and his critical stance toward the ruling elite.

105. S. Quṭb, *Ma'arakat al-islām*, 14.

106. Ibid., 16.

107. Almost three decades later, a respected *'ālim* and a prominent thinker of the Ikhwan echoes similar thoughts on the plight of modern Islam. "The only form of Islam allowed is that upheld by the dervishes and the professional traders in religion; the 'Islam' of the ages of backwardness and decadence; the 'Islam' which only celebrates occasions, supports despotic rulers, and prays for them to have a long life. It is an 'Islam' based on Divine predetermination and 'no-choice' in belief." Yūsuf al-Qaraḍāwī, *Islamic Awakening*, 92.

108. S. Quṭb, *Ma'arakat al-islām*, 63.

109. Ibid., 85.

110. Ibid., 53.

111. Ibid., 95.

112. *Ibid.*, 98.

113. Ibid., 99.

114. Ibid., 99.

115. Ibid., 106.

116. Ibid., 17.

117. P. Chatterjee, "More on Modes of Power and the Peasantry." *Selected Subaltern Studies*, ed. Ranajit Guha and Gayatri Spivak (New York 1988) 359.

118. Ibid., 388.

119. Quṭb, *Islam and Universal Peace*, 1.

120. Ibid., 2.

121. Ibid., 3.

122. Ibid., 55.

123. Ibid., 57–60.

124. Ibid., 61.

125. Ibid., 61–67.

126. Ibid., 68–69.

127. Sayyid Quṭb, "The Ideological Bankruptcy of Europe and the Future Prospects of Islam, I," *The Voice of Islam*, vol. 12(1), October 1963, 5.

128. Ibid., 11.

129. Ibid., 69.

130. Sayyid Quṭb, *Dirāsāt Islāmiyah* (Cairo 1967) 11.

131. Ibid., 31.

132. Ibid., 87.

133. Ibid., 119.

134. Ibid., 120.

135. Ibid.

136. Ibid., 123.

137. See chapter eight of this study.

138. Maḥmūd Amīn al-ʿĀlim, *al-Waʿy wa'l waʿy al-mafqūd fi'l fikr al-ʿarabī al-muʿāṣir* (Cairo 1986), especially chapter 2.

139. See H. Barakat, The *Arab World*, especially chapter 1.

140. Ibid., 160.

141. Quṭb, *Dirāsāt Islāmiyah*, 159.

142. Ibid., 159–160.

143. Ibid., 160–161.

144. Ibid., 161.

145. Ibid., 162.

146. Ibid., 162–163.

147. S. Quṭb, "ʿAduwunna al-awwal: al-rajul al-abyaḍ" ("Our First Enemy is the White Man." In S. Quṭb, *Ayuha al-ʿarab: istayqidhu wa iḥdharu* (Amman 1990) 208.

148. See S. Quṭb, *al-Risāla*, vol. 2(957), November 5, 1951, 1245–1247; and vol. 2(959), November 19, 1951, 1301–1306. These articles are reprinted in Ṣalāḥ D. al-Khālidī, *Amerīca minā al-dākhil bimindhār Sayyid Quṭb* [America from within as Seen by Sayyid Quṭb] (Jeddah 1986) 97–114.

149. Khālidī, ibid., 99.

150. Quṭb, "ʿAduwunna al-awwal: al-rajul al-abyaḍ." *al-Risāla*, vol. 2(1009), November 3, 1952, 1217. Also, Khālidī, 135.

151. Khālidī, 137.

152. Ibid., 163–164. Ḥasan al-Bannā, on his side, tackles the whole issue of Arab nationalism and Islam. He argues that, "The Muslim Brothers do not reject their nationality, which is the first step required for the sought-after awakening. They do not see any harm in having any person work for his/her nation . . . Furthermore, they wholeheartedly support Arab unity, which is a step required for awakening. The final goal of the Muslim Brothers is to work for an Islamic League that comprises the whole Muslim world." Quoted by Muḥammad ʿImārah, "Al-Waṭaniyya wa'l-islām." *Majallat al-ʿArabī*, December 1983, 76.

153. Ibid., 169–170.

154. Ibid., 170.

155. Ibid.

156. Ibid.

157. See especially Ranajit Guha, "Discipline and Punish." *Subaltern Studies VII: Writings on South Asian History and Society*, ed. P. Chatterjee and G. Pandey (New Delhi 1992) 69.

158. N. Abercrombie, S. Hill, B. Turner, *The Dominant Ideology Thesis* (London 1985) 12.

159. For an elaboration on that, see, I. M. Abu-Rabiʿ, "Discourse, Power, and Ideology in Modern Islamic Revivalist Thought: Sayyid Quṭb." *The Muslim World*, vol. 81(3–4), July–October 1991, especially 293–298.

160. See L. Althusser, *Essays on Ideology* (London 1984).

161. On the concept of *ummah* in both the Qur'ān and Muslim history, see Abdullah al-Ahsan, *Ummah or Nation? Identity Crisis in Contemporary Muslim Society* (Leicester 1992), especially chapter 1.

Chapter 5

1. See M. Diyāb, *Sayyid Quṭb: al-Khiṭāb wa'l idiūlujiyyā* (Casablanca 1992) 105–107. William Shepard's account of Quṭb's ideological shift also seems to be disjointed. "Sayyid Quṭb appears to have moved from a Muslim secularist position in the 1930s to a moderate radical Islamism (if I might use such an expression) in the late 1940s and then to an extreme radical Islamism during the last years of his life." William Shepard, "The Development," 201. This type of analysis blurs the discursive continuities in Quṭb's thought and its tenacious consistency, especially in relation to such notions as justice, the poor, imperialism, alienation, authenticity, and change.

2. Ḥasan Ḥanafī, *al-Ḥarakāt al-dinīyya al-mu*ʿāṣira (Cairo 1988) 168.

3. Ibid., 169.

4. Yvonne Haddad contends that, "During this period [the mid-1950s], Qutb was influenced by the writings of Muḥammad Asad (Leopold Weiss) and Abū al-Ala Mawdūdī, writings which became available in Egypt in 1951. His early Islamic writings are filled with their references to their work. His later works continue where they left off, and in fact are the radical conclusion of ideas expressed by them." Yvonne Y. Haddad, "Sayyid Quṭb: Ideologue of Islamic Revival." In John L. Esposito, ed., *Voices of Resurgent Islam* (New York 1983) 70.

5. Olivie Carre, *Mystique et politique-Lecture révolutionnaire du Coran par Sayyid Qutb-frère musulman radical* (Paris 1984).

6. Muḥammad Aḥmad Khalafallah maintains that Sayyid Quṭb, during this period, was subject to two patterns of cultural influence. The first was represented by the nascent thought of Nadwī and Mawdūdī of India and Pakistan which tackled the themes of Jahiliyya and the lack of divine political sovereignty in the modern Muslim world, while the second was represented by the work of Alexis Carrel that considered the modern secular Western civilization to be a deviant political and human system. Muḥammad A. Khalafallah, "al-Sahwah al-islamiyyah fi misr." In Ismāʿil S. ʿAbdallah, ed. *al-Ḥarakāt al-islāmiyya al-muʿāṣirah fī al-waṭan al-ʿarabī* [*Contemporary Islamic Movements in the Arab World*] (Beirut 1989) 61.

7. E. Sivan, *Radical Islam: Medieval Theology and Modern Politics* (New Haven 1990).

8. William Shepard maintains that, "Quṭb's later writing was undoubtedly influenced by the writings of the Indo-Pakistani Abu Aʿla Mawdūdī, which became available in Arabic in the 1950s. This is reflected in some of the new terminology and probably in the increased stress on the 'systematic' nature of Islam (both the assertion that Islam is a system and the tendency to describe and treat as such), which is very characteristics of Mawdudi's writings." William, Shepard, "The Development," 217.

9. I have consulted both the Arabic original and the translation. All quotations, however, are from the English translation. Sayyid Quṭb, *Hādha al-dīn* (Cairo 1962), translated as S. Quṭb, *This Religion of Islam* (Delhi 1974).

10. Ibid., 6.

11. Ibid., 9.

12. Ibid., 17.

13. Ibid., 23.

14. Ibid., 29–30.

15. Ibid., 32.

16. Ibid., 32–33.

17. Ibid., 35.

18. Ibid., 59.

19. Ibid., 87.

20. Sayyid Quṭb, *Islam: The Religion of the Future* (Delhi 1976) 7.

21. Ibid., 9.

22. On Turkish Secularism and the Role of Kemal Ataturk, see the following: Niyazi Berkes, *The Development of Secularism in Turkey* (Montreal 1964); Bernard Lewis, *The Emergence of Modern Turkey* (New York 1968); and Walter F. Weiker, *The Modernization of Turkey: From Ataturk to the Present Day* (New York 1981).

23. Quṭb, *Islam: The Religion of the Future*, 10.

24. See, Sayyid Quṭb, *Khaṣā'iṣ al-taṣawwur al-islāmī wa muqawimātuhū*, vol. 1 (Cairo 1962); English Translation by Mohammed M. Siddiqui, *The Islamic Concept and its Characteristics* (Indianapolis: 1991); and Sayyid Quṭb, *Muqawimāt al-taṣawwur al-islāmī* (Cairo 1986). This book was published by Muhammad Quṭb, Sayyid's brother, many years after the death of the author.

25. In a recent book on the same theme, the Egyptian author Muḥammad 'Imārah borrows a lot from Sayyid Quṭb's work on the Islamic concept without even referring to him by name. See, Muḥammad 'Imārah, *Ma'ālim al-manhaj al-islāmī* [*The Salient Features of the Islamic Method*] (Herndon Va. 1991). 'Imārah justifies writing such a book by saying that there are many competing Islamic discourses occuping the intellectual map of modern Islam, and it is necessary to idenitify and define the basic features of the archetypal method (*al-manhaj al-umm*) in Islam. Ibid., 18.

26. Sayyid Quṭb, *Kahṣā'*is, 4.

27. Ibid., 6.

28. Ibid., 8.

29. Modern leftist and Liberal Arab intelligentsia do not share these views. See, Aḥmad Amīn, *Fajr al-islām* (Beirut 1975); and Adonis ('Alī Aḥmad Sa'īd), *al-Thābit wa'l mutaḥawwil*, vol. 1 (Beirut 1983). Amin proposes that the mixture of cultures and philosophies in the formative phase of Islam created a unique intellectual synthesis that universalized the Arabo-Islamic civilization of the time. Adonis, on the other hand, argues that modernity and innovation (*taḥdīth wa ibdā'*) were the hallmark of the Arabo-Islamic civilization.

30. Quṭb, *Khaṣā'is*, 11.

31. Ibid., 12.

32. Quṭb argues that, "Today, knowledge that does not get transformed into activity is useless . . . There is no value attached to Islamic studies or to the accumulation of religious books on shelves, or the mental preservation of the contents of these books [if these contents do not get transformed into activity]. This is neither Islam or religious science. Religious sciences should be practiced in life and applied in society. It should live in reality and get

represented in a system. Islam is the symbol of the sovereignty of this system." Sayyid Quṭb, *Muqawimmāt al-taṣawwur al-islāmī* (Cairo 1986) 24–25.

33. Richard Rorty, *Philosophy and the Mirror of Nature* (Princeton 1979) 136. Rorty discusses the emerging demarcation, beginning with the seventeenth century, between philosophy, on the one hand, and other disciplines, including religion, on the other. "The secularization of moral thought, which was the dominant concern of European intellectuals in the seventeenth and eighteenth centuries, was not then viewed as a search for a new metaphysical foundation to take the place of theistic metaphysics. Kant, however, managed to transform the old notion of philosophy—metaphysics as 'queen of sciences' because of its concern with what was universal and least material—into the notion of a 'most basic' discipline—a foundational discipline. Philosophy becomes 'primary,' no longer in the sense of the 'highest' but in the sense of the 'underlying.'" Rorty, *Philosophy*, 132.

34. Sayyid Quṭb, *Muqawimāt*, 17.

35. Many Muslim scholars do not share this attitude. See, Muhsin S. Mahdi, *The Political Orientation of Islamic Philosophy* (Georgetown 1982); and Seyyed Hossein Nasr, *Knowledge and the Sacred* (Albany 1989).

36. Quṭb, *Khaṣāi'ṣ*, 14.

37. Ibid., 18–20.

38. Ibid., 9.

39. Ibid., 24.

40. Ibid., 25.

41. Quṭb seems to agree with some of the major philosophers and theologians of the West who hold similar pessimistic views about the achievements of the Western mind. See, Huston Smith, *Beyond the Post-Modern Mind*. Updated and revised edition (New York 1989).

42. Karl Popper, *The Open Society and its Enemies* (Princeton 1962).

43. See G. Hegel, *The Phenomenology of Mind* (New York: Harper 1967).

44. Quṭb, *Maqawimmāt*, 53.

45. Quṭb would agree with the following assessment of religion in nineteenth-century Europe made by Hegel. "It no longer gives our age any concern that it knows nothing of God; on the contrary, it is regarded as a mark of the highest intelligence to hold that such knowledge is not even possible. What is laid down by the Christian religion as the supreme, absolute commandment, 'Ye shall know God,' is regarded as a piece of folly." G. Hegel, *Lectures on the Philosophy of Religion* (London 1895) 36.

46. One of the best assessments of the Renaissance as a historical and intellectual movement is rendered by the American theologian Reinhold Niebuhr, who argues that "The Renaissance as a spiritual movement is best understood as a tremendous affirmation of the limitless possibilities of human existence, and as a rediscovery of the sense of a meaningful history. This affirmation takes many forms, not all of which are equally consistent with the fundamental impulse of the movement. But there is enough consistency in the movement as a whole to justify the historian in placing in one historical category such diverse philosophical, religious and social movements as the early Italian Renaissance, Cartesian rationalism and the French enlightenment; as the liberal idea of progress and Marxist catastrophism [?]; as sectarian perfectionism and secular utopianism. In all of these multifarious expressions there is a unifying principle. It is the impulse toward the fulfillment of life in history." Reinhold Niebuhr, *The Nature and Destiny of Man*, vol. 2 (New York 1943) 160.

47. Here, he relies heavily on Muḥammad al-Bahiy's famous work, *al-Fikr al-islāmī al-ḥadīth wa ṣilatuhu bi'l istiʿmār al-gharbī* (*The Connection of Modern Islamic Thought to Western Imperialism*) (Beirut 1970).

48. Quṭb, *Muqawimmāt*, 67.

49. The following comment by Jurgen Habermas points to the Hegelian contribution to the issue. "Hegel was the first philosopher to develop a clear concept of modernity. We have to go back to him if we want to understand the internal relationship between modernity and rationality, which, until Max Weber, remained self-evident and which today is being called into question. We have to get clear on the Hegelian concept of modernity to be able to judge whether the claim of those who base their analyses on other premise is legitimate." Jurgen Habermas, *The Philosophical Discourse of Modernity* (Cambridge 1987) 4.

50. Quṭb, *Muqawimmāt*, 83.

51. Ibid.

52. Ibid., 90.

53. Yvonne Haddad, "Sayyid Quṭb: Ideologue of Islamic Revival." In John L. Esposito, ed., *Voices of Resurgent Islam* (New York 1983) 75.

54. Quṭb, *Khaṣāi'ṣ*, 28.

55. Ibid., 130.

56. Ibid.

57. Fazlur Rahman has done an excellent job in examining the connection between *ʿibādāt* and *muʿāmalāt* in the Qur'ān. See, Fazlur Rahman, *Major Themes of the Qur'ān* (Minneapolis 1980).

58. Quṭb, *Khaṣāi'ṣ*, 155.

59. Ibid., 182.

60. Ibid., 186.

61. Ibid., 204.

62. Ibid., 205.

63. Ibid., 22.

64. Ibid., 234. Quṭb elaborates on the same theme in *Milestones*. He notes: "The Muslim community today is neither capable of nor is required to present before mankind great genius in material inventions, which will make the world bow its head before its supremacy and thus re-establish once more its world leadership. Europe's creative mind is far ahead in this area, and at least for a few centuries to come, we cannot expect to compete with Europe and attain supremacy over it in these fields." Sayyid Quṭb, *Milestones*, tr. Mohammed M. Siddiqui (Kuwait 1989) 13.

65. Sayyid Quṭb, *Muqawimāt*, 18.

66. Ibid., 22.

67. Ibid., 24.

68. Quṭb would agree with the following statement made by a leading American theologian. "Man, unlike animal existence, not only has a center but he has a center beyond himself. Man is the only animal which can make itself its own object. This capacity for self-transcendence which distinguishes spirit in man from soul . . . , is the basis of discrete individuality, for this self-consciousness involves consciousness of the world as 'the other.'" Reinhold Niebuhr, *The Nature and Destiny of Man*, vol. 1 (New York 1943) 55.

69. Quṭb, *Muqawimmāt*, 29.

70. Ibid., 152.

71. Ibid., 156.

72. Hegel, *Lectures*, 246–247.

73. Paul Tillich, *Systematic Theology*, vol. 1 (Chicago 1954) 211.

74. Sayyid Quṭb, *al-Islām wa mushkilat al-ḥaḍāra* (Cairo 1962) 183.

75. Ibid., 184.

76. Sayyid Quṭb, *al-Islām wa mushkilat al-ḥaḍāra* (Cairo 1962). Quṭb does not like to be referred to as a philosopher. I cannot see how he can escape this categorization when he is busy presenting a comprehensive system

of thought. It is true, as William James says, that philosophy bakes no bread, so to speak, "but it can inspire our souls with courage; . . . no one of us can get along without the far-flashing beams of light it sends over the world's perspective." William James, *Pragmatism: A New Name for Some Old Ways of Thinking* (New York 1913) 6. Quṭb's "far-flashing beams of light" are affecting us in spite of the fact that some have interpreted him in a narrow and dogmatic way.

77. Other attempts have been made by Muslim philosophers and thinkers. See, Seyyed Hossein Nasr, *Islam and the Plight of Modern Man* (London 1975).

78. Alexis Carrel, *Man the Unknown* (New York 1935).

79. William James, *Pragmatism*, 16.

80. Alexis Carrel, *Man the Unknown*, 21.

81. Ibid., 23.

82. Sayyid Quṭb, *al-Islām wa mushkilat*, 32.

83. Ibid., 36–37.

84. Ibid., 49.

85. Ibid., 70.

86. Ibid., 73.

87. Quṭb, *al-Islām wa mushkilat*, 85.

88. Ibid., 89.

89. Ibid., 91.

90. Ibid., 94.

91. Ibid., 95.

92. "The bourgeois individuals who initiated the age with such blithe confidence in the power of human decisions over historical fate see an historical process unfold in which individuals appear as hapless and impotent victims of an ineluctable destiny. Most of their decisions tend, in fact, to aggravate the difficulties of modern society; for those who hold significant economic and social power make decisions in the interest of maintaining their power so that the decisions fall into a general pattern of social anarchy. Thus the bourgeois individual who emerges from the social cohesions, restraints and inertias of medievalism and imagines himself master of nature and history, perishes ingloriously in the fateful historical necessities and the frantically constructed tribal solidarity of the age of decay." Reinhold Niebuhr, *The Nature and Destiny of Man*, 67.

93. Quṭb, *al-Islām wa mushkilat*, 97.

94. Ibid., 97.

95. Ibid., 102.

96. Ibid., 168.

97. Ibid., 179.

98. Ibid., 174.

99. George W. Hegel, *Lectures on the Philosophy of Religion*, 19.

100. See J. Crabbs, Jr., "Politics, History, and Culture in Nasser's Egypt." *International Journal of Middle East Studies*, vol. 6(4), 1975, 386–420.

101. Yvonne Y. Haddad, "Sayyid Quṭb," 67–68.

CHAPTER 6

1. On that, see the following: Issa J. Boullata, *Trends and Issues in Contemporary Arab Thought* (Albany 1990), especially chapter 3; Yvonne Haddad, "Sayyid Quṭb: Ideologue of Islamic Revival." In John L. Esposito, ed., *Voices of Resurgent Islam* (New York 1983), 67–98; Ahmad S. Moussalli, *Radical Islamic Fundamentalism: The Ideological and Political Discourse of Sayyid Quṭb* (Beirut 1992); and Emmanuel Sivan, *Radical Islam: Medieval Theology and Modern Politics*, enlarged ed. (New Haven 1990), chapter 2.

2. S. Quṭb, *Fī Ẓilāl al-Qur'ān*, six vols. (Beirut 1974).

3. Compare Quṭb's main objective behind exegesis to the following: "A legitimately Islamic response to the challenges facing modern Muslim societies will have to be based on the Qur'an and Sunna, which would necessarily mean an interpretation of these fundamental sources of Islam in a way that is consistent with the totality of their content and message." Abdullahi Ahmed An-Na'im, *Toward Islamic Reformation: Civil Liberties, Human Rights, and International Law* (Syracuse 1990) 51.

4. On this point, see the following Arabic sources: Nabīl 'Abd al-Fattāḥ, *al-Misḥaf wa'l sayf: sirā'* al-dīn wa'l dawla fī miṣr [*The Qur'ān and the Sword: Religion-State Conflict in Egypt*] (Cairo 1984), 42; Aḥmad Kamāl Abū al-Majd, *Ḥiwār lā muwājaha* [*Dialogue: Not confrontation*] (Cairo 1988); Ṣalāḥ D. al-Jourshī, *al-Ḥaraka al-islāmiyya fī duwāmma: hiwār ḥawla fikr Sayyid Quṭb* [*The Islamic Movement in the Whirlwind: Debating Sayyid Quṭb's Ideas*] (Tunis 1985); and 'Abdallah al-Nafīsī, *al-Ikhwān al-muslimūn: al-tajriba wa'l khaṭa'* [*The Muslim Brothers: Trial and Error*] (Cairo 1989). Aḥmad Kamāl Abū al-Majd points out that Quṭb wrote most of the *Ẓilāl* in prison while living in a state of physical, mental, and emotional siege. Many resort to the famous

distinction drawn by Quṭb between *jāhiliyah* and Islam and that all contemporary Muslim societies live in a state of *jāhiliyah*. On the influence of Sayyid Quṭb on Muslim students in Afghanistan in the 1960s and 1970s, see David B. Edwards, "Summoning Muslims: Print, Politics, and Religious Ideology in Afghanistan." *The Journal of Asian Studies*, vol. 52(3), August 1993, 609–628.

5. On the tragic life of Sayyid Quṭb, see ʿĀdil Ḥamūdda, *Sayyid Quṭb: min al-qarya ilā al-mashnaqa* (Cairo 1990), especially chapter 7.

6. Leo Strauss, *Persecution and the Art of Writing* (Chicago 1988) 143–144.

7. A. al-Khālidī, *al-Manhaj al-ḥarakī fī Ẓilāl al-Qur'ān*, vol. 2 (Jeddah 1986) 33.

8. al-Jourshī, *al-Ḥaraka*, 89.

9. Sivan, *Radical Islam*, 25–30

10. Sayyid Quṭb, *Milestones*, tr. Siddiqui, 176.

11. On the meaning of the intellectual as critic, see, Enrico Mario Santi, "Politics, Literature and the Intellectual in Latin America." *Salmagundi*, 82–83 (Spring–Summer 1989) 97.

12. See the fine analysis of the circumstances surrounding Quṭb's writing of the *Ẓilāl* in Ṣalāḥ A. al-Khālidī, *al-Manhaj*, 13–32.

13. Fredric Jameson, *The Political Unconscious: Narrative as a Socially Symbolic Act* (Ithaca 1981); and F. Jameson, *The Ideologies of Theory*, vols., 1 and 2 (Minneapolis 1988).

14. Edward Said, *Orientalism* (New York 1978).

15. Robert D'Amico proposes historicism as a method to uncover the main ideas behind the text and their historical relevance. "What we are struggling with in understanding are not the literal words or sentences, nor some simple logical relationships, but the entrenched concepts, presuppositions, and standards which must be teased to the surface and patiently uncovered." Robert D'Amico, *Historicism and Knowledge* (London 1989) xiii. D'Amico adds, "historicism pursues a complex reconstruction of the purposes, functions, and contexts of the various intellectual expressions. And philosophical reflection, for the historicist, is no exception to these historical limitations. Consistently, historicism treats its own reflections as bounded by interests, assumptions, and contexts." Ibid., xi.

16. E. Said, *Orientalism*, 9–10.

17. Teshahero Izutsu, *God and Man in the Qur'ān: Semantics of the Qur'ānic Weltanshauung* (Tokyo 1964) 19.

18. Ibid., 29.

19. Fazlur Rahman considers the central message of the Qur'ān to be that of establishing "a viable social order on earth that will be just and ethically based. Whether ultimately it is the individual that is significant and society merely the necessary instrument for his creation or vice versa is academic, for individual and society appear to be correlates." Fazlur Rahman, *Major Themes of the Qur*'ān (Minneapolis 1989) 37.

20. Quṭb, *Ẓilāl*, vol. 1, 139.

21. Ibid., 129.

22. In this, Quṭb agrees with the late Sudanese activist, Ustādh Maḥmoud Ṭāha. According to An-Na'īm, Ustādh Maḥmoud argued that the Qur'ān and Sunnah reveal "two levels or stages of the message of Islam, one of the earlier Mecca period and the other of the subsequent Medina stage. Furthermore, he maintained that the earlier message of Mecca is in fact the eternal and fundamental message of Islam, emphasizing the inherent dignity of all human beings, regradless of gender, religious belief, race and so forth." Abdullahi Ahmed An-Na'im, *Toward Islamic Reformation*, 52. An-Na'im, however, draws attention to the notion that, after immigration to Medina, a substantial shift in the thinking of the Qur'ān occurred. "The Qur'ān of Medina and accompanying Sunna began to distinguish between men and women, Muslims and non-Muslims, in their legal status and rights before the law." Ibid., 54. For further elaboration on the difference between the first and second messages in Islam see Maḥmoud M. Ṭāha, *The Second Message of Islam*, tr. A. An-Na'im (Syracuse 1987), especially chapters 5 and 6. See also Olivier Carre, *Mystique et politique: Lecture révolutionnaire du Coran par Sayyid Quṭb, frère musulman radical* (Paris 1984) 46.

23. Quṭb, *Ẓilāl*, vol. 1, 47.

24. Quṭb, *Ẓilāl*, vol. 1, 1010.

25. Ibid., 1010.

26. Quṭb, *Milestones*, tr. M. Siddiqui, 77. Quṭb argues that the Qur'ān spent thirteen years in training the believers how to grasp the issue of doctrine (*Ẓilāl*, vol. 2, 1004). These views are corroborated by M. Watt who contends that, in spite of the social and economic changes enveloping Meccan society on the eve of Islam, "The Qur'ān . . . envisages the troubles of the time as due primarily to religious causes, despite their economic, social, and moral undercurrents, and as capable of being remedied only by means that are primarily religious." W. Montgomery Watt, *Muhammad at Mecca* (Oxford 1960) 80.

27. Quṭb, *Ẓilāl*, vol. 1, 1011.

28. Ibid., 1012.

29. Quṭb, *Ẓilāl*, vol. 2, 1009.

30. Quṭb, *Ẓilāl*, vol. 1, 1012.

31. Fazlur Rahman, *Islamic Methodology in History*, second printing (Islamabad 1984) 11. See, also, F. Rahman, "The Religious Situation of Mecca from the Eve of Islam up to the Hijra." *Islamic Studies*, vol. 16(4), Winter 1977, 289–301.

32. Quṭb, *Ẓilāl*, vol. 3, 1217.

33. Ibid., 1213–1216.

34. Quṭb, *Ẓilāl*, vol. 1, 139.

35. Ibid.

36. Quṭb, *Ẓilāl*, vol. 4, 1936–1937.

37. Quṭb, *Ẓilāl*, vol. 1, 28.

38. Ibid.

39. Ibid.

40. Quṭb, *Ẓilāl*, vol. 1, 29.

41. Ibid., 304.

42. Ibid., 181.

43. Ibid., 305.

44. Ibid., 304.

45. Quṭb, *Ẓilāl*, vol. 3, 1437–1439.

46. Ibid., 1439.

47. Ignaz Goldziher, "Catholic Tendencies and Particularism in Islam." In *Studies on Islam*, ed. M. Swartz (New York 1981) 124.

48. Quṭb, *Ẓilāl*, vol. 1, 143.

49. Ibid., 145.

50. Ibid., 146.

51. Ibid., 486.

52. Ibid., 149.

53. Ibid.

54. Ibid., 353.

55. Ibid., 355.

56. Ibid., 32.

57. One must not forget that Quṭb comments with great insight on some biblical themes as narrated by the Qur'ān, such as the story of Moses and the burning bush, and, according to one scholar, one must appreciate "the story of Moses in the evolution of radical Islam." A. H. Johns, "Let My People Go! Sayyid Quṭb and the Vocation of Moses." *Islam and Christian-Muslim Relations*, vol. 1(2), December 1990, 145.

58. Quṭb, *Ẓilāl*, vol. 2, 672–73.

59. Ibid., 673.

60. Ibid.

61. Goldziher has this to say about *jāhiliyah*, "The Jahiliyya . . . is nothing but the time in which jahl . . . was prevalent, i.e. barbarism and cruelty. When the proponents of Islam say that it has ended the customs and habits of the Jahiliyya, they are thinking of these barbaric customs and the wild mentality which distinguish Arab paganism from Islam, and through the abolition of which Muhạmmad intended to become the reformer of his people's morality—the arrogance of Jahiliyya (*ḥamiyyat al-Jāhiliyah*), the tribal pride and the eternal feuds, the cult of revenge, rejection of forgiveness, and all other particularities of Arab paganism which were to be superseded by Islam." Ignaz Goldziher, *Muslim Studies*, vol. 1 (Chicago 1967) 206.

62. Quṭb, *Milestones*, tr. M. Siddiqui, 236.

63. Ibid., 32.

64. Quṭb, *Ẓilāl*, vol. 1, 180.

65. Quṭb, *Ẓilāl*, vol. 4, 2096.

66. Ibid., 2167.

67. Ibid., 2245

68. See the works of I. Boullata, E. Sivan, and others referred to in note 1.

69. O. Carre, *Mystique et politique*, 171.

70. Quṭb, *Ẓilāl*, vol. 5, 2720–2722.

71. Quṭb, *Ẓilāl*, vol. 3, 3589.

72. Quṭb, *Ẓilāl*, vol. 1. 189.

73. O. Carre, *Mystique*, 171.

74. Quṭb, *Ẓilāl*, vol. 5, 2721.

75. Quṭb, *Ẓilāl*, vol. 3, 1496.

76. Ibid., 1497.

77. Ibid., 1538–1539.

78. Ibid., 1556.

79. Ibid., 1557.

80. Ibid., 1570–1571, and 1703–1704.

81. Quṭb, *Ẓilāl*, vol. 4, 1866.

82. Ibid., 1893.

83. G. Hegel, *Lectures on the Philosophy of Religion* (London 1895), vol. 1, 117.

84. *Ẓilāl*, vol. 3 1443.

85. C. Geertz, *The Interpretation of Cultures* (Now York 1973) 90.

86. Quṭb, *Ẓilāl*, vol. 1, 105.

87. Ibid., 108.

88. Quṭb, *Ẓilāl*, vol. 3, 1648.

89. Quṭb, *Ẓilāl*, vol. 1, 40.

90. Ibid., 61.

91. Ibid., 69.

92. Ibid., 59.

93. Ibid., 111. Quṭb elaborates here on the Qur'anic notion of "*umm al-Kitāb*" (Mother of the Book). On this notion, see F. Rahman, *Major Themes*; and Martin Lings, *Symbol and Archetype: A Study of the Meaning of Existence* (Cambridge 1991), especially chapter 1.

94. Quṭb, *Ẓilāl*, vol. 1, 117.

95. Ibid., 128–129.

96. Ibid., 129.

97. The Qur'ān discusses, somewhat at length, the meaning of *qibla*, and the selection of Mecca as the place toward which Muslims turn their faces when praying. After the death of Muhammad in A.D.632 and the dramatic expansion of Islam beyond its Arabian origins, Muslims were in direct contact

with people who held different religious and cultural views. Muslims accepted, for a while, the idea of worshipping in non-Muslim places of worship, such as Christian churches, and recent research indicates that the early Muslim prayer was toward the east. *Ṣalāt*, as the institution of worship, became one of the main manifestations of the power of nascent Islam. This might be corraborated by the Qur'anic verse, "To Allah Belong the East and the West: Whithersoever ye turn, there is Allah's countenance, for Allah is All-Embracing, All-Knowing." (Qur'an 2: 115) In the opinion of Sulayman Bashear, although the church, as a non-Muslim place of worship, was not favored by the Prophet as the place of worship for Muslims, he definitely did not prohibit Muslims from using it as such. Sulayman Bashear, "Qibla Mushariqqa and Early Muslim Prayer in Churches." *The Muslim World*, vol. 81 (3–4), July–October 1991, 274. With the further evolution of Islam and the establishment of a large empire in the second and third centuries, Muslims became more conscious of the need to establish their own separate places for worship, and, thus, the idea of praying in non-Muslim places was forsaken gradually. Bashear contends that "as far as the first century is concerned, one cannot speak of 'one original *qibla* of Islam,' but rather of several currents in the search for one. It is also plausible that this search was eventually decided after Islam acquired a central sanctuary, prayer places, and religious concepts and institutions of its own." Ibid., 382. On *qibla*, see Tor Andrea, *Der Ursprung des Islams und Christentum* (Uppsala and Stockholm, 1926); and A. J. Wensinck, "Kibla." *Encylopedia Islamica*, vol. 5 (Leiden 1972).

98. Quṭb, *Ẓilāl*, vol. 1, 181.

99. Ibid., 181–182.

100. Ibid., 182.

101. Quṭb, *Ẓilāl*, vol. 2, 806–807.

102. Ibid., 806.

103. Ibid.

104. Ibid., 806–807.

105. Quṭb, *Milestones*, tr. M. Siddiqui, 103.

106. Ibid., 138. This is taken directly from volume 3 of Quṭb's *Ẓilāl*, 1443.

107. Quṭb, *Ẓilāl*, vol. 3, 1433.

108. Quṭb, *Ẓilāl*, vol. 1, 187.

109. Quṭb, *Ẓilāl*, vol. 3, 1434. See, also, Quṭb's *Milestones*, R. M. Siddiqui, 104.

110. Quṭb, *Ẓilāl*, vol. 3, 1436.

111. Ibid., 1441.

112. Abūl ʿAla Mawdūdī, *Jihad in Islam* (Kuwait n.d.).

113. Quṭb, *Ẓilāl*, vol. 3, 1445.

114. Ibid., 1449. See, also, Mawdūdī's exact formulation in *Jihad in Islam*, 16–17.

115. Quṭb, *Ẓilāl*, vol. 1, 305.

116. Abdullahi Ahmed An-Naʿim contends that "One of the major factors requiring and conditioning the proposed process of adapting and adjusting to contemporary life has to do with the reality of the modern nation/state. Despite the supposed religious unity of all Muslims and the consequent theoretical universal application of Shari'a throughout the Muslim world, the Muslim people are now organized in nation/states and are likely to remain so for the forseeable future." Abdullahi Ahmed An-Naʿim, *Toward Islamic, Reformation*, 7. Qutb opposes this view because of what he considers as the inherent un-Islamicity of the nation/state.

117. Quṭb, *Ẓilāl*, vol. 1, 400.

118. Ibid., 400–401.

119. Quṭb, *Ẓilāl*, vol. 2, 623.

120. Quṭb, *Ẓilāl*, vol. 3, 1743.

121. Quṭb, *Ẓilāl*, vol. 4, 2006.

122. Ibid., 2012.

123. Quṭb, *Ẓilāl*, vol. 3, 1631.

124. Ibid., 1634.

125. Quṭb, *Ẓilāl*, vol. 4, 2006.

126. Quṭb, *Ẓilāl*, vol. 2, 849.

127. Quṭb, *Ẓilāl*, vol. 4, 2122.

128. A good deal of interesting writing has appeared on imperialism and its political and cultural impact on non-Western people. Perhaps one of the most significant works to appear lately is Edward Said, *Culture and Imperialism* (New York 1993). See also: G. Arrighi, *The Geometry of Imperialism* (London 1978); M. Bennabi, *Islam in History and Society*, tr. Asma Rashid (Islamabad 1988); P. Darby, *The Three Faces of Imperialism: British and American Approaches to Asia and Africa, 1870–1970* (New Haven 1987); Rana Kabbani,

Europe's Myths of the Orient: Devise and Rule (Bloomington 1986); Benita Parry, "Problems in Current Theories of Colonial Discourse." *Oxford Literary Review*, 7(1–2): 25–58; Paul Rabinow, *Symbolic Domination: Cultural Form and Historical Change in Morocco* (Chicago 1975); Gauri Viswanathan. "Raymond Williams and British Colonialism." *The Yale Journal of Criticism*, vol. 4(2), Spring 1991, pp. 47–67, and E. Wolf, *Europe and the People without History* (Berkeley 1982).

129. The following gives a clear definition of both imperialism and colonialism: "Traditionally imperialism was, and in some circles still is, regarded as the formal acquisition of colonies. Thus at one time the term was interchangeable with colonialism, but at present, while most writers continue to define colonialism as the formal establishment of colonies, the term imperialism is used to cover both formal and informal political, economic, and social control. Imperialism in both its preindustrial and industrial capitalist manifestations can be defined in a general way as the effective domination by a relatively strong state over a weaker population, or as the effort to secure such domination. In political terms a relationship is imperial when a weaker people cannot act with respect to what it regards as fundamental domestic or foreign concenrs for fear of foreign reprisals that it believes itself unable to successfully encounter." Mark T. Berger, "Review Essay: From Commerce to Conquest: The Dynamics of British Mercantile Imperialism in Eighteenth-Century Bengal, and the Formation of the British Indian Empire." *Bulletin of Concerned Asian Scholars*, vol. 22(1), January–March 1990, 45.

130. For a list of questions on colonialism and its cultural effects, see Richard Roth, "The Colonial Experience and Its Postmodern Fate." *Salmagundi*, no. 84, Fall 1989, 248–266.

131. Sayyid Quṭb, "Lughat al-ʿabīd." *Al-Risāla*, Number 709, year 15, February 1947, 134.

132. Ibid., 136.

133. See Renato Constantino, *Neocolonial Identity and Counter-consciousness: Essays on Cultural Decolonization* (White Plains, N.Y. 1978).

134. See M. Bennabi, *Islam in History and Society*, especially chapters 1 and 3.

135. Malek Bennabi, "Islam in History and Society, III," *Islamic Studies*, vol. 19(1), Spring 1980, 44.

136. Mohammed Arkoun, *Essais sur la penśee islamique* (Paris 1977), especially chapter 9.

137. Quṭb, *Ẓilāl*, vol. 1, 136.

138. Ibid., 440.

139. E. Said, *Orientalism*, 2–3.

140. Ibid., 5

141. D. Wadada Nabudere, *Imperialism: The Social Sciences and the National Question* (Dar Es Salaam 1977) 48.

142. Quṭb, *Ẓilāl*, vol. 1, 414.

143. Ibid., 415.

144. Ibid., 414.

145. Quṭb, *Ẓilāl*, vol. 3, 1221.

146. Ibid., 1379.

147. O. Carre, *Mystique*, 32.

148. Quṭb, *Ẓilāl*, vol. 2, 1061.

149. Ibid., 1062.

150. S. Quṭb, *al-'Adāla* (Cairo 1949) 97.

151. Ibid., 247.

152. Quṭb (New York 1980) 235.

153. S. Quṭb, *Fī al-tārīkh: fikra wa minhāj* (Beirut 1974) 7. See, Y. Haddad's translation in *Islam and the Challenge of History*, 162.

154. Quṭb, Ibid., 8.

155. Ibid., 22.

156. Ibid., 38–42.

157. Quṭb in Haddad, *Islam and the Challenge* (Albany 1982) 165–166.

158. Quṭb, *Fī al-Tārīkh*, 58.

159. Quṭb, *Ẓilāl*, vol. 2, 1032–1033.

160. Ibid., 1033.

161. Ibid., 1033.

162. Quṭb, *Ẓilāl*, vol. 3, 1379.

163. "Intellectuals are the aggregate of persons in any society who employ in their communication and expression, and with relatively higher frequency than most other members of their society, symbols of general scope and abstract refrence, concerning man, nature, and the cosmos. The high

frequency of their use of such symbols may be a function of their subjective propensity or of the obligations of an occupational role, the performance of which entails such use." Edward Shils, "Intellectuals," in David Sills, ed., *International Encyclopedia of the Social Sciences*, vol. 7 (New York 1968) 399. On the intellectual in the Third World, see Syed Hussein Alatas, *Intellectuals in Developing Societies* (London 1977); S. N. Eisenstadt, "Intellectuals and Tradition." *Daedalus*, vol. 102(2), Spring 1972; Herbert J. Gans, *Popular Culture and High Culture* (New York 1974); Nikki R. Keddi, "Intellectuals in the Modern Middle East: A Brief Historical Consideration." *Daedalus*, vol. 101(3), Summer 1972, 39–57; Yogendra K. Malik, ed., *South Asian Intellectuals and Social Change: A Study of the Role of Vernacular-Speaking Intelligentsia* (New Delhi 1982); Menahem Milson, "Medieval and Modern Intellectual Traditions in the Arab World." *Daedalus*, vol. 101(3), Summer 1972, 17–37; Edward Shils. "The Intellectuals in the Political Development of the New States." In Jadson L. Finkle and Richard W. Gable, eds., *Political Development and Social Change* (New York 1968) 338–364, and Edward Shils, *The Intellectuals and Power and Other Essays* (Chicago 1972).

164. Julien Benda argues that the clerics, including the men of religion, artists, philosophers and others engaged in abstract and theoretical activities, have betrayed their mission of spreading justice and spirituality by involving themselves in the mundane matters of politics and society "Now, at the end of the nineteenth century a fundamental change occurred: the 'clerc' began to play the game of political passions. . . . We have to admit that the 'clercs' now exercise political passions with all the characteristics of passion—the tendency to action, the thirst for immediate results, the exclusive preoccupation with the desired end, the scorn for arguemnt, the excess, the hatred, the fixed ideas. The modern 'clerc' has entirely ceased to let the layman alone descend to the market place. The modern 'clerc' is determined to have the soul of a citizen and to make vigorous use of it; he is proud of that soul; his literature is filled with his contempt for the man who shuts himself up with art or science and takes no interest in the passions of the State." (Benda, *The Betrayal of The Intellectuals* (La Trahison Des Clercs) (Boston 1959) 31–33.

165. To elaborate on these points, see S. al-Jourshi, *al-Ḥaraka*, 29–31.

166. See Sivan, *Radical Islam*, 27.

167. Ḥasan al-Huḍaybī, *Du'āt lā qudāt* (Kuwait 1985).

168. Ibid., 19–20.

169. E. Sivan, *Radical Islam*, 27.

170. Ibid., chapter 1; and H. al-Huḍaybī, *Du'āt lā qudāt*, chapter 1.

171. Sivan, Ibid., 94. K. Cragg argues in a similar vein and proposes that Quṭb "has close mentors and associates elsewhere in the Islamic world,

like Abū-l-'Ala al-Maudūdī and Abu-1-Hasan Ali Nadwi, protagonists of a strongly conservative Islam in Lahore and Lucknow. With them he shared a deep discipleship to the medieval champion of the doctrine that Jihad may have to be pursued against ostensibly Muslim rulers who behave untruly, the redoubtable Ibn Taimiyyah of the seventh Muslim century." Kenneth Cragg, *The Pen and the Faith: Eight Modern Muslim Writers and the Qur'ān* (London 1985) 53–54.

172. Al-Jourshī, *al-Ḥarakā*, 13.

173. Ibid., 17.

174. Ibid., 18–19.

175. Ibid., 73.

176. Ibid., 74–75.

177. Ibid., 76.

178. Fathi Yakan, *Islamic Movement: Problems and Perspectives*, tr. Maneh al-Johani (Indianapolis 1984) 1–2.

179. Ibid., 3.

180. Ibid., 73.

181. Ibid., 23.

182. Ibid., 21.

183. Quṭb, *Ẓilāl*, vol. 2, 679.

184. A. Abercombie, S. Hill, and B. Turner, *The Dominant Ideology Thesis* (London 1985) 12.

185. Antonio Gramsci, *The Modern Prince and Other Writings*, (New York 1957) 122.

186. In his pioneering study of the Ikhwan, the late Richard Mitchell observes that the members of the organization were drawn from all walks of life. "Precise information on the socioeconomic distribution of the membership is just as difficult to amass as on its geographical distribution. But some hard, albeit random, statistical evidence from the numerous legal entanglements of the Society is available to suggest a membership drawn from all sectors of society." Richard Mitchell, *The Society* (New York 1993) 328. On the other hand, Ishak Husaini notes that the main reasons that helped the Ikhwan attract a large following from different social strata was their economic principle, which encouraged, "the growth of national wealth, its protection and its liberation, raising the standard of living, the realization of social justice between individual and classes, social security for all citizens, and the guarantee of

equal opportunity for all. This puts a limit to foreign influences in the Egyptian economy, animates local industries, and sets up labor unions to work toward the raising of the financial and social standards of the workers." I. M. Husaini, *The Moslem Brethren* (Beirat 1956) 42.

187. H. Hanafi, "The Relevance of the Islamic Alternative in Egypt." *Arab Studies Quarterly*, vol. 4(1 and 2) (1982) 60–61.

188. Yvonne Haddad, "The Qur'anic Justification of an Islamic Revolution: The View of Sayyid Quṭb." *The Middle East Journal*, vol. 37(1), Winter 1983, 17 and 23. According to K. Cragg, Quṭb "was no crude muqallid, a pundit incapable of relating to modernity. On the contrary, he was a thinker who expressly rejected a West he had come to know. . . . If Sayyid Quṭb's life and story give point movingly to these perennial issues in faith and for religion, he stands squarely thereby in the central themes of Islam, that of truth and power. His whole biography can be seen as a reading of the Qur'an, a commentary given in a personality." K. Cragg, *The Pen and the Talth*, 54 and 70.

189. "[T]he problems the process [of modernity] poses—economic, social, above all moral—are thought of as the problems of 'Western civilization,' and the future many are troubled about is the future of 'Western civilization.' The problems of other societies are thought of to be essentially different, to be interpreted primarily in terms of their own past traditions, which would be more static or spiritual, depending on the point of view. . . . [S]ome Muslims persuade themselves that if they can avoid both Westernization and Western control, they can escape the modern 'Western' problems." Marshall G. Hodgson, "Modernity and the Islamic Tradition." *Islamic Studies*, vol. 1(2), June 1962, 91.

Chapter 7

1. The most thorough biography of Faḍlallah is ʿAlī H. Surour's *al-ʿAllāma Faḍlallah: Taḥadī al-Mamnūʿ* (Beirut 1992). See, also, Mājid Fāris, "Muqabāla maʿ al-Sayyid Muḥammad Ḥusayn Faḍlallah" *al-Umma*, 16 (Beirut June 1993) 23–27; Martin Kramer, "Muhammad Husayn Fadlallah." *Orient*, vol. 26(2), June 1985, 147–149; and Fouad Ajami, *The Vanished Imam: Musa al-Sadr and the Shia of Lebanon* (Ithaca 1986), especially 213–218.

2. In addition to being a reflection on the painful conditions of community in distress, Faḍlallah's liberation theology is a reflection of the hard life he lived as a boy in the Najaf. In his authorized biography, *Taḥaddī al-Mamnūʿ*, Faḍlallah recounts how his father lived in poverty to the point of starving his family. He says, "In Najaf, we lived in complete poverty, and the only solution available to [our] financial predicament was that my father resort to some *ʿulamāʾ*, whom he never trusted. He always refused to approach and,

consequently we knew starvation in our childhood. I have learned this matter from him. I grew up with a complex against wealthy. . . .When I began my [economic] projects, I never tried to approach these wealthy people, . . . since they never felt any respect for the money they possessed." ʿAlī H. Surour, *Taḥadī al-Mamnūʿ*, 37. Olivier Carre considers the thought of Fadlallah to belong to "the modern, narrow-minded, fundamentalist trend," and not to that of liberation theology. See Olivier Carre, "La revolution islamique selon Muhammad Husayn Fadlallah." *Orient*, 1, March 1988, 68–84.

3. M. B. Sadr was executed by the Iraqi state in 1980 for his Shiʿī activism. See the following sources on al-Sadr: T. M. Aziz, "The Meaning of History: A Study of the Views of Muḥammad Bāqir al-Ṣadr." *Islamic Studies*, vol. 31(2) Summer 1992; T. M. Aziz, "The Role of Muḥammad Bāqir al-Ṣadr in Shiʿī Political Activism in Iraq from 1958 to 1980." *International Journal of Middle East Studies*, vol. 25(2), May 1993; Chibli Mallat, *The Renewal of Islamic Law: Muhammad Baqer As-Sadr and the Shiʿi International* (Cambridge 1993); and A. A. Nayed, "The Unitary Qur'anic Hermeneutics of Muḥammad Bāqir al-Ṣadr." *Islamic Studies*, vol. 31(4), Winter 1992.

4. Faḍlallah counts the following major *ʿulamāʾ* in al-Najaf as among his teachers: Sayyid Abū al-Qāsim al-Khūʾī; Sayyid Muḥsin al-Ḥakīm; Sayyid Mahmoud al-Shahroudi; and Shaykh Ḥusayn al-Hillī. He said "all of them are the most important religious scholars in the Holy Najaf." Surour, *Taḥadī al-Mamnūʿ*, 33.

5. A. H. al-Ghazālī, *The Book of Knowledge*, tr. N. A. Faris (Lahore 1987) 1.

6. In another verse, the Qur'ān states, "Say, 'Are those who know and those who do not know equal'?" (Qur'ān 39:9).

7. According to Edward Lane, *ʿilm*, *maʿrifa*, and *shuʿūr* are made to have one meaning, this being nearly what is said by most of the lexicologists. However, most of the critics discriminate every one of these forms from the others, and *ʿilm*, according to them, denotes the highest quality, because it is that which they allow to be an attribute of God." E. W. Lane, *Arabic-English Lexicon* (Cambridge 1984) 2138. See, also, the entry *ʿilm* in H. A. Gibb and J. H. Kramers, *Shorter Encylopedia of Islam* (Leiden 1953) 163–164. On the meaning of knowledge in Shadhiliyya's Sufism, see, Ibrahim M. Abu-Rabiʿ, ed., *The Mystical Teachings of al-Shadhili, Including his Life, Prayers, Letters, and Followers*, tr. Elmer H. Douglas (Albany, N.Y. 1993), especially chapter 4.

8. M. H. Faḍlallah, *Khuṭuwāt ʿalā ṭarīq al-islām* (Beirut 1986) 115.

9. Richard Hosfstadter, *Anti-Intellectualism in American Life* (New York 1963) 25.

10. Faḍlallah, *Khuṭuwāt*, 116.

11. Faḍlallah, who does narrate the applicable *ḥadīth* seems to be refering to this one: "As long as the *'ulamā'* do not associate with the power-elite, they are the trustess of the prophets of God over His servants [people]. However, when they associate with the power elite, beware of and avoid them." Abū Ḥāmid al-Ghazālī, *Ihyā' 'ulūm al-dīn*, vol. 1 (Beirut n.d.) 68. See, also, A. Ghazālī, *The Book of Knowledge*, tr. N. A. Faris (Lahore 1987) 180.

12. A slight variation of this *ḥadīth* is reported by Ghazali, "If you see the learned cherishing this world, then entrust not your religion into his hands because everyone is captivated by what he loves." M. H. Faḍlallah, *Min ajl al-islām* (*For the Sake of Islam*) (Beirut 1989) 215 (Fāris's translation, 159).

13. One *ḥadīth* stipulates, "The learned [*'ulamā'*] are the heirs of the prophets. The prophets have not bequeathed dinar nor dirham, but have only left Sacred Knowledge [*'ilm*], and whoever takes it has taken an enormous share." Aḥmād Ibn Naqīb al-Miṣrī, *The Reliance of the Traveller*, tr. and ed. Noah H. M. Keller (Evanston, Ill. 1993) 4.

In his *Book of Knowledge* (vol. 1 of the *Ihyā'*), the celebrated Ghazālī devotes a major chapter to the evils of what he calls, "the ulama of this world." Ghazālī remarks "By the learned men of this world, we mean the teachers of falsehood whose sole purpose in pursuing knowledge is to enjoy the luxuries of this life and to achieve power and prestige among its people." Ghazali, *Book of Knowledge*, 154. "Another characteristic expected of the learned man is that he keeps away from the power holders, and, as long as he can help it, not to come near them at all, and rather avoid their company despite any efforts on their part to seek him out, because the world is attractive and inviting, while the power to dispense with its riches is in their hands. To associate with them, therefore, would necessarily involve the learned man in seeking their approval and winning their hearts, although they are unjust and unrighteous. It is, then, the duty of every religious man to censor and twit them by exposing their tyranny and decrying their practices. For he who frequents their [palaces] will either seek their favor and consequently forget the blessings which God has bestowed upon him, or hold his peace and allow their misdeeds to go uncensored, thereby courting their favor. He may also undertake to justify [their sins] and improve their standing in order to gain their pleasure, which is the limit in perjury and falsehood." Ghazali, *Book of Knowledge*, 179. Also, "If you see a learned man frequent the houses of the rulers, beware of him because he is a thief. . . . There is nothing more hateful to God than a learned man who frequents the house of a governor." Ghazali, *Book of Knowledge*, 180.

According to Victor Turner, the function of the priest is as follows: "The priest is concerned with the conservation and maintenance of a deposit of beliefs and practices handed down as a sacred trust from the founders of the social and religious system." Victor W. Turner, "Religious Specialists." In

Arthur C. Lehmann and James E. Myers, eds., *Magic, Witchcraft and Religion: An Anthropological Study of the Supernatural*, 2d ed. (Mountain View 1989) 85–92.

14. M. H. Faḍlallah, *Min ajl al-islām*, 217.

15. Qur'ān 3:114.

16. Faḍlallah, *Min ajl al-islām*, 219.

17. Ibid., 341–342.

18. M. H. Faḍlallah, *Khuṭuwāt*, 404.

19. Ibid., 47.

20. Ibid.

21. Jean-Paul Sartre, *Search For a Method* (New York 1968) 18.

22. K. Marx, "The Eighteenth Brumaire of Louis Bonaparte," in K. Marx, *Surveys from Exile*, ed. D. Fernbach (Harmondsworth 1973) 146.

23. Karl Marx and Frederick Engels, *Collected Works*, vol. 5 (New York 1976) 59.

24. Faḍlallah, *Khuṭuwāt*, 52.

25. Ibid., 76. For an elaboration on this, see Olivier Carre, "Quelques mots-chefs de Muhammad Husayn Fadlallah." *Revue Francaise de Science Politique*, 37:4 (August 1987), especially 481–486.

26. According to Michael Gilsenan, the *'ulamā'* "have been preeminently guardians and interpreters of the sacred texts. They performed the great historical function of organizing a body of law and practice derived from the Qur'ān and the traditions of the Prophet and the Companions." M. Gilsenan, *Recognizing Islam* (New York 1982) 30.

27. M. H. Faḍlallah, *al-Muqāwama al-islāmiyya* [*The Islamic Resistance Movement*] (Beirut 1986) 40.

28. Ibid., 16.

29. Ibid., 47.

30. Compare to, "I am talking of millions of men who have been skillfully injected with fear, inferiority complexes, trepidation, servility, despair, abasement." Aime Cesaire, *Discours du Colonialisme*. Quoted by F. Fanon, *Black Skin, White Masks* (New York 1967) 7.

31. M. H. Faḍlallah, *Ma' al-ḥikmā fī khaṭī'l islām* [*Heeding Wisdom in the Way of Islam*] (Beirut 1985) 46.

32. Marx defines "estranged labor" as the devaluation of the world of workers who, because they do not own the economic means of production, are estranged from their products. See "Economic and Philosophic Manuscripts of 1844" in *Collected Works of Karl Marx and Frederick Engles*, vol. 3 (New York 1975), especially 270–282.

33. Paulo Freire, *Pedagogy of the Oppressed* (New York 1988) 28.

34. M. H. Faḍlallah, *Maʿ al-ḥikmā*, 47.

35. Ibid.

36. Ibid.

37. Ibid., 48.

38. Ibid., 54.

39. Ibid., 52.

40. M. H. Faḍlallah, *al-Islām wa manṭiq al-quwwā* [*Islam and the Logic of Power*] (Beirut 1987) i.

41. Ibid., 234.

42. Ibid., i.

43. Ibid., g.

44. Bernard Lewis, *The Political Language of Islam* (Chicago 1988) 72.

45. George Orwell, *A Collection of Essays* (New York 1981) 40.

46. M. H. Faḍlallah, *al-Islām wa manṭiq*, 16.

47. Ibid., 28. F. Rahman echoes similar thoughts by saying that the primary aim of the Qur'ān is to maximize freedom from any form of slavery and moral energy. F. Rahman, *Major Themes of the Qur*'ān (Minneapolis 1989) 27.

48. M. H. Faḍlallah, *al-Islām wa manṭiq*, 114. Faḍlallah seems to refer here to the major work by Ḥussain Muruwwa, *al-Nazaʿāt al-mādiyah fī al-falsafah al-ʿarabiyah al-islāmiyah* (Beirut 1978). He believes that Muruwwa, although Marxist in orientation, was working on behalf of the poor and the oppressed. Surour, *Taḥaddī al-Mamnūʿ*, 62.

49. M. H. Faḍlallah, *al-Islām wa manṭiq*, 16.

50. Ibid., 114–118.

51. Ibid., 112.

52. P. Freier, *Pedagogy*, 55.

53. Faḍlallah, *al-Islām wa manṭiq*, 171.

54. Ibid., 171–172. Malcolm X echoed the same sentiment when visiting Egypt on his way to pilgrimage in 1966. He said that "Egypt's rising industrialization was one of the reasons why Western powers were so anti-Egypt, [because] it was showing other African countries what they should do." Malcolm X, *The Autobiography of Malcolm X* (New York 1965) 322.

The concept of *fitnah* was discussed in chapter 6 in relation to Qutb's work. As a Qur'anic term, *fitnah* is subject to several meanings that are, in the final analysis, interchangeable. Generally, it means causing the believers, or the masses in Faḍlallah's view, to enter into a permanent state of psychological and mental affliction, trial, and punishment. On the linguistic meaning of the term, see E. Lane, *Arabic-English Lexicon*, 2334–2336.

The following Qur'anic verses illustrate the meaning of *fitnah* as well: "*Fitnah* is worse than slaughter." (Qur'ān 2:191); "And fight them until there is no more *fitnah*." (Qur'ān 2:193); "And know ye that your possessions and progeny are but a *fitnah* [trial]; and that it is Allah with whom lies your highest reward." (Qur'ān 8:28); "The unbelievers are protectors, one of another: unless you do this [protect each other], there would be *fitnah* and great mischief." (Qur'ān 8:73).

In a number of writings by classical theologians, *fitnah* "became the commonest term for any serious challenge, whether intellectual or military, to the existing order." B. Lewis, *The Political Language of Islam* (Chicago 1988) 96.

It should be noted however that Faḍlallah does not see that as *fitnah* but as an Islamic-mandated revolution. Fazlur Rahman defines the term *fitnah* as follows: "As for *fitnah*, although the term is used in the very early Madinan days to describe the active pressure, including physical violence and even fighting of Meccans to bring back those new Muslim converts who had left Mecca and joined the Prophet in Madina, its standard use refers to the persecution of the Muslims by Meccan pagans in Mecca itself. Large-scale *fitnah* undoubtedly occured either just before the Emigration to Abyssinia or during the last phase of the Prophet's life in Mecca, and particularly during the Emigration to Medina." F. Rahman, *Major Themes*, 159.

According to Ghazālī, as well as Faḍlallah, *fitnah* can result from associating with the power elite. Ghazālī reports that "Sufyān [al-Thawrī] said, 'There is in hell a valley which is not inhabited except by the Qur'ān-readers who frequent the palaces of the kings.' Hudhayfah said, 'Expose not yourselves to *fitnah* [temptation]'! He was asked, 'What temptation?' 'The gates of the rulers,' he replied, 'into which you enter giving your approval to their lies and praising them for virtues they do not possess.'" Abū Ḥāmid al-Ghazālī, *The Book of Knowledge*, 180.

55. F. Fanon, *The Wretched of the Earth* (New York 1972) 109.

56. Faḍlallah, *al-Islām wa manṭiq*, 182.

57. "We therefore oppose colonialism, because it robs man of his freedom, exploiting his economic, social, and cultural existence to colonialism's benefit. All exploited people have the right to live in freedom and dignity. This is why we oppose colonialism, be it American, European, or Soviet. We oppose all repressive regimes and repressive leaders, because we believe in justice for all people, including sinners." Muḥammad Ḥ. Faḍlallah in George Nader, "Interview with Sheikh Muḥammad Ḥussein Faḍl Ạllah." *Middle East Insight*, vol. 4(2), June/July 1985, 12.

58. Faḍlallah, *al-Islām wa manṭiq*, 293.

59. Faḍlallah does not consider martyrdom to be a form of suicide in the classical sense. On suicide, see F. Rosenthal, "On Suicide in Islam." *Journal of the American Oriental Society*, 66 (1946), 239–259.

60. René Girard, *Violence and the Sacred*, ed. Patrick Gregory (Baltimore 1977) 1.

61. For an elaboration on the philosophy of violence as a necessary tool to replace the existing order, see Eric Weil, *Logique de la philosophie* (Paris 1967), especially 54–77.

62. R. Girard, *Violence*, 7.

63. M. H. Faḍlallah, *Khuṭuwā*t, 29.

64. Ibid., 35.

65. Ibid., 88.

66. Ibid., 105.

67. Ibid., 165.

68. Ibid., 166.

69. Ibid., 167.

70. Ibid., 350.

71. Ibid., 303.

72. For a different opinion, see Samuel P. Huntington, "The Clash of Civilizations?" *Foreign Affairs*, Summer 1993, 22–49.

73. Faḍlallah, *Kuṭuwāt*, 528. According to Fouad Ajami, "As in Ayatollah Khomeini's thought, there is in Faḍlallah's a curiously Sunni orientation—the sense that *taqiyya*, dissimulation, should be abandoned, that men should create a Muslim order and defend it." F. Ajami, *The Vanished Islam*, 215.

74. M. H. Faḍlallah, *Min ajl al-Islām*, 62.

75. Mājid Fāris, "Muqābala," 24.

76. Faḍlallah, *Min ajl al-Islām*, 113.

77. Ibid., 129.

78. Ibid.

79. Ibid., 143.

80. Ibid., 144.

81. Ibid., 48.

82. Ibid., 51.

83. Ibid., 49.

84. Martin Kramer, "Sacrifice and Fratricide in Shiite Lebanon." In Mark Juergensmeyer, ed., *Violence and the Sacred in the Modern World* (London 1992) 42.

85. Faḍlallah, *Min ajl al-Islām*, 186–187.

86. Mājid Faris, "Muqābala," 24.

87. Ibid.

88. Ibid., 25.

89. M. H. Faḍlallah, "Abʻād itifāq 'Ghaza-Arīḥa' fi'l wāqiʻ al-filasṭīnī, wa'l ʻarabī, wa'l islāmī." *Qira'āt Siyāsiyya*, vol. 4(1), Winter 1994, 87.

90. Ibid., 91.

91. M. Fāris, "Muqābala," 27.

92. "When negotitations [with Israel] lead to positive results in the arena of peace, the Islamic resistance has to face a new formidable situation." M. H. Faḍlallah, quoted by Dalāl al-Bizrī, "al-Islamiyūn fi Lubnan." *Abā'd: Majallat al-Dirāsāt al-Lubnaniyyah wa'l ʻArabiyyah*, No. 1, May 1994, 110.

93. John Esposito, *The Islamic Threat* (New York 1992) 149.

94. For a thorough analysis, see Martin Kramer, "The Pan-Islamic Premise of Hizballah." In David Menashri, ed., *The Iranian Revolution and the Muslim World* (Boulder, Colo. 1990) 121.

95. Martin Kramer, "Sacrifice and Fratricide," In M. Juergensmeyer, ed., *Violence and the Sacred in the Modern World* (London 1992) 35.

96. Bruce B. Lawrence, "The Islamic Idiom of Violence: A View From Indonesia." In Mark Juergensmeyer, ed., *Violence and the Sacred in the Modern World* (London 1992) 84.

97. Martin Kramer, "The Moral Logic of Hizballah." In Walter Reich, ed., *Origins of Terrorism: Psychologies, Ideologies, Theologies, States of Mind* (Cambridge 1990) 132.

98. L. Goldmann, *Cultural Creation in Modern Society*, tr. B. Grahl (Saint Louis 1976).

99. Anni Goldmann, "Lucien Goldmann on Democracy and Culture." *The Philosophical Forum: A Quarterly*, vol. 33(1–2), Fall-Winter 1991–1992, 82.

100. M. H. Faḍlallah, *Risālat al-ta'ākhī* (Beirut n.d.) 88.

101. Faḍlallah has written extensively concerning Christian-Muslim dialogue in Lebanon. See A. H. Surour, *al-'Allāma Faḍlallah*, 111–118.

Chapter 8

1. Islamism does often try to Islamize modernity. "In Morocco, between 1979 and 1981, Abd Assalam Yassin was editor of Al-Jama'a, a review which extolled the virtues of the Prophet Muhammad and glorified the 'original' Islam . . . In 1979, A. Yassin published, in French, *Revolution à l'heure de l'Islam* [Marseille 1979] . . . The stated purpose of Yassin's [book] was to define both the 'Islamic ideal,' as well as the 'Islamic method' (*minhāj*), which would, by means of a rereading of the Qur'ān and a reevaluation of Muḥammad's teachings, induce the Islamic revolution . . . The issue was, he wrote in his preface, 'to Islamicize modernity not to modernize Islam.'" Jean-Claude Vatin, "Seduction and Sedition: Islamic Polemical Discourse in the Maghreb." In William R. Roff, ed., *Islam and the Political Economy of Meaning: Comparative Studies of Muslim Discourse* (Berkeley 1987) 162–163.

2. "Islamic radicalism is not a traditional plea to return to a premodern era. Quite the contrary, it is a product of the contradictions of Third-World modernization and represents a postmodern reaction to the specific form of modernization experienced by the Islamic Third World. In the Islamic countries, where modernization has been synonymous with Westernization, the response to the contradiction of modernization has taken the form of a 'politics of identity.'" Haldun Gulalp, "A Postmodern Reaction to Dependent Modernization: The Social and Historical Roots of Islamic Radicalism." *New Perspectives on Turkey*, 8, Fall 1992, 15.

3. This thesis is highlighted mainly by Burhān Ghalyoun, *Ightiyāl al-'aql: miḥnat al-thaqāfah al-'arabiyya bayna al-salafiyya wa'l taba'iyya* (Cairo 1990).

4. Zakī Najīb Mahmūd, *Tajdīd al-fikr al-'arabī* [*Renewal of Arab Thought*] (Beirut 1978).

5. Ibid., 239.

6. Ibid., 110.

7. Z. N. Mahmūd, *al-Maʿqūl wa'l lā maʿqūl fī ḥayātina al-fikriyyā* (Cairo 1978) 26.

8. Ibid., 62. Ghālī Shukrī, an Egyptian socialist thinker, agrees basically with Mahmūd's basic theses. Shukrī is interested in the analysis of the social composition of the modern Egyptian intelligentsia. Although he reaches the conclusion that the national bourgoisie has been an important vehicle of change, it has failed to put an end to the problem of religion. Many a nationalist intellectual resorted to religion when faced with a crisis. See Ghālī Shukrī, *al-Nahḍa wa'l suqūt fi'l fikr al-miṣrī al-ḥadīth* [*Renaissance and Decline in Modern Egyptian Thought*] (Beirut 1976).

9. Yāssin al-Ḥāfiz, *al-Hazīma wa'l idiulūjiyya al-mahzūmā* [*Defeat and Defeat Ideology*] (Beirut 1979) 188–190.

10. Fu'ād Zakariyyā, *al-Ḥaqīqa wa'l khayāl fi'l ḥaraka al-islāmiyya al-muʿāṣira* [*Reality and Myth in the Contemporary Islamic Movement*] (Cairo 1988). Zakariyyā has this to say about secularism: "The European secular movement was not a reaction against religion but against a method of thinking. Europeans were advancing in science and industrialization. They aimed to expand and dominate the entire world. The biggest obstacle to these advances was the closed religious thinking of the church. The secularists opposed intellectual rigidity while remaining committed to their own faith." Quoted by Nancy E. Gallagher, "Islam v. Secularism in Cairo: An Account of the Dar al-Hikma Debate." *Middle Eastern Studies*, vol. 25(2), April 1989, 210.

11. Ibid., 7.

12. Ibid., 10.

13. Ibid., 11.

14. Ibid., 15. In another place, Zakariyyā comments on extremism. "The true reason surrounding these extreme phenomena is, in my view, the political use made of Islam. The young extremists are part of a huge bureaucracy which continues to grow and swell since the early seventies. Its aim is to exploit Islam in order to achieve political goals. Like any small part of a huge bureaucracy, it knows its aim well and marches to execute its mission relentlessly. Since these youngsters were taught that the commandments of religion bid them to lead society and since they heard from their counsellors that society will not be set right unless it places itself under their tutelage, they, therefore, allow themselves to take the law into their own hands according to their law and methods . . . Just imagine how society could attain perfection if every individual within it has the right to be a lawgiver, judge and a policeman at one and the same time." Fu'ād Zakariyyā, *al-Ahrām*, March 1988, translated and quoted by David Sagiv, "Judge Ashmawi and Militant Islam in Egypt." *Middle Eastern Studies*, vol. 28(3), July 1992, 541.

15. Zakariyyā, *al-Ḥaqīqa*, 17.

16. Ibid., 19.

17. Ibid., 22.

18. Ibid., 22.

19. Ibid., 23. See also F. Zakariyyā, "People Direct Islam in any Direction they Wish." *Middle East Times*, May 28–June 3, 1991, 15.

20. Zakariyyā, *al-Ḥaqīqa*, 23.

21. Ibid., 24.

22. Ibid., 24.

23. Ibid., 25.

24. Ibid., 25–26.

25. L. Binder, *Islamic Liberalism: A Critique of Development Ideologies* (Chicago 1988) 80–81.

26. Leo Strauss, *What Is Political Philosophy?* (Chicago 1988) 13.

27. Karl Popper, *The Open Society and Its Enemies*, two vols. (Princeton 1962).

28. Alexander Flores, "Egypt: A New Secularism?" *Middle East Report*, 153, July–August 1988, 28.

29. F. Fūdā, *Qabla al-ṣuqūt* (Cairo 1985), especially chapter one.

30. F. Fūdā, *al-Ḥaqīqa al-gāi'bā* [*The Absent Reality*] (Casablanca 1989) 14.

31. F. Fūdā, *Ḥiwār ḥawla al-'ilmāniyya* (Cairo 1987).

32. F. Fūdā, *Qabla al-Ṣuqūt*, 9; and *Ḥattā lā yakūna kalāman fi'l hawā'* (Cairo 1993) 17. I have consulted two books that respond to Fouda's analysis of Islam: Munīr Shafīq, *Bayna al-nuḥūḍ wa'l ṣuqūt: radd 'alā kitāb Faraj Fūdā* (Tunisia 1992); and 'Abd al-Majīd Ṣubḥ, *Tahāfut qabla al-ṣuqūt wa ṣuqūt ṣāḥibihī* (al-Manṣūra 1985).

33. Fūdā, *Ḥattā lā*, 27.

34. Ibid., 32.

35. Ibid., 33

36. Ibid., 134.

37. Ibid., 135.

38. F. Fūdā, *Qabla al-suqūt*, 12. Munīr Shafīq criticizes this view. See *Bayna al-nuhūḍ*, 53.

39. Fūdā, *Qabla al-suqūt*, 13.

40. M. Shafīq, *Bayna al-nuhūḍ*, 27.

41. M. Shafīq, *Rudūd ʿala utrūḥāt ʿilmāniyya* [*Responses to Secularist Theses*] (Tunisia 1992) 7–71.

42. F. Fūdā, *al-Nadhīr* [*The Clarion; The Warning*] (Cairo 1992) 8–27.

43. Ibid., 28.

44. Fūdā, *Ḥatta*, 37.

45. See L. Althusser's article, "Ideology and Ideologial State Apprartuses," in L. Althusser, *Essays on Ideology* (London 1984) chapter one.

46. Adonīs, *al-Thābit wa'l mutaḥawwil: Ṣadmat al-ḥadātha*, vol. 3. (Beirut 1979) 239–240.

47. Ibid., 240.

48. Hādī al-ʿUlwī, *Fī al-dīn wa'l turāth* (Jerusalem 1975) 14.

49. B. Ghalyoun, *Ightiyāl*, 203.

50. Ibid., 240.

51. Ibid., 247.

52. Ibid., 198.

53. Ibid., 300.

54. Ibid., 302.

55. Ibid., 303.

56. B. Ghalyoun, *Naqd al-siyāssa: al-dawla wa'l dīn* (Beirut 1991) 192.

57. Ayubi, *Political Islam: Religion and Politics in the Arab World* (London 1991) 5.

58. Ghalyoun, *Naqd*, 239–240.

59. Ibid., 262.

60. Ibid.

61. This is the crux of Qaraḍāwī's argument in his, *al-Ḥall al-Islāmī: farīḍa wa ḍarūrā* [*Islamic Solution: Duty and Necessity*] (Beirut 1989).

62. I have in mind the following: Ḥasan Ḥanafī, and Muḥammad ʿImārah.

63. Yūsuf al-Qaraḍāwī, *al-Islām wa'l ʿilmāniyya wajhan li wajh* [*Islam and Secularism: Face to Face*] (Cairo 1987) 21.

64. Ibid., 33. Qaraḍāwī argues that "Islam was not meant to be only one dimension of life but rather a comprehensive guide that regulated all aspects of life from birth until death. For example, Islamic laws governed the life of a Muslim while he was still in the cradle. Islamic laws defined the period of nursing. After death Islamic laws regulated the ceremony of washing, burial and prayer for him and even the settling of his debts." Quoted by Nancy E. Gallagher, Islam v. Secularism in Cairo, 211.

65. *al-Islām wa'l ʿilmāniyya*, p. 35.

66. Ibid., 36–47.

67. Ibid., 52.

68. Yūsuf al-ʿAzm, *al-Munhazimūn: dirāsa fī al-fikr al-mutakhlif wa'l ḥaḍāra al-munhāra* [*The Defeated: A Study in Backward Thought and Disintegrating Civilization*] (Damascus 1979) 82.

69. Ibid., 111.

70. Ibid., 216.

Bibliography

ʿAbd al-Fattāḥ, N. *al-Miṣḥaf wa'l sayf: sirā'* al-dīn wa'l dawla fi miṣr [*The Qur*'ān and the Sword: Religion-State Conflict in Egypt] (Cairo: Madbūlī, 1984).

ʿAbd al-Rāziq, M. *Tamhīd li tārikh al-falsafah al islāmiyyah*, 3 ed. (Cairo: Matbaʿat Lajnat al-Ta'līf, 1966).

ʿAbdalallah, I. S., et al., eds. *al-Ḥarakat al-islāmiyya al-mʿūṣira fī al-ʿālam al-ʿarabī* (Beirut: Markaz al-Dirasāt al-ʿArabiyyah, 1989).

Abdel-Malek, A. "Foundations and Fundamentalism." *Die Welt des Islams*, vol. 28, 1988.

Abdul Ghani, M. "Practicality and Realism in the Islamic Movement in Sudan." *Inquiry* (Tampa), vol. 1(4), August 1992.

Abercrombie, A.; S. Hill; and B. S. Turner. *The Dominant Ideology Thesis* (London: George Allen and Unwin, 1985).

Abidin, A. Z. "The Political Thought of Ḥasan al-Bannā." *Islamic Studies*, vol. 28(3), Autumn 1989.

Abou-El-Haj, R. *Formation of the Modern State: The Ottoman Empire Sixteenth to Eighteenth Centuries* (Albany: State University of New York Press, 1991).

Abraham, M. D. "Mahmud Shaltut (1893–1963), A Muslim Reformist: His Life, Works and Religious Thought." (Unpulished doctoral dissertation, Hartford Seminary: Hartford, 1976).

Abū al-Majd, A. *Ḥiwār lā muwājaha* [*Dialogue: Not confrontation*] (Cairo: Dār al-Shurūq, 1988).

Abu-Deeb, K. "Cultural Creation in a Fragmented Society." In Hisham

Sharabi, ed., *The Next Arab Decade: Alternative Futures* (Boulder, Colo.: Westview Press, 1988).

Abu-Rabiʿ, I. M. "Al-Azhar and Rationalism in Modern Egypt: The Philosophical Contributions of Shaykhs Musṭafa ʿAbd al-Rāziq and ʿAbd al-Ḥalīm Maḥmūd," *Islamic Studies*, vol. 27(2), Summer 1988.

———. "Discourse, Power, and Ideology in Modern Islamic Revivalist Thought: Sayyid Qutb." *The Muslim World*, vol. 81(3–4), July–October 1991.

———, ed. *The Mystical Teachings of al-Shadhili, Including His Life, Prayers, Letters and Followers*, tr. Elmer Douglas (Albany: State University of New York Press, 1993).

———, ed. *Islamic Resurgence: Challenges, Directions, and Future Perspetives: A Round Table with Khurshid Ahmad* (Tampa: The World and Islam Studies Enterprise, 1994).

Abubakar, M. "Sayyid Quṭb's Interpretation of the Islamic View of Literature," *Islamic Studies*, vol. 23(2), Summer 1984.

Adams, C. *Islam and Modernism in Egypt* (New York: Oxford University Press, 1933).

Adonīs, [ʿAlī Ahmad Saʿīd]. "Reflections on the Manifestations of Intellectual Backwardness in Arab Society." In *Cemam Reports* (Beirut: St. Joseph University, 1974).

———. *Al-Thābit Wa'l mutaḥawwil*, 3 vols. (Beirut; Dār al-ʿAwdah, 1983).

Ahmad, K. "The Nature of the Islamic Resurgence." In John L. Esposito, ed., *Voices of Resurgent Islam* (New York: Oxford University Press, 1983).

Ahmad, K.; and Z. I. Ansari, eds. *Islamic Perspectives: Studies in Honor of Sayyid Abul Aʿla Mawdūdī* (Leicester: The Islamic Foundation, 1980).

Aḥmad, M. H. *al-Ikhwān al-muslimūn fī mizān al-ḥaqq* (Cairo: al-Ikhā' Press, 1946).

Ahsan, A. *Ummah or Nation? Identity Crisis in Contemporary Muslim Society* (Leicester: The Islamic Foundation, 1992).

Ajami, F. *The Vanished Imam: Musa al-Sadr and the Shia of Lebanon* (Ithaca N.Y.: Cornell University Press, 1986).

al-ʿAlim, M. A. *al-Waʿy wa'l waʿy al-mafqūd fi'l fikr al-ʿarabī al-muʿasir* [*Consciousness and Lost Consciousness in Contemporary Arab Thought*] (Cairo: Dār al-Thāqafa al-Jadīda, 1986).

Alatas, S. H. *Intellectuals in Developing Societies* (London: Frank Cass, 1977).

Al-Azmeh, A. *Islams and Modernities* (London: Verso, 1993).

Alcoff, L. "Foucault as Epistemologist." *The Philosophical Forum*, vol. 25(2), Winter 1993.

ʿAlī, Ḥ. I. *Azmat al-islām al-siyāsī* [*The Crisis of Political Islam*] (Casablanca: Dār Qurṭuba, 1991).

Althusser, L. *Essays on Ideology* (London: Verso, 1976).

Amīn, A. *Fajr al-islām* (Beirut: Dār al-Kitāb al-ʿArabī, 1975).

———. *Ḍuḥā al-islām*, three vols. (Beirut: Dār al-Kitāb al-ʿArabī, 1976).

———. *Dhuhr al-islām*, four vols. (Beirut: Dār al-Kitāb al-ʿArabī, 1976).

Amin, S. *The Arab Nation: Nationalism and Class Struggle* (London: Zed Press, 1978).

———. *Azmat al-mujtamaʿ ʿal-ʿarabī* (Cairo: Dār al-Mustaqbal al-ʿArabī, 1985).

———. "Is There a Political Economy of Islamic Fundamentalism?" In his *Delinking* (London: Zed Press, 1990).

Amin, U. *Mohammad Abduh: essai sur ses idées philosophiques et religieuse* (Cairo: Dār al-Kitāb, 1944).

Anawati, G. C. "Un Plaidoyer pour un Islam éclairé: Le livre du Juge Mohammad Saʿ*id al-ʿAshmawi, al-islam al-siyasi*." *MELANGES*, vol. 19, 1989.

Anawati, G. C.; and M. Borrmans. *Tendances et courants de l'Islam arabe contemporaine* (München: Kaiser Verlag, 1982).

Anderson, B. *Imagined Communities: Reflections on the Origin and Spread of Nationalism* (London: Verso, 1991).

Andrea, T. *Der Ursprung des Islams und Christentum* (Uppsala and Stockholm: n.p., 1926).

An-Naʿim, A. A. *Toward Islamic Reformation: Civil Liberties, Human Rights, and International Law* (Syracuse: Syracuse University Press, 1990).

Antoun, R. *Muslim Preacher in the Modern World: A Jordanian Case Study in Comparative Perspective* (Princeton: Princeton University Press, 1989).

Arberry, A. J. *The Doctrines of the Sufis* (Cambridge: Cambridge University Press, 1935).

Arkoun, M. *Essais sur la pensée islamique* (Paris: Editions Maisonneuve et Larose, 1984).

———. *Pour une critique de la raison islamique* (Paris: Editions Maisonneuve et Larose, 1984).

———. *Arab Thought*, tr. Jasmer Singh (New Delhi: S. Chand and Company, 1988).

———. "New Perspectives for a Jewish-Christian-Muslim Dialogue." In Leonard Swidler, ed., *Muslims in Dialogue: The Evolution of a Dialogue* (Lewiston: [New York] The Edwin Mellen Press, 1992).

———. *Rethinking Islam: Common Questions to Uncommon Answers*, tr. R. D. Lee (Boulder, Colo.: Westview Press, 1994).

Aroua, A. *l'Islam à la croisée des chemins* (Algiers: Societie Nationale d'Editions et de Diffusion, 1969).

Arrighi, G. *The Geometry of Imperialism* (London: New Left Books, 1978).

Asad, M. *Islam at the Crossroads*. Fourteenth revised edition (Gibraltar: Dar al-Andalus, 1982).

Asad, T. "Ideology, Class, and the Origins of the Islamic State." *Economy and Society*, vol. 9, number 4, 1980.

———. *Genealogies of Religion: Discipline and Reasons of Power in Christianity and Islam* (Baltimore: The Johns Hopkins University Press, 1993).

Awda, A. Q. *Islam Between Ignorant Followers and Incapable Scholars* (Riyadh: International Islamic Publishing House, 1991).

Ayubi, N. *Political Islam: Religion and Politics in the Arab World* (London: Routledge, 1991).

Aziz, T. M. "The Meaning of History: A Study of the Views of Muhammad Baqir al-Sadr." *Islamic Studies*, vol. 31(2) Summer 1992.

———. "The Role of Muhammad Baqir al-Sadr in Shi'i Political Activism in Iraq from 1958 to 1980." *International Journal of Middle East Studies*, vol. 25(2), May 1993.

al-'Azm, S. J. *Naqd al-fikr al-dīnī* (Criticism of Religious Thinking) (Beirut: Dār al-Ṭalī'ah, 1969).

———. *al-Naqd al-dhātī ba'*d al-hazīma (Beirut: Dār al-Talī'ah, 1969).

al-'Azm, Y. *Al-Munhazimūn: Dirāsa fī al-fikr al-mutakhalif wa'l ḥaḍāra al-munhāra* (Damascus: Dār al-Qalam, 1979).

Badawī, A. *Sayyid Quṭb* (Cairo: al-Hay'a al-Miṣriyyah al-'Āmmah li'l Kitāb, 1992.

Badran, I., et al. *al-Falsafah fi'l waṭan al-ʿarabī al-muʿāṣir* (Beirut: Markaz Dirasāt al-Wiḥdah al-ʿArabiyah, 1985).

Bahiy, M. *al-Fikr al-islāmī al-ḥadīth wa ṣilatihī bi'l istiʿmār al-gharbī* [*Modern Islamic Thought and Its Relation to Western Colonialism*], 5th ed. (Beirut: Dar Al-Fikr, 1970).

al-Bannā, H. *Daʿwatuna* (Cairo: Maṭbaʿat al-Ikhwān al-Muslimīn, 1943).

———. "New Renaissance." In Kemal H. Karpat, ed., *Political and Social Thought in the Contemporary Middle East* (New York: Frderick A. Praeger, 1968).

———. Mudhakarāt al-daʿ*wa wa'l dāʿiya* (Beirut: al-Maktab al-Islāmī, 1970).

———. *Majmuʿāt rasā'il al-imām al-shahīd Ḥasan al-Bannā* (Beirut: al-Muʿsassa al-Islāmiyya, 1981).

al-Bannā, H.; A. al-Sukkari; and H. ʿAskariyya. *Mudhakarra fi'l taʿlīm al-dīnī* (Cairo: al-Maṭbaʿa al-Salafiyya, 1929).

Barakat, H. *The Arab World: Society, Culture, and Change* (Berkeley: University of California Press, 1993).

———. ed. *Contemporary North Africa: Issues of Development and Integration* (Washington, D.C.: Center for Contemporary Arab Studies, 1985).

Bashear, S. "Qibla Mushariqqa and Early Muslim Prayer in Churches." *The Muslim World*, vol. 81(3–4), July–October 1991.

Bayyumi, M. ("The Islamic Ethic of Social Justice and the Spirit of Modernization: An Application of Weber's Thesis to the Relationship between Religious Values and Social Change in Modern Egypt)". An unpublished doctoral dissertation (Philadelphia: Temple University, 1976).

Beinin, J. "Islamic Responses to the Capitalists Penetration of the Middle East." In Barbara F. Stowasser, ed., *The Islamic Impulse* (London: Croom Helm, 1987).

Bell, D. *The End of Ideology: On the Exhaustion of Political Ideas in the Fifties* (New York: Free Press, 1960).

———. "The Return of the Sacred?" *British Journal of Sociology*, vol. 28:4, 1977.

Bello, I. "The Society of Muslim Brethren: An Ideological Study." *Islamic Studies*, vol. 20(2), 1981.

Benda, J. *The Betrayal of the Intellectuals [La Trahison des Clercs]* (Boston: The Beacon Press, 1959).

Bennabi, M. *Mémoires d'un témoin du siècle* (Algiers: Editions Nationales Algeriennes, 1965).

———. "Islam in History and Society, III," *Islamic Studies*, vol. 19(1), Spring 1980.

———. *Islam in History and Society*, tr. Asma Rashid (Islamabad: Islamic Research Institute, 1988).

Berger, M. T. "Review Essay: From Commerce to Conquest: The Dynamics of British Mercantile Imperialism in Eighteenth-Century Bengal, and the Formation of the British Indian Empire." *Bulletin of Concerned Asian Scholars*, vol. 22(1), January–March 1990.

Berger, P. *Facing Up to Modernity: Excursion in Society, Politics, and Religion* (New York: Basic Books, 1977).

Berkes, N. *The Development of Secularism in Turkey* (Montreal: McGill University Press, 1964).

Berman, M. *All That Is Solid Melts Into Air: The Experience of Modernity* (New York: Penguin Books, 1982).

Binder, L. *Islamic Liberalism: A Critique of Development Ideologies* (Chicago: University of Chicago Press, 1988).

al-Bizrī, D. "al-Islamiyūn fī Lubnān." *Abā'ad: Majallat al-Dirāsāt al-Lubnaniyyah wa'l 'Arabiyyah*," 1, May 1994.

Boulares, H. *Islam: The Fear and the Hope* (London: Zed Books, 1990).

Boullata, I. "Challenges to Arab Cultural Authenticity." In Hisham Sharabi, ed., *The Next Arab Decade: Alternative Futures* (Boulder, Colo.: Westview Press, 1988).

———. *Trends and Issues in Contemporary Arab Thought* (Albany: State University of New York Press, 1990).

Brightman, E. S. "Personalism (Including Personal Idealism)." In V. Ferm, ed., *A History of Philosophical Systems* (New York, 1950).

Brunschvig, R. "Problème de la décadence." In G. E. von Grunebaum and R. Brunschvig, eds., *Classicisme et déclin culturel dans l'histoire de l'islam* (Paris: Maisonneuve, 1957).

Buheiry, M. R. "Colonial Scholarship and Muslim Revivalism in 1900." In Lawrence I. Conrad, ed., *The Formation and Perception of the Modern Arab World: Studies by Marwan R. Buheiry* (Princeton: The Darwin Press, Inc., 1989).

Burgat, F.; and W. Dowell. *The Islamic Movement in North Africa* (Austin: University of Texas Press, 1993).

Carre, O. *Mystique et politique: Lecture révolutionnaire du Coran par Sayyid Qutb, frère musulman radical* (Paris: Presse de la Fondation Nationale de Science Politique, 1984).

———. "Quelques mots-chefs de Muhammad Husayn Fadlallah." Revue Française de Science Politique, 37:4, August 1987.

———. "*La révolution islamique selon Muhammad Husayn Fadlallah.*" *Orient*, 1, March 1988.

Carrel, A. *Man the Unknown* (New York: Halcyon House, 1935).

Caspar, R. "*Un aspect de la pensée musulmane moderne: Le renouveau du Mo'tazilisme.*" *MELANGES*, vol. 4, 1957.

Cesaire, A. *Discours du colonialisme* (Paris: Maisonville, 1957).

Charnay, J. "*L'intellectuel arabe entre le pouvoir et la culture.*" *Diogenes*, 83, July–September 1973.

Chatterjee, P. *Nationalist Thought and the Colonial World: A Derivative Discourse* (London: Zed Books, 1986).

———. "More on Modes of Power and the Peasantry." In R. Guha and G. Spivak, eds., *Selected Subaltern Studies* (New York: University of Oxford Press, 1988).

Chatterjee, P.; and G. Pandey, eds. *Subaltern Studies VII: Writings on South Asian History and Society* (New Delhi: Oxford University Press, 1992).

Cherif-Chergui, A. "*El principio de armonia en Sayyid Qutb.*" In J. M. Barral, *Orientalia Hispanica* (Leiden: Brill, n.d.).

Conrad, L. I., ed. *The Formation and Perception of the Modern Arab World: Studies by Marwan R. Buheiry* (Princeton: The Darwin Press, Inc., 1989).

Constantino, R. *Dissent and Counter-Consciousness* (Quezon City, Philippines: n.p., 1970).

———. *Neocolonial Identity and Counter-Consciousness: Essays on Cultural Decolonization* (White Plains, N.Y.: M. E. Sharpe, Inc., 1978).

Corbin, H. *History of Islamic Philosophy* (London: Kegan Paul International, 1993).

Crabbs, J. Jr. "Politics, History, and Culture in Nasser's Egypt." *International Journal of Middle East Studies*, vol. 6(4), 1975.

———. *The Study of History in Nineteenth Century Egypt: A Study in National Transformation* (Detroit: Wayne State University Press, 1984).

Cragg, K. *The Pen and the Faith: Eight Modern Muslim Writers and the Qur'an* (London: George Allen and Unwin, 1985).

Cutler, D. R., ed. *The Religious Situation 1968* (Boston: Beacon Press, 1968).

D'Amico, R. *Historicism and Knowledge* (London: Routledge, 1989).

Dajani, Z. R. *Egypt and the Crisis of Islam* (New York: Peter Lang Publishers, 1990).

Daher, A. *Current Trends in Arab Intellectual Thought* (Washington: Rand, 1969).

Dallal, A. "Islamic Revivalist Thought, 1750–1850." *Journal of the American Oriental Society*, vol. 113(3), July–September 1993.

Darby, P. *The Three Faces of Imperialism: British and American Approaches to Asia and Africa, 1870–1970* (New Haven: Yale University Press, 1987).

Darnton, R. "Intellectual and Cultural History." In Michael Kammen, ed., *The Past Before Us: Contemporary Historical Writing in the United States* (Ithaca: Cornell University Press, 1980).

Daud, W. *The Concept of Knowledge in Islam* (London: Mansell, 1989).

Davis, E. "The Concept of Revival and the Study of Islam and Politics." In Barbara Stowasser, ed., *The Islamic Impulse* (Georgetown: Center For Contemporary Arab Studies, 1987).

Dawn, C. E. "The Formation of Pan-Arab Ideology in the Interwar Years." *International Journal of Middle East Studies*, vol. 20(1), February 1988.

Dekmejian, R. H. *Islam in Revolution: Fundamentalism in the Arab World* (Syracuse: State University of New York Press, 1985).

Diyāb, M. Ḥ. *Sayyid Quṭb: al-khiṭāb wa'l idiulūjiyya* (Casablanca: Matbaʿat al-Najāḥ al-Jadīdā, 1992).

Djait, H. *La personnalité et le devenir arabo-islamique* (Paris: Seuil, 1974).

———. *Europe and Islam: Cultures and Modernity* (Berkeley: University of California Press, 1985).

———. *al-Kūfā: Naissance de la ville islamique* (Paris: Editions Maisonneuve Larose, 1991).

Dunn, M. C. *Renaissance or Radicalism? Political Islam: The Case of Tunisia's Al-Nahda* (Washington, D.C., 1992).

Eaglton, T. *Ideology* (London: Verso, 1992).

Edwards, D. "Summoning Muslims: Print, Politics, and Religious Ideology in Afghanistan." *The Journal of Asian Studies*, vol. 52(3), August 1993.

Eickelman, D. F. *Knowledge and Power in Morocco: The Education of a Twentieth-Century Notable* (Princeton: Princeton University Press, 1985).

———. "Traditional Islamic Learning and Ideas of the Person in the Twentieth Century." In M. Kramer, ed., *Middle Eastern Lives: The Practice of Biography and Self-Narrative* (Syracuse: Syracuse University Press, 1991).

Eisenstadt, S. N. "Intellectuals and Tradition." *Daedalus: Journal of the American Academy of Arts and Sciences*, vol. 102(2), Spring 1972.

———. "Post-Traditional Societies and the Continuity and Reconstruction of Tradition." *Daedalus: Journal of the American Academy of Arts and Sciences*, vol. 102(1), Winter 1973.

El-Affendi, A. *Turabi's Revolution: Islam and Power in Sudan* (London: Grey Seal Books, 1991).

El-Kenz, A. *Algerian Reflections on Arab Crises*, tr. Robert W. Stookey (Austin: University of Texas Press, 1991).

Enayat, H. *Modern Islamic Political Thought* (Austin: University of Texas Press, 1982).

Ennaifer, H. "*La pensée sociale dans les écrits musulmans modernes.*" *IBLA: Revue de l'Institut des Belles Lettres Arabes*, vol. 50(160), 1987.

Esposito, J. L. *The Islamic Threat: Myth or Reality?* (New York: Oxford University Press, 1992).

———, ed. *Voices of Resurgent Islam* (New York: Oxford University Press, 1983).

Faḍlallah, M. H. *Afāq islāmiyya* [*Islamic Horizons*] (Beirut: Dār al-Zahrā', 1980).

———. *M'a al-ḥikmā fī khaṭi'l islām* [*Heeding Wisdom in the Way of Islam*] (Beirut: Dār al-Wafā', 1985).

———. Khuṭuwāt *'ala ṭarīq al-islām* (Beirut: Dār al-Ta'āruf, 1986).

———. *al-Muqāwama al-islāmiyya* [*The Islamic Resistance Movement*] (Beirut: Imām al-Riḍā Publications, 1986).

———. *al-Islām wa manṭiq al-quwwa* [*Islam and the Logic of Power*] (Beirut: Dār al-Tā'ruf, 1987).

———. *Min ajl al-islām* [*For the Sake of Islam*] (Beirut: Dār al-Tāʿruf, 1989).

———. *al-Ḥaraka al-islāmiyya: humoum wa qaḍāya* [*The Islamic Movement: Concerns and Problematics*] (Beirut: Dār al-Malāk, 1990).

———. "Filasṭīn takhtaṣir ḥarakat al-tārikh al-islāmī" [Palestine Summarizes the Process of Islamic History], *al-Ummā* (Beirut) 16, June 1993.

———. "Abʿād itifāq 'Ghaza-Arīḥa' fi'l wāqʿi al-filasṭīnī, wa'l ʿarabī, wa'l islāmī." *Qira'āt Siyāsiyya*, vol. 4(1), Winter 1994.

———. *Risālat al-ta'ākhī* (Beirut: Dār al-Zahrā', n.d.).

Fanon, F. *Black Skin, White Masks* (New York: Grove Press, 1967).

———. *The Wretched of the Earth* (New York: Grove Books, 1972).

Fāris, M. "Muqābala maʿ al-Sayyid Muḥammad Ḥusayn Faḍlallah" *al-Ummā* (Beirut) 16, June 1993.

Fāsī, A. *al-Naqd al-dhātī* (Rabat: Risāla Press, 1979).

Ferm, V., ed. *A History of Philosophical Systems* (New York, 1950).

Filali-Ansary, A. "Hichem Djait: la tyrannie du paradigme." In Hammadi Safi, ed., *Penseurs Maghrébins contemporains* (Tunis: Ceres Productions, 1993).

Findley, C. V. "The Advent of Ideology in the Islamic Middle East." *Studia Islamica*, vol. 55, 1982.

Finkle, J. L.; and R. W. Gable, eds. *Political Development and Social Change* (New York: John Wiley and Sons, 1968).

Fischer, M. M. "Islam and the Revolt of the Petit Bourgeoisie." *Daedalus*, vol. 3, Winter 1982.

Flores, A. "Egypt: A New Secularism?" *Middle East Report*, 153, July–August 1988.

Foucault, M. *Les mots et les choses* (Paris: Gallimard, 1966).

———. *L'archéologie du savoir* (Paris: Gallimard, 1972).

———. *The Archeology of Knowledge and the Discourse on Language* (New York: Pantheon Books, 1972).

Fūdā, F. *Qabla al-ṣuqūt* (Cairo: no publisher, 1985).

———. *Ḥiwār hawla al-ʿilmāniyya* (Cairo: Dār al-Maḥrūsa li'l Nashr, 1987).

———. al-Ḥaqīqa al-gāiʿba [*The Absent Reality*] (Casablanca: ʿUyūn, 1989).

———. *al-Nadhīr* [*The Clarion; The Warning*] (Cairo: al-Hay'a al-Miṣriyya, 1992).

———. Ḥatta lā yakūna kalamān fī al-hawā' (Cairo: Dār al-Mā'rif, 1993).

Freire, P. *Pedagogy of the Oppressed* (New York: Continuum, 1988).

Gallagher, N. E. "Islam v. Secularism in Cairo: An Account of the Dar Hikma Debate." *Middle Eastern Studies*, vol. 25(2), April 1989,

Gans, H. J. *Popular Culture and High Culture* (New York: Basic Books, 1974).

Gardet, L. "*De quelle manière s'est ankylose la pensée religieuse de l'islam.*" In G. E. V. Grunebaum and R. Brunschwick, eds., *Classicisme et déclin culturel dans l'histoire de l'islam* (Paris: Maisonneuve, 1957).

Geertz, C. *The Interpretation of Cultures* (New York: Basic Books, 1973).

Ghalyoun, B. *Ightiyāl al-'aql: miḥnat al-thaqāfah al-'arabiyya bayna al-salafiyya wa'l taba'iyya* (Cairo: Madbūlī, 1990).

———. *Naqd al-siyāssa: al-dawla wa'l dīn* (Beirut: al-Mu'asasa al-'Arabiyya li'l Dirasāt wa'l Nashr, 1991).

Ghani, M. A. "Practicality and Realism in the Islamic Movement in Sudan." *Inquiry*, vol. 1(4), August 1992.

Ghānim, I. B. *al-Fikr al-siyāsī li'l imām Ḥasan al-Bannā* (Cairo: Dar al-Tawzī' wa'l Nashr al-Islāmiyya, 1992).

Ghanoushī, R. *Da'wa ilā al-rushd* (Tunis: Dar Tunis, 1982).

———. *The Right to Nationality Status of non-Muslim Citizens in a Muslim Nation*, tr. M. El Arian (Washington, D.C.: Islamic Foundation of America, 1990).

———. "People of the State or State of the People in the Muslim Nation-States?" *Crescent International*, 19:17, 1990.

Ghazali, A. H. *The Book of Knowledge*, tr. N. A. Faris (Lahore: Ashraf, 1987).

———. *Iḥyā' 'ulūm al-dīn*, vol. 1 (Beirut: Dār Ihyā' al-Turāth al-'Arabī, n.d.).

Ghazālī, M. *al-Islām al-muftara 'alayhī bayna al-shuyui'yīn wa'l ra'smaliyīn* (Cairo: Dār al-Kutub, 1952).

———. *Our Beginning is Wisdon*, tr. Ismai'l R. al-Faruqi (Washington, D.C.: American Council of Learned Societies, 1953).

———. *al-Ghazw al-thaqāfī yamtadu fi farāghina* [*The Cultural Invasion Expands through Our Vacuum*] (Amman: Mu'assasat al-Sharq, 1985).

———. *al-Sunna al-nabawiyya bayna ahl al-fiqh wa ahl al-ḥadīth* (Beirut: Dar al-Shurūq, 1989).

Gibb, H. "Whither Islam?" In H. Gibb, ed., *Whither Islam? A Survey of Modern Movements in the Moslem World* (London: Gollancz, 1932).

———. *Modern Trends in Islam* (Chicago: University of Chicago Press, 1947).

———. "Islamic Biographical Literature." In B. Lewis and P. O. Holt, eds., *Historians of the Middle East* (London, 1962).

———. "The Heritage of Islam in the Modern World (1)." *International Journal of Middle East Studies*, vol. 1(1), January 1970.

Gibb, H.; and J. H. Kramers. *Shorter Encylopedia of Islam* (Leiden: E. J. Brill, 1953).

Giddens, A. *The Consequences of Modernity* (Stanford: Stanford University Press, 1990).

Gilbert, F. "Intellectual History: Its Aims and Methods." *Daedalus*, vol. 100(1), Winter 1971.

Gilsenan, M. *Recognizing Islam: Religion and Society in the Modern Arab World* (New York: Pantheon, 1982).

Girard, R. *Violence and the Sacred*, ed. Patrick Gregory (Baltimore: The Johns Hopkins University Press, 1977).

Goldmann, A. "Lucien Goldmann on Democracy and Culture." *The Philosophical Forum: A Quarterly*, vol. 23(1–2), Fall–Winter 1991–1992.

Goldmann, L. *The Philosophy of the Enlightenment*, tr. H. Maas (London: Routledge and Kegan Paul, 1973).

———. *Cultural Creation in Modern Society*, tr. B. Grahl (Saint Louis: Telos Press, 1976).

Goldziher, I. *Muslim Studies*, vol. 1 (Chicago: Aldine Publishing Company, 1967).

———. "Catholic Tendencies and Particularism in Islam." In *Studies on Islam*, ed. M. Swartz (New York: Oxford University Press, 1981).

Gramsci, A. *The Modern Prince and Other Writings* (New York: International Publishers, 1957).

Guha, R. "Discipline and Punish." *Subaltern Studies VII: Writings on South*

Asian History and Society, eds. Partha Chatterjee and Gyanendra Pandey (New Delhi: Oxford University Press, 1992).

Guha, R.; and G. Spivak, eds. *Selected Subaltern Studies* (New York, 1988).

Gulalp, H. "A Postmodern Reaction to Dependent Modernization: The Social and Historical Roots of Islamic Radicalism." *New Perspectives on Turkey*, 8, Fall 1992.

Habermas, J. *The Philosophical Discourse of Modernity* (Cambridge: MIT Press, 1987).

Haddad, Y. Y. *Contemporary Islam and the Challenge of History* (Albany: State University of New York Press, 1982).

———. "Sayyid Qutb: Ideologue of Islamic Revival." In John L. Esposito, ed., *Voices of Resurgent Islam* (New York: Oxford University Press, 1983).

———. "The Qur'anic Justification of an Islamic Revolution: The View of Sayyid Quṭb." *The Middle East Journal*, vol. 37(1), Winter 1983.

Haddad, Y. Y., et al. *The Contemporary Islamic Revival: A Critical Survey and Bibliography* (New York: Greenwood Press, 1991).

Ḥafīẓ, Y. *al-Hazīma wa'l idiulūjiyya al-mahzūma* [*Defeat and Defeat Ideology*] (Beirut: Dār al-Ṭalīʿah, 1979).

Ḥamūdda, A. *Sayyid Quṭb: min al-qarya ila al-mashnaqa* (Cairo: Dār Sinā', 1990).

Hanafi, H. "The Relevance of the Islamic Alternative in Egypt." *Arab Studies Quarterly*, vol. 4(1, 2), 1980.

———. *al-Harakāt al-dīniyya al-muʿāṣira* (Cairo: Madbūlī, 1988).

Hanna, S. A. "Khayr al-Dīn of Tunisia: The Impact of his Book *Aqwam al-Masālik* on the Arab and Ottoman Reformers." *Islamic Culture*, vol. 65(2, 3), April–July 1991.

Harris, C. *Nationalism and Revolution in Egypt: The Role of the Muslim Brotherhood* (The Hague: Mouton and Co., 1964).

Hasan, Z. *Philosophy: A Critique* (Lahore: Institute of Islamic Culture, 1988).

Ḥawwa, S. *al-Madkhal ilā daʿwat al-ikhwān al-muslimīn* (Amman: al-Matbaʿa al-Taʿāwuniyya, 1979).

———. *Hādhihi tajribatī wa hādhihī shahādatī* (Cairo: Muʿsasat al-Khalīj al-ʿArabī, 1988).

Hegel, G. *Lectures on the Philosophy of Religion*, tr. E. B. Speirs (London: Kegan Paul, Trench, Trubner, & Co., 1895).

———. *The Phenomenology of Mind*, tr. George Lichtheim (New York: Harper and Row, 1967).

———. *Lectures on the Philosophy of World History*, tr. H. B. Nisbet (Cambridge: Cambridge University Press, 1975).

Hirmasī, M. B. "al-Islām al-iḥtijājī fi Tūnis." In Ismā'il S. 'Abdalallah et al., eds., *al-Ḥarakāt al-islāmiyya al-mu'āṣira fi al-'ālam al-'arabī* (Beirut: Markaz al-Dirāsat al-'Arabiyya, 1989).

Hobsbawm, E. "Introduction: Inventing Traditions." In Eric Hobsbawm and Terence Ranger, eds., *The Invention of Tradition* (Cambridge: Cambridge University Press, 1984).

Hodgson, M. H. "Modernity and the Islamic Tradition." *Islamic Studies*, vol. 1(2), June 1962.

Hoffer, E. *The True Believer: Thoughts on the Nature of Mass Movements* (New York: Harper & Row, 1951).

Hosfstadter, R. *Anti-Intellectualism in American Life* (New York: Alfred A. Knopf, 1963).

Hourani, A. *Arabic Thought in the Liberal Age: 1798–1939* (Cambridge: Cambridge University Press, 1970).

———. *Islam in European Thought* (New York: Cambridge University Press, 1991).

———. *A History of the Arab People* (Cambridge: Harvard University Press, 1991).

Huḍaybī, H. *Du'āt lā qudāt* (Kuwait: International Islamic Federation of Student Organizations, 1985).

Huntington, S. P. "The Clash of Civilizations?" *Foreign Affairs*, Summer 1993.

Husain, T. *An Egyptian Childhood*, tr. E. H. Oaxton (London: Routledge, 1932).

Husaini, I. M. *The Moslem Brethren: The Greatest of Modern Islamic Movements* (Beirut: Khayat's College Book Cooperative, 1956).

Ḥussain, T. *Mustaqbal al-thaqāfa fi miṣr*, vol. 1 (Cairo: Maṭba'at al-Ma'ārif, 1938).

Ḥussayn, A. B. *Sayyid Quṭb: Ḥayātuhūwa adabuhū* (Al-Manṣūra, Egypt: Dār al-Wafā', 1986).

Hussayn, T. *The Stream of Days*, tr. H. Waymont (London: Longmans, 1948).

Hussein, T. "Le cheikh Mosṭafa 'Abd el-Razeq tel que je l'ai connu," *MELANGES*, vol. 4, 1957.

———. *The Future of Culture*, tr. S. Glazer (New York: Octagon Books, 1975).

'Imārah, M. *al-A'māl al-kāmilah li'l imām Muḥammad 'Abduh*, vol. 3 (Beirut: al-Mu'asasah al-'Arabiyyah li'l Dirāsat wa'l Nashr, 1972).

———. "Al-Waṭaniyya wa'l islām." *Majallat al-'Arabī*, December 1983.

Izutso, T. *God and Man in the Qur'ān: Semantics of the Qur'anic Weltanshauung* (Tokyo: n.p., 1964).

———. *Ethico-Religious Concepts of the Qur'*ān (Montreal: McGill University Press, 1966).

al-Jābirī, M. A. *Al-Khiṭab al-'arabī al-mu'āṣir* (Beirut: Dār al-Ṭali'āh, 1982).

———."Ishkaliyat al-aṣālah wa'l mu'aṣarah fi'l fikr al-'arabī al-ḥadīth wa'l mu'āṣir." In Sayyid Yāssin et al., *al-Turāth wa taḥadiyāt al-'aṣr* (Beirut: Markaz Dirāsat al-Wiḥdah al-'Arabiyah, 1985).

———. *Takwīn al-'aql al-'arabī* [*The Constitution of the Arab Mind*] (Beirut: Markaz Dirasāt al-Wihdah al-'Arabiyah, 1988).

James, W. *Pragmatism: A New Way for Some Old Ways of Thinking* (New York: Longmans, Green and Co., 1913).

Jameson, F. *The Political Unconscious: Narrative as a Socially Symbolic Act* (Ithaca: Cornell University Press, 1981).

———. *The Ideologies of Theory*, vols. 1 and 2 (Minneapolis: University of Minnesota Press, 1988).

Jansen, J. G. "Hasan al-Banna's Earliest Pamphlet." *Die Welt des Islams*, vol. 32(2), 1992.

Johns, A. J. "Let My People Go! Sayyid Qutb and the Vocation of Moses." *Islam and Christian-Muslim Relations*, vol. 1(2), December 1990.

Jourshī, S. D. "al-Ḥaraka al-islāmiyya mustaqbaluha rahīn al-tagayurrāt al-jazriyya." [The Future of the Islamic Movement Depends on Fundamental Changes]. In 'Abd Allah al-Nafīsī, *al-Ḥaraka al-Islāmiyya: ru'yā mustaqbaliyyā* (Cairo: Madbuli, 1981).

———. "*al-Ḥaraka al-islāmiyya fi duwamma: ḥiwār hawla fikr Sayyid Quṭb*

[*The Islamic Movement in the Whirlwind: Debating Sayyid Qutb's Ideas*] (Tunis: Dār al-Burāq, 1985).

Juergensmeyer, M., ed. *Violence and the Sacred in the Modern World* (London: Frank Cass, 1992).

———. *The New Cold War? Religious Nationalism Confronts the Secular State* (Berkeley: University of California Press, 1993).

Kabbani, R. *Europe's Myths of the Orient: Devise and Rule* (Bloomington: Indiana University Press, 1986).

Kalabādhī, A. B. *At-ta'rruf li-madhab ahl al-taṣawwuf*, ed. A. J. Arberry (Cairo: al-Maṭaba'ah al-Misriyah, 1934).

Kammen, M., ed. *The Past Before Us: Contemporary Historical Writing in the United States* (Ithaca: Cornell University Press, 1980).

Karbal, M. "Western Scholarship and the Islamic Resurgence in the Arab World." *American Journal of the Islamic Social Sciences*, vol. 10(1), Spring 1993.

Karpat, K., ed. *Political and Social Thought in the Contemporary Middle East* (New York: Frederick A. Praeger, 1968).

Keddi, N. *Sayyid Jamal al-Din al-Afghani: A Biography* (Berkeley: University of California Press, 1972).

———. "Intellectuals in the Modern Middle East: A Brief Historical Consideration." *Daedalus*, vol. 101(3), Summer 1972.

Kedourie, E. *Afghani and Abduh: An Essay on Religious Unbelief and Political Activism in Modern Islam* (New York: The Humanities Press, 1962).

Kerr, M. *Islamic reform: The Political and Legal Theories of Muhammad Abduh and Rashid Rida* (Berkeley: University of California Press, 1966).

Khalafallah, M. A. "al-Ṣaḥwa al-islāmiyya fi miṣr" [Islamic Reawakening in Egypt]. In Ismai'l S. 'Abdallah, ed., *al-Ḥarakāt al-islāmiyya al-mu'āṣira fi'l waṭan al-'arabī* [*Contemporary Islamic Movements in the Arab World*] (Beirut: Markaz Dirasāt al-Wiḥda al-'Arabiyya, 1989).

Khalid, D. "Aḥmad Amīn and the Legacy of Muḥammad 'Abduh." *Islamic Studies*, vol. 9(1), March 1970.

Khalid, K. M. *From Here We Start*, tr. Isma'il R. al-Faruqi (Washington, D.C.: American Council of Learned Societies, 1953).

Khālidī, M.; and O. Farrūkh. *Al-Tabshīr wa'l isti'mār fi'l bilād al-'arabiyya* (Beirut: Manshūrāt al-Maktaba al-'Asriyya, 1986).

Khālidī, S. D. *al-Manhaj al-ḥarakī fī Ẓilāl al-Qur'ān*. vol. 2 (Jeddah: Dār al-Manāra, 1986).

———. *Amerīca mina al-dākhil bimindhār Sayyid Quṭb* [*America from within as Seen by Sayyid Qutb*] (Jeddah: Dār al-Manāra, 1986).

———. *Sayyid Quṭb: Minā al-milād ila al-istishhād* (Damascus: Dār al-Qalam, 1991).

Khan, M. A., ed. *Proceedings of the International Conference* (Islamabad: Islamic Research Institute, 1970).

Khatibi, A. K. "Double Criticism: The Decolonization of Arab Sociology," In H. Barakat, ed., *Contemporary North Africa: Issues of Development and Integration* (Washington, D.C.: Center for Contemporary Arab Studies, 1985).

Khoury, P. *Traditions et modernité: thèmes et tendances de la pensée arabe actuelle* (Beirut: n.p., 1983).

Khoury, P. S. "Islamic Revivalism and the Crisis of the Secular State in the Arab World: A Historical Appraisal." In Ibrahim Ibrahim, ed., *Arab Resources: The Transformation of a Society* (Washington, D.C.: Georgetown University, 1983).

Khūrī, R. *Modern Arab Thought: Channels of the French Revolution to the Arab East*, tr. Iḥsān ʿAbbās (Princeton: The Kingston Press, Inc., 1983).

Kojeve, A. *Introduction to the Reading of Hegel: Lectures on the Phenomenology of Spirit* (Ithaca, N.Y.: Cornell University Press, 1980).

Koprülü, M. F. *The Origins of the Ottoman Empire*, tr., and ed., Gary Leiser (Albany: State University of New York Press, 1992).

Kramer, M. "Muḥammad Ḥusayn Faḍlallah." *Orient*, vol. 26(2), June 1985.

———. "The Moral Logic of Ḥizballah." In Walter Reich, ed. *Origins of Terrorism: Psychologies, Ideologies, Theologies, States of Mind* (Cambridge: Cambridge University Press, 1990).

———. "Sacrifice and Fratricide in Shiite Lebanon." In Mark Juergensmeyer, ed., *Violence and the Sacred in the Modern World* (London: Frank Cass, 1992).

———, ed. *Middle Eastern Lives: The Practice of Biography and Self-Narrative* (Syracuse: Syracuse University Press, 1991).

Labdaoui, M. *Les nouveaux intellectuels arabes* (Paris: l'Harmattan, 1993).

Lahbabi, M. A. *De l'Etre à la personne: Essai de personnalisme réaliste* (Paris: PUF, 1954).

———. *Liberté ou libération* (Paris: Montagne, 1956).

———. *Du clos à l'ouvert: Vingt propos sur les cultures nationales et la civilization humaine* (Casablanca: Dār al-Kitāb, 1961).

———. Le personnalisme musulman (Paris: PUF, 1964).

———. *Le monde de demain: Le Tiers-monde accuse* (Casablanca: Sherbrooke, 1980).

Lalande, J. *La raison et les normes* (Paris: Hachette, 1963).

Lane, E. W. *Arabic-English Lexicon* (Cambridge: The Islamic Texts Society, 1984).

Laoust, H. "Le Réformisme orthodoxe des 'Salafiyya,' et les caractères généraux de son organisation actuelle," *Revue des Etudes Islamiques*, 6:175–224 (1932).

Laroui, A. *L'idéologie arabe contemporaine* (Paris: Maspero, 1970).

———. *The Crisis of the Arab Intelligentsia: Traditionalism or Historicism?* (Berkeley: University of California Press, 1976).

Lawrence, B. B. *Defenders of God: The Fundamentalist Revolt Against the Modern Age* (New York: Harper and Row, 1989).

———. "The Islamic Idiom of Violence: A View From Indonesia." In Mark Juergensmeyer, ed., *Violence and the Sacred in the Modern World* (London: Frank Cass, 1992).

Lehmann, A. C.; and J. E. Myers, eds. *Magic, Witchcraft and Religion: An Anthropological Study of the Supernatural*, 2d ed. (Mountain View: [Ill] Mayfield Publishing Company, 1989).

Leiden, C., ed. *The Conflict of Traditionalism and Modernism in the Muslim Middle East* (Austin: University of Texas Press, 1966).

Lewis, B. *The Emergence of Modern Turkey* (New York: Oxford University Press, 1968).

———. The Political Language of Islam (Chicago: University of Chicago Press, 1988).

Lewis, B.; and P. O. Holt, eds. *Historians of the Middle East* (London: Oxford University Press, 1962).

Lindner, R. P. *Nomads and Ottomans in Medieval Anatolia* (Bloomington, Ind.: Research Institute for Inner Asian Studies, 1983).

Lings, M. *Symbol and Archetype: A Study of the Meaning of Existence* (Cambridge: Quinta Essentia, 1991).

Louca, A. *L'or de Paris: Relation de voyage, 1826–1831* (Paris, 1988).

Lowrie, A., ed. *Islam, Democracy, The State and the West: A Round Table with Dr. Hasan Turabi* (Tampa: World and Islam Studies Enterprise, 1993).

Macdonell, D. *Theories of Discourse: An Introduction* (London: Basil Blackwell, 1986).

Mahdī, M. *al-Ṣaḥwa al-islāmiyyah: al-dawāfiʿ wa'l ʿawāʾiq* (Manṣūrah: al-Wafā', 1992).

Mahdi, S. M. "Islamic Philosophy in Contemporary Islamic Thought." In C. Malik, ed., *God and Man in Contemporary Islamic Thought* (Beirut: American University Press, 1972).

———. *The Political Orientation of Islamic Philosophy* (Georgetown: Center for Contemporary Arab Studies, 1982).

Mahmūd, Z. N. *Tajdīd al-fikr al-ʿarabī* [*Renewal of Arab Thought*] (Beirut: Dār al-Shurūq, 1978).

———. *al-Maʿqūl wa'l la maʿqūl fi ḥayatina al-fikriyya* (Cairo: Dār al-Shurūq, 1978).

Makdisi, G. "The Juridical Theory of Shafiʿi—Origins and Significance of *Uṣūl al-Fiqh*." *Studia Islamica*. vol. 59, 1984.

———. "Ṭabaqāt-Biography: Law and Orthodoxy in Classical Islam." *Islamic Studies*, vol. 32(4), Winter 1993.

Makki, A. T. *Qūt al-qulūb fi muʿamalat al-maḥbūb*, 2 vols. (Cairo: al-Bābī 1310 h./1892–1893).

Malcolm, X. *The Autobiography of Malcolm X* (New York: Ballantine Books, 1965).

Malik, C., ed. *God and Man in Contemporary Islamic Thought* (Beirut: American University Press, 1972).

Malik, Y. K. ed. *South Asian Intellectuals and Social Change: A Study of the Role of Vernacular-Speaking Intelligentsia* (New Delhi: Heritage Publishers, 1982).

Mallat, C. *The Renewal of Islamic Law: Muhammad Baqer As-Sadr, Najaf and the Shiʿi International* (Cambridge: Cambridge University Press, 1993).

Mannheim, K. *Ideology and Utopia: An Introduction to the Sociology of Knowledge* (New York: Harcourt, Brace & World, Inc., 1936).

Marsot, A. L. *Protest Movements and Religious Undercurrents in Egypt:*

Past and Present. Occasional Papers Series (Georgetown: Center for Contemporary Arab Studies, 1984).

Marty, M. E.; and R. S. Appleby, eds. *Fundamentalisms Observed* (Chicago: University of Chicago Press, 1992).

Marx, K. "The Eighteenth Brumaire of Louis Bonaparte." In K. Marx, *Surveys from Exile*, ed. D. Fernbach (Harmondsworth: Center for Economic Research, 1973).

Marx, K., and F. Engels. *Collected Works of Karl Marx and Frederick Engles*, vol. 3 (New York: International Publishers, 1976).

———. *Collected Works*, vol. 5 (New York: International Publishers, 1976).

Mawdudi, A. A. *Jihad in Islam* (Kuwait: al-Faisal Printing Co., n.d.).

Menashri, D., ed. *The Iranian Revolution and the Muslim World* (Boulder, Colo.: Westview Press, 1990).

Miller, J. "The Challenge of Radical Islam." *Foreign Affairs*, Spring 1993.

Miller, S. G., trans. and ed. *Disorienting Encounters, Travels of a Moroccan Scholar in France in 1845–1846: The Voyage of Muhammad As-Saffar* (Berkeley: University of California Press, 1992).

Milson, M. "Medieval and Modern Intellectual Traditions in the Arab World." *Daedalus*, vol. 101(3), Summer 1972.

Miṣrī, A. N. *The Reliance of the Traveller*, tr. and ed. Noah H. M. Keller (Evanston, Ill.: Sunna Books, 1993).

Mitchell, R. P. *The Society of the Muslim Brothers*, new ed. (New York: Oxford University Press, 1993).

Moughrabi, F. "The Arab Basic Personality: A Critical Survey of the Literature." *International Journal of Middle East Studies*, vol. 9(1), February 1978.

Mounier, E. *Qu'est-ce que le personnalisme?* (Paris: PUF, 1961).

Moussalli, A. S. "Contemporary Islamic Political Thought: Sayyid Qutb." Doctoral dissertation (College Park: University of Maryland, 1985).

———. "Sayyid Quṭb: The Ideologist of Islamic Fundamentalism." *Al-Abḥāth* (American University of Beirut), vol. 38, 1990.

———. *Radical Islamic Fundamentalism: The Ideological and Political Discourse of Sayyid Quṭb* (Beirut: American University of Beirut Press, 1992).

———. "Ḥasan al-Bannā's Islamist Discourse on Democracy and Shūra." *Middle Eastern Studies*, vol. 30(1), January 1994.

Muruwwa, H. *Al-Naza'āt al-m̃adiyah fī al-falsafah al-'arabiyah al-islāmiyah* (Beirut: Dār al-Farābī, 1978).

Mūsā, S. *The Education of Salāma Mūsā*, tr. L. O. Schuman (Leiden: Brill, 1961).

Musallam, A. "The Formative Stages of Sayyid Quṭb's Intellectual Career and his Emergence as an Islamic Dāi'yah, 1906–1952." Doctoral dissertation (Ann Arbor: University of Michigan, 1983).

———. "Sayyid Quṭb's Literary and Spiritual Orientation(1932–1938)." *The Muslim World*, vol. 80(3–4), July–October 1990.

———."Sayyid Quṭb and Social Justice, 1945–1948." *Journal of Islamic Studies*, vol. 4(1), 1993

Mustafa, S. "Arab Cultural Crisis and the Impact of the Past." *The Jerusalem Quarterly*, 11, Spring 1979.

Nabudere, D. W. *Imperialism: The Social Sciences and the National Question* (Dar Es Salaam: Tanzania Publishing House, 1977).

Nader, G. "Interview with Sheikh Muhammad Hussein Fadl Allah." *Middle East Insight*, vol. 4(2), June–July 1985.

Nadwī, A. H. *Islam and the World*, tr. Mohammad Kidawi (Kwrait: IIFSO, 1977).

Nafīsī, A. *al-Ḥaraka al-Islāmiyya: ru'yā mustaqbaliyya* (Cairo: Madbūlī, 1981).

———. *al-Ikhwān al-muslimūn, al-tajriba wa*'l khaṭa': awrāq fi'l naqd al-ẓātī [*The Muslim Brothers, Trial and Error: Readings in Self-Criticism*] (Cairo: Madbūlī, 1989).

al-Nāshif, T. *Mufakirroun falasṭiniyūn fi'l al-qarn al-'ishrīn* (Baghdād: Markaz al-Dirāsāt al-Filasṭiniyyah, 1981).

Nasr, S. H. *Islam and the Plight of Modern Man* (London: Longman, 1975).

———. "Decadence, Deviation, and Renaissance in the Context of Contemporary Islam." In Khurshid Ahmad and Zafar Ishaq Ansari, eds., *Islamic Perspectives: Studies in Honor of Sayyid Abul A'la Mawdūdī* (Leicester: The Islamic Foundation, 1980).

———. *Knowledge and the Sacred* (Albany: State University of New York Press, 1989).

Nayed, A. A. "The Radical Qur'anic Hermeneutics of Sayyid Qutb." *Islamic Studies*, vol. 31(3), Autumn 1992.

———. "The Unitary Qur'anic Hermeneutics of Muhammad Baqir al-Sadr." *Islamic Studies*, voi. 31(4), Winter 1992.

Nicholls, W., ed. *Modernity and Religion* (Waterloo, Canada: Wilfrid Laurier University Press, 1987).

Nicholson, R. A., *A Literary History of the Arabs* (Cambridge: Cambridge University Press, 1953).

Niebuhr, R. *The Nature and Destiny of Man*, vol. 1 (New York: Charles Scribner's Sons, 1943).

———. *The Nature and Destiny of Man*, vol. 2 (New York: Scribner's, 1964).

Nietzsche, F. *The Will to Power*, tr. Walter Kaufmann and R. J. Hollingdale (New York: Vintage Books, 1968).

O'Brien, C. C. *God Land: Reflections on Religion and Nationalism* (Cambridge: Harvard University Press, 1988).

Orwell, G. *A Collection of Essays* (New York: Harcourt, 1981).

Owen, R. "The Middle East in the Eighteenth Century—an Islamic Society in Decline?: A Critique of Gibb and Bowen's *Islam Society and the West*." *Review of Middle Eastern Studies* 1(1975).

Parry, B. "Problems in Current Theories of Colonial Discourse." *Oxford Literary Review*, 7(1–2): 25–58.

Pelletreau, R. H., Jr., et al. "Political Islam. Symposium: Resurgent Islam in the Middle East." *Middle East Policy*, vol. 3(2), 1994.

Peters, F. E. *Muhammad and the Origins of Islam* (Albany: State University of New York Press, 1994).

Polk, W. R. "Sir Hamilton Gibb Between Orientalism and History." *International Journal of Middle East Studies*, vol. 6(2), April 1975.

Popper, K. *The Poverty of Historicism* (New York: Harper, 1957).

———. *The Open Society and Its Enemies*, two vols. (Princeton: Princeton University Press, 1962).

Pruett, G. "The Escape from Seraglio: Anti-Orientalist Trends in Modern Religious Studies." *Arab Studies Quarterly*, vol. 2:4, Fall 1980.

Qaraḍāwī, Y. *al-Islām wa'l ʿilmāniyya wajhan li wajh* [*Islam and Secularism: Face to Face*] (Cairo: Dār al-Ṣahwa, 1987).

———. *Al-Ḥall al-islāmī, farīḍa wa darūra* (Beirut: Mu'asasat al-Risālah, 1989).

———. *Islamic Awakening Between Rejection and Extremism*, tr. A. S. al-Shaikh Ali and Mohamed Wasfy (Herndon, Va.: The International Institute of Islamic Thought, 1991).

Qashani, A. R. *A Glossary of Sufi Technical Terms*, tr. N. Safwat (London: The Octagon Press, 1991).

Qureshi, S. A. *Selected Writings of Hasan al-Banna Shaheed* (Karachi: International Islamic Publishers, 1983).

Quṭb, S. "Bayna al-'Aqqād wa'l Rāfi'ī." *Al-Risāla*, 251, April 1938.

———. "al-Dalalah al-nafsiyah li'l alfāẓ wa'l tarākīb al-'arabiyah." *Ṣaḥifat Dār al-'Ulūm*, 3(3), January 1938.

———. "al-Dalalah al-nafsiyah li'l asālīb wa'l itijahāt al-ḥadīthah." *Ṣahīfat Dār al-'Ulūm*, 5(1), July 1938.

———. "Naqd mustaqbal al-thaqāfa fi miṣr." *Ṣaḥifat Dār al-'Ulūm*, vol. 4, April 1939.

———. *al-Naqd al-adabī: uṣūluhu wa manāhajihū* (Cairo: Dār al-Fikr al-'Arabī, 1947).

———. "Lughat al-'abīd." *Al-Risāla*, Number 709, year 15, February 1947.

———. *al-'Adāla al-ijtimā'iyya fi'l islām* (Cairo: Lajnat al-Nashr li'l Jāmi'yyīn, 1949). English translation by John B. Hardie, *Social Justice in Islam* (New York: Octagon Books, 1980).

———. "'Aduwunna al-awwal: al-rajul al-abyaḍ." *al-Risāla*, vol. 2(1009), November 3, 1952.

———. al-Taṣwār al-fannā fi'l qur'ān (Cairo: Dar al-Ma'ārif, 1962).

———. *Hādha al-dān* (Cairo: Dār al-Qalam, 1962).

———. *Al-Islām wa mushkilāt al-haḍāra* (Cairo: al-Bābā al-Ḥalabī, 1962).

———. *Khaṣā'iṣ al-taṣawwur al-islāmā wa muqawimatuhū* (Beirut: Dār Iḥyā' al-Kutub al-'Arabiyah, 1962).

———. "The Ideological Bankruptcy of Europe and the Future Prospects of Islam, I," *The Voice of Islam*, vol. 12(1), October 1963.

———. *Mashāhid al-qiyama fi'l qur'ān* (Cairo: Dār al-Ma'ārif, 1966).

———. Dirāsāt Islāmiyya (Cairo: Dār al-Fatḥ, 1967).

———. "The Bases of Social Justice in Islam." *The Criterion: Journal of the Islamic Research* Academy. vol. 3(4), 1969.

———. *Ma'ālām fi al-ṭarāq* (Beirut: Dār al-Shurūq, 1973).

———. *Kutub wa shakhṣiyāt* (Beirut: Dār al-Shurūq, 1974).

———. *Ma'arakat al-islām wa'l ra'smāliyya* (Cairo: Dār al-Shurūq, 1974).

———. *Fā Ẓilāl al-Qur'ān*, 6 vols, rev. ed. (Beirut: Dār al-Shurūq, 1974).

———. *This Religion of Islam* [*Hādaha al-dān*] (Delhi: Markazi Maktaba Islami, 1974).

———. Islam: The Religion of the Future (Delhi: Markaz Maktaba Islami, 1976).

———. *Milestones* (Karachi: International Islamic Publishers, 1981).

———. *Muqawimāt al-taṣawwur al-islāmā* (Cairo: Dār al-Shurūq, 1986).

———. *Milestones*, tr. M. M. Siddiqui (Kuwait: International Islamic Federation of Student Organizations, 1989).

———. "'Aduwunna al-awwal: al-rajul al-abyad" [Our First Enemy is the White Man]." In S. Qutb, *Ayuha al-'arab: istayqidhu wa ihdharu* (Amman: Dar al-Isra', 1990).

———. *The Islamic Concept and its Characteristics*, tr. M. M. Siddiqui (Indianapolis: American Trust Publications, 1991).

———. *Muhimmat al-shā'ir fi'l ḥayāt wa shi'r al-jāl al-ḥādir* (Beirut: Dār al-Shurūq, n.d.).

———. Ṭifl min al-qarya (Beirut: Dār al-Ḥikmah, n.d.).

Rabinow, P. *Symbolic Domination: Cultural Form and Historical Change in Morocco* (Chicago: University of Chicago Press, 1975).

———, ed. *The Foucault Reader* (New York: Pantheon Books, 1984).

Rahman, F. "Islamic Modernism: Its Scope, Method and Alternative." In *International Journal of Middle Eastern Studies*, vol. 1(4), October 1970.

———. "Revival and Reform in Islam." In P.M. Holt, Ann Lambton, and Bernard Lewsi, eds. *The Cambridge History of Islam*, 2 vols. (Cambridge: Cambridge University Press, 1970).

———. "The Religious Situation of Mecca from the Eve of Islam up to the Hijra." *Islamic Studies*, vol. 16(4), Winter 1977.

———. *Major Themes of the Qur'ān* (Minneapolis: Bibliotheca Islamica, 1980).

———. *Islam and Modernity: Transformation of an Intellectual Tradition* (Chicago: University of Chicago Press, 1982).

———. *Islamic Methodology in History*, second printing (Islamabad: Islamic Research Institute, 1984).

Reich, W., ed. *Origins of Terrorism: Psychologies, Ideologies, Theologies, States of Mind* (Cambdrige: Cambridge University Press, 1990).

Reid, D. M. *Cairo University and the Making of Modern Egypt* (Cambridge: Cambridge University Press, 1990).

Renan, E. *Averroes et l'Averroisme: Essai historique* (Paris: Ancienne Maison, 1882).

Riad, I. "Factors Contributing to the Political Ascendancy of the Muslim Brethren in Sudan." *Arab Studies Quarterly*, vol. 12(3), 1990.

Rida, R. *Tārīkh al-ustādh al-imām* al-Shaykh Muḥammad ʿAbduh (Cairo: Maṭbaʿat al-Manār, 1933).

Rizq, J. *Ḥasan al-Bannā* (Manṣūra: al-Wafā' Press, 1986).

Roff, W. R., ed. *Islam and the Political Economy of Meaning: Comparative Studies of Muslim Discourse* (Berkeley: University of California Press, 1987).

Rorty, R. *Philosophy and the Mirror of Nature* (Princeton: Princeton University Press, 1979).

———. *Essays on Heidegger and Others: Philosophical Papers*, vol. 2 (Cambridge: Cambridge University Press, 1991).

Rosenau, M. P. *Post-Modernism and the Social Sciences: Insights, Inroads, and Intrusions* (Princeton: Princeton University Press, 1992).

Rosenthal, F. "On Suicide in Islam." *Journal of the American Oriental Society*, 66 (1946).

———. "The 'Muslim Brethren' in Egypt." *The Muslim World*, vol. 37(4), October 1947.

Roth, R. "The Colonial Experience and Its Postmodern Fate." *Salmagundi*, 84, Fall 1989.

Roy, O. *The Failure of Political Islam* tr. Carol Vol, (Cambridge: Harvard University Press, 1994).

Sachedina, A. "Activist Shiʿism in Iran, Iraq, and Lebanon." In *Fundamentalism Observed*, ed. Martin E. Marty and R. Scott Appleby (Chicago: University of Chicago Press, 1992).

Ṣafadī, M. *"al-Qawmiyya al-'arabiyya wa'l islām al-thawrī"* (Arab Nationalism and Revolutionary Islam) *al-Fikr al-'Arabī al-Mu'āṣir* (June 1980), 6. Quoted and Translated by Bassam Tibi, "Islam and Arab Nationalism." In Barbara F. Stowasser, ed., *The Islamic Impulse* (Georgetown, 1987).

Safi, H., ed. *Penseurs Maghrébins contemporains* (Tunis: Ceres Productions, 1993).

Sagiv, D. "Judge Ashmawi and Militant Islam in Egypt." *Middle Eastern Studies*, vol. 28(3), July 1992.

Sāi'd, R. *Ḥasan al-Bannā: Kayfa wa limādha?* (Cairo: Dār al-Thaqāfa al-Jadīda, 1984).

Said, E. *Orientalism* (New York: Vintage Books, 1978).

———. *Culture and Imperialism* (New York: Alfred A. Knopf, 1993).

Salwādī, H. *al-Doktor Isḥāk Musah al-Ḥusainī, 'amīd al-adab al-'arabī* (Taybeh: Markaz Ihyā' al-turāth al-'Arabī, 1991).

Santi, E. M. "Politics, Literature, and the Intellectual in Latin America." *Salmagundi*, 82–83 (Spring-Summer 1989).

Sarrāj, A. N. *Kitāb al Luma' fi al Taṣawwuf*, ed. Reynold A. Nicholson (Leiden and London: Brill, 1914);

Sartre, J. P. *Search For a Method* (New York: Vintage Books, 1968)

Schacht, J. *An Introduction to Islamic Law* (Oxford: Oxford University Press, 1964).

Schimmel, A. "The Origin and Early Development of Sufism." *Journal of the Pakistan Historical Society*, 1958.

———. *Mystical Dimensions of Islam* (Chapel Hill: The University of North Carolina Press, 1975).

Shafīq, M. *Bayna al-nuhūḍ wa'l suqūṭ: radd 'alā kitāb Faraj Fūdā* (Tunisia: Al-Nāshir, 1992).

———. *Rudūd 'ala utrūḥāṭ 'ilmāniyya* [*Responses to Secularist Theses*] (Tunisia: al-Nāshir, 1992).

Shaikh, N. M. *Memoirs of Ḥasan al-Bannā Shaheed* (Karachi: International Islamic Publishers, 1982).

Sharabi, H. *Arab Intellectuals and the West: The Formative Years, 1875–1914* (Baltimore: The Johns Hopkins University Press, 1970).

———. *Neopatriarchy: A Theory of Distorted Change in Arab Society* (New York: Oxford University Press, 1988).

———, ed. *The Next Arab Decade: Alternative Futures* (Boulder Colo.: Westview Press, 1988).

Shari'ati, A. *On the Sociology of Islam*, tr. Hamid Algar (Berkeley: Mizan Press, 1979).

Shayegan, D. *Le regard mutilé: Schizophrénie culturelle: pays traditionnels face à la modernité* (Paris: Albin Michel, 1989).

Shepard, W. "Islam and Ideology: Toward a Typology." *International Journal of Middle Eastern Studies*, vol. 19(3), August 1987.

———. "The Development of the Thought of Sayyid Qutb as Reflected in Earlier and Later Editions of 'Social Justice in Islam'." *Die Welt Des Islams*, vol. 32(2), 1992.

Shils, E. "Intellectuals." In David Sills, ed., *International Encyclopedia of the Social Sciences*, vol. 7 (New York: Macmillan, 1968).

———. "The Intellectuals in the Political Development of the New States." In J. L. Finkle and R. W. Gable, eds. *Political Development and Social Change* (New York: Pantheon, 1968).

———. *The Intellectuals and Power and Other Essays* (Chicago: The University of Chicago Press, 1972).

———. *Tradition* (Chicago: The University of Chicago Press, 1981).

Shukrī, G. *al-Nahḍah wa'l suqūt fi'l fikr al-miṣrī al-ḥadīth* [*Renaissance and Decline in Modern Egyptian Thought*] (Beirut: Dār al-Ṭal'iāh, 1976).

Sibā'ī, M. *al-Islām wa'l ishtirākiyya* (Cairo: al-Dār al-Qaqmiyya li'l Tiba'ā wa'l Nashr, 1960).

———. "Islamic Socialism." In Kemal H. Karpat, *Political and Social Thought in the Contemporary Middle East* (New York: Praeger, 1968).

Siddiqi, M. *Modern Reformist Thought in the Muslim World* (Islamabad: Islamic Research Institute, 1982).

Sills, D., ed. *International Encyclopedia of the Social Sciences*, vol. 7 (New York: Macmillan, 1968).

Sīsī, A. *Ḥasan al-Bannā: Mawāqif fi'l da'wa wa'l tarbiya* (Cairo: Dār Qabas, 1982).

Sivan, E. "Sunni Radicalism in the Middle East and the Iranian Revolution," *International Journal of Middle East Studies*, 21(1), February 1989.

———. *Radical Islam: Medieval Theology and Modern Politics*, enlarged ed. (New Haven: Yale University Press, 1990)

Smith, C. D. "The 'Crisis of Orientation': The Shift of Egyptian Intellectuals to Islamic Subjects in the 1930s." *International Journal of Middle East Studies*, vol. 4(4), October 1974.

———. *Islam and the Search for Social Order in Modern Egypt: A Biography of Muhammad Husayn Haykal* (Albany: State University of New York Press, 1983).

Smith, W. C. *Islam in Modern History* (New York: New American Library, 1957).

———. *The Meaning and End of Religion: A New Approach to the Religious Traditions of Mankind* (New York: The Macmillan Company, 1963).

Smith, H. *Beyond the Post-Modern Mind* (Wheaton Ill.: The Theosophical Publication House, 1989).

Smyth, W. "The Making of a Textbook." *Studia Islamica*, vol. 78, 1994.

Stowasser, B. F., ed. *The Islamic Impulse* (Georgetown: Center for Contemporary Arab Studies, 1987).

Strauss, L. *Persecution and the Art of Writing* (Chicago: University of Chicago Press, 1988).

———. *What Is Political Philosophy and Other Studies* (Chicago: University of Chicago Press, 1988).

Ṣubḥ, A. M. *Tahāfut qabl al-ṣuqūt wa ṣuqūt ṣāḥibihī* (al-Manṣūra: Dār al-Wafā', 1985).

Surour, A. H. *al-ʿAllāma Faḍlallah: Taḥadī al-Mamnūʿ* (Beirut: Dār al-Malak, 1992).

Swidler, L., ed. *Muslims in Dialogue: The Evolution of a Dialogue* (Lewiston: [New York] The Edwin Mellen Press, 1992).

Ṭāhā, M. M. *The Second Message of Islam*, tr. A. An-Naʿim (Syracuse: Syracuse University Press, 1987).

Ṭahṭāwī, R. R. *Kitāb takhlīṣ al-ibrīz fi talhīs Bārīz*. In M. ʿImārah, ed., *Al-aʿmāl al-kāmila li-Rifaʿā Rāfiʿ at-Ṭahṭāwī* (Beirut: al-Muʿasasah al-ʿArabiyah, 1973).

Tibi, B. "Islam and Arab Nationalism," In Barbara F. Stowasser, ed., *The Islamic Impulse* (Georgetown: Center for Contemporary Arab Studies, 1987).

———. *The Crisis of Modern Islam* (Salt Lake City: University of Utah Press, 1988).

———. "The Worldview of Sunni Arab Fundamentalists: Attitudes toward Modern Science and Technology." In Martin E. Marty and R. Scott Appleby, eds., *Fundamentalisms and Society* (Chicago: The University of Chicago Press, 1993).

Tillich, P. *Systematic Theology*. 3 vols. (Chicago: University of Chicago Press, 1953–1962).

———. *On the Boundary: An Autobiographical Sketch* (New York: Charles Scribner's Sons, 1966).

———. *A History of Christian Thought* (New York: Simon and Schuster, 1967).

Tūrabī, H. *al-Ḥaraka al-islāmiyya fi'l Sūdān* (Khartoum: n.p., 1989).

———. "Challenging times, but Madinah is Our Model." Impact International, vol. 23(3–4), 1993.

———. "Islam as a Pan-National Movement and Nation-States: An Islamic Doctrine on Human Association." Islamica, vol. 1(2), 1993.

Turan, O. "The Need of Islamic Renaissance." In M. A. Khan, ed., *Proceedings of the International Conference* (Islamabad: Islamic Research Institute, 1970).

Turner, V. W. "Religious Specialists." In Arthur C. Lehmann and James E. Myers, eds., *Magic, Witchcraft and Religion: An Anthropological Study of the Supernatural*, 2d ed. (Mountain View Ill.: Mayfield Publishing Company, 1989).

'Ulwī, H. *Fī al-dīn wa'l turāth* (Jerusalem: Ṣalāḥ al-Dīn, 1975).

Vatin, J. "Seduction and Sedition: Islamic Polemical Discourse in the Maghreb." In William R. Roff, ed., *Islam and the Political Economy of Meaning: Comparative Studies of Muslim Discourse* (Berkeley: University of California Press, 1987).

Vattimo, G. *The End of Modernity: Nihilism and Hermeneutics in Postmodern Culture* (Baltimore: The Johns Hopkins University Press, 1988).

Veitch, J. "Muslim Activism, Islamization or Fundamentalism: Exploring the Issues." *Islamic Studies*, vol. 32(3), Autumn 1993.

Viswanathan, V. "Raymond Williams and British Colonialism." *The Yale Journal of Criticism*, vol. 4(2), Spring 1991.

Voll, J. "Renewal and Reform in Islamic History: Tajdid and Islah." In John Esposito, ed. *Voices of Resurgent Islam* (New York: Oxford University Press, 1983).

———. "The Revivalist Heritage." In Yvonne Y. Haddad, et al., *The Contemporary Islamic Revival: A Critical Survey and Bibliography* (New York: Greenwood Press, 1991).

———. "Fundamentalism in the Sunni Arab World: Egypt and the Sudan." In *Fundamentalisms Observed*, ed. Martin E. Marty and R. Scott Appleby (Chicago: University of Chicago Press, 1992).

von Grunebaum, G. E. *Modern Islam: The Search for Cultural Identity* (Berkeley: University of California Press, 1962).

———. "Some Recent Constructions and Reconstructions of Islam." In Carl Leiden, ed. *The Conflict of Traditionalism and Modernism in the Muslim Middle East* (Austin: University of Texas Press, 1966).

von Grunebaum, G. E., and R. Brunschwig, eds. *Classicisme et déclin culturel dans l'histoire de l'Islam* (Paris: Maisonneuve, 1957).

Watt, W. M. *Muhammad at Mecca* (Oxford: Clarendon Press, 1960).

———. *The Faith and Practice of al-Ghazali* (Chicago: Kazi Publications, 1982).

Weiker, W. F. *The Modernization of Turkey: From Ataturk to the Present Day* (New York: Holmes and Meier, 1981).

Weil, E. *Logique de la philosophie* (Paris: J. Vrin, 1967).

Weintraub, K. J. "Autobiography and Historical Consciousness," *Critical Inquiry*, vol. 1(4), 1974–1975.

Wendell, C. tr. *Five Tracts of Hasan al-Banna, 1906–1949* (Berkeley: University of California Press, 1978).

Wensinck, A. J. "Kibla." *Encylopedia Islamica*, vol. 5 (Leiden: Brill, 1972).

Wesmann, I. "Saʿid Hawwa: The Making of a Radical Muslim Thinker in Modern Syria." *Middle Eastern Studies,* vol. 29(4), October 1993.

Wolf, E. *Europe and the People without History* (Berkeley: University of California Press, 1982).

Yāfut, S. "Al-Hājis al-thālith fi falsafat Muḥammad ʿAzīz al-Ḥabābī." In I. Badrān, et al., *al-Falsafah fi'l waṭan al-ʿarabī al-muʿāṣir* (Beirut: Markaz Dirāsāt al-Wiḥdah al-ʿArabiyah, 1985).

Yakan, F. *Islamic Movement: Problems and Perspectives*, tr. Maneh al-Johani (Indianapolis: American Trust Publications, 1984).

Yassin, A. *Révolution à l'heure de l'Islam* (Marseille: Presses de L'Imprime du Collège, 1979).

Yāssin, S., et al. *al-Turāth wa taḥadiyāt al-ʿaṣr* (Beirut: Markaz Dirāsāt al-Wiḥdah al-ʿArabiyah, 1985).

Zakariyyā, F. *al-Ḥaqīqa wa'l khayāl fi'l haraka al-islāmiyya al-muʿāṣira* [*Reality and Myth in the Contemporary Islamic Movement*](Cairo: Dār al-Fikr, 1988).

———. "People Direct Islam in any Direction they Wish." *Middle East Times*, May 28–June 3, 1991.

Zayn, S. *al-Ṣūfiyya fī naẓar al-islām* (Beirut: Dār al-Turāth, 1976).

Zebiri, K. *Maḥmūd Shaltūt and Islamic Modernism* (Oxford: Clarendon Press, 1993).

Zghal, A. "The Reactivation of Tradition in a Post-Traditional Society." *Daedalus: Journal of the American Academy of Arts and Sciences*, vol. 102(1), Winter 1973.

Zurayk, K. *Tensions in Islamic Civilization* (Georgetown: Center for Contemporary Arab Studies, 1978).

Index

A

B

C

L

M

N

O

P

Q

R

S

T

U

V

W

Y

Z